20.00

WHAT EVERY VETERA

72nd EDIT

BOOK PRICE - $20)0 – I' ..UDES SHIPPING

This is the 72nd edition of the book "WHAT EVERY VETERAN SHOULD KNOW," a service officer's guide since 1937.

Monthly supplements are available from the publisher, which provide updates to the information contained in this book. A one-year subscription to the supplement service is $30.00.

The material herein covers veterans' benefits, rights, privileges, and services over which the Department of Veterans Affairs has jurisdiction. All references to "VA" pertain to the Department of Veterans Affairs. Revised and new laws passed by the 110th Congress as of December 31, 2007, are incorporated in this text. Chapter 1 of the book contains a brief summary of some of the important legislative changes affecting veterans' benefits during 2007.

This guide was prepared solely for convenient reference purposes, and does not have the effect of law. Although diligent effort has been made to ensure its accuracy, in the event of any conflict between this book and any regulation, the latter is, of course, controlling.

You will find a Table of Contents, listing the main subject headings. For your convenience, there is also a complete index in the back of the book, as well as an Edge Index on the back cover.

Veterans and the dependents of deceased veterans are advised to contact their local veterans organization service officers, or the nearest Veterans Administration Office, for help in completing any valid claim.

VETERANS INFORMATION SERVICE
P.O. Box 111
East Moline, Illinois 61244-0111
Telephone and Fax: (309) 757-7760
Email: help@vetsinfoservice.com
www.vetsinfoservice.com

WHAT EVERY VETERAN SHOULD KNOW

VETERANS INFORMATION SERVICE
P.O. Box 111
East Moline, Illinois 61244-0111

Phone and Fax: (309) 757-7760
E-mail: help@vetsinfoservice.com
www.vetsinfoservice.com

A NOTE TO THE READER:

Revised and new laws passed by the 110th Congress as of December 31, 2007, are incorporated in the text of this book. Chapter 1 of the book contains a brief summary of some of the important legislative changes affecting veterans' benefits during 2007.

You will find a Table of Contents, listing the main subject headings. For your convenience there is also a complete index in the back of the book, as well as an Edge Index on the back cover.

We hope you enjoy this edition of **WHAT EVERY VETERAN SHOULD KNOW**. Any comments or suggestions for future improvements are welcome.

What Every Veteran Should Know
Library of Congress Cataloging in Serials
ISSN 1532-8112
ISBN 0-9670331-95

Publisher:

Veterans Information Service
P.O. Box 111
East Moline, IL 61244-0111

TABLE OF CONTENTS

CHAPTER 1

IMPORTANT NDAA UPDATE

In late 2007, President Bush unexpectedly vetoed the 2008 National Defense Authorization Act (NDAA) due to a section that would "allow the immediate freezing of Iraqi assets and would expose Iraq to massive liability in lawsuits concerning the misdeeds of the Saddam Hussein regime," according to White House spokesman Scott Stanzel. The White House also said it was likely that Iraq would withdraw billions of dollars from American banks to protect them from the possible lawsuits.

The White House stated that while they were not happy with some other sections of the NDAA, this was the only section that was causing the veto and that when Congress returned in January, they hoped to quickly have a new NDAA passed.

This unexpected veto has affected publication of this book. As this book is going to press, the House & Senate have passed a new version of the 2008 NDAA, removing the language President Bush opposed. However, it still has not been signed into law, and it was necessary to move forward with the printing of the book, even though it would not include provisions from the 2008 NDAA.

The consesus is that the new version of the 2008 NDAA will include the following key provisions affecting veterans:

- Rejects the Pentagon plan for steep increases in TRICARE fees and pharmacy copayments for retirees under age 65 and their families;
- Approves a 3.5% military pay raise;
- Extends Combat Related Special Compensation (CRSC) to all combat-related disabled veterans;
- Authorizes full, immediate concurrent receipt of Disability Pay for all 100% disabled retirees rated Individual Unemployability (IU). Payments are expected to begin October 1, 2008.
- Lowers Guard/Reserve retirement age by 3 months for every aggregate 90 days served on active duty under certain mobilization authorities. This change would only apply to assignments after September 2007;

- Extends the time for using GI Bill benefits - Guard & Reserve personnel will have 10 years to use their education benefits after separation – no longer must they remain in drill status;
- Expands Guard/Reserve education benefits;
- Guarantees combat veterans mental health evaluations within 30 days of their request;
- Requires DoD to use the VA Schedule for Rating Disabilities in determining service member disabilities;
- Increases from 2 to 5 years the period during which recently separated combat veterans may seek care from the VA;
- Increase from 12 to 26 weeks, the amount of leave caregivers of seriously injured service members may take under the Family Medical Leave Act;
- Authorizes a Special Survivor Indemnity Allowance of $50 a month beginning October 2008, and increasing to $100 by Oct. 2012.

Veterans Information Service will keep readers advised in the monthly newsletter. For customers who do not subscribe to the monthly newsletter, see the website at www.vetsinfoservice.com for updated information.

2007 LEGISLATIVE CHANGES

Following is a brief summary of some of the important legislative changes, as well as VA-policy changes, affecting veterans' benefits during 2007.

Joshua Omvig Veterans Suicide Prevention Act
Public Law 110-110

- Directs the VA Secretary to develop and carry out a comprehensive program designed to reduce the incidence of suicide among veterans. The program is required to include:
    - Mandatory training for appropriate staff and contractors of the Department of Veterans Affairs who interace with veterans;
    - Mental health assessments of veterans;
    - Designation of a suicide prevention counselor at each Department medical facility;
    - Research on the best practices for suicide prevention;
    - Mental health care for veterans who have experienced sexual trauma while in military service;
    - 24-hour veterans' mental health care availability;
    - A toll-free hotline; and
    - Outreach and education for veterans and their families.

Veterans' Compensation Cost-Of-Living Adjustment Act Of 2007

Public Law 110-111

- Increases, effective December 1, 2007, the rates of Disability Compensation for veterans with service-connected disabilities, and the rates of dependency and indemnity compensation for survivors of certain service-connected disabled veterans. (The COLA was 2.3%) (These increases are reflected in all appropriate tables included throughout the book.)

Dr. James Allen Veteran Vision Equity Act of 2007

Public Law 110-157

- Modifies the standard for awarding disability compensation to veterans for loss of vision to require payment of compensation for impairment of vision (currently, blindness) involving both eyes due to a service-connected and non service-connected disability.
- Defines such impairment as a visual acuity of 20/200 or less or of a peripheral field of 20 degrees or less.
- Requires the Secretary of Veterans Affairs to provide the Secretary of Health and Human Services with information for comparison with the National Directory of New Hires for income verification purposes with respect to individuals under age 65 in order to determine eligibility for certain veteran benefits and services.
- Requires:
  - Independent verification of information so acquired prior to terminating, denying, or reducing a benefit or service; and
  - The opportunity for an individual to contest negative findings.
- Extends, through June 30, 2009, VA authority to provide an educational allowance to persons performing qualifying work-study activities.
- Authorizes the Secretary, in lieu of furnishing a headstone or marker for the grave of certain individuals buried in a private cemetery, to furnish a bronze representation of the letter "V" to be attached to a headstone or marker furnished at private expense.

Army Makes Changes to its Program offering Transferability of GI Bill to Dependents

- Effective November 1, 2007 the ***Army*** has made changes to its GI Bill transferability program. Eligible soldiers may now transfer up to 18 months of their GI Bill to spouses or children.

  This pilot program is authorized under Title 38, U.S. Code, Chapter 30 (amended by PL 107-107), the Montgomery GI Bill (MGIB).

Participants must ensure they meet the following eligibility requirements and take the following actions to participate in the program:

- MGIB-era Soldiers who are eligible for MGIB must have enrolled in the MGIB upon initial entry to active duty and paid the $1,200 for MGIB enrollment. (Not eligible are Vietnam Ear-Rollover, VEAP conversion, and Involuntary Separation.)
- Completed at least 6 years of service in the Armed Forces at the time of reenlistment.
- Reenlist for a period of at least 4 years and complete DD Form 2366-2 with their servicing Army Retention Career Counselor.
- Qualify for a MOS Specific Selective Reenlistment Bonus (SRB) and entitled to a Zone B or Zone C bonus at the time of reenlistment.

OJT & Apprenticeship Rates to Change January 1, 2008

- Effective October 1, 2005 Public Law 108-454, Section 103 temporarily increased the reimbursement rates for On the Job Training & Apprenticeship training. This temporary rate increase was effective from October 1, 2005 to December 31, 2007. Congress has not extended this temporary increase, therefore effective January 1, 2008 reimbursement rates will decrease.

Both sets of rates have been included, where applicable, throughout this book.

CHAPTER 2

MEMBERS OF THE 110TH CONGRESS

SENATE MEMBERS OF THE VETERANS AFFAIRS COMMITTEE

Democrats

Daniel K. Akaka, HI (Chairman)
Sherrod Brown, OH
Patty Murray,WA
Barack Obama, IL
John D. Rockefeller IV, WV
Jon Tester, MT
Jim Webb, VA

Independent

Bernard Sanders, VT

Republicans

Richard Burr, NC (Ranking Member)
Larry Craig, ID
Lindsey Graham, SC
Kay Bailey Hutchison, TX
Johnny Isakson, GA
Alren Specter, PA
Roger Wicker, MS

HOUSE MEMBERS OF THE VETERANS AFFAIRS COMMITTEE

Democrats

Bob Filner, CA (Chairman)
Shelley Berkley, NV
Corrine Brown, FL
Joe Donnelly, IN
Michael R. Doyle, PA
John J. Hall, NY
Phil Hare, IL
Stephanie Herseth Sandlin, SD
Jerry McNerney, CA
Michael H. Michaud, ME
Harry E. Mitchell, AZ
Ciro D. Rodriguez, TX

John T. Salazar, CO
Vic Snyder, AR
Zachary T. Space, OH
Timothy J. Walz, MN

Republicans
Steve Buyer, IN (Ranking Republican Member
Richard H. Baker, LA
Brian P. Bilbray, CA
Gus M. Bilirakis, FL
John Boozman, AR
Henry E. Brown, Jr., SC
Vern Buchanan, FL
Doug Lamborn, CO
Jeff Miller, FL
Jerry Moran, KS
Cliff Stearns, FL
Michael R. Turner, OH
Ginny Brown-Waite, FL

SENATE MEMBERS

State	Name	Party	Prior Experience	First took office	Born
Alabama	Jeff Sessions	Republican	State Attorney General	1997	1946
Alabama	Richard Shelby	Republican	U.S. House (AL-7)	1987	1934
Alaska	Lisa Murkowski	Republican	State House of Representatives	2002	1957
Alaska	Ted Stevens	Republican	military, attorney, State House of Representatives	1968	1923
Arizona	Jon Kyl	Republican	attorney, U.S. House (AZ-4)	1995	1942
Arizona	John McCain	Republican	military, U.S. House (AZ-1)	1987	1936
Arkansas	Blanche Lincoln	Democratic	U.S. House (AR-1)	1999	1960
Arkansas	Mark Pryor	Democratic	State Attorney General	2003	1963
California	Barbara Boxer	Democratic	U.S. House (CA-6)	1993	1940
California	Dianne Feinstein	Democratic	Mayor of San Francisco	1992	1933
Colorado	Wayne Allard	Republican	U.S. House (CO-4)	1997	1943
Colorado	Ken Salazar	Democratic	State Attorney General	2005	1955
Connecticut	Chris Dodd	Democratic	U.S. House (CT-2)	1981	1944
Connecticut	Joe Lieberman	Independent Democratic	State Attorney General	1989	1942
Delaware	Joe Biden	Democratic	New Castle County Council	1973	1942
Delaware	Tom Carper	Democratic	Governor; U.S. House (DE-At Large)	2001	1947

State	Name	Party	Prior Experience	First took office	Born
Florida	Mel Martinez	Republican	U.S. Secretary of Housing and Urban Development	2005	1946
Florida	Bill Nelson	Democratic	State Treasurer	2001	1942
Georgia	Saxby Chambliss	Republican	U.S. House (GA-8)	2003	1943
Georgia	Johnny Isakson	Republican	U.S. House (GA-6)	2005	1944
Hawaii	Daniel Akaka	Democratic	U.S. House (HI-2)	1991	1924
Hawaii	Daniel Inouye	Democratic	U.S. House (HI-At Large)	1963	1924
Idaho	Larry Craig	Republican	U.S. House (ID-1)	1991	1945
Idaho	Mike Crapo	Republican	U.S. House (ID-2)	1999	1951
Illinois	Dick Durbin	Democratic	U.S. House (IL-20)	1997	1944
Illinois	Barack Obama	Democratic	State Senate	2005	1961
Indiana	Evan Bayh	Democratic	Indiana Secretary of State, Governor	1999	1955
Indiana	Dick Lugar	Republican	Mayor of Indianapolis	1977	1932
Iowa	Chuck Grassley	Republican	U.S. House (IA-3)	1981	1933
Iowa	Tom Harkin	Democratic	U.S. House (IA-5)	1985	1939
Kansas	Sam Brownback	Republican	U.S. House (KS-2)	1996	1956
Kansas	Pat Roberts	Republican	U.S. House (KS-1)	1997	1940
Kentucky	Jim Bunning	Republican	U.S. House (KY-4)	1999	1931
Kentucky	Mitch McConnell	Republican	Jefferson County Executive	1985	1942
Louisiana	Mary Landrieu	Democratic	State Treasurer	1997	1955
Louisiana	David Vitter	Republican	U.S. House (LA-1)	2005	1961
Maine	Susan Collins	Republican	Deputy State Treasurer	1997	1952
Maine	Olympia Snowe	Republican	U.S. House (ME-2)	1995	1947
Maryland	Ben Cardin	Democratic	U.S. House (MD-3)	2007	1943
Maryland	Barbara Mikulski	Democratic	U.S. House (MD-3)	1987	1936
Massachusetts	Ted Kennedy	Democratic	lawyer	1962	1932
Massachusetts	John Kerry	Democratic	Lieutenant Governor	1985	1943
Michigan	Carl Levin	Democratic	Detroit City Council	1979	1934
Michigan	Debbie Stabenow	Democratic	U.S. House (MI-8)	2001	1950
Minnesota	Norm Coleman	Republican	Mayor of St. Paul	2003	1949
Minnesota	Amy Klobuchar	Democratic-Farmer-Labor	Hennepin County Attorney	2007	1960
Mississippi	Thad Cochran	Republican	U.S. House (MS-4)	1979	1937
Mississippi	Roger Wicker	Republican	U.S. House (MS-1)	2007	1951

State	Name	Party	Prior Experience	First took office	Born
Missouri	Kit Bond	Republican	Governor	1987	1939
Missouri	Claire McCaskill	Democratic	State Auditor	2007	1953
Montana	Max Baucus	Democratic	U.S. House (MT-1)	1979	1941
Montana	Jon Tester	Democratic	State Senator	2007	1956
Nebraska	Chuck Hagel	Republican	electronics executive, investment banker	1997	1946
Nebraska	Ben Nelson	Democratic	Governor	2001	1941
Nevada	John Ensign	Republican	U.S. House (NV-1)	2001	1958
Nevada	Harry Reid	Democratic	U.S. House (NV-1)	1987	1939
New Hampshire	Judd Gregg	Republican	Governor	1993	1947
New Hampshire	John E. Sununu	Republican	U.S. House (NH-1)	2003	1964
New Jersey	Frank Lautenberg	Democratic	U.S. Senate, Class 1	2003	1924
New Jersey	Bob Menendez	Democratic	U.S. House (NJ-13)	2006	1954
New Mexico	Jeff Bingaman	Democratic	State Attorney General	1983	1943
New Mexico	Pete Domenici	Republican	Albuquerque City Commission Chairman	1973	1932
New York	Hillary Rodham Clinton	Democratic	First Lady	2001	1947
New York	Chuck Schumer	Democratic	U.S. House (NY-9)	1999	1950
North Carolina	Richard Burr	Republican	U.S. House (NC-5)	2005	1955
North Carolina	Elizabeth Dole	Republican	Secretary of Labor, President of the American Red Cross	2003	1936
North Dakota	Kent Conrad	Democratic	State Tax Commissioner	1987	1948
North Dakota	Byron Dorgan	Democratic	U.S. House (ND-At Large)	1993	1942
Ohio	Sherrod Brown	Democratic	U.S. House (OH-13)	2007	1952
Ohio	George Voinovich	Republican	Governor	1999	1936
Oklahoma	Tom Coburn	Republican	U.S. House (OK-2)	2005	1948
Oklahoma	Jim Inhofe	Republican	U.S. House (OK-1)	1995	1934
Oregon	Gordon Smith	Republican	State Senate President	1997	1952
Oregon	Ron Wyden	Democratic	U.S. House (OR-3)	1997	1949
Pennsylvania	Bob Casey, Jr.	Democratic	State Treasurer	2007	1960
Pennsylvania	Arlen Specter	Republican	Philadelphia District Attorney	1981	1930
Rhode Island	Jack Reed	Democratic	U.S. House (RI-2)	1997	1949
Rhode Island	Sheldon Whitehouse	Democratic	State Attorney General	2007	1955

State	Name	Party	Prior Experience	First took office	Born
South Carolina	Jim DeMint	Republican	U.S. House (SC-4)	2005	1951
South Carolina	Lindsey Graham	Republican	U.S. House (SC-3)	2003	1955
South Dakota	Tim Johnson	Democratic	U.S. House (SD-At Large)	1997	1946
South Dakota	John Thune	Republican	U.S. House (SD-At Large)	2005	1961
Tennessee	Lamar Alexander	Republican	U.S. Secretary of Education	2003	1940
Tennessee	Bob Corker	Republican	Mayor of Chattanooga	2007	1952
Texas	Kay Bailey Hutchison	Republican	State Treasurer	1993	1943
Texas	John Cornyn	Republican	State Attorney General	2003	1952
Utah	Robert Bennett	Republican	businessman	1993	1933
Utah	Orrin Hatch	Republican	attorney	1977	1934
Vermont	Patrick Leahy	Democratic	Chittenden County State's Attorney	1975	1940
Vermont	Bernie Sanders	Independent	US Rep (VT-At Large)	2007	1941
Virginia	John Warner	Republican	U.S. Secretary of the Navy	1979	1927
Virginia	Jim Webb	Democratic	Secretary of the Navy	2007	1946
Washington	Maria Cantwell	Democratic	U.S. House (WA-1)	2001	1958
Washington	Patty Murray	Democratic	State Senate	1993	1950
West Virginia	Robert Byrd	Democratic	U.S. House (WV-6)	1959	1917
West Virginia	Jay Rockefeller	Democratic	Governor	1985	1937
Wisconsin	Russ Feingold	Democratic	State Senate	1993	1953
Wisconsin	Herb Kohl	Democratic	State Democratic Party chairman	1989	1935
Wyoming	John Barrasso	Republican	State Senate	2007	1952
Wyoming	Mike Enzi	Republican	State Senate	1997	1944

HOUSE OF REPRESENTATIVES

District	Name	Party	Prior Experience	First Took Office	Born
Alabama 1	Jo Bonner	Republican	congressional aide	2003	1959
Alabama 2	Terry Everett	Republican	journalist, newspaper publisher	1993	1937
Alabama 3	Mike D. Rogers	Republican	Calhoun County Commissioner, State House of Representatives	2003	1957
Alabama 4	Robert Aderholt	Republican	Haleyville Municipal Judge	1997	1965
Alabama 5	Bud Cramer	Democratic	Madison County District Attorney	1991	1947
Alabama 6	Spencer Bachus	Republican	state Republican Party chairman	1993	1947
Alabama 7	Artur Davis	Democratic	Assistant U.S. Attorney	2003	1967
Alaska At Large	Don Young	Republican	State Senate, ship captain, mayor of Fort Yukon	1973*	1933
Arizona 1	Rick Renzi	Republican	insurance executive	2003	1958
Arizona 2	Trent Franks	Republican	non-profit program manager, policy consultant	2003	1957
Arizona 3	John Shadegg	Republican	lawyer	1995	1949
Arizona 4	Ed Pastor	Democratic	Maricopa County Board of Supervisors, Teacher	1991*	1943
Arizona 5	Harry Mitchell	Democratic	Mayor of Tempe, State Senate	2007	1947
Arizona 6	Jeff Flake	Republican	non-profit program manager	2001	1962
Arizona 7	Raúl M. Grijalva	Democratic	Pima County Board of Supervisors	2003	1948
Arizona 8	Gabrielle Giffords	Democratic	State Senate	2007	1970
Arkansas 1	Marion Berry	Democratic	pharmacist, farmer	1997	1942
Arkansas 2	Vic Snyder	Democratic	physician, State Senate	1997	1947
Arkansas 3	John Boozman	Republican	optometrist	2001	1950
Arkansas 4	Mike Ross	Democratic	financial executive, State Senate	2001	1961
California 1	Mike Thompson	Democratic	military, State Senate	1999	1951
California 2	Wally Herger	Republican	State Assembly	1987	1945
California 3	Dan Lungren	Republican	State Attorney General	2005	1946
California 4	John Doolittle	Republican	State Senate	1991	1950
California 5	Doris Matsui	Democratic	law firm director	2005*	1944
California 6	Lynn Woolsey	Democratic	Petaluma City Council member,Teacher	1993	1937
California 7	George Miller	Democratic	State Senate	1975	1945

District	Name	Party	Prior Experience	First Took Office	Born
California 8	Nancy Pelosi	Democratic	San Francisco Board of Supervisors	1987	1940
California 9	Barbara Lee	Democratic	State Senate	1998*	1946
California 10	Ellen Tauscher	Democratic	investment banker	1997	1951
California 11	Jerry McNerney	Democratic	engineering executive	2007	1951
California 12	Tom Lantos	Democratic	U.S. Senate aide	1981	1928
California 13	Pete Stark	Democratic	Banking executive	1973	1931
California 14	Anna Eshoo	Democratic	San Mateo County Board of Supervisors	1993	1942
California 15	Mike Honda	Democratic	State Assembly	2001	1941
California 16	Zoe Lofgren	Democratic	Santa Clara County Board of Supervisors	1995	1947
California 17	Sam Farr	Democratic	State Assembly	1993	1941
California 18	Dennis Cardoza	Democratic	State Assembly	2003	1959
California 19	George Radanovich	Republican	Mariposa County Board of Supervisors	1995	1955
California 20	Jim Costa	Democratic	State Assembly	2005	1952
California 21	Devin Nunes	Republican	Director of Rural Development with the United States Department of Agriculture	2003	1973
California 22	Kevin McCarthy	Republican	State Assembly	2007	1965
California 23	Lois Capps	Democratic	nurse, teacher	1998*	1938
California 24	Elton Gallegly	Republican	City Council Member	1987	1944
California 25	Howard McKeon	Republican	Santa Clarita City Council Member	1993	1938
California 26	David Dreier	Republican	director of corporate relations	1981	1952
California 27	Brad Sherman	Democratic	lawyer, accountant	1997	1954
California 28	Howard Berman	Democratic	State Assembly	1983	1941
California 29	Adam Schiff	Democratic	State Senate	2001	1960
California 30	Henry Waxman	Democratic	State Assembly	1975	1939
California 31	Xavier Becerra	Democratic	State Assembly	1993	1958
California 32	Hilda Solis	Democratic	State Senate	2001	1957
California 33	Diane Watson	Democratic	U.S. Ambassador to Micronesia	2001	1933
California 34	Lucille Roybal-Allard	Democratic	public relations executive	1993	1941
California 35	Maxine Waters	Democratic	State Assembly	1991	1938
California 36	Jane Harman	Democratic	professor of public policy	2001	1945
California 37	Laura Richardson	Democratic	Long Beach City Council and assistant speaker pro tempore of the California State Assembly	2007	1962

District	Name	Party	Prior Experience	First Took Office	Born
California 38	Grace Napolitano	Democratic	State Assembly	1999	1936
California 39	Linda Sánchez	Democratic	attorney	2003	1969
California 40	Edward R. Royce	Republican	State Senate	1993	1951
California 41	Jerry Lewis	Republican	State Assembly	1979	1934
California 42	Gary Miller	Republican	State Assembly	1999	1948
California 43	Joe Baca	Democratic	State Senate	1999	1947
California 44	Ken Calvert	Republican	real estate executive	1993	1953
California 45	Mary Bono	Republican	congressional aide	1998	1961
California 46	Dana Rohrabacher	Republican	special assistant to Ronald Reagan	1989	1947
California 47	Loretta Sanchez	Democratic	financial analyst	1997	1960
California 48	John Campbell	Republican	State Assembly	2005	1955
California 49	Darrell Issa	Republican	electronics executive	2001	1953
California 50	Brian Bilbray	Republican	U.S. House, lobbyist	2006	1951
California 51	Bob Filner	Democratic	congressional aide	1993	1942
California 52	Duncan Hunter	Republican	attorney	1981	1946
California 53	Susan Davis	Democratic	State Assembly	2001	1944
Colorado 1	Diana DeGette	Democratic	State House of Representatives	1997	1957
Colorado 2	Mark Udall	Democratic	State House of Representatives	1999	1950
Colorado 3	John Salazar	Democratic	State House of Representatives	2005	1953
Colorado 4	Marilyn Musgrave	Republican	State House of Representatives	2003	1949
Colorado 5	Doug Lamborn	Republican	State Senate	2007	1954
Colorado 6	Thomas Tancredo	Republican	State House of Representatives	1999	1945
Colorado 7	Ed Perlmutter	Democratic	State Senate	2007	1953
Connecticut 1	John Larson	Democratic	State Senate	1999	1948
Connecticut 2	Joe Courtney	Democratic	State House of Representatives	2007	1953
Connecticut 3	Rosa DeLauro	Democratic	EMILY's List director	1991	1953
Connecticut 4	Christopher Shays	Republican	State House of Representatives	1987	1945
Connecticut 5	Chris Murphy	Democratic	State Senate	2007	1973
Delaware At Large	Michael Castle	Republican	Governor	1993	1939
Florida 1	Jeff Miller	Republican	real estate broker, deputy sheriff	2001	1959
Florida 2	Allen Boyd	Democratic	State House of Representatives	1997	1945
Florida 3	Corrine Brown	Democratic	State House of Representatives	1993	1946
Florida 4	Ander Crenshaw	Republican	State Senate	2001	1944
Florida 5	Ginny Brown-Waite	Republican	State Senate	2003	1943
Florida 6	Cliff Stearns	Republican	military	1989	1941
Florida 7	John Mica	Republican	State House of Representatives	1993	1943

District	Name	Party	Prior Experience	First Took Office	Born
Florida 8	Ric Keller	Republican	attorney	2001	1964
Florida 9	Gus Bilirakis	Republican	State House of Representatives	2007	1963
Florida 10	Bill Young	Republican	State Senate	1971	1930
Florida 11	Kathy Castor	Democratic	Hillsborough County Board of Commissioners	2007	1966
Florida 12	Adam Putnam	Republican	State House of Representatives	2001	1974
Florida 13	Vern Buchanan	Republican	auto dealer	2007	1951
Florida 14	Connie Mack IV	Republican	State House of Representatives	2005	1967
Florida 15	Dave Weldon	Republican	military	1995	1953
Florida 16	Tim Mahoney	Democratic	COO of assest management company	2007	1956
Florida 17	Kendrick Meek	Democratic	State Senate	2003	1966
Florida 18	Ileana Ros-Lehtinen	Republican	State Senate	1989	1952
Florida 19	Robert Wexler	Democratic	State Senate	1997	1961
Florida 20	Debbie Wasserman Schultz	Democratic	State Senate	2005	1966
Florida 21	Lincoln Diaz-Balart	Republican	lawyer	1993	1954
Florida 22	Ron Klein	Democratic	lawyer, State House of Representatives	2007	1957
Florida 23	Alcee Hastings	Democratic	lawyer, District Court judge	1993	1936
Florida 24	Tom Feeney	Republican	lawyer; State House of Representatives	2003	1958
Florida 25	Mario Diaz-Balart	Republican	aide to Miami Mayor Xavier Suarez; State House of Representatives	2003	1961
Georgia 1	Jack Kingston	Republican	agribusiness, insurance executive	1993	1955
Georgia 2	Sanford Bishop	Democratic	State Senate	1993	1947
Georgia 3	Lynn Westmoreland	Republican	State House of Representatives	2003	1950
Georgia 4	Hank Johnson	Democratic	lawyer, DeKalb County Commission	2007	1954
Georgia 5	John Lewis	Democratic	Atlanta City Council	1987	1944
Georgia 6	Tom Price	Republican	State Senate	2005	1954
Georgia 7	John Linder	Republican	State House of Representatives	1993	1942
Georgia 8	Jim Marshall	Democratic	Mayor of Macon	2005	1948
Georgia 9	Nathan Deal	Republican	State Senate	1993	1942
Georgia 10	Paul Broun[C]	Republican	physician	2007	1946
Georgia 11	Phil Gingrey	Republican	State Senate	2003	1942
Georgia 12	John Barrow	Democratic	Athens-Clarke County city/county commissioner	2005	1955

District	Name	Party	Prior Experience	First Took Office	Born
Georgia 13	David Scott	Democratic	State Senate	2003	1946
Hawaii 1	Neil Abercrombie	Democratic	Honolulu City Council; State Senate	1991	1938
Hawaii 2	Mazie Hirono	Democratic	Lieutenant Governor	2007	1947
Idaho 1	William Sali	Republican	State House of Representatives	2007	1954
Idaho 2	Michael K. Simpson	Republican	dentist	1999	1950
Illinois 1	Bobby Rush	Democratic	Chicago City Council, insurance agent	1993	1946
Illinois 2	Jesse Jackson, Jr.	Democratic	community organizer	1995	1965
Illinois 3	Dan Lipinski	Democratic	college professor	2005	1966
Illinois 4	Luis Gutierrez	Democratic	Chicago City Council, teacher, social worker	1993	1953
Illinois 5	Rahm Emanuel	Democratic	investment banker	2003	1959
Illinois 6	Peter Roskam	Republican	State Senate	2007	1961
Illinois 7	Danny K. Davis	Democratic	Chicago City Council, Cook County Board of Commissioners	1997	1941
Illinois 8	Melissa Bean	Democratic	consulting firm director	2005	1962
Illinois 9	Janice D. Schakowsky	Democratic	State House of Representatives	1999	1944
Illinois 10	Mark Steven Kirk	Republican	Counsel to House International Relations Committee	2001	1959
Illinois 11	Jerry Weller	Republican	State House of Representatives	1995	1957
Illinois 12	Jerry Costello	Democratic	chief investigator, Illinois State Attorney's office	1988*	1949
Illinois 13	Judy Biggert	Republican	State House of Representatives	1999	1937
Illinois 14	Vacant[D]				
Illinois 15	Timothy V. Johnson	Republican	attorney	2001	1946
Illinois 16	Donald Manzullo	Republican	attorney	1993	1944
Illinois 17	Philip Hare	Democratic	congressional aide, union leader	2007	1949
Illinois 18	Ray LaHood	Republican	State House of Representatives	1995	1945
Illinois 19	John Shimkus	Republican	Madison County treasurer	1997	1958
Indiana 1	Peter Visclosky	Democratic	attorney, congressional staff member	1985	1949
Indiana 2	Joe Donnelly	Democratic	lawyer, printing executive	2007	1955
Indiana 3	Mark Souder	Republican	U.S. Senate staff member	1995	1950

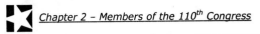

District	Name	Party	Prior Experience	First Took Office	Born
Indiana 4	Steve Buyer	Republican	legal counsel, military	1993	1958
Indiana 5	Dan Burton	Republican	State Senate	1983	1938
Indiana 6	Mike Pence	Republican	attorney, radio talk show host	2001	1959
Indiana 7	Vacant[F]				
Indiana 8	Brad Ellsworth	Democratic	Sheriff of Vanderburgh County	2007	1958
Indiana 9	Baron Hill	Democratic	State House of Representatives, U.S. House	2007	1953
Iowa 1	Bruce Braley	Democratic	lawyer	2007	1957
Iowa 2	David Loebsack	Democratic	political science professor at Cornell College	2007	1952
Iowa 3	Leonard L. Boswell	Democratic	State Senate	1997	1934
Iowa 4	Tom Latham	Republican	agribusiness	1995	1948
Iowa 5	Steve King	Republican	State Senate	2003	1949
Kansas 1	Jerry Moran	Republican	State Senate Majority Leader	1997	1954
Kansas 2	Nancy Boyda	Democratic	analytical chemist	2007	1955
Kansas 3	Dennis Moore	Democratic	attorney	1999	1945
Kansas 4	Todd Tiahrt	Republican	State Senator, Kansas	1995	1951
Kentucky 1	Ed Whitfield	Republican	attorney	1995	1943
Kentucky 2	Ron Lewis	Republican	State House of Representatives, minister	1994*	1946
Kentucky 3	John Yarmuth	Democratic	newspaper publisher	2007	1947
Kentucky 4	Geoff Davis	Republican	manufacturing consultant	2005	1958
Kentucky 5	Harold Rogers	Republican	attorney	1981	1937
Kentucky 6	Ben Chandler	Democratic	Attorney General, Kentucky	2004*	1959
Louisiana 1	Vacant[D]				
Louisiana 2	William J. Jefferson	Democratic	State Senate	1991	1947
Louisiana 3	Charlie Melancon	Democratic	industry association president	2005	1947
Louisiana 4	Jim McCrery	Republican	corporate attorney	1988*	1949
Louisiana 5	Rodney Alexander	Republican	State House of Representatives	2003	1946
Louisiana 6	Richard H. Baker	Republican	State House of Representatives	1987	1948
Louisiana 7	Charles Boustany	Republican	general surgeon	2005	1956
Maine 1	Tom Allen	Democratic	Mayor of Portland	1997	1945
Maine 2	Mike Michaud	Democratic	State Senate	2001	1955
Maryland 1	Wayne Gilchrest	Republican	teacher	1991	1946
Maryland 2	Dutch Ruppersberger	Democratic	Baltimore County Executive	2003	1946
Maryland 3	John Sarbanes	Democratic	lawyer	2007	1962
Maryland 4	Albert Wynn	Democratic	State Senate	1993	1951

District	Name	Party	Prior Experience	First Took Office	Born
Maryland 5	Steny Hoyer	Democratic	State Senate President	1981	1939
Maryland 6	Roscoe Bartlett	Republican	education, private sector	1993	1926
Maryland 7	Elijah Cummings	Democratic	State House of Delegates	1996	1951
Maryland 8	Chris Van Hollen	Democratic	State Senate	2003	1959
Massachusetts 1	John Olver	Democratic	college professor	1991*	1936
Massachusetts 2	Richard Neal	Democratic	Mayor of Springfield	1989	1949
Massachusetts 3	Jim McGovern	Democratic	congressional staff member	1997	1959
Massachusetts 4	Barney Frank	Democratic	Massachusetts House of Representatives	1981	1940
Massachusetts 5	Niki Tsongas	Democratic	Dean of External Affairs at Middlesex Community College	2007	1946
Massachusetts 6	John Tierney	Democratic	attorney	1997	1951
Massachusetts 7	Ed Markey	Democratic	State House of Representatives	1976	1946
Massachusetts 8	Mike Capuano	Democratic	Mayor of Somerville	1999	1952
Massachusetts 9	Stephen Lynch	Democratic	State Senate	2001*	1955
Massachusetts 10	Bill Delahunt	Democratic	Norfolk County District Attorney	1997	1941
Michigan 1	Bart Stupak	Democratic	attorney, State House of Representatives	1993	1952
Michigan 2	Peter Hoekstra	Republican	manufacturing executive	1993	1953
Michigan 3	Vern Ehlers	Republican	State Senate	1993	1934
Michigan 4	David Lee Camp	Republican	State House of Representatives	1991	1953
Michigan 5	Dale Kildee	Democratic	State Senate	1977	1929
Michigan 6	Fred Upton	Republican	U.S. government administrator	1987	1953
Michigan 7	Tim Walberg	Republican	State House of Representatives	2007	1951
Michigan 8	Mike J. Rogers	Republican	State Senate	2001	1963
Michigan 9	Joe Knollenberg	Republican	insurance agent	1993	1933
Michigan 10	Candice S. Miller	Republican	State Secretary of State	2003	1954
Michigan 11	Thaddeus McCotter	Republican	State Senate	2003	1965
Michigan 12	Sander Levin	Democratic	U.S. Government administrator	1983	1931
Michigan 13	Carolyn Cheeks Kilpatrick	Democratic	State House of Representatives	1997	1945
Michigan 14	John Conyers	Democratic	congressional aide	1965	1929
Michigan 15	John Dingell	Democratic	asst. prosecutor, Wayne County]]	1955*	1926
Minnesota 1	Tim Walz	Democratic-Farmer-Labor	Command Sergeant Major in the National Guard, teacher	2007	1964

District	Name	Party	Prior Experience	First Took Office	Born
Minnesota 2	John Kline	Republican	U.S. Marine Corps colonel	2003	1947
Minnesota 3	Jim Ramstad	Republican	State Senate	1991	1946
Minnesota 4	Betty McCollum	Democratic-Farmer-Labor	State House of Representatives	2001	1954
Minnesota 5	Keith Ellison	Democratic-Farmer-Labor	State House of Representatives	2007	1963
Minnesota 6	Michele Bachmann	Republican	Education adviser for Minnesota Family Institute, State Senate	2007	1956
Minnesota 7	Collin Peterson	Democratic-Farmer-Labor	Certified Public Accountant	1991	1944
Minnesota 8	Jim Oberstar	Democratic-Farmer-Labor	U.S. Marine Corps, chief staff assistant to Representative John Blatnik	1975	1934
Mississippi 1	Vacant				
Mississippi 2	Bennie Thompson	Democratic	alderman, mayor of Bolton, Hinds County Board of Supervisors	1993*	1948
Mississippi 3	Chip Pickering	Republican	congressional aide	1997	1963
Mississippi 4	Gene Taylor	Democratic	U.S. Coast Guard, State Senate	1989*	1953
Missouri 1	William Lacy Clay, Jr.	Democratic	State Senate	2001	1956
Missouri 2	Todd Akin	Republican	State House of Representatives	2001	1947
Missouri 3	Russ Carnahan	Democratic	State House of Representatives	2005	1958
Missouri 4	Ike Skelton	Democratic	State Senate	1977	1931
Missouri 5	Emanuel Cleaver	Democratic	Mayor of Kansas City, pastor, radio show host	2005	1944
Missouri 6	Sam Graves	Republican	State Senate	2001	1963
Missouri 7	Roy Blunt	Republican	State Secretary of State	1997	1950
Missouri 8	Jo Ann Emerson	Republican	professional advocate	1996*	1950
Missouri 9	Kenny Hulshof	Republican	Assistant State Attorney General	1997	1958
Montana At Large	Denny Rehberg	Republican	Lieutenant Governor, rancher	2001	1955
Nebraska 1	Jeff Fortenberry	Republican	Lincoln city council, businessman	2005	1960
Nebraska 2	Lee Terry	Republican	Omaha City Council, attorney	1999	1962
Nebraska 3	Adrian Smith	Republican	State Legislator	2007	1970
Nevada 1	Shelley Berkley	Democratic	State Assembly; attorney	1999	1951
Nevada 2	Dean Heller	Republican	State Secretary of State	2007	1960
Nevada 3	Jon Porter	Republican	Nevada Senate; insurance executive	2003	1955

District	Name	Party	Prior Experience	First Took Office	Born
New Hampshire 1	Carol Shea-Porter	Democratic	social worker, Rochester, New Hampshire, Rochester City Council	2007	1955
New Hampshire 2	Paul Hodes	Democratic	lawyer	2007	1951
New Jersey 1	Rob Andrews	Democratic	Camden County Board of Chosen Freeholders	1990	1957
New Jersey 2	Frank LoBiondo	Republican	New Jersey General Assembly	2003	1946
New Jersey 3	Jim Saxton	Republican	New Jersey Senate	1984	1943
New Jersey 4	Chris Smith	Republican	retail executive	1980	1953
New Jersey 5	Scott Garrett	Republican	New Jersey General Assembly	2003	1959
New Jersey 6	Frank Pallone	Democratic	New Jersey Senate	1989	1951
New Jersey 7	Mike Ferguson	Republican	teacher	2001	1970
New Jersey 8	Bill Pascrell	Democratic	Mayor of Paterson	1989	1937
New Jersey 9	Steve Rothman	Democratic	Bergen County Surrogate Court judge	1997	1952
New Jersey 10	Donald M. Payne	Democratic	Newark City Council	1989	1934
New Jersey 11	Rodney Frelinghuysen	Republican	New Jersey General Assembly	1995	1946
New Jersey 12	Rush D. Holt, Jr.	Democratic	physicist	1999	1948
New Jersey 13	Albio Sires	Democratic	New Jersey General Assembly	2006*	1951
New Mexico 1	Heather Wilson	Republican	business development planner	1999	1960
New Mexico 2	Steve Pearce	Republican	State House of Representatives	2003	1947
New Mexico 3	Tom Udall	Democratic	State Attorney General	1999	1948
New York 1	Tim Bishop	Democratic	Provost of Southampton College	2003	1950
New York 2	Steve Israel	Democratic	Huntington Town Board	2001	1958
New York 3	Peter T. King	Republican	Nassau County Comptroller	1993	1944
New York 4	Carolyn McCarthy	Democratic	Practical Nurse	1997	1944
New York 5	Gary Ackerman	Democratic	New York State Senator; newspaper publisher	1983	1942
New York 6	Gregory W. Meeks	Democratic	New York Assemblyman	1999	1953
New York 7	Joseph Crowley	Democratic	New York Assemblyman	1999	1962
New York 8	Jerrold Nadler	Democratic	New York Assemblyman	1993	1947
New York 9	Anthony D. Weiner	Democratic	New York City Councilman	1999	1964

District	Name	Party	Prior Experience	First Took Office	Born
New York 10	Ed Towns	Democratic	Brooklyn Deputy Borough President	1983	1934
New York 11	Yvette D. Clarke	Democratic	New York City Councilwoman	2007	1964
New York 12	Nydia Velázquez	Democratic	Director, Dept. of Puerto Rican Community Affairs	1993	1953
New York 13	Vito Fossella	Republican	New York City Councilman	1997	1965
New York 14	Carolyn B. Maloney	Democratic	New York City Councilman	1993	1948
New York 15	Charles B. Rangel	Democratic	New York Assemblyman	1971	1930
New York 16	José Serrano	Democratic	New York Assemblyman	1990	1943
New York 17	Eliot L. Engel	Democratic	New York Assemblyman	1989	1947
New York 18	Nita Lowey	Democratic	New York Assistant Secretary of State	1989	1937
New York 19	John Hall	Democratic	musician Ulster County Legislature; Saugerties School Board	2007	1948
New York 20	Kirsten Gillibrand	Democratic	lawyer	2007	1966
New York 21	Michael R. McNulty	Democratic	NY Assemblyman; Mayor of Green Island	1989	1945
New York 22	Maurice Hinchey	Democratic	New York Assemblyman	1993	1938
New York 23	John M. McHugh	Republican	New York Senator	1993	1948
New York 24	Michael Arcuri	Democratic	Oneida County District Attorney	2007	1959
New York 25	Jim Walsh	Republican	Syracuse Common Council	1989	1947
New York 26	Tom Reynolds	Republican	New York Assemblyman	1999	1950
New York 27	Brian Higgins	Democratic	New York Assemblyman	2005	1959
New York 28	Louise McIntosh Slaughter	Democratic	New York Assemblyman	1987	1929
New York 29	Randy Kuhl	Republican	New York Senator	2005	1943
North Carolina 1	G. K. Butterfield	Democratic	North Carolina Supreme Court Justice	2004*	1947
North Carolina 2	Bob Etheridge	Democratic	Public Schools Administrator, North Carolina	1997	1941
North Carolina 3	Walter B. Jones	Republican	State Representative, North Carolina	1995	1943
North Carolina 4	David Price	Democratic	college professor	1997	1940
North Carolina 5	Virginia Foxx	Republican	State Senator, North Carolina	2005	1943

District	Name	Party	Prior Experience	First Took Office	Born
North Carolina 6	Howard Coble	Republican	NC Secretary of Revenue, state representative	1985	1931
North Carolina 7	Mike McIntyre	Democratic	attorney	1997	1956
North Carolina 8	Robin Hayes	Republican	North Carolina House of Representatives	1999	1945
North Carolina 9	Sue Wilkins Myrick	Republican	Business owner	1995	1941
North Carolina 10	Patrick McHenry	Republican	North Carolina House of Representatives	2005	1975
North Carolina 11	Heath Shuler	Democratic	National Football League quarterback, real estate developer	2007	1971
North Carolina 12	Mel Watt	Democratic	attorney, State Senate	1993	1945
North Carolina 13	Brad Miller	Democratic	State Senate	2003	1953
North Dakota At Large	Earl Pomeroy	Democratic	State Insurance Commissioner	1993	1952
Ohio 1	Steve Chabot	Republican	Hamilton County Commissioner	1995	1953
Ohio 2	Jean Schmidt	Republican	State Senate	2005*	1951
Ohio 3	Michael R. Turner	Republican	Mayor of Dayton	2003	1960
Ohio 4	Jim Jordan	Republican	State General Assembly	2007	1964
Ohio 5	Bob Latta	Republican	Ohio House of Representatives, Ohio State Senator	2007	1956
Ohio 6	Charlie Wilson	Democratic	Ohio House of Representatives	2007	1943
Ohio 7	David L. Hobson	Republican	Ohio State Senator	1991	1936
Ohio 8	John A. Boehner	Republican	State House of Representatives	1991	1949
Ohio 9	Marcy Kaptur	Democratic	Domestic Policy Advisor, Carter Adm.	1983	1946
Ohio 10	Dennis J. Kucinich	Democratic	Mayor of Cleveland	1997	1946
Ohio 11	Stephanie Tubbs Jones	Democratic	Cuyahoga County Prosecutor	2000	1949
Ohio 12	Pat Tiberi	Republican	Ohio House of Representatives	2001	1962
Ohio 13	Betty Sutton	Democratic	Ohio House of Representatives	2007	1963
Ohio 14	Steve LaTourette	Republican	Lake County Prosecutor	2003	1954
Ohio 15	Deborah Pryce	Republican	Franklin County Judge	1993	1951
Ohio 16	Ralph S. Regula	Republican	U.S. Navy veteran, State Legislator	1973	1924
Ohio 17	Tim Ryan	Democratic	Ohio State Senator	2003	1973
Ohio 18	Zack Space	Democratic	attorney	2007	1961

District	Name	Party	Prior Experience	First Took Office	Born
Oklahoma 1	John Sullivan	Republican	State House of Representatives	2003	1965
Oklahoma 2	Dan Boren	Democratic	State House of Representatives	2005	1973
Oklahoma 3	Frank Lucas	Republican	State House of Representatives	2003	1960
Oklahoma 4	Tom Cole	Republican	college professor	2003	1949
Oklahoma 5	Mary Fallin	Republican	Lieutenant Governor	2007	1954
Oregon 1	David Wu	Democratic	attorney	1999	1955
Oregon 2	Greg Walden	Republican	State Senate	1999	1957
Oregon 3	Earl Blumenauer	Democratic	Portland City Commissioner	1996*	1948
Oregon 4	Peter DeFazio	Democratic	Lane County Commissioner, Chair	1987	1947
Oregon 5	Darlene Hooley	Democratic	Clackamas County Commissioner	1997	1939
Pennsylvania 1	Bob Brady	Democratic	congressional aide; Pennsylvania Turnpike Commission	1998*	1945
Pennsylvania 2	Chaka Fattah	Democratic	State Senator, Pennsylvania	1995	1956
Pennsylvania 3	Phil English	Republican	Chief of Staff, U.S. Senate	1995	1956
Pennsylvania 4	Jason Altmire	Democratic	hospital executive	2007	1968
Pennsylvania 5	John E. Peterson	Republican	State Senator, Pennsylvania	1997	1938
Pennsylvania 6	Jim Gerlach	Republican	State Senator, Pennsylvania	2003	1955
Pennsylvania 7	Joe Sestak	Democratic	Vice Admiral, U.S. Navy	2007	1951
Pennsylvania 8	Patrick Murphy	Democratic	Captain, U.S. Army	2007	1973
Pennsylvania 9	Bill Shuster	Republican	businessman	2001*	1961
Pennsylvania 10	Chris Carney	Democratic	Professor, army officer	2007	1959
Pennsylvania 11	Paul Kanjorski	Democratic	community solicitor, judge	1985	1937
Pennsylvania 12	John Murtha	Democratic	State Representative	1974*	1932
Pennsylvania 13	Allyson Schwartz	Democratic	State Senator	2005	1948
Pennsylvania 14	Michael F. Doyle	Democratic	State Senator Chief of Staff	1995	1953
Pennsylvania 15	Charlie Dent	Republican	State Senate	2005	1960
Pennsylvania 16	Joseph R. Pitts	Republican	State Representative, Pennsylvania	1997	1939
Pennsylvania 17	Tim Holden	Democratic	Sheriff, Schuylkill County, Pennsylvania	1993	1957
Pennsylvania 18	Tim Murphy	Republican	State Senator, Pennsylvania	2003	1952
Pennsylvania 19	Todd Platts	Republican	State Representative, Pennsylvania	2001	1962

District	Name	Party	Prior Experience	First Took Office	Born
Rhode Island 1	Patrick Kennedy	Democratic	State Legislature	1995	1967
Rhode Island 2	Jim Langevin	Democratic	Secretary of State, Rhode Island	2001	1964
South Carolina 1	Henry E. Brown, Jr.	Republican	State Representative, South Carolina	2001	1935
South Carolina 2	Joe Wilson	Republican	State Senator, South Carolina	2001	1947
South Carolina 3	Gresham Barrett	Republican	State Representative, South Carolina	2003	1961
South Carolina 4	Bob Inglis	Republican	attorney	2005	1959
South Carolina 5	John Spratt	Democratic	attorney	1983	1942
South Carolina 6	Jim Clyburn	Democratic	state government; teacher	1993	1940
South Dakota At Large	Stephanie Herseth Sandlin	Democratic	attorney	2004	1970
Tennessee 1	David Davis	Republican	State Representative	2007	1959
Tennessee 2	John James Duncan, Jr.	Republican	state court judge	1988*	1947
Tennessee 3	Zach Wamp	Republican	Business owner, real estate broker	1995	1957
Tennessee 4	Lincoln Davis	Democratic	State Senator, Tennessee	2003	1943
Tennessee 5	Jim Cooper	Democratic	college professor	2003	1954
Tennessee 6	Bart Gordon	Democratic	Tennessee Democratic Party State Chair	1985	1949
Tennessee 7	Marsha Blackburn	Republican	State Senator, Tennessee	2003	1952
Tennessee 8	John S. Tanner	Democratic	State Representative, Tennessee	1989	1944
Tennessee 9	Steve Cohen	Democratic	Attorney	2007	1949
Texas 1	Louie Gohmert	Republican	Texas appeals court judge	2005	1953
Texas 2	Ted Poe	Republican	federal court judge	2005	1948
Texas 3	Sam Johnson	Republican	Texas state legislator	1991	1930
Texas 4	Ralph Hall	Republican	attorney; financial executive	1981	1923
Texas 5	Jeb Hensarling	Republican	energy executive	2003	1957
Texas 6	Joe Barton	Republican	oil industry consultant	1985	1949
Texas 7	John Culberson	Republican	State representative, Texas	2001	1956
Texas 8	Kevin Brady	Republican	Beaumont, Texas Chamber of Commerce executive	1997	1955
Texas 9	Al Green	Democratic	Houston NAACP president	2005	1947

District	Name	Party	Prior Experience	First Took Office	Born
Texas 10	Michael McCaul	Republican	attorney, federal prosecutor	2005	1962
Texas 11	Mike Conaway	Republican	oil exploration executive	2005	1948
Texas 12	Kay Granger	Republican	Mayor, Fort Worth	1999	1943
Texas 13	Mac Thornberry	Republican	rancher, attorney	1995	1958
Texas 14	Ron Paul	Republican	physician	1997	1935
Texas 15	Rubén Hinojosa	Democratic	food processing executive	1997	1940
Texas 16	Silvestre Reyes	Democratic	U.S. Immigration and Naturalization Service administrator	1997	1944
Texas 17	Chet Edwards	Democratic	State Senator, Texas	1991	1951
Texas 18	Sheila Jackson-Lee	Democratic	City Council, Houston	1995	1950
Texas 19	Randy Neugebauer	Republican	real estate developer	2003	1949
Texas 20	Charlie Gonzalez	Democratic	district court judge	1999	1945
Texas 21	Lamar S. Smith	Republican	Bexar County, Texas commissioner	1987	1947
Texas 22	Nick Lampson	Democratic	US Congressman, Texas 9th district	1997	1945
Texas 23	Ciro Rodriguez	Democratic	US Congressman, Texas 28th district	1993	1946
Texas 24	Kenny Marchant	Republican	State Representative, Texas	2005	1951
Texas 25	Lloyd Doggett	Democratic	Texas state supreme court justice, college professor	1995	1946
Texas 26	Michael C. Burgess	Republican	physician	2003	1950
Texas 27	Solomon P. Ortiz	Democratic	Nueces County Sheriff	1983	1937
Texas 28	Henry Cuellar	Democratic	Secretary of State, Texas	2005	1955
Texas 29	Gene Green	Democratic	State Senator, Texas	1993	1947
Texas 30	Eddie Bernice Johnson	Democratic	State Senator, Texas	1991	1935
Texas 31	John Carter	Republican	district judge	2003	1941
Texas 32	Pete Sessions	Republican	marketing executive	1997	1955
Utah 1	Rob Bishop	Republican	Chairman of the Utah Republican Party	2003	1951
Utah 2	Jim Matheson	Democratic	Business owner	2001	1960
Utah 3	Chris Cannon	Republican	attorney; ventural capitalist	1997	1950
Vermont At Large	Peter Welch	Democratic	Vermont Senate President Pro Tempore	2007	1947

District	Name	Party	Prior Experience	First Took Office	Born
Virginia 1	Rob Wittman	Republican	Virginia State House	2007	1959
Virginia 2	Thelma Drake	Republican	Virginia State House	2005	1949
Virginia 3	Robert C. Scott	Democratic	Virginia State Senate	1993	1947
Virginia 4	Randy Forbes	Republican	Virginia State Senate	2001	1952
Virginia 5	Virgil Goode	Republican	Virginia State Senate	1997	1946
Virginia 6	Bob Goodlatte	Republican	Private legal practice	1993	1952
Virginia 7	Eric Cantor	Republican	Virginia State House	2001	1963
Virginia 8	Jim Moran	Democratic	Mayor of Alexandria	1991	1945
Virginia 9	Rick Boucher	Democratic	Virginia State Senate	1983	1946
Virginia 10	Frank Wolf	Republican	Assistant to the Secretary of the Interior	1981	1939
Virginia 11	Thomas M. Davis	Republican	chief elected official in Fairfax county	1995	1949
Washington 1	Jay Inslee	Democratic	Attorney	1999	1951
Washington 2	Rick Larsen	Democratic	Snohomish County Council	2001	1965
Washington 3	Brian Baird	Democratic	Psychologist	1999	1956
Washington 4	Richard Doc Hastings	Republican	Washington State House	1995	1941
Washington 5	Cathy McMorris	Republican	Washington State House	2005	1969
Washington 6	Norm Dicks	Democratic	Legislative Assistant	1977	1940
Washington 7	Jim McDermott	Democratic	Psychiatrist	1989	1936
Washington 8	Dave Reichert	Republican	King County Sheriff	2005	1950
Washington 9	Adam Smith	Democratic	Washington State Senate	1997	1965
West Virginia 1	Alan Mollohan	Democratic	attorney	1983	1943
West Virginia 2	Shelley Moore Capito	Republican	West Virginia House of Delegates	2001	1953
West Virginia 3	Nick Rahall	Democratic	Senate Staff Member; media executive	1977	1949
Wisconsin 1	Paul Ryan	Republican	Legislative Director	1999	1970
Wisconsin 2	Tammy Baldwin	Democratic	Wisconsin State Assembly	1999	1962
Wisconsin 3	Ron Kind	Democratic	County Prosecutor	1997	1963
Wisconsin 4	Gwen Moore	Democratic	Wisconsin State Senate	2005	1951
Wisconsin 5	Jim Sensenbrenner	Republican	Wisconsin State Senate	1979	1943
Wisconsin 6	Tom Petri	Republican	Wisconsin State Senate	1979	1940
Wisconsin 7	Dave Obey	Democratic	Wisconsin State Assembly	1969	1939
Wisconsin 8	Steve Kagen	Democratic	allergist	2007	1949

District	Name	Party	Prior Experience	First Took Office	Born
Wyoming At Large	Barbara Cubin	Republican	Wyoming State Senate; Wyoming State House	1995	1946
American Samoa	Eni Fa'aua'a Hunkin Faleomavaega, Jr.	Democratic	Lieutenant Governor of American Samoa	1989	1943
District of Columbia	Eleanor Homes Norton	Democrat	EEO Commission	1991	1937
Guam	Madeleine Bordallo	Democrat	Lieutenant Governor of Guam	2003	1933
Puerto Rico	Luis Fortuno	New Progressive Party & Republican	National Committee	2005	1960
United States Virgin Islands	Donna Christian-Christensen	Democrat	Commissioner of Health	1997	1945

CHAPTER 3

PERIODS OF WAR

Indian Wars:
The period January 1, 1817 through December 31, 1898. Service must have been rendered with the United States military forces against Indian tribes or nations.

Spanish-American War:
The period April 21, 1898 through July 4, 1902. In the case of a veteran who served with the United States military forces engaged in hostilities in the Moro Province the ending date is July 15, 1903.

Mexican Border Period:
The period May 9, 1916 through April 5, 1917, in the case of a veteran who during such period served in Mexico, on the borders thereof, or in the waters adjacent thereto.

World War I:
The period April 6, 1917, through November 11, 1918. In the case of a veteran who served with the United States military forces in Russia, the ending date is April 1, 1920. Service after November 11, 1918 and before July 2, 1921 is considered World War I for compensation or pension purposes, if the veteran served in the active military, naval, or air service after April 5, 1917 and before November 12, 1918.

World War II:
The period December 7, 1941through December 31, 1946. If the veteran was in service on December 31, 1946, continuous service before July 26, 1947 is considered World War II service.

Korean Conflict:
The period June 27, 1950 through January 31, 1955.

Vietnam Era:
The period August 5, 1964 (February 28, 1961 for Veterans who served "in country" before August 5, 1964), and ending May 7, 1975.

Persian Gulf War:
The period August 2, 1990 through a date to be set by law or Presidential Proclamation.

Future Dates:
The period beginning on the date of any future declaration of war by the Congress, and ending on a date prescribed by Presidential Proclamation or concurrent resolution of the Congress. (Title U.S.C. 101)

CHAPTER 4

DISABILITY COMPENSATION FOR SERVICE-CONNECTED DISABILITIES (TITLE 38, CHAPTER 11)

BENEFIT DESCRIPTION

In grateful recognition of their dedication and sacrifice, the United States, through the Veterans Administration has provided its former servicemen and women with compensation and pension programs designed to assist disabled veterans and their dependents. The disability compensation program provides financial assistance to veterans with service-connected disabilities to compensate them for the loss of, or reduction in earning power resulting from comparable injuries and disease in civil life.

Disability compensation payments vary in amount, depending on the impairment of earning capacity suffered by the veteran. The degree is assessed in multiples of 10, from 10 percent to 100 percent, with special statutory rates for such disabilities as blindness and loss of use of limbs.

Disability compensation payments vary in amount, depending on the impairment of earning capacity suffered by the veteran. The degree is assessed in multiples of 10, from 10 percent to 100 percent, with special statutory rates for such disabilities as blindness and loss of use of limbs.

The VA shall adopt and apply a schedule of ratings in reductions in earning capacity from specific injuries or combination of injuries. The rating shall be based, as far as practicable, upon the average impairments of earning capacity resulting from such injuries in civil occupations. The Administrator shall from time to time readjust this schedule or ratings in accordance with experience. The rates of compensation payments are not automatically adjusted for inflation, and they can be increased only if Congress passes specific enabling legislation. However, almost without exception, each Congress has acted to grant an increase equal to the consumer price index or the cost-of-living formula that determines the social security old-age increase.

If a veteran is evaluated as having a service-connected disability of 30 percent or more, the veteran is entitled to additional allowances for his or her dependents. In addition, in cases where a veteran has suffered certain severe disabilities, the veteran may be entitled to *special monthly compensation* (SMC), which can provide compensation payments at a rate much greater than the 100 percent rate. Severely disabled veterans in need of regular aid and attendance, or daily health-care services may be eligible for additional compensation.

WAR TIME DISABILITY COMPENSATION

ELIGIBILITY

A veteran may be entitled to VA disability compensation for any medical condition or injury that was incurred in, or aggravated by his or her military service. The veteran must have been discharged or released under conditions other than dishonorable from the period of service in which the injury or disease was incurred or aggravated.

There is no time limit for applying for VA disability compensation. However, veterans are encouraged to apply within one year of release from active duty. If a claim is filed within this period, entitlement may be established retroactively to the date of separation from service. If a claim is filed beyond one year of release from active duty, the effective date of eligibility for benefits will be based upon the date of the claim, not the date of separation.

No compensation shall be paid if the disability is a result of the person's own willful misconduct or abuse of alcohol or drugs.

There is no time limit for applying for VA disability compensation. However, veterans are encouraged to apply within one year of release from active duty. If a claim is filed within this period, entitlement may be established retroactively to the date of separation from service. If a claim is filed beyond one year of release from active duty, the effective date of eligibility for benefits will be based upon the date of the claim, not the date of separation.

INDIVIDUAL UNEMPLOYABILITY

There is a benefit administered by the U.S. Department of Veterans Affairs (VA) that is payable under certain conditions when a veteran has one or more service connected disabilities rated less than 100% that interfere with his or her ability to secure or retain employment. This benefit is known as Individual Unemployability (I.U.). I.U. must be established on a factual basis.

I.U. establishes entitlement to compensation at the 100% disability rate even though a veteran's combined disabilities are less than a scheduler 100% rating.

To apply for I.U. benefits VA form 21-8940, Application for Increased Compensation Based on Unemployability, must be submitted to the VA with current medical evidence on the extent of the service connected disabilities.

When an application for I.U. benefits is received by the VA, VA must first decide whether the veteran meets the requirements for a scheduler 100% rating before considering I.U.

The scheduler requirements for I.U. benefits are provided in the Code of Federal Regulations (38 CFR 4.16), which states in essence, that total disability ratings for compensation may be assigned when there is one disability rated at 60% or more, or two or more disabilities combined at 70% or more, with at least one of the combined disabilities rated at least 40%.

In addition, for the purpose of one 60% disability, or one 40% disability in the case of combined disabilities, the following will be considered one disability:

- Disabilities of one or both upper or lower extremities, including the bilateral factor if applicable.
- Disabilities resulting from common etiology or a single accident
- Disabilities affecting a single body system, such as, orthopedic, digestive, respiratory, cardiovascular-renal, neuropsychiatric
- Multiple injuries incurred in action
- Multiple disabilities incurred as a Prisoner of War (POW)

When considering I.U., the VA looks at the following evidence:

- Current degree of service connected disability
- Employment status
- Results of VA examination(s)
- Hospital reports and/or outpatient treatment records
- Current physical and mental status
- Nature of employment
- Reason employment was terminated
- Whether disabilities meet scheduler consideration (38 CFR 4.16)
- Whether Extra Scheduler consideration is warranted (38 CFR 3.321(b)(1)

In addition, VA will take in to consideration the veteran's previous type of occupation (such as physical or non physical) and his or her level of formal education.

Factors that may not be taken in to account when considering I.U. are:

- Age
- Non service connected (NSC) disabilities
- Injuries occurring after military service
- Availability of work

In certain situations where a veteran does not meet the percentage standards under 38 CFR 4.16 for scheduler consideration of I.U but the evidence supports that the veteran is unemployable due to his or her service connected conditions, VA rating boards may submit to the Director of Compensation and Pension Service for an Extra Scheduler consideration.

Once an I.U. rating is granted, VA will pay service connected compensation at the 100% rate.

Receipt of I.U. benefits does not mean that a veteran is never allowed to work again; however, if a veteran receiving I.U. benefits obtains substantially gainful employment, I.U. benefits can be terminated.

VA's definition of substantial gainful employment is basically any amount earned above the annual poverty limit for one person set by the U.S. Census Bureau. In 2007 the poverty limit for one person was $10,210.

Amounts earned below the Census Bureau annual poverty limit are considered marginal employment and do not affect receipt of I.U. benefits.

Each year after the U.S. Census Bureau sets the new poverty limit, VA publishes notice in the Federal Register.

Other Benefits Or Payments That May Affect VA Disability Compensation

By law, receipt of certain types of military pay may affect an individual's eligibility for VA Disability Compensation. Following are the categories of pay that may affect eligibility:

VA Pension Benefits

Occasionally, a veteran may be entitled to both VA Compensation benefits, and VA Pension benefits. The VA is prohibited from paying both benefits concurrently. In the event a veteran is entitled to both, he or she must elect to receive one benefit or the other. This election prevails, even if the option paying a lower benefit is chosen, and even if the election reduces the benefits payable to his or her dependents.

Selected Reserve and National Guard

Since September 11, 2001, numerous members of the Armed Forces Reserves have been called to active duty. Some of these individuals had already filed claims for VA compensation, based on earlier periods of active service. In September 2004, the VA General Counsel issued a precedent opinion that discussed the effect of a return to active service on a pending disability compensation claim.

In general, a veteran's return to active duty does not affect his or her claim for VA benefits, and does not alter either the veteran's right or the VA's duty to develop and adjudicate the claim. If the veteran is temporarily unable to report for a medical examination, or take some other required action because of his or her return to active duty, the VA must defer processing the claim until the veteran can take the required action. The VA cannot deny a claim because a veteran is temporarily unavailable due to a return to active duty.

A veteran is not entitled to receive both active duty pay and VA disability compensation for the same period of time. However, he or she is permitted to elect the higher benefit. If a veteran with a pending claim dies on active duty before the claim is decided, an eligible survivor may be entitled to any accrued benefits payable.

Military Retired Pay

Historically, veterans were not permitted to receive ***full*** military retirement pay and VA compensation benefits at the same time. Veterans who were entitled to both had to either elect one of the benefits, or waive the amount of retirement pay which equaled the amount of VA disability compensation to which he or she was entitled. (This issue was commonly known as "concurrent receipt".)

Because there was often a tax advantage to receive VA disability compensation, which is tax free, rather than military retirement pay, most disabled retirees chose to have a $1 reduction in their retired pay for each $1 of VA disability compensation they received.

Since this type of rule against "concurrent receipt" does not apply to any other group of federal or state retirees, may individuals and service organizations felt this was unfair discrimination against disabled military retirees.

This has been a very hot topic for the last several years, and Congress and the President have taken several steps toward eliminating the bar to concurrent receipt of full military retired pay and full disability compensation.

Since this type of rule against "concurrent receipt" does not apply to any other group of federal or state retirees, many individuals and service organizations felt this was unfair discrimination against disabled military retirees.

This has been a very hot topic for the last several years, and Congress and the President have taken several steps toward eliminating the bar to concurrent receipt of full military retired pay and full disability compensation.

Following is a summary of the steps taken from 1999 to the present.

Special Compensation For Severely Disabled Length Of Service Military Retirees

Section 658 of the National Defense Authorization Act for Fiscal Year 1999, Public Law 106-65, dated October 5, 1999, and (Title 10 U.S.C.1413) provided a "special compensation" for severely disabled length of service retirees of the Uniformed Services. This benefit was administered by the Department of Defense (DoD). The "special compensation" was paid to retirees with at least 20 years of regular service, who incurred VA disability ratings of 60% or higher within 4 years after retiring. (Payments ranged from $50 per month to $325 per month.)

This "special compensation" was repealed as of January 1, 2004, since the first increment of concurrent receipt (described below) is bigger than the "special compensation" for all recipients.

National Defense Authorization Act for Fiscal Year 2003

The National Defense Authorization Act for ***Fiscal Year 2003*** instituted a program called **Combat-Related Special Compensation (CRSC)**, which became effective with benefits payable June 1, 2003. Under the CRSC program, a new, tax-free, special compensation benefit was made available to the following military retirees:

- Veterans rated at least 10% disabled due to a combat wound for which they received the Purple Heart; or
- Veterans rated at least 60% disabled, and the disability was directly attributed to combat situations, combat-related training, hazardous duty, or instrumentalities of war.

Details Of CRSC Payments

- CRSC payments will be in the amount of the VA disability compensation paid for whatever percentage of the member's disability rating is due to combat-related disabilities, as determined by the parent service.
- Retirees must apply to their parent service for CRSC payments.
- There is no phase-in period for CRSC.
- CRSC is not subject to taxation.
- Individuals must apply for CRSC. For detailed information, individuals should contact the following:

ARMY:
DEPARTMENT OF THE ARMY
U.S. Army Physical Disabilities Agency/
Combat Related Special Compensation (CRSC)
200 Stovall Street
Alexandria, VA 22332-0470
(866) 281-3254

NAVY AND MARINE CORPS:
Department of Navy Naval Council of Personnel Boards
Combat-Related Special Compensation Branch
720 Kennon Street S.E., Suite 309
Washington Navy Yard, DC 20374-5023
(877) 366-2772

AIR FORCE:
United States Air Force Personnel Center Disability Division (CRSC)
550 C Street West, Suite 6
Randolph AFB TX 78150-4708
(866)229-7074

National Defense Authorization Act for Fiscal Year 2004

The National Defense Authorization Act for Fiscal Year 2004 further authorized that:

- Beginning January 1, 2004, all retirees with at least 20 years of service and VA disability ratings of 50% or higher began having their military retired pay offsets phased out over a ten-year period. (This is referred to as ***Concurrent Receipt*** throughout the remainder of this section.)

- The Combat Related Special Compensation (CRSC) (as outlined above) was expanded to include all combat-or-operations-related disabilities (from 10% to 100% ratings), effective January 1, 2004. In effect, this fully eliminated the offset to retired pay for any combat-or-operations-related disability.

In both of the above cases, Guard and Reserve retirees with 20 qualifying years of service (including those with less than 7,200 retirement points) are considered eligible.

Details Of Concurrent Receipt

For those retirees eligible for concurrent receipt (50% - 100%), there is to be a ten-year phase-out of the disability offset. For 2004, qualifying retirees should have seen their retired pay increase by a flat monthly amount for these ratings:

Disability Rating	Amount Of Monthly Increase
100%	$750
90%	$500
80%	$350
70%	$250
60%	$125
50%	$100

The remaining retired pay offset is then to be phased out over the following nine years:

Year	Remaining Offset To Be Reduced By
2005	10%
2006	20%
2007	30%
2008	40%
2009	50%
2010	60%
2011	70%
2012	80%
2013	90%
2014	100%

By January 2014, disabled retirees with 50% and higher ratings weree entitled to full concurrent receipt of military retired pay and VA disability compensation.

Because Concurrent Receipt is the restoration of retired pay, it is thus subject to the same tax provisions as a veteran's retired pay. If an individual's retired pay is taxable, concurrent receipt payments are taxable. If an individual's retired pay is non-taxable, concurrent receipt payments are to be non-taxable.

The changes approved in the 2005 NDAA did not apply to retirees who were rated 100 percent disabled because they are Individually Unemployable (IU) due to a service-connected disability.

However, the 2006 NDAA reduced the phase-in time from 10 years to 5 years for these individuals.

Concurrent Receipt is automatic. If you qualify you will automatically see an increase in your monthly retirement check.

National Defense Authorization Act of 2005:

The National Defense Authorization Act of 2005 eliminated the 9 year phase-in for full concurrent receipt payments to eligible retirees rated at 100% disabled by the VA, as of January 1, 2005. However the 9-year phase-in schedule ***is*** still in effect for retirees with disabilities rated at 50% to 90%, and, at that time, ***was*** still in effect for retirees who are rated 100 percent disabled because they are Individually Unemployable (IU) due to a service-connected disability.

National Defense Authorization Act of 2006:

The National Defense Authorization Act of 2006 reduced the phase-in time for full concurrent-receipt payments from 10 years to five years, for retirees who are rated 100 percent disabled because they are Individually Unemployable (IU) due to a service-connected disability

What If A Retiree Is Eligible For Both The CRSC And Concurrent Receipt Programs?

Retirees eligible for both programs will be able to make an election between the two programs, depending on which one is more advantageous.

Because the CRSC program provides full payment immediately, versus the 10—year phase in for concurrent receipt, the election can be changed each year. (This recognizes that a retiree who is 100% disabled, but only 60% of that is due to combat-related conditions, may find it advantageous to elect full CRSC payments for a few years until the concurrent receipt payment rises to a level that exceeds the CRSC payment. Because CRSC payments are tax-free, and non-disability retired pay is not, this could also figure into a retiree's election decision.)

BENEFIT RATES FOR SERVICE-CONNECTED DISABILITY COMPENSATION

The first chart shows the basic monthly benefit payable. However, depending on the disability rating of the veteran, there are additional allowances for a spouse, children, children over age 18 & attending school, and parents. The additional charts show these rates in detail.

Basic Rates of Disability Compensation –
Rates Effective December 1, 2007:

Title 38, USC 1114 subsection:	Disability Rating	Monthly Benefit
(a)	10 percent	$ 117.00
(b)	20 percent	230.00
(c)	30 percent	356.00
(d)	40 percent	512.00
(e)	50 percent	728.00
(f)	60 percent	921.00
(g)	70 percent	1161.00
(h)	80 percent	1349.00
(i)	90 percent	1517.00
(j)	100 percent	2527.00

Detailed Rates of Disability Compensation –
Rates Effective December 1, 2007:

DEPENDENT STATUS	DISABILITY RATING									
	10%	20%	30%	40%	50%	60%	70%	80%	90%	100%
Veteran Alone	$117	$230	$356	$512	$728	$921	$1161	$1349	$1517	$2527
Veteran & Spouse	117	230	398	568	799	1006	1260	1462	1644	2669
Veteran & Spouse & 1 Child	117	230	429	610	850	1068	1332	1545	1737	2772
Veteran & No Spouse & 1 Child	117	230	384	550	776	978	1228	1425	1603	2623

Detailed Rates of Disability Compensation - (Continued from previous page)
Rates Effective December 1, 2007

DEPEN-DENT STATUS	DISABILITY RATING									
	10%	20%	30%	40%	50%	60%	70%	80%	90%	100%
Veteran & Spouse & No Children & 1 Parent	117	230	432	613	856	1074	1339	1553	1746	2783
Veteran & Spouse & 1 Child & 1 Parent	117	230	463	655	907	1136	1411	1636	1839	2886
Veteran & Spouse & No Children & 2 Parents	117	230	466	658	913	1142	1418	1644	1848	2897
Veteran & Spouse & 1 Child & 2 Parents	117	230	497	700	964	1204	1490	1727	1941	3000
Veteran & No Spouse & No Children & 1 Parent	117	230	390	557	785	989	1240	1440	1619	2641
Veteran & No Spouse & 1 Child & 1 Parent	117	230	418	595	833	1046	1307	1516	1705	2737
Veteran & No Spouse & No Children & 2 Parents	117	230	424	602	842	1057	1319	1531	1721	2755
Veteran & No Spouse & 1 Child & 2 Parents	117	230	452	640	890	1114	1386	1607	1807	2851

Additional Amount Payable For Spouse Requiring Aid & Attendance
(Rates Effective December 1, 2007)

Disability Rating	30%	40%	50%	60%	70%	80%	90%	100%
Monthly Benefit	$39	$52	$64	$77	$90	$103	$116	$129

Additional Amount Payable For Each Additional Child Under Age 18 (Rates Effective December 1, 2007)								
Disability Rating	30%	40%	50%	60%	70%	80%	90%	100%
Monthly Benefit	$21	$28	$35	$42	$49	$56	$63	$71

Additional Amount Payable For Each Additional Child Over Age 18 Attending School (Rates Effective December 1, 2007)								
Disability Rating	30%	40%	50%	60%	70%	80%	90%	100%
Monthly Benefit	$68	$90	$113	$136	$158	$181	$204	$227

Notes:
Rates for Children over age 18 attending school are shown separately in the above chart. All other entries in the above charts reflect rates for children under age 18, or helpless.

All references in the preceding charts to parents refer to parents who have been determined to be dependent by the Secretary of Veterans Affairs.

Higher Statutory Awards for Certain Multiple Disabilities

Title 38, USC 1114 subsection (k)

If a veteran, as the result of a service-connected disability, has suffered the anatomical loss or loss of use of one or more creative organs, or one foot, or one hand, or both buttocks, or 25 percent or more tissue from a single breast or from both breasts in combination (loss by mastectomy or partial mastectomy or following radiation treatment), or blindness of one eye, having only light perception, or has suffered complete organic aphonia with constant inability to communicate by speech, or deafness of both ears, having absence of air and bone conduction, the rate of compensation shall be **$91** per month for each such loss or loss of use.

This additional amount is independent of any other disability compensation provided in subsections (a) through (j) of the above table, or subsection (s) described below; however, in no event may the total amount exceed **$3,145** per month.

In the event the veteran has suffered one or more of the disabilities previously specified in this subsection, in addition to the requirement for any of the rates specified in subsections (l) through (n), described below, the rate of compensation shall be increased by **$91** per month for each such loss or loss of use, but in no event may exceed **$4,412** per month.

Title 38, USC 1114 subsection (l)
If the veteran, as the result of a service-connected disability, has suffered the anatomical loss or loss of use of both feet, or of one hand and one foot, or is blind in both eyes, with 5/200 visual acuity or less, or is permanently bedridden or so helpless as to be in need of regular aid and attendance, the monthly compensation shall be **$3,145**.

Title 38, USC 1114 subsection (m)
If the veteran, as the result of a service-connected disability, has suffered the anatomical loss or loss of use of both hands, or of both legs at a level, or with complications, preventing natural knee action with prostheses in place, or of one arm and one leg at levels, or with complications, preventing natural elbow and knee action with prostheses in place, or has suffered blindness in both eyes, having only light perception, or has suffered blindness in both eyes, rendering such veteran so helpless as to be in need of regular aid and attendance, the monthly compensation shall be **$3,470**.

Title 38, USC 1114 subsection (n)
If the veteran, as the result of a service-connected disability, has suffered the anatomical loss or loss of use of both arms at levels, or with complications, preventing natural elbow action with prostheses in place, has suffered the anatomical loss of both legs so near the hip as to prevent the use of prosthetic appliances, or has suffered the anatomical loss of one arm and one leg so near the shoulder and hip as to prevent the use of prosthetic appliances, or has suffered the anatomical loss of both eyes, or has suffered blindness without light perception in both eyes, the monthly compensation shall be **$3,948**.

Title 38, USC 1114 subsection (o)
If the veteran, as the result of a service-connected disability, has suffered disability under conditions which would entitle such veteran to two or more of the rates provided in one or more subsections (l) through (n) of this section, no condition being considered twice in the determination, or if the veteran has suffered bilateral deafness (and the hearing impairment in either one or both ears is service connected) rated at 60% or more disabling, and the veteran has also suffered service-connected total blindness with 5/200 visual acuity or less, or if the veteran has suffered service-connected total deafness in one ear or bilateral deafness (and the hearing impairment in either one or both ears is service connected) rated at 40% or more disabling, and the veteran has also suffered service-connected blindness having only light perception or less, or if the veterans has suffered the anatomical loss of both arms so near the shoulder as to prevent the use of prosthetic appliances, the monthly compensation shall be **$4,412**.

Title 38, USC 1114 subsection (p)
In the event a veteran's service-connected disabilities exceed the requirements for any of the rates previously prescribed in this section, the Secretary of Veterans Affairs may allow the next higher rate, or an intermediate rate, but in no event in excess of **$4,412**.

In the event a veteran has suffered service-connected blindness with 5/200 visual acuity or less, and (1) has also suffered bilateral deafness (and the hearing impairment in either one or both ears is service connected) rated at no less than 30% disabling, the Secretary of Veterans Affairs shall allow the next higher rate, or (2) has also suffered service-connected total deafness in one ear or service-connected anatomical loss or loss of use of one hand or one foot, the

Secretary shall allow the next intermediate rate, but in no event in excess of **$4,412**.

In the event a veteran has suffered service-connected blindness, having only light perception or less, and has also suffered bilateral deafness (and the hearing impairment in either one or both ears is service-connected) rated at 10 or 20% disabling, the Secretary shall allow the next intermediate rate, but in no event in excess of **$4,412**.

In the event a veteran has suffered the anatomical loss or loss of use, or a combination of anatomical loss and loss of use, of three extremities, the Secretary shall allow the next higher rate or intermediate rate, but in no event in excess of **$4,412**.

Any intermediate rate under this subsection shall be established at the arithmetic mean, rounded down to the nearest dollar, between the two rates concerned.

Title 38, USC 1114 subsection (q)
This subsection was repealed by Public Law 90-493.

Title 38, USC 1114 subsection (r)
If a veteran is entitled to compensation under (o) of this section, at the maximum rate authorized under (p) of this section, or at the intermediate rate authorized between the rates authorized under subsections (n) and (o) of this section and at the rate authorized under subsection (k) of this section, is in need of regular aid and attendance, then, in addition to such compensation:

- The veteran shall be paid a monthly aid and attendance allowance at the rate of **$1,1893**; or
- If the veteran, in addition to such need for regular aid and attendance, is in need of a higher level of care, such veteran shall be paid a monthly aid and attendance allowance at the rate of **$2,820**, in lieu of the allowance authorized in the previous paragraph. (Need for a higher level of care shall be considered to be need for personal health-care services provided on a daily basis in the veteran's home by a person who is licensed to provide such services or who provides such services under the regular supervision of a licensed health-care professional. The existence of the need for such care shall be determined by a physician employed by the VA, or in areas where no such physician is available, by a physician carrying out such function under contract or fee arrangement based on an examination by such physician).

Title 38, USC 1114 subsection (s)
If a veteran has a service-connected disability rated as total, and:

- Has additional service-connected disability or disabilities independently ratable at 60% or more; or
- By reason of such veteran's service-connected disability or disabilities, is permanently housebound, and then the monthly compensation shall be **$2,829**.

For the purposes of this subsection, the requirement of "permanently housebound" will be considered to have been met when the veteran is substantially confined to such veteran's house (ward or clinical areas, if institutionalized) or immediate premised due to a service-connected disability or disabilities which it is reasonable certain will remain throughout such veteran's lifetime.

Title 38, USC 1114 subsection (t)
This subsection was repealed by Public Law 99-576.

Additional Compensation For Dependents (38 USC 1115)

Any veteran entitled to compensation under 38 USC 1114, and whose disability is rated not less than 30%, shall be entitled to additional compensation for dependents in the following monthly amounts:

If and while the veteran is rated totally disabled and:

1.	Has a spouse but no child living:	$142.00
2.	Has a spouse and one child living:	245.00
	(plus for each additional living child under age 18):	71.00
3.	Has no spouse, but one child living:	96.00
	(plus for each additional living child under age 18):	71.00
4.	Has a mother or father, either or both dependent upon him for support - for each parent so dependent:	114.00
5.	For a spouse who is a patient in a nursing home, or who is so helpless or blind as to require the regular aid and attendance of another person:	129.00 for a totally disabled veteran, and proportionate amounts for partially disabled veterans.
6.	For each child who is between the ages of 18-23, and who is pursuing a course of instruction at an approved educational institution:	227.00 for a totally disabled veteran, and proportionate amounts for partially disabled veterans.

Adjustment To Individual VA Awards

There will be no adjustment of VA awards. Special Compensation paid under 10 USC 1413 is provided under chapter 71, title 10, USC, "Computation of Retired Pay." However, it is NOT RETIRED PAY. It is to be paid from funds appropriated for pay and allowances of the recipient member's branch of service. Eligible retirees in receipt of VA disability compensation may receive this special compensation in addition to their VA disability compensation.

PRESUMPTIONS

Presumption Of Sound Condition

Every veteran will be assumed to have been in sound medical condition when examined, accepted, and enrolled for service, except any defects, infirmities, or disorders noted at the time of the examination, acceptance, and enrollment, or if there is clear and unmistakable evidence showing that the injury or disease did exist before acceptance and enrollment, and the injury or disease was not aggravated by such service.

Presumptions Of Service-Connection Relating To Certain Chronic Diseases And Disabilities

In the case of any veteran who served for 90 days or more during a period of war, any of the following shall be considered to have been incurred in, or aggravated by such service, notwithstanding there is no record of evidence of such disease during the period of service:

- A chronic disease (detailed below), becoming manifest to a degree of 10% or more within one year from the date of separation from such service.
- A tropical disease (detailed below), and the resultant disorders or disease originating because of therapy, administered in connection with such diseases, or as a preventative thereof, becoming manifest to a degree of 10% or more within one year from the date of separation from such service. Additionally, if it is shown to exist at a time when standard and accepted treatises indicate that the incubation period thereof commenced during active service, it shall be deemed to have incurred during such service.
- Active tuberculosis disease developing a 10% degree of disability or more within 3 years from the date of separation from such service.
- Multiple sclerosis developing a 10% degree of disability or more within seven years from the date of separation from such service.
- Hansen's disease developing a 10% degree of disability or more within three years from the date of separation from such service.

Chronic Diseases:

- Anemia, primary
- Arteriosclerosis
- Arthritis
- Atrophy, progressive muscular
- Brain hemorrhage
- Brain thrombosis
- Bronchiectasis
- Calculi of the kidney, bladder, or gallbladder
- Cardiovascular-renal disease, including hypertension
- Cirrhosis of the liver
- Coccidiodomycosis
- Diabetes mellitus
- Encephalitis lethargica residuals
- Endocarditis
- Endocrinopathies
- Epilepsies
- Hansen's disease
- Hodgkin's disease
- Leukemia
- Lupus erythematosus, systemic
- Myasthenia gravis
- Myelitis
- Myocarditis
- Nephritis
- Organic diseases of the nervous system
- Osteitis deformans (Paget's disease)
- Osteomalacia
- Palsy, bulbar
- Paralysis agitans
- Psychoses
- Purpura idiopathic, hemorrhagic
- Raynaud's disease
- Sarcoidosis
- Scleroderma
- Sclerosis, amyotrohpic lateral
- Sclerosis, multiple
- Syringomyelia
- Thromboangiitis obilterans (Buerger's disease)
- Tuberculosis, active
- Tumors, malignant, or of the brain or spinal cord or peripheral nerves
- Ulcers, peptil (gastric or duodenal)
- Other chronic diseases the Secretary of Veterans Affairs may add to this list.

Tropical Diseases:

- Amebiasis
- Blackwater fever
- Cholera
- Dracontiasis
- Dysentery
- Filiariasis

- Hansen's disease
- Leishmaniasis, including kala-azar
- Loiasis
- Malaria
- Onchocerciasis
- Oroya fever
- Pinta
- Plague
- Schistosomiasis
- Yaws
- Yellow fever
- Other tropical diseases the Secretary of Veterans Affairs may add to this list.

Presumptions Of Service-Connection Relating To Certain Diseases And Disabilities For Former Prisoners Of War

In the case of any veteran who is a former prisoner of war, and who was detained or interned for not less than thirty days, any of the following which became manifest to a degree of 10% or more after active military, naval or air service, shall be considered to have been incurred in or aggravated by such service, notwithstanding that there is no record of such disease during the period of service:

Starting October 7, 2005, VA expanded benefits to all former POWs with strokes and common heart diseases. Affected veterans will automatically be eligible for disability compensation for those common ailments, and their spouses and dependents will be eligible for service-connected survivors' benefits if these diseases contribute to the death of a former POW.

Public Law 108-183, The Veterans Benefits Act of 2003, eliminated the requirement that a veteran was a POW for at least 30 days for certain conditions. Therefore, there are now two categories of presumptive conditions - those that include the 30-day requirement, and those that do not.

In the case of any veteran who is a former prisoner of war, and **who was detained or interned for not less than thirty days,** any of the following which became manifest to a degree of 10% or more after active military, naval or air service, shall be considered to have been incurred in or aggravated by such service, notwithstanding that there is no record of such disease during the period of service:

- Avitaminosis

- Beriberi (including beriberi heart disease, which includes Ischemic Heart Disease-coronary artery disease-for former POWs who suffered during captivity from edema-swelling of the legs or feet- also known as "wet" beriberi)

- Chronic dysentery

- Helminthiasis

- Malnutrition (including optic atrophy associated with malnutrition)
- Pellagra
- Any other nutritional deficiency
- Peripheral neuropathy, except where directly related to infectious causes
- Irritable bowel syndrome
- Peptic ulcer disease
- Cirrhosis of the liver (This condition was added as part of Public Law 108-183, The Veterans Benefit Act of 2003.)
- Atherosclerotic heart disease or hypertensive vascular disease (including hypertensive heart disease) and their complications (including myocardial infarction, congestive heart failure and arrhythmia) (These conditions were added as part of Public Law 109-233.)
- Stroke and its complications (This condition was added as part of Public Law 109-233.)

In the case of any veteran who is a former prisoner of war, and **who was detained or interned for any period of time,** any of the following which became manifest to a degree of 10% or more after active military, naval or air service, shall be considered to have been incurred in or aggravated by such service, notwithstanding that there is no record of such disease during the period of service:

- Psychosis
- Any of the anxiety states
- Dysthymic disorder (or depressive neurosis)
- Organic residuals of frostbite, if the VA determines the veteran was interned in climatic conditions consistent with the occurrence of frostbite
- Post-traumatic osteoarthritis

Update:
Starting October 7, 2005, VA expanded benefits to all former POWs with strokes and common heart diseases. Affected veterans will be automatically eligible for disability compensation for those common ailments, and their spouses and dependents will be eligible for service-connected survivors' benefits if these diseases contribute to the death of a former POW.

Presumptions Relating To Certain Diseases Associated With Exposure To Radiation

VA may pay compensation for radiogenic diseases under two programs specific to radiation-exposed veterans and their survivors:

Statutory List

Veterans who participated in nuclear tests by the U.S. or its allies, who served with the U.S. occupation forces in Hiroshima or Nagasaki, Japan, between August 1945 and July 1946, or who were similarly exposed to ionizing radiation while a prisoner of war in Japan, are eligible for compensation for cancers specified in legislation.

The definition of radiation-risk activities was expanded in March 2002 to include service at Amchitka Island, Alaska, prior to January 1, 1974, if a veteran was exposed while performing duties related to certain underground nuclear tests.

The new definition also included service at gaseous diffusion plants located in Paducah, Ky., Portsmouth, Ohio and an area known as K25 at Oak Ridge, Tenn.

The types of cancer covered by these laws are:

- All forms of leukemia except chronic lymphocytic leukemia;
- Cancer of the thyroid,
- Cancer of the breast,
- Cancer of the pharynx,
- Cancer of the esophagus,
- Cancer of the stomach,
- Cancer of the small intestine,
- Cancer of the pancreas,
- Cancer of the bile ducts,
- Cancer of the gall bladder,
- Cancer of the salivary gland,
- Cancer of the urinary tract,
- Lymphomas (except Hodgkin's disease),
- Multiple myeloma,
- Primary liver cancer.

In March 2002, VA announced the addition of five new cancers to the list of diseases presumed to be connected to the exposure of veterans to radiation during their military service:

- Bone Cancer
- Brain Cancer
- Colon Cancer
- Lung Cancer
- Ovary Cancer

The new rules apply to those veterans who participated in "radiation-risk activities" while on active duty, during active duty for training or inactive duty training as a member of a reserve component.

Regulatory List

Disability compensation claims of veterans who were exposed to radiation in service and who develop a disease within specified time periods not specified in the statutory list are governed by regulation. Under the regulations, various additional factors must be considered in determining service-connection, including amount of radiation exposure, duration of exposure, and elapsed time between exposure and onset of the disease. VA regulations identify all cancers as potentially radiogenic, as well as certain other non-malignant conditions: posterior subcapsular cataracts; non-malignant thyroid nodular disease; parathyroid adenoma; and tumors of the brain and central nervous system.

A final rule that expanded the regulatory list from more than a dozen specific cancers to add "any other cancer" (any malignancy) was published Sept. 24, 1998. The rulemaking began following a 1995 review of the radiogenicity of cancer generally by the Veterans Advisory Committee on Environmental Hazards. It concluded that, on the basis of current scientific knowledge, exposure to ionizing radiation can be a contributing factor in the development of any malignancy. VA also will consider evidence that diseases other than those specified in regulation may be caused by radiation exposure.

Presumptions Of Service-Connection For Diseases Associated With Exposure To Certain Herbicide Agents

A disease specified below, becoming manifest in a veteran, who, during active military, naval, or air service, served in the Republic of Vietnam during the period beginning on January 9, 1962, and ending on May 7, 1975 shall be considered to have been incurred in or aggravated by such service, notwithstanding that there is no record of evidence of such disease during the period of such service.

The diseases referred to above are:

- Non-Hodgkin's lymphoma becoming manifest to a degree of disability of 10% or more.
- Each soft-tissue sarcoma becoming manifest to a degree of disability of 10% ore more other than osteosarcoma, chondrosarcoma, Kaposi's sarcoma, or mesothelioma.
- Chloracne or another acne form disease consistent with chloracne becoming manifest to a degree of disability of 10% or more within one year after the last date on which the veteran performed active military, naval, or air service in the Republic of Vietnam during the period beginning on January 9, 1962, and ending on May 7, 1975.
- Type 2 diabetes (also known as Type II diabetes mellitus or adult-onset diabetes)

- Hodgkin's disease becoming manifest to a degree of disability of 10% ore more.
- Porphyria cutanea tarda becoming manifest to a degree of disability of 10% ore more within a year after the last date on which the veteran performed active military, naval, or air service in the Republic of Vietnam during the period beginning on January 9, 1962, and ending on May 7, 1975.
- Respiratory cancers (cancer of the lung, bronchus, larynx, or trachea) becoming manifest to a degree of 10% or more.
- Multiple myeloma becoming manifest to a degree of disability of 10% or more.
- Acute and subacute peripheral neuropathy.
- Prostate cancer.
- Chronic Lymphocytic Leukemia.
- Each additional disease (if any) that the Secretary of the VA determines warrants a presumption of service-connection by reason of having positive association with exposure to an herbicide agent, becomes manifest within the period (if any) prescribed in such regulations in a veteran who, during active military, naval, or air service, served in the Republic of Vietnam during the period beginning on January 9, 1962 and ending on May 7, 1975, and while so serving was exposed to that herbicide agent.

Veterans having a disease referred to above, shall be presumed to have been exposed during such service to an herbicide agent containing dioxin or 2,4-dichlorophenoxyacetic acid, and may be presumed to have been exposed during such service to any other chemical compound in an herbicide agent, unless there is affirmative evidence to establish that the veteran was not exposed to any such agent during that service.

If the Secretary of the VA later determines that a previously established presumption of service-connection for one of the above diseases is no longer warranted, all veterans currently awarded compensation on the basis of the presumption shall continue to be entitled to receive compensation. Additionally, all survivors of any such veterans who were awarded dependency and indemnity compensation shall continue to be entitled to receive dependency and indemnity compensation on that basis.

Presumptions Of Service-Connection For Illnesses Associated With Service In The Persian Gulf During The Persian Gulf War

Like all other veterans, veterans of the Persian Gulf War can receive service-connected compensation for mental and physical disabilities that were incurred during, or aggravated by their service in the armed forces.

Recent legislation also authorized disability compensation for Persian Gulf veterans with chronic, **undiagnosed** illness resulting in a permanent disability that developed after they left the Persian Gulf.

Congress created this legislation after many Persian Gulf War veterans reported they were suffering from multi-symptom disabilities that are poorly understood by the medical profession, and may be classified as "undiagnosed" by one physician, or referred to as "chronic fatigue syndrome" by another physician.

Public Law 107-103, signed by President Bush on December 27, 2001, extended the presumptive period for disabilities associated with Persian Gulf War service until December 31, 2011, or such later date as prescribed by VA.

To be entitled to disability compensation due to an undiagnosed illness, the claimant must meet the following requirements:

1. The veteran must qualify as a Persian Gulf War veteran.

   VA considers an individual to be a Persian Gulf War veteran if he or she served on active military, naval, or air service in the Southwest Asia theater of operations during the Persian Gulf War. This includes service in Iraq, Kuwait, Saudi Arabia, the neutral zone between Iraq and Saudi Arabia, Bahrain, Qatar, the United Arab Emirates, Oman, the Gulf of Aden, the Gulf of Oman, the Persian Gulf, the Arabian Sea, the Red Sea, and the airspace above these locations.

   The veteran's period of service must have included service in the designated area after August 2, 1990. Since members of the armed services are still serving in the area of operations, they qualify as Persian Gulf veterans because the end date for the Persian Gulf War has not been set.

2. The veteran must suffer from a "qualifying chronic disability."

   A "qualifying chronic disability" can be any of the following (or combination of the following):

   a. An undiagnosed illnesses;
   b. A medically unexplained chronic multi-symptom illness (such as chronic fatigue syndrome, fibromyalgia, or irritable bowel syndrome) that is defined by a cluster of signs or symptoms;
   c. Any diagnosed illness that the VA Secretary determines warrants a pres

   (VA considers disabilities to be chronic if they have existed for 6 months or more, or if they have exhibited intermittent episodes of improvement and worsening over a 6-month period. The 6-month period is measured from the earliest date that the signs or symptoms manifested.)

3. The "qualifying chronic disability" must have appeared either during active duty in the Southwest Asia Theater of Operations during the Gulf War or it must have manifested to a degree of at least 10 percent during the presumptive period.

The following symptoms may be manifestations of an undiagnosed illness:

- Fatigue

- Skin disorders
- Headaches
- Muscle pain
- Joint pain
- Neurological symptoms
- Neuropsychological symptoms
- Symptoms involving the respiratory system
- Sleep disturbances
- Gastrointestinal symptoms
- Cardiovascular symptoms
- Abnormal weight loss
- Menstrual disorders
- Any poorly defined chronic multi-symptom illness of unknown etiology characterized by 2 or more of the above symptoms.

Rates of compensation depend upon the degree of disability, and follow a payment schedule that is adjusted annually and applies to all veterans. Please refer to the charts in detailed earlier in this chapter for the current rates payable.

LOU GEHRIG'S DISEASE
AMYOTROPHIC LATERAL SCLEROSIS (ALS)

VA has evidence that veterans who deployed to the Gulf War are nearly twice as likely as their non-deployed counterparts to develop Lou Gehrig's Disease, technically known as amyotrohpic lateral sclerosis, or ALS.

Based on new research, VA now has evidence that veterans who deployed to the Gulf War are nearly twice as likely as their non-deployed counterparts to develop Lou Gehrig's Disease, technically known as amyotrohpic lateral sclerosis, or ALS.

On December 10, 2001, VA reported that veterans who served in the Gulf during the period from August 2, 1990 through July 31, 1991, and who subsequently developed Lou Gehrig's Disease will be compensated.

Anyone seeking more information should contact the VA Gulf War Helpline at (800) 749-8387.

VA has established a national ALS registry to identify veterans with the disease – regardless of when they served – and track their health status. Veterans with

ALS who enroll will complete an initial telephone interview covering their health and military service, and will be interviewed twice yearly thereafter.

For more information about VA's ALS registry, call toll free (877) 342-5257.

Presumptions Rebuttable

If there is affirmative evidence to the contrary, or evidence to establish that an intercurrent injury or disease which is a recognized cause of any of the diseases or disabilities mentioned in the above sections, has been suffered between the date of separation from service and the onset of any such diseases or disabilities, or if the disability is due to the veteran's own willful misconduct, payment of compensation shall not be made.

Special Provisions Relating To Claims Based Upon Effects Of Tobacco Products

Effective June 10, 1998, a veteran's death or disability will not be considered to have resulted from personal injury suffered, or disease contracted in the line of duty if the injury or disease is attributable to the use of tobacco products by the veteran during the veteran's service.

PEACETIME DISABILITY COMPENSATION

Basic Entitlement

A veteran may be entitled to VA disability compensation for any medical condition or injury that was incurred in, or aggravated by his or her military service, during any period other than a period of war. The veteran must have been discharged or released under conditions other than dishonorable from the period of service in which the injury or disease was incurred or aggravated.

No compensation shall be paid if the disability is a result of the person's own willful misconduct or abuse of alcohol or drugs.

Presumption of Sound Condition

Every person employed in the active military, naval, or air service during any period other than a period of war, for 6 months or more, will be assumed to have been in sound medical condition when examined, accepted, and enrolled for service, except any defects, infirmities, or disorders noted at the time of the examination, acceptance, and enrollment, or if there is clear and unmistakable evidence showing that the injury or disease did exist before acceptance and enrollment, and the injury or disease was not aggravated by such service.

Presumptions Relating to Certain Diseases

If a veteran who served in the active military, naval, or air service after December 31, 1946, during any period other than a period of war, for 6 months or more, contracts any of the following, it shall be considered to have been incurred in, or aggravated by such service, notwithstanding there is no record of evidence of such disease during the period of service:

- A chronic disease, becoming manifest to a degree of 10% or more within one year from the date of separation from such service.
- A tropical disease, and the resultant disorders or disease originating because of therapy, administered in connection with such diseases, or as a preventative thereof, becoming manifest to a degree of 10% or more within one year from the date of separation from such service. Additionally, if it is shown to exist at a time when standard and accepted treatises indicate that the incubation period thereof commenced during active service, it shall be deemed to have incurred during such service.
- Active tuberculosis disease developing a 10% degree of disability or more within 3 years from the date of separation from such service.
- Multiple sclerosis developing a 10% degree of disability or more within seven years from the date of separation from such service.
- Hansen's disease developing a 10% degree of disability or more within three years from the date of separation from such service.

In the case of any veteran who served for 90 days or more during a period of war, service-connection will not be granted in any case where the disease or disorder is shown by clear and unmistakable evidence to have had its inception before or after active military, naval, or air service.

Presumptions Rebuttable

If there is affirmative evidence to the contrary, or evidence to establish that an intercurrent injury or disease which is a recognized cause of any of the diseases or disabilities mentioned in the above sections, has been suffered between the date of separation from service and the onset of any such diseases or disabilities, or if the disability is due to the veteran's own willful misconduct, payment of compensation shall not be made.

Rates Of Peacetime Disability Compensation

The compensation payable shall be the same as the compensation payable for Wartime Disability Compensation. Please refer to the charts presented earlier in this chapter.

Additional Compensation For Dependents

Any veteran entitled to peacetime disability compensation, and whose disability is rated as 30% or greater, will be entitled to additional monthly compensation for dependents in the same amounts payable for Wartime Disability Compensation. Please refer to the charts presented earlier in this chapter.

GENERAL DISABILITY COMPENSATION PROVISIONS

How To Apply For Disability Compensation Benefits

In order to apply for disability compensation benefits from the VA, Form 21-526, Veteran's Application for Compensation or Pension, must be completed and returned to the VA Regional Office serving the veteran's area (refer to Chapter 37 for a listing of regional offices). In addition to the application, the following documents must be submitted:

- Service Medical Records: In order to expedite processing of the claim, if an applicant has his or her service medical records, they should be submitted with the application. If not included with the application, VA will contact the veteran's service department to obtain them.
- Other Medical Records: Any medical records from private doctors or hospitals pertaining to the claim should be submitted along with the application.
- Dependency Documents: Copies of pertinent birth, marriage, death and divorce certificates should be submitted along with the application.
- Military Discharge / DD Form 214-Copy 4-Member Copy: In order to expedite processing of the claim, if an applicant has a copy of his or her DD-214, it should be submitted with the application. If not included with the application, VA will attempt to obtain verification from the veteran's service department.
- Copies of missing DD Forms 214 may be obtained form the National Personnel Records Center - 9700 Page Blvd. - St. Louis, MO - 63132-5100.

If any of the pertinent supporting evidence is not immediately available, the applicant should send in the application anyway. The date VA receives the application is important! If VA approves the claim, benefit payments usually begin from the date the application is received, regardless of when the claim is approved.

Adjudication

Adjudication means a judicial decision made by the Veterans Administration in claims filed within their jurisdiction. There is an Adjudication Division in each regional office, under the direction of an adjudication officer, who is responsible for the preparation of claims.

Upon the receipt of an original application in the Adjudication Division, it will be referred to the Authorization Unit for review and development in accordance with established procedures. All reasonable assistance will be extended a claimant in the prosecution of his or her claim, and all sources from which information may be elicited will be thoroughly developed prior to the submission of the case to the rating board. Every legitimate assistance will be rendered a claimant in obtaining any benefit to which he or she is entitled, and the veteran will be given every opportunity to substantiate his or her claim. Information and advice to claimants will be complete, and will be given in words that the average person can understand.

VA personnel must at all times give to claimants and other properly interested and recognized individuals courteous and satisfactory service which is essential to good public relations. It is incumbent upon the claimant to establish his or her case in accordance with the law. This rule, however, should not be highly technical and rigid in its application. The general policy is to give the claimant every opportunity to substantiate the claim, to extend all reasonable assistance in its prosecution, and to develop all sources from which information may be obtained. Information and advice to claimants will be complete and expressed, so far as possible, in plain language, which can be easily read and understood by persons not familiar with the subject matter.

Benefits For Persons Disabled By Treatment Or Vocational Rehabilitation

Compensation shall be awarded for a qualifying additional disability or a qualifying death of a veteran in the same manner as if such additional disability or death were service-connected, provided:

- The disability or death was caused by hospital care, medical or surgical treatment, or examination was furnished under any law administered by the VA, either by a VA employee, or in a VA facility, and the proximate cause of the disability or death was:
- Carelessness, negligence, lack of proper skill, error in judgment, or similar instance of fault on the part of the VA in furnishing the hospital care, medical treatment, surgical treatment, or examination; or
- An event not reasonably foreseeable.
- The disability or death was proximately caused by the provision of training and rehabilitation services by the VA (including a service-provider used by the VA) as part of an approved rehabilitation program.

Effective December 1, 1962, if an individual is awarded a judgment against the United States in a civil action brought pursuant to Section 1346(b) of Title 28, or enters into a settlement or compromise under Section 2672 or 2677 of Title 28 by reason of a disability or death treated pursuant to this section as if it were service-connected, then no benefits shall be paid to such individual for any month beginning after the date such judgment, settlement, or compromise on account of such disability or death becomes final until the aggregate amount of benefits which would be paid out for this subsection equals the total amount included in such judgment, settlement, or compromise.

Person Heretofore Having A Compensable Status

The death and disability benefits outlined in this chapter, shall, notwithstanding the service requirements thereof, be granted to persons heretofore recognized by law as having a compensable status, including persons whose claims are based on war or peacetime service rendered before April 21, 1898.

Aggravation

A preexisting injury or disease will be considered to have been aggravated by active military, naval, or air service, if there is an increase in disability during such service, unless there is a specific finding that the increase in disability is due to the natural progress of the disease.

Consideration To Be Accorded Time, Place And Circumstances Of Service

Consideration shall be given to the places, types, and circumstances of each veteran's service. The VA will consider the veteran's service record, the official history of each organization in which such veteran served, such veteran's medical records, and all pertinent medical and lay evidence. The provisions of Public Law 98-542 – *Section 5 of the Veterans' Dioxin and Radiation Exposure Compensation Standards Act* shall also be applied.

In the case of any veteran who engaged in combat with the enemy in active service with a military, naval, or air organization of the United States during a period of war, campaign, or expedition, the Secretary shall accept as sufficient proof of service-connection of any disease or injury alleged to have been incurred in or aggravated by such service, if consistent with the circumstances, conditions, or hardships of such service. This provision will apply even if there is no official record of such incurrence or aggravation in such service. Every reasonable doubt in such instance will be resolved in favor of the veteran.

Service-connection of such injury or disease may be rebutted only by clear and convincing evidence to the contrary. The reasons for granting or denying service-connection in each case shall be recorded in full.

Disappearance

If a veteran who is receiving disability compensation disappears, the VA may pay the compensation otherwise payable to the veteran to such veteran's spouse, children, and parents. Payments made to such spouse, child, or parent shall not exceed the amounts payable to each if the veteran had died from a service-connected disability.

Combination Of Certain Ratings

The VA shall provide for the combination of ratings and pay compensation at the rates prescribed previously in this chapter to those veterans who served during a period of war and during any other time, who have suffered disability in the line of duty in each period of service.

Combined ratings can be figured out by the following formula:

1. Subtract the highest rating, for the major disability, from 100%
2. Multiply the rating for the next lower disability by the sum remaining after the first subtraction.
3. Add the product to the major rating to arrive at the combined rating for two disabilities.

If there are three rated service-connected disabilities, then, after the combined rating for the two larger ratings has been calculated, subtract such combined rating from 100% and multiply the rating for the third disability times the remainder, and add the resulting product to the combined rating of the first two disabilities to arrive at the combined rating for the three disabilities.

Thus, if a veteran has a 60% disability, a 40% disability, and a 20% disability, the following calculation would be done to arrive at the combined rating of 81%:

1. 100 - 60 = 40
2. 40 X .40 = 16
3. 16 + 60 = 76
4. 100 - 76 = 24
5. 24 X .20 = 4.8 (round up to 5)
6. 76 + 5 = 81%

Tax Exemption

Compensation and pension may not be assigned to anyone, and are exempt from taxation (including income tax). No one can attach, levy, or seize a compensation or pension check either before or after receipt. Property purchased with money received from the government is not protected.

Protection Of Service Connection

Service connection for any disability or death granted under this title which has been in force for ten or more years shall not be severed on or after January 1, 1962, unless it is shown that the original grant of service connection was based on fraud, or it is clearly shown from military records that the person concerned did not have the requisite service or character of discharge. The mentioned period shall be computed from the date determined by the VA as the date on which the status commenced for rating purposes.

Preservation of Ratings

Public Law 88-445, approved August 19, 1964, effective the same date, amends Section 110, Title 38, U.S. Code as follows:

The law provides that a disability which has been continuously rated at or above a given percentage for 20 years or longer for the purpose of service connection compensation under laws administered by the VA shall not thereafter be rated at any lesser percentage except upon showing that the rating was based on fraud.

Special Consideration For Certain Cases Of Loss Of Paired Organs Or Extremities

If a veteran has suffered any of the following, the VA shall assign and pay to the veteran the applicable rate of compensation, as if the combination of disabilities were the result of a service-connected disability:

- Blindness in one eye as a result of a service-connected disability, and blindness in the other eye as a result of a non-service-connected disability not the result of the veteran's own willful misconduct; or
- The loss or loss of use of one kidney as a result of a service-connected disability, and involvement of the other kidney as a result of a non-service connected disability not the result of the veteran's own willful misconduct; or
- Total deafness in one ear as a result of a service-connected disability, and total deafness in the other ear as the result of non-service-connected disability not the result of the veteran's own willful misconduct; or
- The loss or loss of use of one hand or one foot as a result of a service-connected disability and the loss or loss of use of the other hand or foot as a result of non-service-connected disability not the result of the veteran's own willful misconduct; or
- Permanent service-connected disability of one lung, rated 50% or more disabling, in combination with a non-service-connected disability of the other lung that is not the result of the veteran's own willful misconduct.

If a veteran described above receives any money or property of value pursuant to an award in a judicial proceeding based upon, or a settlement or compromise of, any cause of action for damages for the non-service-connected disability, the increase in the rate of compensation otherwise payable shall not be paid for any month following a month in which any such money or property is received until such time as the total of the amount of such increase that would otherwise have been payable equals the total of the amount of any such money received, and the fair market value of any such property received.

Payment Of Disability Compensation In Disability Severance Cases

The deduction of disability severance pay from disability compensation, as required by Section 1212(c) of Title 10, shall be made at a monthly rate not in excess of the rate of compensation to which the former member would be entitled based on the degree of such former member's disability, as determined on the initial Department rating.

Trial Work Periods And Vocational Rehabilitation For Certain Veterans With Total Disability Ratings

The disability rating of a qualified veteran who begins to engage in a substantially gainful occupation after January 31, 1985, may not be reduced on the basis of the veteran having secured and followed a substantially gainful occupation unless the veteran maintains such an occupation for a period of 12 consecutive months.

("Qualified Veteran" means a veteran who has a service-connected disability or disabilities, not rated as total, but who has been awarded a rating of total of disability by reason of inability to secure or follow a substantially gainful occupation as a result of such disability or disabilities.)

Counseling services, placement, and post placement services shall be available to each qualified veteran, whether or not the veteran is participating in a vocational rehabilitation program.

CHAPTER 5

MISCELLANEOUS BENEFITS

(AUTOMOBILES, ADAPTIVE EQUIPMENT, CLOTHING ALLOWANCE AND MEDAL OF HONOR PENSION)

AUTOMOBILE ASSISTANCE PROGRAM

The VA offers an automobile assistance program for eligible veterans, or eligible members of the Armed Forces serving on active duty who are suffering from a disability as described below, if such disability is the result of an injury incurred or disease contracted in or aggravated in the line of duty in the active military, naval, or air service. Following are highlights of the VA program:

Financial Assistance

Qualified veterans may receive a ***one-time*** payment from VA of up to $11,000 to be used toward the purchase of an automobile or other conveyance. (This grant was increased from $9,000 to $11,000 as part of Public Law 108-183, the Veterans Benefits Act of 2003, which became law December 16, 2003.)

Eligibility Requirements For Receipt Of One-Time Payment:

Veterans or service members who are entitled to Disability Compensation under Chapter 11 of Title 38 due to one of the following service-connected losses:

- The loss or permanent loss of use of one or both feet; or
- The loss or permanent loss of use of one or both hands; or
- The permanent impairment of vision of both eyes of the following status:
- Central visual acuity of 20/200 or less in the better eye, with corrective glasses, or central visual acuity of more than 20/200 if there is a field defect in which the peripheral field has contracted to such an extent that the widest diameter of visual field subtends an angular distance no greater than twenty degrees in the better eye.

ADAPTIVE EQUIPMENT

In addition to the one-time payment described above, VA will also pay for installation of adaptive equipment deemed necessary to insure that the eligible veteran will be able to safely operate the vehicle, and to satisfy the applicable State standards of licensure.

VA will also repair, replace, or reinstall adaptive equipment determined necessary for the operation of a vehicle acquired under this program, or for the operation of a vehicle an eligible veteran may previously or subsequently have acquired.

Eligibility Requirements For Receipt Of Adaptive Equipment:

- The loss or permanent loss of use of one or both feet; or
- The loss or permanent loss of use of one or both hands; or
- The permanent impairment of vision of both eyes of the following status:
- Central visual acuity of 20/200 or less in the better eye, with corrective glasses, or central visual acuity of more than 20/200 if there is a field defect in which the peripheral field has contracted to such an extent that the widest diameter of visual field subtends an angular distance no greater than twenty degrees in the better eye; or
- Ankylosis (immobility) of one or both knees; or
- Ankylosis (immobility) of one or both hips.

Adaptive Equipment Available for Installation

The term adaptive equipment, means generally, any equipment which must be part of or added to a vehicle manufactured for sale to the general public in order to make it safe for use by the claimant, and to assist him or her in meeting the applicable standards of licensure of the proper licensing authority.

Following is a partial list of adaptive equipment available under this program:

- Power steering;
- Power brakes;
- Power window lifts;
- Power seats;
- Special equipment necessary to assist the eligible person into and out of the automobile or other conveyance;
- Air-conditioning equipment, if such equipment is necessary to the health and safety of the veteran and to the safety of others, regardless

of whether the automobile or other conveyance is to be operated by the eligible person or is to operated for such person by another person;

- Any modification of the size of the interior space of the automobile or other conveyance if necessary for the disabled person to enter or operate the vehicle;

- Other equipment, not described above, if determined necessary by the Chief Medical Director or designee in an individual case.

Eligible veterans are not entitled to adaptive equipment for more than 2 vehicles at any one time during any four-year period. (In the event an adapted vehicle is no longer available for use by the eligible veteran due to circumstances beyond his or her control, i.e. loss due to fire, theft, accident, etc., an exception to this four-year provision may be approved.)

SPECIALLY ADAPTED HOMES

Disabled persons may be entitled to a ***one-time*** grant from VA for a home specially adapted to their needs, or for adaptations. There are two types of grants that may be payable:

$50,000 Grant

The VA may approve a grant of not more than 50% of the cost of building, buying, or remodeling adapted homes, or paying indebtedness on homes previously acquired, up to a maximum of $50,000. (This grant was increased from $48,000 to $50,000 as part of Public Law 108-183, the Veterans Benefits Act of 2003, which became law December 16, 2003.)

To qualify for this grant, veterans must be entitled to compensation for permanent and total service-connected disability due to:

- Loss or loss of use of both lower extremities, which prevents movement without the aid of braces, crutches, canes, or a wheelchair; or
- Disability which includes:
- Blindness in both eyes, having only light perception; **with**
- Loss or loss of use of one lower extremity; or
- Loss or loss of use of one lower extremity together with:
- Residuals of organic disease or injury; **or**
- The loss or loss of use of one upper extremity, which so affects the functions of balance or propulsion as to preclude locomotion without using braces, canes, crutches, or a wheelchair.
- Loss of, or loss of use, of both upper extremities such as to preclude use of the arms at or above the elbows. (This disability was added as part of the Veterans Benefits Act of 2005.)

Eligibility For Active Duty Members

Public Law 108-183, The Veterans Benefits Act of 2003, which became law on December 16, 2003, extended eligibility for the $50,000 grant to members of the Armed Forces serving on ***active duty*** who are suffering from a disability as described above, if such disability is the result of an injury incurred or disease contracted in or aggravated in the line of duty in the active military, naval, or air service.

IMPORTANT UPDATE:

On June 15, 2006, the President signed Public Law 109-233, the Veterans Housing Opportunity and Benefits Act of 2006. One section of the law made several significant changes to the Specially Adapted housing (SAH) benefits.

Benefit Changes

- An eligible veteran or active duty service member can now use his or her benefit up to **three times**, as long as the aggregate amount of assistance does not exceed the maximum amounts allowable. (Prior to this law, grant recipients could only receive their SAH benefit from VA one time, regardless of the grant amount.)
- This benefit extends to previous grant recipients, however, they cannot obtain a subsequent grant(s) to pay for adaptations made prior to June 15, 2006, or to reduce an existing mortgage principal balance for properties acquired prior to June 15, 2006.
- The Law authorizes VA to provide a **TEMPORARY RESIDENCE ADAPTATION GRANT** of up to $14,000 (for those eligible for the $50,000 grant) to assist a veteran in adapting a family member's home to meet the veteran's special needs.
- The Law authorizes VA to provide a **TEMPORARY RESIDENCE ADAPTATION GRANT** of up to $2,000 (for those eligible for the $10,000 grant) to assist a veteran in adapting a family member's home to meet the veteran's special needs.

  Note: The Temporary Residence Adaptation Grant does not apply to active duty personnel, and no Temporary Adaptation Grant can be provided after June 15, 2011.

$10,000 Grant

VA may approve a grant for the actual cost, up to a maximum of $10,000, for adaptations to a veteran's residence that are determined by VA to be reasonable necessary. (This grant was increased from $9,250 to $10,000 as part of Public Law 108-183, the Veterans Benefits Act of 2003, which became law December 16, 2003.)

The grant may also be used to assist veterans in acquiring a residence that already has been adapted with special features for the veteran's disability.

To qualify for this grant, veterans must be entitled to compensation for permanent and total service-connected disability due to:

- Blindness in both eyes, with 5/200 visual acuity or less; or
- Anatomical loss or loss of use of both hands.

Supplemental Financing – Loan Guaranty

Veterans who have available loan guaranty entitlement may also obtain a guaranteed loan or possibly a direct loan from VA to supplement the grant to acquire a specially adapted home. Please refer to Chapter 22 of this book for specific information on VA Loan Guaranties.

CLOTHING ALLOWANCE

The VA shall pay a clothing allowance of $677.00 per year (rate effective December 1, 2007 but not payable until August 1, 2008 to each veteran who:

- Because of a service-connected disability, wears or uses a prosthetic or orthopedic appliance (including a wheelchair) which the VA determines tends to wear out or tear the clothing of the veteran; or
- Uses medication prescribed by a physician for a skin condition that is due to a service-connected disability, and which the VA determines causes irreparable damage to the veteran's outer garments.

MEDAL OF HONOR PENSION

VA administers pensions to holders of the Medal of Honor. In December 1998, Congress set the monthly pension at $600. Public Law 107-330 (signed by President Bush on December 6, 2002) increased this monthly amount to $1,000, effective September 1, 2003.

As of December 1, 2007, the Medal of Honor pension is $1,129 per month.

Public Law 107-330 also directed the VA to increase the amount of the monthly Medal of Honor Pension December 1 of each year by the same percentage as the percentage by which benefit amounts payable under Title II of the Social Security Act are increased. As of December 1, 2007, the Medal of Honor pension is $1,129 per month.

The Law further states that VA shall pay, in a lump sum, to each person who is in receipt of the Medal of Honor Pension, an amount equal to the total amount of special pension that the person would have received during the period beginning on the 1st day of the 1st month beginning after the date of the act for which the person was awarded the Medal of Honor, and ending on the last day of the month preceding the month in which the person's special pension commenced.

For each month of a period referred to in the previous paragraph, the amount of special pension payable shall be determined using the rate of special pension that was in effect for such month.

The Secretary of the Department of the Army, the Department of the Navy, the Department of the Air Force, or the Department of Transportation will determine the eligibility of applicants to be entered on the Medal of Honor Roll and will deliver to the Secretary of the Department of Veterans Affairs a certified copy of each certificate issued in which the right of the person named in the certificate to the special pension is set forth. The special pension will be authorized on the basis of such certification.

The special pension will be paid in addition to all other payments under laws of the United States. However, a person awarded more than one Medal of Honor may not receive more than one special pension.

CHAPTER 6

NON-SERVICE CONNECTED DISABILITY PENSION

BENEFIT DESCRIPTION

Non-Service Connected Disability Pension is a Department of Veterans Affairs benefits program that provides financial support to wartime veterans having limited income. The amount payable under this program depends on the type and amount of income the veteran and family members receive from other sources. Monthly payments are made to bring a veteran's total annual income (including other retirement and Social Security income) to an established support level. (Unreimbursed medical expenses may reduce countable income.)

DEFINITIONS

The following definitions apply only to CHAPTER 6 – NON-SERVICE CONNECTED DISABILITY PENSION:

Indian Wars: means the campaigns, engagements, and expeditions of the United States military forces against Indian tribes or nations, service in which has been recognized heretofore as pensionable service.

World War I: means the period April 6, 1917, through November 11, 1918. In the case of a veteran who served with the United States military forces in Russia, the ending date is April 1, 1920. Service after November 11, 1918 and before July 2, 1921 is considered World War I for compensation or pension purposes, if the veteran served in the active military, naval, or air service after April 5, 1917 and before November 12, 1918.

Civil War Veteran: includes a person who served in the military or naval forces of the Confederate States of America during the Civil War, and the term "active military or naval service" includes active service in those forces.

Period of War: means the Mexican border period, World War I, World War II, the Korean conflict, the Vietnam era, the Persian Gulf War, and the period beginning on the date of any future declaration of war by the Congress and ending on the date prescribed by Presidential proclamation or concurrent resolution of the Congress.

Permanently and Totally Disabled: for the purposes of this chapter, a person shall be considered to be permanently and totally disabled if such person is unemployable as a result of a disability reasonably certain to continue throughout the life of the disabled person, or:

- Suffering from any disability which is sufficient to render it impossible for the average person to follow a substantially gainful occupation, but only if it is reasonably certain that such disability will continue throughout the life of the disabled person; or

- Suffering from any disease or disorder determined by the VA Secretary to be of such a nature or extent as to justify a determination that persons suffering therefrom are permanently and totally disabled; or

- Is a patient in a nursing home for long-term care because of disability; or

- Is disabled, as determined by the Social Security Administration (SSA) for purpose of benefits administered by the SSA; or

- Is unemployable, as a result of suffering from any disability which is sufficient to render it impossible for the average person to follow a substantially gainful occupation, but only if it is reasonable certain that such disability will continue throughout the life of the person, or otherwise justifying a determination of permanent and total disability.

Regular Aid and Attendance: for the purposes of this chapter, a person shall be considered to be in need of regular aid and attendance if such person is:

- A patient in a nursing home; or

- Helpless or blind, or so nearly helpless or blind as to need or require the aid and attendance of another person.

Permanently Housebound: for the purposes of this chapter, the requirement of "permanently housebound" will be considered to have been met when the veteran is substantially confined to such veteran's house (ward or clinical areas, if institutionalized) or immediate premises due to a disability or disabilities, which it is reasonably certain will remain throughout such veteran's lifetime.

Annual Income: In determining annual income under this chapter, all payments of any kind or from any source (including salary, retirement or annuity payments, or similar income, which has been waived, irrespective of whether the waiver was made pursuant to statue, contract, or otherwise) shall be included except:

- Donations from public or private relief or welfare organizations;

- Payments under this chapter;

- Amounts equal to amounts paid by a spouse of a veteran for the expenses of such veteran's last illness, and by a surviving spouse or child of a deceased veteran for:

- Such veteran's just debts;

- The expenses of such veteran's last illness; and

- The expenses of such veteran's burial to the extent such expenses are not reimbursed through Chapter 23 of Title 38, United States Code (Burial Benefits);
- Amounts equal to amounts paid:
- By a veteran for the last illness and burial of such veteran's deceased spouse or child; or
- By the spouse of a living veteran or the surviving spouse of a deceased veteran for the last illness and burial of a child of such veteran;
- Reimbursements of any kind for any casualty loss, but the amount excluded under this clause may not exceed the greater of the fair market value or reasonable replacement value of the property involved at the time immediately preceding the loss;
- Profit realized from the disposition of real or personal property other than in the course of a business;
- Amounts in joint accounts in banks and similar institutions acquired by reason of death of other joint owner;
- Amounts equal to amounts paid by a veteran, veteran's spouse, or surviving spouse, or by or on behalf of a veteran's child for unreimbursed medical expenses, to the extent that such amounts exceed 5% of the maximum annual rate of pension (including any amount of increased pension payable on account of family members but not including any amount of pension payable because a person is in need of regular aid and attendance, or because a person is permanently housebound) payable to such veteran surviving spouse, or child.
- In the case of a veteran or surviving spouse pursuing a course of education or vocational rehabilitation or training, amounts equal to amounts paid by such veteran or surviving spouse for such course of education or vocational rehabilitation or training, including:
- Amounts paid for tuition, fees, books, and materials; and
- In the case of such a veteran or surviving spouse in need of regular aid and attendance, unreimbursed amounts paid for unusual transpiration expenses in connection with the pursuit of such course of education or vocational rehabilitation or training, to the extent that such amounts exceed the reasonable expenses which would have been incurred by a nondisabled person using an appropriate means of transportation (public transportation, if reasonably available); and
- In the case of a child, or any current-work income received during the year, to the extent that the total amount of such income does not exceed an amount equal to the sum of:
- The lowest amount of gross income for which an income tax return is required under section 6012(a) of the Internal Revenue Code of 1986, to be filed by an individual who is not married, is not a surviving spouse, and is not a head of household; and

- If the child is pursuing a course of postsecondary education or vocational rehabilitation or training, the amount paid by such child for such course of education or vocational rehabilitation or training, including the amount paid for tuition, fees, books, and materials.

Note: Where a fraction of a dollar is involved, annual income shall be fixed at the next lower dollar.

ELIGIBILITY

- Veteran was discharged from service under other than dishonorable conditions; and
- Veteran served 90 days or more of active duty with at least 1 day during a period of war time. However, 38 CFR 3.12a requires that anyone who enlisted after 9/7/80 generally has to serve at least 24 months or the full period for which a person was called or ordered to active duty in order to receive any benefits based on that period of service; and
- Veteran is permanently and totally disabled, or is age 65 or older; and
- Veteran's countable family income is below a yearly limit set by law.

AMOUNT OF VA PAYMENTS

If eligible, VA pays the difference between a recipient's countable family income and the annual income limit set by law (see following charts) for his or her status. This difference is generally paid in 12 equal monthly installments.

Family Income Limits

Improved Pension Annual Rates (PL-95-588) Effective December 1, 2007	
STATUS OF VETERAN:	**ANNUAL INCOME LIMITATION:**
Permanently & totally disabled veterans:	
Veteran alone	*$11,181.00*
Veteran with one dependent	*14,643.00*
Each additional dependent child	*1,909.00*
Veteran – Aid and Attendance:	
Veteran alone	*18,654.00*
Veteran with one dependent	*22,113.00*
Each additional dependent child	*1,909.00*
Veteran – Housebound:	
Veteran alone	*13,664.00*
Veteran with one dependent	*17,126.00*
Each additional dependent child	*1,909.00*
Two veterans married to one another:	*14,643.00*
Each additional dependent child	*1,909.00*
Add for Mexican Border Period or World War I Veterans:	*2,538.00*
Child Earned Income Exclusion effective 1-1-2008 –	*$8,950.00*

Maximum Annual Income Limitations For Protected Pensions - (Effective December 1, 2007)

Pensioners entitled to benefits as of December 31, 1978, who do not elect to receive a pension under the Improved Pension Program, may continue to receive pension benefits at the rates they were entitled to receive on December 31, 1978 or June 30, 1960, as long as they remain permanently and totally disabled, do not lose a dependent, and their income does not exceed the income limitation, adjusted annually. Under the Old Law Disability Pensions, all veterans whose income was under the annual limitation received the same monthly amount. These monthly amounts are also listed below, following the annual income limitation charts.

Pension Law in Effect on December 31, 1978 (Section 306):

The rate entitled to on December 31, 1978 may be continued if the recipient's IVAP for 2007 is below the following limits:

STATUS OF RECIPIENT:	ANNUAL INCOME LIMITATION:
Veteran / widow with no dependents	*$ 12,718.00*
Veteran / widow with one or more dependent	*17,095.00*
Child (no entitled veteran or surviving spouse)	*10,397.00*
Veteran with no dependents in receipt of A&A	*13,218.00*
Veteran with one dependent in receipt of A&A	*17,595.00*
Surviving spouse's income exclusion	*4,059.00*

Pension Law in Effect on June 30, 1960 (Old Law):

The rate entitled to on June 30, 1960 may be continued if the recipient's IVAP for 2007 is below the following limits:

STATUS OF RECIPIENT:	ANNUAL INCOME LIMITATION:
Veteran / widow with no dependents	*$ 11,134.00*
Veteran / widow with one or more dependents	*16,051.00*
Child (no entitled veteran or surviving spouse)	*11,134.00*

Monthly Benefit Payable To Eligible Veterans Receiving Disability Pension Under Laws In Effect

June 30, 1960 Or December 31, 1978

VETERAN'S ENTITLEMENT:	RATE PAYABLE:
Basic Rates	*$ 66.15*
10 Years or Age 65	*78.75*
If Entitled To Aid & Attendance	*135.45*
If Entitled To Housebound	*100.00*

APPLYING FOR BENEFITS

> *If any of the pertinent supporting evidence is not immediately available, the applicant should send in the application anyway. The date VA receives the application is important! If VA approves the claim, benefit payments usually begin from the date the application is received, regardless of when the claim is approved.*

Veterans can apply for a Disability Pension by completing VA Form 21-526, Veteran's Application for Compensation or Pension. If available, the applicant should attach copies of dependency records (marriage and children's birth certificates) and current medical evidence (doctor and hospital reports). The completed form should be sent to the veteran's VA Regional Office. (Refer to Chapter 37 for a listing of all VA regional offices.)

If any of the pertinent supporting evidence is not immediately available, the applicant should send in the application anyway. The date VA receives the application is important! If VA approves the claim, benefit payments usually begin from the date the application is received, regardless of when the claim is approved.

NET WORTH LIMITATION

The VA shall deny or discontinue the payment of pension to a veteran under this chapter when the corpus of the estate of the veteran, or, if the veteran has a spouse, the corpus of the estates of the veteran and of the veteran's spouse is such that under all the circumstances, including consideration of the annual income of the veteran, the veteran's spouse, and the veteran's children, it is reasonable that some part of the corpus of such estates be consumed for the veteran's maintenance.

The VA shall deny or discontinue the payment of increased pension under this chapter on account of a child when the corpus of such child's estate is such that under all the circumstances, including consideration of the veteran's and spouse's income, and the income of the veteran's children, it is reasonable that some part of the corpus of such child's estate be consumed for the child's maintenance. During the period such denial or discontinuance remains in effect, such child shall not be considered as the veteran's child for purposes of this chapter.

PROOF OF INCOME AND OVERPAYMENT ADJUSTMENTS

As a condition of granting, or continuing payment of a Disability Pension for a Non-Service-Connected Disability, the VA:

- May require from any person who is an applicant or recipient, such information, proof, and evidence the VA determines to be necessary in order to determine the annual income and the value of the corpus of the estate of such person, and of any spouse or child for whom the person is receiving, or is to receive increased pension, and in the case of a child applying for or in receipt of benefits, of any person with whom such child is residing who is legally responsible for such child's support.

- May require that any such applicant or recipient file for a calendar year with the VA, a report showing:
- The annual income which such applicant or recipient (and any spouse or dependent child) received during the preceding year, the corpus of the estate of such applicant or recipient (and of any such spouse or dependent child) at the end of such year, and in the case of a surviving child, the income and corpus of the estate of any person with whom such child is residing who is legally responsible for such child's support.
- Such applicant's or recipient's estimate for the current year of the annual income such applicant or recipient (and any such spouse or dependent child) expects to receive, and of any expected increase in the value of the corpus of the estate of such applicant or recipient (and for any such spouse or dependent child); and
- In the case of a surviving child, an estimate of the annual income of any person with whom such child is residing who is legally responsible for such child's support, and of any expected increase in the value of the corpus of the estate of such person;
- Shall require that any such applicant or recipient promptly notify the VA whenever there is a material change in the annual income of such applicant or recipient (or of any such spouse or dependent child) or a material change in the value of the corpus of the estate of such applicant or recipient (or of any such spouse or dependent child), an din the case of a surviving child, a material change in the annual income or value of the corpus of the estate of any person with whom such child is residing who is legally responsible for such child's support; and
- Shall require that any such applicant or recipient applying for or in receipt of increased pension on account of a person who is a spouse or child of such applicant or recipient promptly notify the VA if such person ceases to meet the applicable definition of spouse or child.

COMBINATION OF RATINGS

The VA shall provide that, for the purpose of determining whether or not a veteran is permanently and totally disabled, ratings for service-connected disabilities may be combined with ratings for non-service-connected disabilities.

Where a veteran is found to be entitled to a Non-Service-Connected Disability Pension, and is also entitled to Service-Connected Disability Compensation, the VA shall pay the veteran the greater benefit.

VOCATIONAL TRAINING FOR CERTAIN PENSION RECIPIENTS

In the case of a veteran who is awarded a Non-Service-Connected Disability Pension, the VA shall, based on information on file with the VA, make a preliminary finding whether such veteran, with the assistance of a vocational training program, has a good potential for achieving employment. If such potential is found to exist, the VA shall solicit from the veteran an application for vocational training. If the veteran thereafter applies for such training, the VA shall provide the veteran with an evaluation, which may include a personal interview, to determine whether the achievement of a vocational goal is reasonably feasible.

If the VA, based on the evaluation, determines that the achievement of a vocational goal by a veteran is reasonably feasible, the veteran shall be offered, and may elect to pursue a vocational training program.

If the veteran elects to pursue such a program, the program shall be designed in consultation with the veteran in order to meet the veteran's individual needs, and shall be set forth in an individualized written plan of vocational rehabilitation.

A vocational training program under this section:

- May not exceed 24 months unless, based on a determination by the VA that an extension is necessary in order for the veteran to achieve a vocational goal identified in the written plan formulated for the veteran, the VA grants an extension for a period not to exceed 24 months.
- May not include the provision of any loan or subsistence allowance, or any automobile adaptive equipment.
- May include a program of education at an institution of higher learning, only in a case in which the Secretary of the VA determines that the program involved is predominantly vocational in content.

When a veteran completes a vocational training program, the VA may provide the veteran with counseling, placement and post-placement services for a period not to exceed 18 months.

A veteran may not begin pursuit of a vocational training program under this chapter after the later of:

- December 31, 1995; or
- The end of a reasonable period of time, as determined by the VA, following either the evaluation of the veteran or the award of pension to the veteran.

In the case of a veteran who has been determined to have a permanent and total non-service-connected disability and who, not later than one year after the date the veteran's eligibility for counseling under this chapter expires, secures employment within the scope of a vocational goal identified in the veteran's individualized written plan of vocational rehabilitation (or in a related field which requires reasonably developed skills, and the use of some or all of the training or services furnished the veteran under such plan), the evaluation of the veteran as having a permanent and total disability may not be terminated be reason of the veteran's capacity to engage in such employment until the veteran first maintains such employment for a period of not less than 12 consecutive months.

PROTECTION OF HEALTH-CARE ELIGIBILITY

In the case of a veteran whose entitlement to pension is terminated after January 31, 1985, by reason of income from work or training, the veteran shall retain for a period of three years, beginning on the date of such termination, all eligibility for care and services that the veteran would have had if the veteran's entitlement to pension had not been terminated.

DISAPPEARANCE

When a veteran receiving a non-service-connected disability pension from the VA disappears, the VA may pay the pension otherwise payable to such veteran's spouse and children. Payments made to a spouse or child shall not exceed the amount to which each would be entitled if the veteran died of a non-service-connected disability.

CHAPTER 7

DEPENDENCY AND INDEMNITY COMPENSATION FOR SERVICE-CONNECTED DEATHS

Dependency and Indemnity Compensation (DIC) payments may be available for:

- Surviving spouses who have not remarried (please refer to boxes on bottom of this page for important additional information regarding remarriage);
- Surviving spouses who remarry after attaining age 57 (see following "Important Update.")
- Unmarried Children under 18;
- Helpless children;
- Children between 18 and 23, if attending a VA-approved school; and
- Low-income parents of deceased servicemembers or veterans.

IMPORTANT:
Public Law 108-183, The Veterans Benefits Act of 2003, restores DIC eligibility, effective January 1, 2004, for surviving spouses who remarry after age 57.

Qualifying spouses who remarried at age 57 or older prior to enactment of this bill had until December 16, 2004 to apply for reinstatement of these benefits. No retroactive benefits will be paid for any period prior to January 1, 2004.

Public Law 108-183 also provided that, for surviving spouses who remarry after attaining age 57, DIC be paid with no reduction of certain other Federal benefits to which a surviving spouse might be entitled. This provision, in essence eliminates the requirement for DIC to offset military SBP annuities, as was required under prior law. In other words, concurrent receipt of DIC and SBP without an offset of either is now allowed for surviving spouses who remarry after attaining age 57.

DEFINITIONS

The following definitions apply only to CHAPTER 7 – DEPENDENCY AND INDEMNITY COMPENSATION FOR SERVICE-CONNECTED DEATHS:

Veteran: in this chapter, the term includes a person who died in the active military, naval, or air service.

Social Security Increase: in this chapter, the term means the percentage by which benefit amounts payable under Title II of the Social Security Act (42 U.S.C. 401 et seq.) are increased for any fiscal year as a result of a determination under section 215(i) of such Act (42 U.S.C. 415(i)).

Permanently Housebound: for the purposes of this chapter, the requirement of "permanently housebound" will be considered to have been met when the individual is substantially confined to such individual's house (ward or clinical areas, if institutionalized) or immediate premises due to a disability or disabilities, which it is reasonably certain will remain throughout such individual's lifetime.

ELIGIBILITY

To receive Dependency and Indemnity Compensation (DIC), an individual must be an eligible survivor of a veteran who died from:

- A disease or injury incurred or aggravated while on active duty or active duty for training; or
- An injury incurred or aggravated in the line of duty while on inactive duty training; or
- A disability compensable by VA.
- The death cannot be a result of the veteran's willful misconduct.

DIC also may be authorized for survivors of veterans who at the time of death, were determined to be totally disabled as a result of military service, even though their service-connected disabilities did not cause their deaths. The survivor qualifies if:

- The veteran was continuously rated totally disabled for a period of 10 or more years immediately preceding death; or
- The veteran was so rated for a period of at least five years from the date of military discharge; or
- The veteran was a former prisoner of war who died after Sept. 30, 1999, and who was continuously rated totally disabled for a period of at least one year immediately preceding death.

To qualify as an eligible survivor, an individual must have proof of the following:

- Proof that he or she was married to the veteran for at least 1 year (Note: If a child was born, there is no time requirement); AND

- Proof that the marriage was VALID; AND
- Proof that he or she lived with the veteran continuously until his/her death or, if separated, the surviving spouse wasn't at fault; AND
- Proof that he or she did not remarry. (Note: The remarriage of the surviving spouse of a veteran shall not bar the furnishing of DIC if the remarriage is terminated by death, divorce, or annulment, unless the VA determines that the divorce or annulment was secured through fraud or collusion.)

OR

- The individual is an unmarried child of a deceased veteran; AND
- The individual is under age 18, or between the ages of 18 and 23 and attending school.

IMPORTANT UPDATE: Public Law 108-183, The Veterans Benefits Act of 2003, restores DIC eligibility, effective January 1, 2004, for surviving spouses who remarry after age 57. Qualifying spouses who remarried at age 57 or older prior to enactment of this bill had until December 16, 2004 to apply for reinstatement of these benefits. No retroactive benefits will be paid for any period prior to January 1, 2004.

Note: Certain helpless adult children and some parents of deceased veterans are entitled to DIC. Call VA at (800) 827-1000 for the eligibility requirements for these survivors.

AMOUNT OF DIC PAYMENTS TO SURVIVING SPOUSES

- Surviving spouses of veterans who died after January 1, 1993, receive a basic monthly rate of **$1,091 (effective December 1, 2007.)**
- Surviving spouses entitled to DIC based on the veteran's death prior to January 1, 1993, receive the greater of:
- The basic monthly rate of **$1,091**, **or**
- An amount based on the veteran's pay grade. (See following sections for Pay Grade tables and Determination of Pay Grade.)

There are additional DIC payments for dependent children. (Refer to the following charts.)

Additional Allowances For Surviving Spouses

- Add **$233.00** to the basic monthly rate if, at the time of the veteran's death, the veteran was in receipt of, or entitled to receive compensation for a service-connected disability rated totally disabling (including a rating based on individual unemployability) for a continuous period of at least 8 years immediately preceding death AND the surviving spouse was married to the veteran for those same 8 years.

- Add **$271.00** per child to the basic monthly rate for each dependent child under age 18.
- If the surviving spouse is entitled to Aid & Attendance, add **$271.00** to the basic monthly rate.
- If the surviving spouse is Permanently Housebound, add **$128.00** to the basic monthly rate.

SURVIVING SPOUSE DIC RATES IF VETERAN'S DEATH WAS PRIOR TO JANUARY 1, 1993

Rates Effective December 1, 2007

Pay Grade	Monthly Rate	Pay Grade	Monthly Rate
E-1*:	$1091	W-4**:	$1305
E-2*:	$1091	O-1**:	$1153
E-3* (see footnote #1):	$1091	O-2**:	$1191
E-4*:	$1091	O-3**:	$1274
E-5*:	$1091	O-4:	$1349
E-6*:	$1091	O-5:	$1485
E-7**:	$1129	O-6:	$1674
E-8**:	$1191	O-7:	$1808
E-9** (see footnote #2):	$1242 or $1342	O-8:	$1985
W-1**:	$1153	O-9:	$2123
W-2**:	$1198	O-10 (see footnote #3):	$2328 or $2499
W-3**:	$1234		

Footnotes to Table:

* Add $233 if veteran rated totally disabled 8 continuous years prior to death, and surviving spouse was married to veteran those same 8 years.

** Base rate is $1324 if veteran rated totally disabled 8 continuous years prior to death, and surviving spouse was married to vet those same 8 years.

1. A surviving spouse of an Aviation Cadet or other service not covered by this table is paid the DIC rate for enlisted E-3 under 34.

2. $1342 is for a veteran who served as Sergeant Major of the Army or Marine Corps, Senior Enlisted Advisor of the Navy, Chief Master Sergeant of the Air Force, or Master Chief Petty Officer of the Coast Guard.
3. $2499 is for a veteran who served as Chairman of the Joint Chiefs of Staff, Chief of Staff of the Army or Air Force, Chief of Naval Operations, or Commandant of the Marine Corps.

Determination Of Pay Grade

With respect to a veteran who died in the active military, naval, or air service, such veteran's pay grade shall be determined as of the date of such veteran's death, or as of the date of a promotion after death, while in a missing status.

With respect to a veteran who did not die in the active military, naval, or air service, such veteran's pay grade shall be determined as of:

- The time of such veteran's last discharge or release from active duty under conditions other than dishonorable; or

- The time of such veteran's discharge or release from any period of active duty for training or inactive duty training, if such veteran's death results from service-connected disability incurred during such period, and if such veteran was not thereafter discharged or released under conditions other than dishonorable from active duty.

If a veteran has satisfactorily served on active duty for a period of six months or more in a pay grade higher than that specified in the previous paragraphs of this section, and any subsequent discharge or release from active duty was under conditions other than dishonorable, the higher pay grade shall be used if it will result in greater monthly payments to such veteran's surviving spouse under this chapter. The determination as to whether an individual has served satisfactorily for the required period in a higher pay grade shall be made by the Secretary of the department in which such higher pay grade was held.

The pay grade of any person not otherwise described in this section, but who had a compensable status on the date of such person's death under laws administered by the Secretary, shall be determined by the head of the department under which such person performed the services by which such person obtained such status.

DIC PAYMENTS TO CHILDREN

Whenever there is no surviving spouse of a deceased veteran entitled to DIC, DIC shall be paid in equal shares to the children of the deceased veteran at the following monthly rates (effective December 1, 2007):

Number of Children	Total Payable (to be divided in equal shares):
1	$462
2	$663
3	$865
4	$1030
5	$1195
6	$1360

Additional Allowances For ly to such child shall be increased by *$271*.

- If DIC is payable monthly to a person as a surviving spouse, and there is a child (of such person's deceased spouse) who has attained the age of 18, and who, while under such age, became permanently incapable of self-support, DIC shall be paid monthly to each such child, concurrently with the payment of DIC to the surviving spouse, in the amount of ***$462***.

- If DIC is payable monthly to a person as a surviving spouse, and there is a child (of such person's deceased spouse) who has attained the age of 18 and who, while under the age of 23, is pursuing a course of instruction at a VA-approved educational institution, DIC shall be paid monthly to each such child, concurrently with the payment of DIC to the surviving spouse, in the amount of ***$230***.

DIC PAYMENTS FOR PARENTS

Parents whose child died in-service or from a service-connected disability may be entitled to DIC if they are in financial need. Parents may be biological, step, adopted, or *in loco parentis*.

The monthly payment for parents of deceased veterans depends upon their income. The following 3 charts outline the monthly rates payable, **effective December 1, 2007,** under various conditions.

Chart #1
Sole Surviving Parent Unremarried or Remarried Living With Spouse

Income Not Over:	*Monthly Rate:*	*Income Not Over:*	*Monthly Rate:*
$ 800	*$ 537*	*$ 2,500*	*$ 401*
900	*529*	*2,600*	*393*
1,000	*521*	*2,700*	*385*
1,100	*513*	*2,800*	*377*
1,200	*505*	*2,900*	*369*
1,300	*497*	*3,000*	*361*
1,400	*489*	*3,100*	*353*
1,500	*481*	*3,200*	*345*
1,600	*473*	*3,300*	*337*
1,700	*465*	*3,400*	*329*
1,800	*457*	*3,500*	*321*
1,900	*449*	*3,600*	*313*
2,000	*441*	*3,700*	*305*
2,100	*433*	*3,800*	*297*
2,200	*425*	*3,900*	*289*
2,300	*417*	*4,000*	*281*
2,400	*409*	*4,100*	*273*

Chart #1 Continued -			
Income Not Over:	**Monthly Rate:**	**Income Not Over:**	**Monthly Rate:**
$4,200	$265	$6,100	$113
4,300	257	6,200	105
4,400	249	6,300	97
4,500	241	6,400	89
4,600	233	6,500	81
4,700	225	6,600	73
4,800	217	6,700	65
4,900	209	6,800	57
5,000	201	6,900	49
5,100	193	7,000	41
5,200	182	7,100	33
5,300	177	7,200	25
5,400	169	7,300	17
5,500	161	7,400	9
5,600	153	7,449	5.08
5,700	145	7,450 to **	5
5,800	137	If A&A add: 291	
5,900	129	If living w/ spouse: 17,095	
6,000	121	**If not living w/ spouse: 12,718	

Chart #2 - One of Two Parents Not Living With Spouse

Income Not Over:	**Monthly Rate:**	**Income Not Over:**	**Monthly Rate:**
$ 800	$ 389	$ 3,400	$ 185
900	383	3,500	177
1,000	376	3,600	169
1,100	369	3,700	161
1,200	361	3,800	153
1,300	353	3,900	145
1,400	345	4,000	137
1,500	337	4,100	129
1,600	329	4,200	121
1,700	321	4,300	113
1,800	313	4,400	105
1,900	305	4,500	97
2,000	297	4,600	89
2,100	289	4,700	81
2,200	281	4,800	73
2,300	273	4,900	65
2,400	265	5,000	57
2,500	257	5,100	49
2,600	249	5,200	41
2,700	241	5,300	33
2,800	233	5,400	25
2,900	225	5,500	17
3,000	217	5,600	9
3,100	209	5,649	5.08
3,200	201	5,650 to 12,718	5
3,300	193	If A&A add: $291	

Chart #3
1 of 2 Parents Living with Spouse or Other Parent

Income Not Over:	Monthly Rate:	Income Not Over:	Monthly Rate:
$1,000	$365	$3,900	$202
1,100	362	4,000	194
1,200	359	4,100	186
1,300	356	4,200	178
1,400	353	4,300	170
1,500	350	4,400	162
1,600	346	4,500	154
1,700	342	4,600	146
1,800	338	4,700	138
1,900	334	4,800	130
2,000	329	4,900	122
2,100	324	5,000	114
2,200	319	5,100	106
2,300	314	5,200	98
2,400	309	5,300	90
2,500	303	5,400	82
2,600	297	5,500	74
2,700	291	5,600	66
2,800	285	5,700	58
2,900	279	5,800	50
3,000	272	5,900	42
3,100	265	6,000	34
3,200	258	6,100	26
3,300	250	6,200	18
3,400	242	6,300	10
3,500	234	6,362	5.04
3,600	226	6,363 to 17,095	5
3,700	218		
3,800	210	If A&A add:	291

Miscellaneous Information Regarding Income Limitations For Parents

The VA may require, as a condition of granting or continuing DIC to a parent that such parent, other than one who has attained 72 years of age, and has been paid DIC during 2 consecutive calendar years, file for a calendar year with the VA, a report showing the total income which such parent expects to receive in that year, and the total income which such parent received in the preceding year. The parent or parents shall notify the VA whenever there is a material change in annual income.

In determining income under this section, all payments of any kind, or from any source shall be included except:

- Payments of a death gratuity;
- Donations from public or private relief or welfare organizations;
- Payments under this chapter (DIC), Chapter 11 of Title 38, United States Code (Disability Compensation), and Chapter 15 of Title 38, United States Code (Non-Service Connected Disability/Death Pension);
- Payments under policies of servicemembers group life insurance, United States Government life insurance, or national service life insurance, and payments of servicemen's indemnity;
- 10% of the amount of payments to an individual under public or private retirement, annuity, endowment, or similar plans or programs;
- Amounts equal to amounts paid by a parent of a deceased veteran for:
- A deceased spouse's just debts;
- The expenses of the spouse's last illness, to the extent such expenses are not reimbursed under Chapter 51 of Title 38 of the United States Code;
- The expenses of the spouse's burial to the extent that such expenses are not reimbursed under Chapter 23 or Chapter 51 of Title 38 of the United States Code;
- Reimbursements of any kind for any casualty loss (as defined in regulations which the VA shall prescribe), but the amount excluded under this clause may not exceed the greater of the fair market value or the reasonable replacement value of the property involved at the time immediately preceding the loss;
- Amounts equal to amounts paid by a parent of a deceased veteran for:
- The expenses of the veteran's last illness, and
- The expenses of such veteran's burial, to the extent that such expenses are not reimbursed under Chapter 23 of Title 38 of the United States Code;
- Profit realized from the disposition of real or personal property other than in the course of a business;
- Payments received for discharge of jury duty or obligatory civic duties;
- Payments of annuities elected under Subchapter I of Chapter 73 of Title 10.

Where a fraction of a dollar is involved, annual income shall be fixed at the next lower dollar.

The VA may provide by regulation for the exclusion from income under this section of amounts paid by a parent for unusual medical expenses.

SPECIAL PROVISIONS RELATING TO SURVIVING SPOUSES

No Dependency and Indemnity Compensation shall be paid to the surviving spouse of a veteran dying after December 31, 1956, unless such surviving spouse was married to such veteran:

- Before the expiration of 15 years after the termination of the period of service in which the injury or disease causing the death of the veteran was incurred or aggravated; or
- For one year or more; or
- For any period of time if a child was born of the marriage, or was born to them before the marriage.

APPLYING FOR DEPENDENCY AND INDEMNITY COMPENSATION

Eligible surviving spouses and dependent children can apply for DIC by completing VA Form 21-534, *Application for Dependency and Indemnity Compensation or Death Pension by Surviving Spouse or Child.* If available, copies of dependency records (marriage records, divorce records, & children's birth certificates) should be attached to the application. A copy of the veteran's DD Form 214 and a copy of the veteran's death certificate should also be included with the completed application.

The completed form should be sent to the applicable VA Regional Office (refer to Chapter 37 for a listing of all VA regional offices.)

Note:
If any of the pertinent supporting evidence is not immediately available, the applicant should send in the application anyway. The date VA receives the application is important! If VA approves the claim, benefit payments usually begin from the date the application is received, regardless of when the claim is approved.

CHAPTER 8

DEATH PENSIONS TO SURVIVING SPOUSES AND CHILDREN

A Death Pension is a benefit paid to eligible dependents of deceased wartime veterans.

DEFINITIONS

The following definitions apply only to CHAPTER 8 - DEATH PENSIONS TO SURVIVING SPOUSES AND CHILDREN:

Veteran: as used in this chapter, includes a person who has completed at least 2 years of honorable active military, naval, or air service, as certified by the appropriate authority, but whose death in such service was not in line of duty.

Indian Wars: means the campaigns, engagements, and expeditions of the United States military forces against Indian tribes or nations, service in which has been recognized heretofore as pensionable service.

World War I: means the period April 6, 1917, through November 11, 1918. In the case of a veteran who served with the United States military forces in Russia, the ending date is April 1, 1920. Service after November 11, 1918 and before July 2, 1921 is considered World War I for compensation or pension purposes, if the veteran served in the active military, naval, or air service after April 5, 1917 and before November 12, 1918.

Civil War Veteran: includes a person who served in the military or naval forces of the Confederate States of America during the Civil War, and the term "active military or naval service" includes active service in those forces.

Period of War: means the Mexican border period, World War I, World War II, the Korean conflict, the Vietnam era, the Persian Gulf War, and the period beginning on the date of any future declaration of war by the Congress and ending on the date prescribed by Presidential proclamation or concurrent resolution of the Congress.

Regular Aid and Attendance: for the purposes of this chapter, a person shall be considered to be in need of regular aid and attendance if such person is:

- A patient in a nursing home; or
- Helpless or blind, or so nearly helpless or blind as to need or require the aid and attendance of another person.

Permanently Housebound: for the purposes of this chapter, the requirement of "permanently housebound" will be considered to have been met when the surviving spouse is substantially confined to such surviving spouse's house (ward or clinical areas, if institutionalized) or immediate premises due to a disability or disabilities, which it is reasonably certain will remain throughout such surviving spouse's lifetime.

ELIGIBILITY REQUIREMENTS

Eligible dependents may qualify for a Death Pension if:

- The deceased veteran was discharged from service under other than dishonorable conditions; **AND**
- He or she served 90 days or more of active duty with at least 1 day during a war, or must have had a service-connected disability justifying discharge for disability. If the veteran died in service but not in the line of duty, pension may be payable if the veteran had completed at least two years of honorable service; **AND**
- The dependent is the surviving spouse (spouse must not have remarried), or the unmarried child of the deceased veteran (children must be under age 18, or under age 23 if attending a VA-approved school); **AND**
- The dependent's countable income is below an annual limit set by law (See below for 2005 annual income limitations.)

(Children who become incapable of self-support because of a disability before age 18 may be eligible for a pension as long as the condition exists, unless the child marries or the child's income exceeds the applicable limit.)

ADDITIONAL REQUIREMENTS

No Death Pension shall be paid under this chapter to a surviving spouse of a veteran unless the spouse was married to the veteran:

Before:

- December 14, 1944, in the case of a surviving spouse of a Mexican Border period or World War I veteran; or
- January 1, 1957 in the case of a surviving spouse of a World War II veteran; or
- February 1, 1965, in the case of a surviving spouse of a Korean conflict veteran; or
- May 8, 1985, in the case of a surviving spouse of a Vietnam era veteran, or
- January 1, 2001, in the case of a surviving spouse of a veteran of the Persian Gulf War;

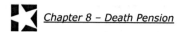

- For one year or more; or
- For any period of time if a child was born of the marriage, or was born to them before the marriage.

ANNUAL INCOME LIMITATIONS

DEATH PENSION RATE TABLE FOR SURVIVING SPOUSES & CHILDREN RATES EFFECTIVE DECEMBER 1, 2007	
Maximum Annual Pension Rate (MAPR) Category	Annual Income Must Be Less Than:
Surviving Spouse Alone (No Dependent Child):	$7,498
Surviving Spouse With One Dependent Child:	$9,818
Child Alone:	$1,909
Housebound Spouse Without Dependents:	$9,164
Housebound Spouse With One Dependent:	$11,478
Surviving Spouse In Need Of Aid And Attendance (No Dependent Child):	$11,985
Surviving Spouse In Need Of Aid And Attendance With One Dependent Child:	$14,298
For Each Additional Child:	$1,909
Child Earned Income Exclusion Effective 1/1/2006:	$8,950

MAXIMUM ANNUAL INCOME LIMITATIONS FOR PROTECTED PENSIONS (EFFECTIVE DECEMBER 1, 2007)

(Pensioners entitled to benefits as of December 31, 1978, who do not elect to receive a pension under the Improved Pension Program, may continue to receive pension benefits at the rates they were entitled to receive on December 31, 1978 or June 30, 1960, as long as they remain permanently and totally disabled, do not lose a dependent, and their income does not exceed the income limitation, adjusted annually.)

Pension Law in Effect on December 31, 1978 (Section 306):

The rate entitled to on December 31, 1978 may be continued if the recipient's IVAP for 2007 is below the following limits:

STATUS OF RECIPIENT:		ANNUAL INCOME LIMITATION:
Surviving spouse with no dependents	*$*	*12,718.00*
Surviving spouse with one or more dependents		*17,095.00*
Child (no entitled veteran or surviving spouse)		*10,397.00*

Pension Law in Effect on June 30, 1960 (Old Law):

The rate entitled to on June 30, 1960 may be continued if the recipient's IVAP for 2007 is below the following limits:

STATUS OF RECIPIENT:		ANNUAL INCOME LIMITATION:
Surviving spouse with no dependents		*11,134.00*
Surviving spouse with one or more dependents		*16,051.00*
Child only (no entitled veteran or surviving spouse)		*11,134.00*

Note: Some income is not counted toward the yearly limit (for example, welfare benefits, some wages earned by dependent children, and Supplemental Security Income).

In determining the annual income of a surviving spouse, if there is a child of the veteran in the custody of the surviving spouse, that portion of the annual income of the child that is reasonably available to or for the surviving spouse shall be considered to be income of the surviving spouse, unless in the judgment of the VA, to do so would work a hardship on the surviving spouse.

AMOUNT PAID BY VA

VA pays eligible spouses and dependents the difference between his or her countable income and the annual income limit outlined in the above table. The difference is generally paid in 12 equal monthly payments rounded down to the nearest dollar.

NET WORTH LIMITATION

The VA shall deny or discontinue payment of pension to a surviving spouse when the corpus of the estate of the surviving spouse is such that under all the circumstances, including consideration of the income of the surviving spouse and the income of any child from whom the surviving spouse is receiving increased pension, it is reasonable that some part of the corpus of such estate be consumed for the surviving spouse's maintenance.

The VA shall deny or discontinue the payment of increased pension on account of a child when the corpus of such child's estate is such that under all the circumstances, including consideration of the income of the surviving spouse and such child and the income of any other child for whom the surviving spouse is receiving increased pension, it is reasonable that some part of the corpus of the child's estate be consumed for the child's maintenance. During the period such denial or discontinuance remains in effect, such child shall not be considered as the surviving spouse's child for purposes of this chapter.

The VA shall deny or discontinue payment of pension to a child when the corpus of the state of the child is such that under all the circumstances, including consideration of the income of the child, the income of any person with whom such child is residing who is legally responsible for such child's support, and the corpus of the estate of such person, it is reasonable that some part of the corpus of such estate be consumed for the child's maintenance.

APPLYING FOR DEATH PENSION BENEFITS

Eligible surviving spouses and dependent children can apply for Death Pension benefits by completing VA Form 21-534, *Application for Dependency and Indemnity Compensation or Death Pension by Surviving Spouse or Child.* If available, copies of dependency records (marriage & children's birth certificates) should be attached to the application. A copy of the veteran's DD Form 214 and a copy of the veteran's death certificate should also be included with the completed application.

The completed forms should be sent to the applicable VA Regional Office. (Refer to Chapter 37 for a listing of all VA regional offices.)

Special Note: If any of the pertinent supporting evidence is not immediately available, the applicant should send in the application anyway. The date VA receives the application is important! If VA approves the claim, benefit payments usually begin from the date the application is received, regardless of when the claim is approved.

CHAPTER 9

MISCELLANEOUS BENEFITS FOR SURVIVING SPOUSES AND CHILDREN

SURVIVOR BENEFIT PLAN (SBP)

The Survivor Benefit Plan (SBP) was established by Congress effective September 21, 1972 (Public Law 92-425) to provide a monthly income to survivors of retired military personnel upon the member's death when retired pay stops. Survivors of members who die while on active duty, and survivors of members recalled to active duty from retirement who die while on active duty may also be protected by the SBP.

The SBP is free for active duty service members with 20 years of qualifying service. The SBP for retirees is paid for by premium payments from a retiree's paycheck. There is a tax break for the retiree in that the amount of the SBP premium is not included in the taxable portion of his or her retired pay.

If you elect to participate in the SBP you will be required to pay a monthly premium. SBP Premiums and benefits are based on the "base amount" or benefit level that you elect.

At retirement, full basic SBP for spouse and children will take effect *automatically* if you make no other valid election. You may not reduce or decline spouse coverage without your spouse's written consent. This means you will have to have your spouses input in the decision and his or her signature is required. You may choose coverage for a former spouse or, if you have no spouse or children, you may be able to cover an "insurable interest" (such as, a business partner or parent).

If you elect to participate in the SBP you will be required to pay a monthly premium. SBP Premiums and benefits are based on the "base amount" or benefit level that you elect.

Your base amount can be any amount from full coverage down to as little as $300 a month. Full coverage is based on your full retired pay meaning your spouse will receive **55 percent** of your retirement pay. If you select lesser coverage then your spouse will receive 55 percent of your elected "base amount."

Note: A surviving spouse's SBP annuity is reduced when they reach age 62 and become eligible for Social Security. This is called the Social Security offset. In the past the offset reduced the SBP annuity to 35 percent of the base amount. The offset created a need for members to purchase a Supplemental Survivor Benefit Plan (SSBP) policy. Fortunately the National Defense Authorization Act of

2005 established a phase out of the offset by 2008. Thus eliminating the need for the SSBP. Details of the National Defense Authorization Act of 2005 are described below.

PHASED-IN INCREASE IN BASIC ANNUITY

One major provision of the Ronald W. Reagan FY2005 National Defense Authorization Act included an increase in the minimum SBP annuity for survivors age 62 and older from 35% to 55% over a 3-year period.

The FY 2005 Defense Authorization Act included provisions to eliminate the social security offset under SBP by increasing the annuities paid to survivors of military retirees who are 62 or older from 35 percent of retired pay to the percentages indicated below:

- For months after September 2005 and before April 2006: 40 percent
- For months after March 2006 and before April 2007: 45 percent
- For months after March 2007 and before April 2008: 50 percent
- For months after March 2008: 55 percent

In addition, a one-year open-enrollment period began on October 1, 2005, allowing retirees not enrolled in SBP to participate, provided they make a lump-sum payment covering all back premiums, plus interest, since their retirement.

Note: Public Law 108-183, The Veterans Benefits Act of 2003 provided that, for surviving spouses who remarry after attaining age 57, Dependency and Indemnity Compensation (DIC) be paid with no reduction of certain other Federal benefits to which a surviving spouse might be entitled. This provision, in essence eliminates the requirement for DIC to offset military SBP annuities, as was required under prior law. In other words, concurrent receipt of DIC and SBP without an offset of either is now allowed for surviving spouses who remarry after attaining age 57.

SURVIVOR BENEFIT PLAN – MINIMUM INCOME ANNUITY

Effective December 1, 2007, the SBP-MIW annuity limitation is $7,498.

Eligible surviving spouses of military retirees who did not participate in the plan, and who died prior to September 21, 1973 are eligible for SBP-MIW (Survivor Benefit Plan – Minimum Income Annuity). To be eligible the surviving spouse must not be remarried, must be eligible for VA death pension, and must have income for VA purposes, excluding any SBP annuity, of less than the MIW-SBP annuity limitation. Effective December 1, 2007, the SBP-MIW annuity limitation is $7,498.

BENEFITS FOR CHILDREN OF WOMEN VIETNAM VETERANS BORN WITH CERTAIN BIRTH DEFECTS

Section 401 of P.L. 106-416, which became law on November 1, 2000 directed the Secretary of VA to identify birth defects of children of female Vietnam veterans that: (1) are associated with service during the Vietnam era; and (2) result in the permanent physical or mental disability of such children. The law excludes from such defects familial or birth-related defects or injuries. The law further directs the Secretary to provide to such children necessary health care to address the defect and any associated disability. It authorizes the Secretary to provide vocational training to such a child if the achievement of a vocational goal is reasonably feasible.

The law also directs the Secretary to pay a monthly allowance to such a child, the amount to be determined through a schedule rating the various defects and disabilities and their degrees. The receipt of such allowance shall not infringe upon the right to receive any other benefit to which the individual is entitled. Such allowance shall not be considered income for purposes of other veterans' benefits for which income limitations exist. In the case of an eligible child whose only covered birth defect is spina bifida, a monetary allowance shall be paid under these provisions only. An eligible individual shall be provided only one program of vocational training.

The monthly allowance is set at four levels, depending upon the degree of disability suffered by the child.

Children of Women Vietnam Veterans Born With Certain Birth Defects (P.L 106-419)

(Rates Effective 12-01-2007)

Disability Level	***Monthly Allowance***
Level I	$123.00
Level II	$270.00
Level III	$930.00
Level IV	$1,586.00

CHAPTER 10

BURIAL BENEFITS

REIMBURSEMENT OF BURIAL EXPENSES

The Veterans Benefits Administration administers a burial benefits program designed to assist claimants in meeting the funeral and burial costs of a deceased veteran. The type and amount of benefits payable depends on the veteran's individual service record and cause of death.

Service-Connected Death

If a veteran's death is service-connected, the VA will pay a burial allowance of up to $2,000 (for deaths on or after 9-11-2001 - prior to 9-11-2001, the burial allowance was $1,500). If the veteran is buried in a VA national cemetery, some or all of the cost of moving the deceased to the national cemetery nearest the veteran's home may also be reimbursed. There is no time limit for applying for a service-connected burial allowance. The person who bore the veteran's burial expense may claim reimbursement from any VA regional office.

Non-Service Connected Death

If a veteran's death is not service-connected, there are two types of payments the VA may make:

Burial and Funeral Expense Allowance

The VA will pay a burial and funeral allowance of $300, provided the veteran was discharged under conditions other than dishonorable; and:

- The veteran was in receipt of VA pension or compensation at the time of death; or
- The veteran was, at the time of death, receiving military retired pay in lieu of compensation; or
- The veteran, at the time of death, had an original or reopened claim pending, and had been found entitled to compensation or pension from a date prior to the date of death; or
- The veteran's death occurred in a VA facility; or
- The veteran died while traveling, under proper authorization and at VA expense, to or from a specified place for the purpose of examination, treatment, or care; or

- The veteran died on or after October 9, 1996, while a patient at an approved State nursing home or while residing in a VA-approved State nursing home, is transferred to a non-VA facility for acute medical care, and then dies at that location. (Contact a VA regional office for a complete listing of approved State nursing homes.); or

- The veteran's remains are being held by a State or political subdivision of a State, there is no next of kin or other person claiming the body and the veteran's estate does not have enough resources to cover the cost of the funeral and burial, and the veteran served during wartime or was released from active service for a disability incurred or aggravated in the line of duty.

Payment may be made to:

- The creditor who provided services or furnished merchandise in connection with burial, funeral, transportation, plot or interment; or

- The person or persons whose personal funds were used to pay such expenses; or

- The representative of the estate of the deceased veteran or claimant when the estate funds were used to pay the expenses or the veteran or claimant prepaid them.

Plot Allowance

If a veteran is not buried in a cemetery that is under U.S. government jurisdiction, the VA may also pay a plot allowance of $300 (for deaths on or after 12-1-2001 - prior to 12-1-2001, the plot allowance was $150), provided that the veteran was discharged under conditions other than dishonorable; and:

- The veteran was discharged from active duty because of a disability incurred or aggravated in the line of duty; or

- The veteran was receiving VA pension or compensation at the time of death, or would have been entitled to receive VA pension or compensation, but for receipt of military retirement or disability pay; or

- The veteran died in a VA facility.

The plot allowance may be paid to the state if a veteran is buried without charge for the cost of a plot or interment in a state-owned cemetery reserved solely for veteran burials. Burial expenses paid by the deceased veteran's employer or a state agency will not be reimbursed.

Reimbursement Of Transportation Costs

The costs of transporting a veteran's body to the place of burial may be authorized if a veteran's death occurs while:

- Enroute for a VA authorized examination, treatment or care; or

- The veteran is properly hospitalized at an approved medical center domiciliary; or

- The veteran is in a nursing home under the direct jurisdiction of the VA; or if the veteran's death occurred on or after October 9, 1996, while a patient at an approved State nursing home; or

- The costs of transporting the veteran's body to the place of burial may also be authorized if the veteran is buried in a national cemetery, and died of a service-connected condition. If burial is not in the national cemetery nearest the veteran's last place of residence, the total reimbursement will not be more than the amount which would have been payable for burial in the nearest national cemetery.

Filing Claim for Reimbursement of Expenses

Reimbursement of burial expenses may be applied for by submitting VA Form 21-530, Application for Burial Allowance. A certified copy of the death certificate, proof of the veteran's military service (Form DD-214), and itemized bills of the funeral and burial expenses must be submitted by the person(s) filing the claim(s).

The itemized bills must clearly show the name of the veteran for whom services were performed, the nature and cost of the service rendered, all credits, and the name(s) of the person or persons by whom payment in whole or in part was made.

If the undertaker's bill is not paid, he is entitled to file claim for reimbursement.

If more than one person is entitled to reimbursement, each claimant must submit a separate VA Form 21-530 containing the signature of the person who authorized services or the responsible official. Any burial allowance awarded will be apportioned according to the proportionate share paid by each, unless a waiver is executed in favor of one of such person by the other person or persons. However, in no case will there be allowed the person in whose favor payment is waived a sum greater than that which was paid by him/her toward the burial, funeral, and transportation expenses. If two or more persons have paid such expenses from their personal funds, and one or more of such persons dies before filing claim, no consideration will be given to the amount paid by the deceased person(s).

The itemized bills must clearly show the name of the veteran for whom services were performed, the nature and cost of the service rendered, all credits, and the name(s) of the person or persons by whom payment in whole or in part was made.

If applying for reimbursement of transportation expenses, a statement of account identifying the charges for transporting the body is required.

Unpaid Balance Due Persons who Performed Services

If there is an unpaid balance due the person who performed burial, funeral, and transportation services, such claim as a creditor for the statutory burial allowance will be given priority over any claim for reimbursement based on use of personal funds, unless there is executed by such creditor a waiver in favor of the person or persons whose personal funds were used in making the partial payment of the account.

No reimbursement may be made to a State, County, or other governmental subdivision.

Veteran's Estate

The representative of a deceased person's estate may file a claim for reimbursement, if estate funds were used to pay the expenses of the veteran's burial, funeral, and transportation. Accordingly, if otherwise in order, reimbursement may be made to the estate, regardless of whether such person pre-deceased the veteran or was deceased at the time the expenses were incurred or paid, or burial of the veteran actually occurred.

Death of Active Duty Personnel

The VA does not pay a burial or plot interment allowance if a veteran dies while on active military duty. However, such veteran is entitled to certain benefits from the military. Information should be obtained from the branch of the armed forces in which the person served at time of death.

Burial of Unclaimed Bodies

If the body of an eligible deceased veteran is unclaimed by relatives or friends, the Director of any regional VA office or any VA medical center is authorized to arrange for burial in either a national cemetery or in a cemetery or section of a cemetery, owned by a state, a state agency, or political subdivision of a state, and used solely for the interment of persons eligible for burial in a national cemetery.

If an organization provides a burial or furnishes a burial plot as a humanitarian measure, and not pursuant to a legal obligation, it may be reimbursed for its actual cost. Reimbursement to such organization cannot exceed the maximum benefits payable based on the veteran's eligibility.

Correction of Discharge to Honorable Conditions

Public Law 88-3 (H.R. 212) provides that where burial allowance was not payable at the time of a veteran's death because of the nature of his discharge from service, but after death his discharge is corrected by competent authority so as to reflect a discharge under conditions other than dishonorable, claim may be filed within two years from the date of correction of the discharge.

Legal Execution

The execution of a veteran as a lawful punishment for a crime does not of itself preclude a payment of the statutory burial allowances.

State Burial Allowance

There are some burial allowances allowed by states or counties for the burial of needy veterans, and in some instances, of their dependents. Check with the veteran's state or county of residence for specific information.

Assistance to Claimants

It is incumbent upon the claimant to establish his case in accordance with the law. This rule, however, will not be highly technical or rigid in its application. The general policy of the VA is to give the claimant every opportunity to substantiate his claim, to extend all reasonable assistance in its prosecution, and develop all sources from which information may be obtained. Assistance may also be secured from post, state, and national service officers or veterans' organizations.

Miscellaneous

If the deceased veteran is entitled to payment in full of burial expenses by the Employees' Compensation Commission, Workman's Compensation, or employer, the Veterans Administration will make no payment.

Appeal

An appeal may be made within one year from the date of denial of a claim. The appeal must be sent to the regional VA office that denied the claim. (For specific information regarding Appeals Procedures, refer to Chapter 36 of this book.)

BURIAL FLAGS

The VA shall furnish a United States flag, at no cost, for burial or memorial purposes in connection with the death of an eligible veteran who served honorably in the U.S. Armed Forces.

Public Law 105-261, added eligibility for former member of the Selected Reserve who:

- Completed at least one enlistment as a member of the Selected Reserve or, in the case of an officer, completed the period of initial obligated service as a member of the Selected Reserve; or
- Was discharged before completion of the person's initial enlistment as a member of the Selected Reserve or, in the case of an officer, period of initial obligated service as a member of the Selected Reserve, for a disability incurred or aggravated in line of duty; or
- Who died while a member of the Selected Reserve.

Burial flags may not be furnished on behalf of deceased veterans who committed capital crimes.

After the burial of the veteran, the flag shall be given to his next of kin. If no claim is made for the flag by the next of kin, it may be given, upon request, to a close friend or associate of the deceased veteran. If a flag is given to a close friend or associate of the deceased veteran, no flag shall be given to any other person on account of the death of such veteran.

When burial is in a national, state or post cemetery, a burial flag will automatically be provided. When burial is in a private cemetery, an American flag may be obtained by a service officer, an undertaker or other interested person from the nearest Veterans Administration office or most U.S. Post Offices. VA Form 2008, Application for United States Flag for Burial Purposes, must be completed and submitted along with a copy of the veteran's discharge papers. Generally, the funeral director will help the next of kin with this process.

The proper way to display the flag depends upon whether the casket is open or closed. VA Form 2008 provides the proper method for displaying and folding the flag. The burial flag is not suitable for outside display, because of its size and fabric.

After burial of a veteran, the flag should be folded in military style and presented to the next of kin at the cemetery. Local veteran organizations, when presenting the flag, usually say something like this:

> "In the name of the United States government and *name of veterans organization,* (such as A.L., D.A.V., V.F.W., and American Veterans of World War II, etc.) we present you this flag, in loving memory of our departed comrade."

Presenting of the flag is sometimes a difficult task when there is a disagreement in the family. However, the Veterans Administration gives the following order of preference to be followed:

1. Widow or widower (even if separated but not divorced)
2. Children according to age (minor child may be issued flag on application signed by guardian)
3. Father, including adopted, step and foster father
4. Mother, including adopted, step and foster mother
5. Brothers or sisters, including brothers and sisters of half blood.
6. Uncles or aunts
7. Nephews or nieces
8. Cousins, grandparents, etc. (but not in-laws)

(If two relatives have equal rights, the flag will be presented to the elder one.)

Following a veteran's burial, the United States flag received by the next of kin may be donated to the VA, for use on national holidays at VA national cemeteries. If the next of kin chooses to make such a donation, it should be given or mailed to the Director of any national cemetery selected by the donor with a written request that the flag be flown at that location. If the flag is brought into a Veterans Service Division, it will be accepted and forwarded to the cemetery chosen by the donor. A Certificate of Appreciation is presented to the donor for providing their loved ones' burial flag to a national cemetery.

Please note that VA cannot provide flag holders for placement on private headstones or markers. These flag holders may be purchased from private manufacturing companies.

The law allows the VA to issue one flag for a veteran's funeral. The VA cannot replace it if it is lost, destroyed, or stolen. However, if this occurs, a local veteran's organization or other community group may be able to assist you in obtaining another flag.

HEADSTONES AND MARKERS IN PRIVATE CEMETERIES

On December 27, 2001, President Bush signed Public Law 107-103, The Veterans Education and Benefits Expansion Act of 2001.

This law included a provision that allows the VA to furnish an appropriate headstone or marker for the graves of eligible veterans buried in private cemeteries, whose deaths occur on or after December 27, 2001, regardless of whether the grave is already marked with a non-government marker. (Headstones or markers may not be furnished on behalf of deceased veterans who committed capital crimes.)

On December 6, 2002, the law was further amended by Public Law 107-330, which changed the effective date to deaths occurring on or after September 11, 2001.

For all deaths occurring prior to September 11, 2001, the VA may provide a headstone or marker only for graves that are not marked with a private headstone.

Spouses and dependents buried in a private cemetery are not eligible for a Government-provided headstone or marker.

Flat markers in granite, marble, and bronze; and upright headstones in granite and marble are available. The style chosen must be consistent with existing monuments at the place of burial. Niche markers are also available to mark columbaria used for cremated remains.

Government-furnished headstones and markers must be inscribed with the name of the deceased, branch of service, and the year of birth and death, in this order. Headstones and markers also may be inscribed with other items, including an authorized emblem of believe and, space permitting, additional text including military grade, rate or rank, war service such as "World War II", complete dates of birth and death, military awards, military organizations, and civilian or veteran affiliations. To apply, and to obtain specific information on available styles, contact the cemetery where the headstone or marker is to be placed.

When burial occurs in a private cemetery, an application for a government-furnished headstone or marker must be made to VA. The government will ship the headstone or marker free of charge, but will not pay for its placement. To apply, complete VA Form 40-1330, Application for Standard Government Headstone or Marker for Installation in a Private or State Veterans' Cemetery, and forward it along with a *copy* of the veteran's military discharge documents (do not send original discharge documents, as they will not be returned) to:

Director
Memorial Programs Service (403)
Department of Veterans Affairs
810 Vermont Avenue, NW
Washington, DC 20420-0001

Eligibility Rules For A Government Headstone Or Marker In a Private Cemetery

1. Veterans and Members of the Armed Forces (Army, Navy, Air Force, Marine Corps, Coast Guard):

a. Any veterans or members of The Armed Forces who dies while on active duty.

b. Any veteran who was discharged under conditions other than dishonorable. With certain exceptions, service beginning after September 7, 1980, as an enlisted person, and service after October 16, 1981, as an officer, must be for a minimum of 24 months or the full period for which the person was called to active duty. (Examples include those serving less than 24 months in the Gulf War or Reservists that were federalized by Presidential Act.) Undesirable, bad conduct, and any other type of discharge other than honorable may or may not qualify the individual for veterans benefits, depending upon a determination made by a VA Regional Office. Cases presenting multiple discharges of varying character are also referred for adjudication to a VA Regional Office.

2. Members of Reserve Components and Reserve Officers' Training Corps:

a. Reservists and National Guard members who, at time of death, were entitled to retired pay under Chapter 1223, Title 10, United States Code, or would have been entitled, but for being under the age of 60.

b. Members of reserve components who die while hospitalized or undergoing treatment at the expense of the United States for injury or disease contracted or incurred under honorable conditions while performing active duty for training or inactive duty training, or undergoing such hospitalization or treatment.

c. Members of the Reserve Officers' Training Corps of the Army, Navy, or Air Force who die under honorable conditions while attending an authorized training camp or on an authorized cruise, while performing authorized travel to or from that camp or cruise, or while hospitalized or undergoing treatment at the expense of the United States for injury or disease contracted or incurred under honorable conditions while engaged in one of those activities.

d. Members of reserve components who, during a period of active duty for training, were disabled or died from a disease or injury incurred or aggravated in the line of duty or, during a period of inactive duty training, were disabled or died from an injury incurred or aggravated in the line of duty.

3. Commissioned Officers, National Oceanic and Atmospheric Administration:

a. A commissioned Officer of the National Oceanic and Atmospheric Administration (formerly titled the Coast and Geodetic Survey and the Environmental Science Services Administration) with full-time duty on or after July 29, 1945.

b. A commissioned Officer who served before July 29, 1945, and:

i. Was assigned to an area of immediate military hazard while in time of war, or of a Presidentially declared national emergency as determined by the Secretary of Defense; or

ii. Served in the Philippine Islands on December 7, 1941, and continuously in such islands thereafter; or

iii. Transferred to the Department of the Army or the Department of the Navy under the provisions of the Act of May 22, 1917.

4. Public Health Service:

a. A Commissioned A Commissioned Officer of the Regular or Reserve Corps of the Public Health Service who served on full-time duty on or after July 29, 1945. If the service of the particular Public Health Service Officer falls within the meaning of active duty for training, as defined in section 101(22), title 38, United States Code, he or she must have been disabled or died from a disease or injury incurred or aggravated in the line of duty.

b. A Commissioned Officer of the Regular or Reserve Corps of the Public Health Service who performed full-time duty prior to July 29, 1945:

i. In time of war;

ii. On detail for duty with the Army, Navy, Air Force, Marine Corps, or Coast Guard; or,

iii. While the Service was part of the military forces of the United States pursuant to Executive Order of the President.

c. A Commissioned Officer serving on inactive duty training as defined in section 101(23), title 38, United States Code, whose death resulted from an injury incurred or aggravated in the line of duty.

5. World War II Merchant Mariners

a. United States Merchant Mariners with oceangoing service during the period of armed conflict, December 7, 1941, to December 31, 1946. Prior to the enactment of Public Law 105-368, United States Merchant Mariners with oceangoing service during the period of armed conflict of December 7, 1941, to August 15, 1945, were eligible. With enactment of Public Law 105-368, the service period is extended to December 31, 1946, for those dying on or after November 11, 1998. A DD-214 documenting this service may be obtained by submitting an application to Commandant (G-MVP-6), United States Coast Guard, 2100 2nd Street, SW, Washington, DC 20593. Notwithstanding, the Mariner's death must have occurred after the enactment of Public Law 105-368 and the interment not violate the applicable restrictions while meeting the requirements held therein.

b. United States Merchant Mariners who served on blockships in support of Operation Mulberry during World War II.

Persons NOT Eligible for a Headstone or Marker

1. Disqualifying Characters of Discharge

A person whose only separation from the Armed Forces was under dishonorable conditions or whose character of service results in a bar to veterans benefits.

2. Discharge from Draft

A person who was ordered to report to an induction station, but was not actually inducted into military service.

3. Person Found Guilty of a Capital Crime

Eligibility for a headstone or marker is prohibited if a person is convicted of a Federal capital crime and sentenced to death or life imprisonment, or is convicted of a State capital crime, and sentenced to death or life imprisonment without parole. Federal officials are authorized to deny requests for headstones or markers to persons who are shown by clear and convincing evidence to have committed a Federal or State capital crime but were not convicted of such crime because of flight to avoid prosecution or by death prior to trial.

4. Subversive Activities

Any person convicted of subversive activities after September 1, 1959, shall have no right to burial in a national cemetery from and after the date of commission of such offense, based on periods of active military service commencing before the date of the commission of such offense, nor shall another person be entitled to burial on account of such an individual. Eligibility will be reinstated if the President of the United States grants a pardon.

5. Active or Inactive Duty for Training

A person whose only service is active duty for training or inactive duty training in the National Guard or Reserve Component, unless the individual meets the following criteria.

a. Reservists and National Guard members who, at time of death, were entitled to retired pay under Chapter 1223, title 10, United States Code, or would have been entitled, but for being under the age of 60. Specific categories of individuals eligible for retired pay are delineated in section 12731 of Chapter 1223, title 10, United States Code.

b. Members of reserve components who die while hospitalized or undergoing treatment at the expense of the United States for injury or disease contracted or incurred under honorable conditions while performing active duty for training or inactive duty training, or undergoing such hospitalization or treatment.

c. Members of the Reserve Officers' Training Corps of the Army, Navy, or Air Force who die under honorable conditions while attending an authorized training camp or on an authorized cruise, while performing authorized travel to or from that camp or cruise, or while hospitalized or undergoing treatment at the expense of the United States for injury or disease contracted or incurred under honorable conditions while engaged in one of those activities.

d. Members of reserve components who, during a period of active duty for training, were disabled or died from a disease or injury incurred or aggravated in line of duty or, during a period of inactive duty training, were disabled or died from an injury incurred or aggravated in line of duty.

6. Other Groups

Members of groups whose service has been determined by the Secretary of the Air Force under the provisions of Public Law 95-202 as not warranting entitlement to benefits administered by the Secretary of Veterans Affairs.

BURIAL IN NATIONAL CEMETERIES

The National Cemetery Administration honors Veterans with a final resting place and lasting memorials that commemorate their service to our nation.

Veterans and service members who meet the eligibility requirements, and their eligible dependents may be buried in one of the VA's national cemeteries. The National Cemetery Administration currently includes 122 national cemeteries. The Department of the Army administers 2 national cemeteries, and the Department of the Interior administers 14 national cemeteries. There are also numerous state cemeteries for veterans throughout the U.S. For a listing of all national cemeteries as well as state veterans cemeteries refer to the listing at the end of this chapter.

UPDATE: Respect for America's Fallen Heroes Act
(Became Public Law 109-228 on May 29, 2006)

On May 29, 2006, President Bush signed the *"Respect For America's Fallen Heroes Act"* into law. This law does the following:

- Prohibits a demonstration on the property of a cemetery under the control of the National Cemetery Administration or on the property of Arlington National Cemetery unless the demonstration has been approved by the cemetery superintendent or the director of the property on which the cemetery is located.

The Respect For America's Fallen Heroes Act prohibits certain demonstrations at cemeteries under the control of the National Cemetery Administration and at Arlington National Cemetery.

- Prohibits, with respect to the above cemeteries, a demonstration during the period beginning 60 minutes before and ending 60 minutes after a funeral, memorial service, or ceremony is held, which:
    - Takes place within 150 feet of a road, pathway, or other route of ingress to or egress from such cemetery property; or
    - Is within 300 feet of such cemetery and impedes access to or egress from such cemetery.

- The term "Demonstration" includes the following:
    - Any picketing or similar conduct.
    - Any oration, speech, use of sound amplification equipment or device, or similar conduct that is not part of a funeral, memorial service, or ceremony.
    - The display of any placard, banner, flag, or similar device, unless the display is part of a funeral, memorial service, or ceremony.
    - The distribution of any handbill, pamphlet, leaflet, or other written or printed matter other than what is distributed as part of a funeral, memorial service, or ceremony.

- Amends the federal criminal code to provide criminal penalties for violations of such prohibitions.

- Express the sense of Congress that each state should enact similar legislation to restrict demonstrations near any military funeral.

Eligibility

The VA national cemetery directors have the primary responsibility for verifying eligibility for burial in VA national cemeteries. A dependent's eligibility for burial is based upon the eligibility of the veteran. To establish a veteran's eligibility, a copy of the official military discharge document bearing an official seal or a DD 214 is usually sufficient. The document must show that release from service was under conditions other than dishonorable. A determination of eligibility is usually made in response to a request for burial in a VA national cemetery.

The cemeteries administered by the National Cemetery Administration and the Department of the Interior use the eligibility requirements that follow. The Department of the Interior can be contacted at:

U.S. Department of the Interior
National Park Service
1849 C Street, N.W.
Washington, D.C. 20240
(202) 208-4621

The Department of the Army should be contacted directly for inquiries concerning eligibility for interment in either of the two cemeteries under its jurisdiction (call 703-695-3250).

Eligibility requirements for burial in state veterans cemeteries are the same, or similar, to the eligibility requirements that follow. However, some states also have residency and other more restrictive requirements. Please contact the specific state cemetery for its eligibility requirements.

The following veterans and members of the Armed Forces (Army, Navy, Air Force, Marine Corps, Coast Guard) are eligible for burial in a VA national cemetery:

Veterans and Members of the Armed Forces

- Any member of the Armed Forces of the U.S. who dies on active duty.
- Any citizen of the U.S. who, during any war in which the U.S. has been engaged, served in the Armed Forces of any U.S. ally during that war, whose last active service terminated honorably by death or otherwise, and who was a citizen of the U.S. at the time of entry into such service and at the time of death.
- Any veteran discharged under conditions other than dishonorable, and who has completed the required period of service. With certain exceptions, service beginning after September 7, 1980, as an enlisted person, and service after October 16, 1981, as an officer, must be for a minimum of 24 months or the full period for which the person was called to active duty.

Members of Reserve Components and Reserve Officers' Training Corps

- Reservists and National Guard members with 20 years of qualifying service, who are entitled to retired pay, or would be entitled, if at least 60 years of age.
- Members of reserve components who die under honorable conditions while hospitalized or undergoing treatment at the expense of the U.S. for injury or disease contracted or incurred under honorable conditions, while performing active duty for training, or inactive duty training, or undergoing such hospitalization or treatment.
- Members of the Reserve Officers' Training Corps of the Army, Navy, or Air Force who die under honorable conditions while attending an authorized training camp or cruise, or while traveling to or from that camp or cruise, or while hospitalized or undergoing treatment at the

expense of the U.S. for injury or disease contracted or incurred under honorable conditions while engaged in one of those activities.

- Members of reserve components who, during a period of active duty for training, were disabled or died from a disease or injury incurred or aggravated in the line of duty, or, during a period of inactive duty training, were disabled or died from an injury incurred or aggravated in the line of duty.

Commissioned Officers, National Oceanic and Atmospheric Administration

- A Commissioned Officer of the National Oceanic and Atmospheric Administration with full-time duty on or after July 29, 1945.
- A Commissioned Officer of the National Oceanic and Atmospheric Administration who served before July 29, 1945, and:
- Was assigned to an area of immediate hazard described in the Act of December 3, 1942 (56 Stat. 1038; 33 U.S.C. 855a), as amended;
- Served in the Philippine Islands on December 7, 1941, and continuously in such islands thereafter.

Public Health Service

- A Commissioned Officer of the Regular or Reserve Corps of the Public Health Service who served on full-time duty on or after July 29, 1945. If the service of such Officer falls within the meaning of active duty for training, he must have been disabled or died from a disease or injury incurred or aggravated in the line of duty.
- A Commissioned Officer of the Regular or Reserve Corps of the Public Health Service who performed full-time duty prior to July 29, 1945:
  a. In time of war; or
  b. On detail for duty with the Army, Navy, Air Force, Marine Corps, or Coast Guard; or
  c. While the service was part of the military forces of the U.S. pursuant to Executive Order of the President.
- A Commissioned Officer of the Regular or Reserve Corps of the Public Health Service serving on inactive duty training as defined in Section 101 (23), title 39, U.S. Code, whose death resulted from an injury incurred or aggravated in the line of duty.

World War II Merchant Mariners

- U.S. Merchant Mariners with oceangoing service during the period of armed conflict, December 7, 1941 to December 31, 1946. Prior to the enactment of Public Law 105-368, United States Merchant Mariners with oceangoing service during the period of armed conflict of December 7, 1941, to August 15, 1945, were eligible. With enactment of Public Law 105-368, the service period is extended to December 31, 1946, for those dying on or after November 11, 1998.

- U.S. Merchant Mariners who served on blockships in support of Operation Mulberry during WWII.

The Philippine Armed Forces

- Any Philippine veteran who was a citizen of the United States or an alien lawfully admitted for permanent residence in the United States at the time of their death; and resided in the United States at the time of their death; and:

- Was a person who served before July 1, 1946, in the organized military forces of the Government of the Commonwealth of the Philippines, while such forces were in the service of the Armed Forces of the United States pursuant to the military order of the President dated July 26, 1941, including organized guerilla forces under commanders appointed, designated, or subsequently recognized by the Commander in Chief, Southwest Pacific Area, or other competent authority in the Army of the United States who dies on or after November 1, 2000; or

- Was a person who enlisted between October 6, 1945, and June 30, 1947, with the Armed Forces of the United States with the consent of the Philippine government, pursuant to Section 14 of the Armed Forces Voluntary Recruitment Act of 1945, and who died on or after December 16, 2003.

Spouses and Dependents

- The spouse or surviving spouse of an eligible veteran is eligible for interment in a national cemetery even if that veteran is not buried or memorialized in a national cemetery. In addition, the spouse or surviving spouse of a member of the Armed Forces of the United States whose remains are unavailable for burial is also eligible for burial.

- The surviving spouse of an eligible veteran who had a subsequent remarriage to a non-veteran and whose death occurred on or after January 1, 2000, is eligible for burial in a national cemetery, based on his or her marriage to the eligible veteran.

- The minor children of an eligible veteran. For the purpose of burial in a national cemetery, a minor child is a child who is unmarried and:

- Under 21 years of age; or

- Under 23 years of age and pursuing a full-time course of instruction at an approved educational institution.

- An unmarried adult child of an eligible veteran if the child became permanently physically or mentally disabled and incapable of self-support before reaching 21 years of age, or before reaching 23 years of age if pursuing a full-time course of instruction at an approved educational institution.

- Any other persons or classes of persons as designated by the Secretary of Veterans Affairs or the Secretary of the Air Force.

The following are not eligible for burial in a VA national cemetery:

- A former spouse of an eligible individual whose marriage to that individual has been terminated by annulment or divorce, if not otherwise eligible.

- Family members other than those specifically described above.

- A person whose only separation from the Armed Forces was under dishonorable conditions, or whose character of service results in a bar to veterans benefits.

- A person ordered to report to an induction station, but not actually inducted into military service.

- Any person found guilty of a capital crime. Interment or memorialization in a VA cemetery or in Arlington National Cemetery is prohibited if a person is convicted of a Federal capital crime and sentenced to death or life imprisonment, or is convicted of a State capital crime, and sentenced to death or life imprisonment without parole. Federal officials are authorized to deny burial in veterans cemeteries to persons who are shown by clear and convincing evidence to have committed a Federal or State capital crime but were not convicted of such crime because of flight to avoid prosecution or by death prior to trial. The Secretary is authorized to provide aid to States for the establishment, expansion and/or improvement of veterans cemeteries on the condition that the State is willing to prohibit interment or memorialization in such cemeteries of individuals convicted of Federal or State capital crimes, or found by clear and convincing evidence to have committed such crimes, without having been convicted of the crimes due to flight to avoid prosecution or death prior to trial.

- Any person convicted of subversive activities after September 1, 1959, shall have no right to burial in a national cemetery from and after the date of commission of such offense, based on periods of active military service commencing before the date of the commission of such offense, nor shall another person be entitled to burial on account of such an individual. Eligibility will be reinstated if the President of the United States grants a pardon.

Requests for Gravesites in National Cemeteries

An eligible veteran or family member may be buried in the VA national cemetery of his choice, provided space is available. A veteran may not reserve a gravesite in his name prior to his death. However, any reservations made under previous programs will be honored. The funeral director or loved one making the burial arrangements must apply for a gravesite at the time of death. No special forms are required when requesting burial in a VA national cemetery. The person making burial arrangement should contact the national cemetery in which burial is desired at the time of need.

If possible, the following information concerning the deceased should be provided when the cemetery is first contacted:

- Full name and military rank;

- Branch of service;
- Social security number;
- VA claim number, if applicable;
- Date and place of birth;
- Date and place of death;
- Date of retirement or last separation from active duty; and
- Copy of any military separation documents (such as DD-214)

When a death occurs and eligibility for interment in a national cemetery is determined, grave space is assigned by the cemetery director in the name of the veteran or family member.

One gravesite is permitted for the interment of all eligible family members, unless soil conditions or the number of family decedents necessitate more than one grave.

There is no charge for burial in a national cemetery.

One gravesite is permitted for the interment of all eligible family members, unless soil conditions or the number of family decedents necessitate more than one grave.

There is no charge for burial in a national cemetery.

The availability of grave space varies among each National Cemetery. In many cases, if a national cemetery does not have space for a full-casket burial, it may still inter cremated remains. Full-casket gravesites occasionally become available in such cemeteries due to disinterment or cancellation of prior reservations. The cemetery director can answer such questions at the time of need.

Most national cemeteries do not typically conduct burials on weekends. However, weekend callers trying to make burial arrangements for the following week will be provided with the phone number of one of three strategically located VA cemetery offices that remains open during weekends.

Burial at Sea

The National Cemetery Administration cannot provide burial at sea. For information, contact the United States Navy Mortuary Affairs office toll-free at (888) 647-6676, and select option 4.

Furnishing and Placement of Headstones and Markers

In addition to the gravesite, burial in a VA national cemetery also includes furnishing and placement of the headstone or marker, opening and closing of the grave, and perpetual care. Many national cemeteries also have columbaria or gravesites for cremated remains. (Some State Veterans' cemeteries may charge a nominal fee for placing a Government-provided headstone or marker.)

***SPECIAL NOTES*:**

- For person's with 20-years service in the National Guard or Reserves, entitlement to retired pay must be subsequent to October 27, 1992 in order to qualify for a Government-provided headstone or marker. A copy of the Reserve Retirement Eligibility Benefits Letter must accompany the application. Active duty service while in the National Guard or Reserves also establishes eligibility.

- Service prior to World War I requires detailed documentation to prove eligibility such as muster rolls, extracts from State files, military or State organizations where served, pension or land warrants, etc.

Flat bronze, granite, or marble grave markers and upright marble or granite headstones are available to mark graves in the style consistent with existing monuments in the national cemetery. Niche markers are also available for identifying cremated remains in columbaria. The following is a brief description of each type:

- *Upright Marble and Upright Granite:* 42 inches long, 13 inches wide, 4 inches thick, approximately 230 pounds.

- *Flat Bronze:* 24 inches long, 12 inches wide, ¾ inch rise, approximately 18 pounds. Anchor bolts, nuts and washers for fastening to base are supplied with marker. The government does not provide the base.

- *Flat Granite and Flat Marble*: 24 inches long, 12 inches wide, 4 inches thick, approximately 130 pounds.

- *Bronze Niche:* 8 ½ inches long, 5 ½ inches wide, 7/16 inch rise, approximately 3 pounds. Mounting bolts and washers are supplied with marker.

- There are also two special styles of upright marble headstones and flat markers available - one for those who served with the Union Forces during the Civil War or the Spanish-American War; and one for those who served with the Confederate Forces during the Civil War.

Inscriptions

Headstones and markers are inscribed with the name of the deceased, branch of service, year of birth, and year of death.

The word "Korea" may be included on Government headstones and markers for the graves of those members and former members of the United States Armed Forces who served within the areas of military operations in the Korean Theater between June 27, 1950 and July 27, 1954; and for headstones and markers for active duty decedents who lost their lives in Korea or adjacent waters as a result of hostile action subsequent to the 1953 Armistice.

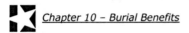

The word "Vietnam" may be included on Government headstones and markers for the graves of those members and former members of the United States Armed Forces who died in Vietnam or whose death was attributable to service in Vietnam, and on the headstones and markers of all decedents who were on active duty on or after August 5, 1964.

The words "Lebanon" or "Grenada" may be included on Government headstones and markers for those killed as a result of those military actions.

The words "Panama" and "Persian Gulf" may be included on Government headstones and markers for those killed as a result of those military actions.

If desired, the following inscriptions can also be made (space permitting):

- Military grade
- Military rank
- Military rate
- Identification of war service
- Months and days of birth and death
- An authorized emblem of religious belief (see following list of available emblems)
- Military awards (documentation of award must be provided)
- Military organizations
- Civilian or veteran affiliations

With the VA's approval, terms of endearment that meet acceptable standards of good taste may also be added. Most optional inscriptions are placed as the last lines of the inscription. No other graphics are permitted on Government-provided headstones and markers, and inscriptions will be in English text only. Civilian titles such as "Doctor or Reverend" are not permitted on the name line of government-provided headstones and markers.

Available Emblems of Belief for Placement on Government Headstones and Markers:

- Christian Cross
- Buddhist (Wheel of Righteousness)
- Hebrew (Star of David)
- Presbyterian Cross
- Russian Orthodox Cross

- Lutheran Cross
- Episcopal Cross
- Unitarian Church (Flaming Chalice)
- United Methodist Church
- Aaronic Order Church
- Mormon (Angel Moroni)
- Native American Church of North America
- Serbian Orthodox
- Greek Cross
- Bahai (9 Pointed Star)
- Atheist
- Muslim (Crescent and Star)
- Hindu
- Konko-Kyo Faith
- Community of Christ
- Sufism Reoriented
- Tenrikyo Church
- Seicho-No-Ie
- Church of World Messianity (Izunome)
- United Church of Religious Science
- Christian Reformed Church
- United Moravian Church
- Eckankar
- Christian Church
- United Church of Christ
- Christian & Missionary Alliance
- Humanist Emblem Of Spirit
- Presbyterian Church (USA)
- Izumo Taishakyo Mission Of Hawaii

- Soka Gakkai International - USA
- Sikh (Khanda)
- Christian Scientist (Cross and Crown)
- Muslim (Islamic 5 Pointed Star)

Ordering a Headstone or Marker

For burial of a veteran in a national, state veteran, or military post cemetery, the cemetery will order the headstone or marker, and can give loved ones information on style, inscription, and shipment. Shipment and placement of the headstone or marker is provided at no cost.

When burial is in a private cemetery, VA Form 40-1330, *Application for Standard Government Headstone or Marker* must be submitted by the next of kin or a representative, such as funeral director, cemetery official or veterans' counselor, along with the veteran's military discharge documents, to request a Government-provided headstone or marker. Do not send original documents, as they will not be returned.

Headstones and Markers for Spouses and Children

The VA will issue a headstone or marker for an eligible spouse or child buried in a national, state veteran or military post cemetery. However, the VA cannot issue a headstone or marker for a spouse or child buried in a private cemetery.

The VA will issue a headstone or marker for an eligible spouse or child buried in a national, state veteran or military post cemetery. However, the VA cannot issue a headstone or marker for a spouse or child buried in a private cemetery.

The applicant can, however, request to reserve inscription space below the veteran's inscription, so that the non-veteran's commemorative information can be inscribed locally, at private expense, when the non-veteran is buried. The applicant may also choose to have his/her name and date of birth added at Government expense, when the headstone or marker is ordered. The date of death may then be added, at private expense, at the time of his/her death.

Commemoration of Unidentified Remains

Many national cemeteries have areas suitable to commemorate veterans whose remains were not recovered or identified, were buried at sea, or are otherwise unavailable for interment. In such instances, the VA will provide a memorial headstone or marker to be placed in that section of the cemetery. The words *"In Memory of"* must precede the authorized inscription.

Checking Order Status

To check the status of a previously ordered headstone or marker for placement in a private cemetery, applicants may call the VA's Applicant Assistance Line at

1-800-697-6947. The line is open weekdays, from 8:00 A.M. to 5:00 P.M., Eastern Standard Time.

Replacement of Headstones and Markers

For guidance on obtaining a replacement headstone or marker, call (800)-697-6947.

The Government will replace a previously furnished headstone or marker if it: becomes badly damaged, is vandalized, is stolen, becomes badly deteriorated, the inscription becomes illegible, is different from that ordered by the applicant, becomes damaged in transit, or the inscription is incorrect.

Government headstones or markers in private cemeteries damaged by cemetery personnel will not be replaced at Government expense.

If a marble or granite headstone or marker is permanently removed from a grave, it must be destroyed. Bronze markers must be returned to the contractor.

MILITARY HONORS

The rendering of Military Funeral Honors is a way to show the Nation's deep gratitude to those who have faithfully defended our country in times of war and peace. It is the final demonstration a grateful Nation can provide to the veterans' families.

The following service members are eligible for Military Funeral Honors:

- Military members on active duty or in the Selected Reserve at time of death;
- Former military members who served on active duty and departed under conditions other than dishonorable;
- Former military members who completed at least one term of enlistment or period of initial obligated service in the Selected Reserve, and departed under conditions other than dishonorable;
- Former military members discharged from the Selected Reserve due to a disability incurred or aggravated in the line of duty.

Military Funeral Honors have always been provided whenever possible. However, effective October 5, 1999, the law, under P.L. 105-261, Section 578, mandates that all eligible veterans receive basic Military Funeral Honors, if requested by the deceased veteran's family. As provided by law, an honor guard detail for the burial of an eligible veteran shall consist of not less than two members of the Armed Forces. One member of the detail shall be a representative of the parent Service of the deceased veteran. The honor detail will, at a minimum, perform a ceremony that includes the folding and presenting of the American flag to the next of kin, and the playing of Taps. Taps will be played by a bugler, if available, or by electronic recording.

In 2003, the Department of Defense announced its approval of the use of a ceremonial bugle as an alternative to the recorded version of Taps played on stereo at military funerals.

The ceremonial bugle consists of a small cone-shaped device inserted deep into the bell of a bugle that plays an exceptionally high-quality rendition of Taps that is virtually indistinguishable from a live bugler.

The ceremonial bugle will be offered to families as an alternative to the pre-recorded Taps played on a stereo, but will not be used as a substitute for a live bugler when one is available. Live buglers will continue to play at veterans' funerals whenever available.

Funeral Directors have the responsibility of assisting loved ones in requesting military honors. A toll-free telephone number has been established for funeral directors requesting military honors.

The Department of Defense (DOD) has provided registered funeral home directors with a military funeral honors kit and information on how to contact the appropriate military organization to perform the honors ceremony.
Questions about the Military Funeral Honors program should be sent to:

Department of Defense
Directorate for Public Inquiry and Analysis
Room 3A750, The Pentagon
Washington, DC 20301-1400

PREPARATIONS WHICH CAN BE MADE PRIOR TO DEATH

It is suggested that veterans and their families prepare in advance by discussing cemetery options, collecting the veteran's military information (including discharge papers), and by contacting the cemetery where the veteran wishes to be buried. If burial will be in a private cemetery and a Government headstone or marker will be requested, VA Form 40-1330 can be completed in advance and placed with the veteran's military discharge papers for use at the time of need.

BURIAL LOCATION ASSISTANCE

The VA National Cemetery Administration can provide limited burial location assistance to family members and close friends of decedents thought to be buried in a VA national cemetery.

The National Cemetery Administration will research its records to determine if the decedent is buried in one of VA's national cemeteries. A request can include a maximum of ten specific names to locate.

The National Cemetery Administration does not have information on persons buried in cemeteries other than its national cemeteries. Its records do not contain any personal, military or family information – only information regarding whether or not an individual is buried in a VA national cemetery, and if so, where, can be provided.

The "Gravesite Locator" tool is available online at the VA's website.

If the online tool is not available or helpful, you may submit a written request. No form is required to request this information, and no fee is charged. The following information should be provided:

- Full name, including any alternate spellings, of decedent;
- Date and place of birth;
- Date and place of death;
- State from which the individual entered active duty;
- Military service branch;
- Mailing address and phone number of individual requesting the information.

Allow approximately 4 weeks for a reply.

Requests should be sent to:

U.S. Department of Veterans Affairs
National Cemetery Administration (41C1)
Burial Location Request
810 Vermont Avenue, N.W.
Washington, D.C. 20420

U.S. MILITARY CEMETERIES AND MONUMENTS OVERSEAS

The *American Battle Monuments Commission (ABMC)* a small, independent agency of the U.S. government's executive branch, maintains 24 American military cemeteries, and 27 memorials, monuments, or markers. (The VA is not responsible for maintaining cemeteries and monuments honoring deceased veterans buried on foreign soil.)

ABMC Cemeteries

- Aisne Marne - South of Belleau, France
- Ardennes – Neupre (Neuville-enCondroz), Belgium
- Brittany – Southeast of St. James (Marche), France
- Brookwood – Brookwood, Surrey, England
- Cambridge – Cambridge, England
- Corozal – North of Panama City, Republic of Panama
- Epinal – Southeast of Epinal (Vosges), France

- Flanders Field – Waregem, Belgium
- Florence – South of Florence, Italy
- Henri-Chapelle – Northeast of Henri-Chapelle, Belgium
- Lorraine – North of St. Avold (Moselle), France
- Luxembourg – Luxembourg City, Luxembourg
- Manila – Southeast of Manila, Republic of Philippines
- Meuse Argonne – East of Romagne –sous-Montfaucon (Meuse), France
- Mexico City – Mexico City, Mexico
- Netherlands – Margraten, Netherlands
- Normandy – Colleville-sur Mer, France
- North Africa – near Carthage
- Oise-Aisne – East of Fere-en-Tardenois (Aisne), France
- Rhone – Draguignan (Var), France
- Sicily-Rome – Nettuno, Italy
- Somme – Southwest of Bony (Aisne), France
- St. Mihil – Thiaacourt, France
- Surresnes – West of Paris, France

ABMC Monuments

- Audenaude Monument – Oudenaarde (Audenarde), Belgium
- Belleau Wood Monument
- Bellicourt Monument – North of St. Quentin (Aisne), France
- Cabanatuan Memorial - Philippines
- Cantigny Monument – Cantigny (Somme), France
- Chateau-Thierry Monument – West of Chateay-Thierry, France
- Chaumont Marker – Chaumont, France
- East Coast Memorial – Battery Park, New York City
- Guadalcanal Memorial – Honiara, Guadalcanal, Solomon Islands
- Honolulu Memorial – Honolulu, Hawaii
- Kemmel Monument – South of Ieper (Ypres), Belgium

- Montfaucan Monument – Northwest of Verdun, France
- Montsec Monument – Montsec (Thiaucourt), France
- Naval Brest Monument – Brest, France
- Naval Gibraltar Monument – Straights of Gibraltar
- Pointe-du-Hoc Monument – Overlooks Omaha Beach, France
- Papua Marker – Papua, New Guinea
- Saipan Memorial – Saipan, Commonwealth of the Mariana Islands
- Santiago Surrender Tree
- Sommepy Monument – Northwest of Sommepy – Tahure (Marne), France
- Souilly Marker – Souilly, France
- Tours Monument – Tours, France
- Utah Beach Monument – Sainte-Marie-du-Mont (Manche), France
- West Coast Memorial – San Francisco, California
- Western Task Force Marker – Casablanca, Morocco

ABMC Services

The ABMC can provide interested parties with:

- Name, location, and information on cemeteries and memorials.
- Plot, row and grave number or memorialization location of Honored War Dead.
- Best in-country routes and modes of travel to cemeteries or memorials.
- Information on accommodations near cemeteries or memorials.
- Escort service for relatives to grave and memorial sites within the cemeteries.
- Letters authorizing fee-free passports for members of the immediate family traveling overseas to visit a grave or memorialization site.
- Black and white photographs of headstones and Tablets of the Missing on which the names of dead or missing are engraved.
- Arrangements for floral decorations placed at graves and memorialization sites.
- An Honor Roll Certificate containing data on a Korean War casualty suitable for framing.
- Polaroid color photographs of donated floral decorations in place.

The Andrews Project

The commission also provides friends and relatives of those interred in its cemeteries or memorialized on its Tablets of the Missing with color lithographs of the cemetery or memorial on which is mounted a photograph of the headstone or commemorative inscription. The Andrews Project, named in honor of its sponsor, the late Congressman George W. Andrews, is ABMC's most popular service.

For further information, contact the ABMC at:

American Battle Monuments Commission
Arlington Court House Plaza II
2300 Clarendon Blvd., Suite 500
Arlington, VA 22201
(703) 696-6897

Passports to Visit Overseas Cemeteries

Family members who wish to visit overseas graves and memorial sites of World War I and World War II veterans are eligible for "no-fee" passports. Family members eligible for the "no-fee" passports include surviving spouses, parents, children, sisters, brothers and guardians of the deceased veteran buried or commemorated in American military cemeteries on foreign soil. For further information contact the American Battle Monuments Commission at the address and phone number indicated in the previous section.

PRESIDENTIAL MEMORIAL CERTIFICATES

A Presidential Memorial Certificate is an engraved paper certificate that has been signed by the current president, honoring the memory of any honorably discharged deceased veteran.

Presidential Memorial Certificates may be distributed to a deceased veteran's next of kin and loved ones. More than one certificate can be provided per family, and there is no time limit for applying for the certificate.

Presidential Memorial Certificates may not be furnished on behalf of deceased veterans who committed capital crimes.

Requests for a Presidential Memorial Certificate can be made in person at any VA regional office, by faxing the request and all supporting documents (copy of discharge and death certificate) to (202) 565-8054, or by U.S. Mail.

There is no form to use when requesting a certificate. A copy of the veteran's discharge documents and a return mailing address should be included with any request. Written requests should be sent to:

Presidential Memorial Certificates (41A1C)
Department of Veterans Affairs
5109 Russell Road
Quantico, VA 22134-3903

LISTS OF NATIONAL CEMETERIES

Some national cemeteries can bury only cremated remains or casketed remains of eligible family members of those already buried. Contact the cemetery director for information on the availability of space

Department Of Veterans Affairs National Cemeteries

Alabama

Fort Mitchell National Cemetery
553 Highway 165
Seale, AL 36875
(334) 855-4731

Mobile National Cemetery
1202 Virginia Street
Mobile, AL 36604
For information please contact: Barrancas National Cemetery (850) 453-4846

Alaska

Fort Richardson National Cemetery
Building #997, Davis Highway
P. O. Box 5-498
Fort Richardson, AK 99505
(907) 384-7075

Sitka National Cemetery
803 Sawmill Creek Road
Sitka, AK 99835
For information please contact:
Fort Richardson National Cemetery
(907) 384-7075

Arizona

National Memorial Cemetery of Arizona
23029 North Cave Creek Road
Phoenix, AZ 85024
(480) 513-3600

Prescott National Cemetery
500 Highway 89 North
Prescott, AZ 86301
For information please contact National Memorial Cemetery of Arizona (480) 513-3600

Arkansas

Fayetteville National Cemetery
700 Government Avenue
Fayetteville, AR 72701
(479) 444-5051

Fort Smith National Cemetery
522 Garland Avenue
Fort Smith, AR 72901
(479) 783-5345

Little Rock National Cemetery
2523 Confederate Boulevard
Little Rock, AR 72206
(501) 324-6401

California

Fort Rosecrans National Cemetery
P. O. Box 6237 Point Loma
San Diego, CA 92106
(619) 553-2084

Golden Gate National Cemetery
1300 Sneath Lane
San Bruno, CA 94066
(650) 761-7737

Los Angeles National Cemetery
950 South Sepulveda Boulevard
Los Angeles, CA 90049
(310) 268-4675

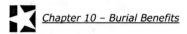

Riverside National Cemetery
22495 Van Buren Boulevard
Riverside, CA 92518
(909) 653-8417

Sacramento Valley National Cemetery
5810 Midway Road
Dixon, CA 95620
(707) 693-2460

San Francisco National Cemetery
P. O. Box 29012
Presidio of San Francisco
San Francisco, CA 94129
For information please contact
Golden Gate National Cemetery
(650) 761-1646

San Joaquin Valley National
Cemetery
32053 West McCabe Road
Gustine, CA 95322
(209) 854-1040

Colorado

Fort Logan National Cemetery
3698 South Sheridan Boulevard
Denver, CO 80235
(303) 761-0117

Fort Lyon National Cemetery
VA Medical Center
Fort Lyon, CO 81038
For information please contact Fort
Logan National Cemetery
(303) 761-0117

Florida

Barrancas National Cemetery
Naval Air Station
80 Hovey Road
Pensacola, FL 32508-1099
(850) 453-4108

Bay Pines National Cemetery
P. O. Box 477
Bay Pines, FL 33504-0477
(727) 398-9426

Florida National Cemetery
6502 SW 102nd Avenue
Bushnell, FL 33513
(352) 793-7740 or 1074

South Florida National Cemetery
6501 S. State Road 7
Lake Worth, FL 33467
Phone: (561) 649-6489

St. Augustine National Cemetery
104 Marine Street
St. Augustine, FL 32084
For information please contact
Florida National Cemetery
(352) 793-7740

Georgia

Georgia National Cemetery
2025 Mount Carmel Church Lane
Canton, GA 30114
(866) 236-8159

Marietta National Cemetery
500 Washington Avenue
Marietta, GA 30060
(866) 236-8159

Hawaii

National Memorial Cemetery of the
Pacific
2177 Puowaina Drive
Honolulu, HI 96813-1729
(808) 523-3720

Illinois

Abraham Lincoln National
Cemetery
27034 South Diagonal Road
Elwood, IL 60421
(815) 423-9958

Alton National Cemetery
600 Pearl Street
Alton, IL 62003
For information please contact
Jefferson Barracks National
Cemetery (314) 260-8691

Camp Butler National Cemetery
5063 Camp Butler Road; RR #1
Springfield, IL 62707
(217) 492-4070

Danville National Cemetery
1900 East Main Street
Danville, IL 61832
(217) 554-4550

Mound City National Cemetery
P. O. Box 128
Mound City, IL 62963
For information please contact
Jefferson Barracks National Cemetery
(314) 260-8691

Quincy National Cemetery
36th and Maine Street
Quincy, IL 62301
For information please contact
Rock Island National Cemetery
(309) 782-2094

Rock Island National Cemetery
Rock Island Arsenal
P. O. Box 737
Moline, IL 61265
Rock Island, IL 61299-7090
(309) 782-2094

Indiana

Crown Hill National Cemetery
700 West 38th Street
Indianapolis, IN 46208
For information please contact
Marion National Cemetery
(765) 674-0284

Marion National Cemetery
VA Medical Center
1700 East 38th Street
Marion, IN 46952
(765) 674-0284

New Albany National Cemetery
1943 Ekin Avenue
New Albany, IN 47150
For information please contact
Zachary Taylor National Cemetery
(812) 948-5234

Iowa

Keokuk National Cemetery
1701 J Street
Keokuk, IA 52632
For information please contact
Rock Island National Cemetery
(309) 782-2094

Kansas

Fort Leavenworth Natl Cemetery
Fort Leavenworth, KS 66027
For information please contact
Leavenworth National Cemetery
(913) 758-4105

Fort Scott National Cemetery
P. O. Box 917
Fort Scott, KS 66701
(620) 223-2840

Leavenworth National Cemetery
P. O. Box 1694
Leavenworth, KS 66048
(913) 758-4105

Kentucky

Camp Nelson National Cemetery
6980 Danville Road
Nicholasville, KY 40356
(859) 885-5727

Cave Hill National Cemetery
701 Baxter Avenue
Louisville, KY 40204
For information please contact
Zachary Taylor National Cemetery
(502) 893-3852

Danville National Cemetery
277 North First Street
Danville, KY 40442
For information please contact
Camp Nelson National Cemetery
(859) 885-5727

Lebanon National Cemetery
20 Highway 208
Lebanon, KY 40033
(502) 893-3852

Lexington National Cemetery
833 West Main Street
Lexington, KY 40508
For information please contact
Camp Nelson National Cemetery
(859) 885-5727

Mill Springs National Cemetery
Nancy, KY 42544
For information please contact
Camp Nelson National Cemetery
(859) 885-5727

Zachary Taylor National Cemetery
4701 Brownsboro Road
Louisville, KY 40207
(502) 893-3852

Louisiana

Alexandria National Cemetery
209 East Shamrock Street
Pineville, LA 71360
For information please contact
Natchez National Cemetery
(318) 449-1793

Baton Rouge National Cemetery
220 North 19th Street
Baton Rouge, LA 70806
For information please contact
Port Hudson National Cemetery
(225) 654-3767

Port Hudson National Cemetery
20978 Port Hickey Road
Zachary, LA 70791
(225) 654-3767

Maine

Togus National Cemetery
VA Medical and Regional Office
Center
Togus, ME 04330
For information please contact
Massachusetts National Cemetery
(508) 563-7113

Maryland

Annapolis National Cemetery
800 West Street
Annapolis, MD 21401
For information please contact
Baltimore National Cemetery
(410) 644-9696

Baltimore National Cemetery
5501 Frederick Avenue
Baltimore, MD 21228
(410) 644-9696

Loudon Park National Cemetery
3445 Frederick Avenue
Baltimore, MD 21228
For information please contact
Baltimore National Cemetery
(410) 644-9696

Massachusetts

Massachusetts National Cemetery
Bourne, MA 02532
(508) 563-7113

Michigan

Fort Custer National Cemetery
15501 Dickman Road
Augusta, MI 49012
(269) 731-4164

Great Lakes National
Cemetery
4200 Belford Road
Holly, MI 48842
(866) 348-8603

Minnesota

Fort Snelling National Cemetery
7601 34th Avenue, South
Minneapolis, MN 55450-1199
(612) 726-1127

Mississippi

Biloxi National Cemetery
P. O. Box 4968
Biloxi, MS 39535-4968
(601) 388-6668

Corinth National Cemetery
1551 Horton Street
Corinth, MS 38834
For information please contact
Memphis National Cemetery
(901) 386-8311

Natchez National Cemetery
41 Cemetery Road
Natchez, MS 39120
(601) 445-4981

Missouri

Jefferson Barracks National Cemetery
2900 Sheridan Road
St. Louis, MO 63125
(314) 260-8691

Jefferson City National Cemetery
1024 East McCarty Street
Jefferson City, MO 65101
For information please contact
Jefferson Barracks National Cemetery
(314) 260-8691

Springfield National Cemetery
1702 East Seminole Street
Springfield, MO 65804
(417) 881-9499

Nebraska

Fort McPherson National Cemetery
HCO1, Box 67
Maxwell, NE 69151
(308) 582-4433

New Jersey

Beverly National Cemetery
R.D. #1, Bridgeboro Road
Beverly, NJ 08010
(609) 877-5460

Finn's Point National Cemetery
RFD # 3, Fort Mott Road, Box 542
Salem, NJ 08079
For information please contact
Beverly National Cemetery
(609) 877-5460

New Mexico

Fort Bayard National Cemetery
P. O. Box 189
Fort Bayard, NM 88036
For information please contact
Fort Bliss National Cemetery
(915) 564-0201

Santa Fe National Cemetery
501 North Guadalupe Street
Santa Fe, NM 87501
(505) 988-6400

New York

Bath National Cemetery
VA Medical Center
Bath, NY 14810
(607) 664-4853

Calverton National Cemetery
210 Princeton Boulevard
Calverton, NY 11933-1031
(631) 727-5410 or 5770

Cypress Hills National Cemetery
625 Jamaica Avenue
Brooklyn, NY 11208
For information please contact
Long Island National Cemetery
(631) 454-4949

Long Island National Cemetery
2040 Wellwood Avenue
Farmingdale, NY 11735-1211
(631) 454-4949

Saratoga National Cemetery
200 Duell Road
Schuylerville, NY 12871-1721
(518) 581-9128

Woodlawn National Cemetery
1825 Davis Street
Elmira, NY 14901
(607) 732-5411

North Carolina

New Bern National Cemetery
1711 National Avenue
New Bern, NC 28560
(252) 637-2912

Raleigh National Cemetery
501 Rock Quarry Road
Raleigh, NC 27610
(252) 637-2912

Salisbury National Cemetery
202 Government Road
Salisbury, NC 28144
(704) 636-2661

Wilmington National Cemetery
2011 Market Street
Wilmington, NC 28403
For information please contact New Bern National Cemetery
(252) 637-2912

Ohio

Dayton National Cemetery
VA Medical Center
4100 West Third Street
Dayton, OH 45428-1008
(937) 262-2115

Ohio Western Reserve National Cemetery
P.O. Box 8
10175 Rawiga Road
Rittman, OH 44270
(330) 335-3069

Oklahoma

Fort Gibson National Cemetery
1423 Cemetery Road
Fort Gibson, OK 74434
(918) 478-2334

Fort Sill National Cemetery
24665 N-S Road 260
Elgin, OK 73538
(580) 492-3200

Oregon

Eagle Point National Cemetery
2763 Riley Road
Eagle Point, OR 97524
(541) 826-2511

Roseburg National Cemetery
VA Medical Center
Roseburg, OR 97470
(541) 826-2511

Willamette National Cemetery
11800 S.E. Mt. Scott Boulevard
Portland, OR 97266-6937
(503) 273-5250

Pennsylvania

Indiantown Gap National Cemetery
R. R. #2, P. O. Box 484
Annville, PA 17003-9618
(717) 865-5254

National Cemetery of the Alleghenies
1158 Morgan Road
Bridgeville, PA 15017
(724) 746-4363

Philadelphia National Cemetery
Haines Street and Limekiln Pike
Philadelphia, PA 19138
For information please contact Beverly National Cemetery
(609) 877-5460

Puerto Rico

Puerto Rico National Cemetery
Avenue Cementario Nacional #50
Bayamon, PR 00960
(787) 798-8400

South Carolina

Beaufort National Cemetery
601 Boundary Street
Beaufort, SC 29902
(843) 524-3925

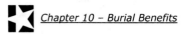

Florence National Cemetery
803 East National Cemetery Road
Florence, SC 29501
(843) 669-8783

South Dakota

Black Hills National Cemetery
P. O. Box 640
Sturgis, SD 57785
(605) 347-3830

Fort Meade National Cemetery
Old Stone Road
Sturgis, SD 57785
For information please contact
Black Hills National Cemetery
(605) 347-3830

Hot Springs National Cemetery
VA Medical Center
Hot Springs, SD 57747
For information please contact
Black Hills National Cemetery
(605) 347-3830

Tennessee

Chattanooga National Cemetery
1200 Bailey Avenue
Chattanooga, TN 37404
(423) 855-6590

Knoxville National Cemetery
939 Tyson Street, N.W.
Knoxville, TN 37917
(423) 855-6590

Memphis National Cemetery
3568 Townes Avenue
Memphis, TN 38122
(901) 386-8311

Mountain Home National Cemetery
P. O. Box 8
Mountain Home, TN 37684
(423) 979-3535

Nashville National Cemetery
1420 Gallatin Road, South
Madison, TN 37115-4619
(615) 860-0086

Texas

Dallas-Fort Worth
National Cemetery
2191 Mountain Creek Parkway
Dallas, TX 75211
(214) 467-3374

Fort Bliss National Cemetery
5200 Fred Wilson Road
P. O. Box 6342
Fort Bliss, TX 79906
(915) 564-0201

Fort Sam Houston National
Cemetery
1520 Harry Wurzbach Road
San Antonio, TX 78209
(210) 820-3891

Houston National Cemetery
10410 Veterans Memorial Drive
Houston, TX 77038
(281) 447-8686

Kerrville National Cemetery
VA Medical Center
3600 Memorial Boulevard
Kerrville, TX 78028
For information please contact
Fort Sam Houston National
Cemetery
(210) 820-3891

San Antonio National Cemetery
517 Paso Hondo Street
San Antonio, TX 78202
For information please contact
Fort Sam Houston National
Cemetery
(210) 820-3891

Virginia

Alexandria National Cemetery
1450 Wilkes Street
Alexandria, VA 22314
For information please contact
Quantico National Cemetery
(703) 221-2183

Balls Bluff National Cemetery
Route 7
Leesburg, VA 22075
For information please contact
Culpeper National Cemetery
(540) 825-0027

City Point National Cemetery
10th Avenue and Davis Street
Hopewell, VA 23860
For information please contact
Fort Harrison National Cemetery
(804) 795-2031

Cold Harbor National Cemetery
Route 156 North
Mechanicsville, VA 23111
For information please contact
Fort Harrison National Cemetery
(804) 795-2031

Culpeper National Cemetery
305 U.S. Avenue
Culpeper, VA 22701
(540) 825-0027

Danville National Cemetery
721 Lee Street
Danville, VA 24541
For information please contact
Salisbury National Cemetery
(704) 636-2661

Fort Harrison National Cemetery
8620 Varina Road
Richmond, VA 23231
(804) 795-2031

Glendale National Cemetery
8301 Willis Church Road
Richmond, VA 23231
For information please contact
Fort Harrison National Cemetery
(804) 795-2031

Hampton National Cemetery
Cemetery Road at Marshall Avenue
Hampton, VA 23667
(757) 723-7104

Hampton National Cemetery
VA Medical Center
Emancipation Drive
Hampton, VA 23667
(757) 723-7104

Quantico National Cemetery
P. O. Box 10
18424 Joplin Road (Route 619)
Triangle, VA 22172
(703) 221-2183 (local)

Richmond National Cemetery
1701 Williamsburg Road
Richmond, VA 23231
For information please contact
Fort Harrison National Cemetery
(804) 795-2031

Seven Pines National Cemetery
400 East Williamsburg Road
Sandston, VA 23150
For information please contact
Fort Harrison National Cemetery
(804) 795-2031

Staunton National Cemetery
901 Richmond Avenue
Staunton, VA 24401
(540) 825-0027

Winchester National Cemetery
401 National Avenue
Winchester, VA 22601
For information please contact
Culpeper National Cemetery
(540) 825-0027

Washington

Tahoma National Cemetery
18600 Southeast 240th Street
Kent, WA 98042-4868
(425) 413-9614

West Virginia

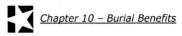

Grafton National Cemetery
431 Walnut Street
Grafton, WV 26354
For information please contact
West Virginia National Cemetery
(304) 265-2044

West Virginia National Cemetery
Route 2, Box 127
Grafton, WV 26354
(304) 265-2044

Wisconsin

Wood National Cemetery
5000 W National Ave, Bldg 1301
Milwaukee, WI 53295-4000
(414) 382-5300

Department Of The Interior National Cemeteries

District Of Columbia

Battleground National Cemetery
C/O Superintendent, Rock Creek Park
3545 Williamsburg Lane, NW
Washington, DC 20008
(202) 282-1063

Georgia

Andersonville National Historic Site
Route 1, Box 800
Andersonville, GA 31711
(912) 924-0343

Louisiana

Chalmette National Cemetery
C/O Jean Lafitte National
Historical Park and Preserve
365 Canal Street, Suite 2400
New Orleans, LA 70130
(504) 589-3882
(504) 589-4430

Maryland

Antietam National Battlefield
Box 158
301) 432-5124
Sharpsburg, MD 21782-0158
(301) 432-5124

Mississippi

Vicksburg National Military Park
3201 Clay Street
Vicksburg, MS 39180
(601) 636-0583

Montana

Little Bighorn Battle
National Monument
Custer National Cemetery
P. O. Box 39
Crow Agency, MT 59022
(406) 638-2621

Pennsylvania

Gettysburg National Military Park
97 Taneytown Road
Gettysburg, PA 17325-2804
(717) 334-1124

Tennessee

Andrew Johnson National
Historic Site
P. O. Box 1088
Greeneville, TN 37744
(423) 638-3551

Fort Donelson National Battlefield
P. O. Box 434
Dover, TN 37058
(615) 232-5348

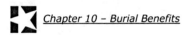

Shiloh National Military Park
Route 1, Box 9
Shiloh, TN 38376-9704
(901) 689-5275

Stones River National Battlefield
3501 Old Nashville Highway
Murfreesboro, TN 37129
(615) 893-9501

Virginia

Fredericksburg and Spotsylvania County Battlefields Memorial National Military Park
120 Chatham Lane
Fredericksburg, VA 22405
(540) 371-0802

Poplar Grove National Cemetery
Petersburg National Battlefield
1539 Hickory Hill Road
Petersburg, VA 23803
(804) 732-3531

Yorktown Battlefield Cemetery
Colonial National Historical Park
P. O. Box 210
Yorktown, VA 23690
(757) 898-3400

Department Of The Army National Cemeteries

United States Soldiers' & Airmen's Home National Cemetery
21 Harewood Road, NW
Washington, DC 20011
(202) 829-1829

Arlington National Cemetery
Interment Services Branch
Arlington, VA 22211
(703) 695-3250 or 3255

STATE VETERANS CEMETERIES

Arizona

Southern Arizona Veterans Memorial
1300 Buffalo Soldier Trail
Sierra Vista, AZ 85635
(520) 458-7144

Arkansas

Arkansas Veterans Cemetery
1501 W Maryland Avenue
North Little Rock, AR 72120
(501) 683-2259

California

Veterans Memorial Grove Cemetery
Veterans Home of California
Yountville, CA 94599
(707) 944-4600

Northern California Veterans Cemetery
P.O. Box 76
11800 Gas Point Road
Igo, CA 96047
(866) 777-4533

Colorado

Colorado State Veterans Cemetery At Homelake
3749 Sherman Avenue
Monte Vista, CO 81144
(719) 852-5118

Veterans Memorial Cemetery Of Western Colorado
2830 D Road
Grand Junction, CO 81505
(970) 263-8986

Connecticut

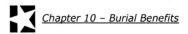

Colonel Raymond F. Gates
Memorial Cemetery
Veterans Home and Hospital
287 West Street
Rocky Hill, CT 06067
(860) 721-5838

Spring Grove Veterans Cemetery
Darien, CT
C/O Veterans Home and Hospital
287 West Street
Rocky Hill, CT 06067
(860) 721-5838

Middletown Veterans Cemetery
C/O Veterans Home and Hospital
287 West Street
Rocky Hill, CT 06067
(860) 721-5838

Delaware

Delaware Veterans Memorial
Cemetery
2465 Chesapeake City Road
Bear, DE 19701
(302) 834-8046

Delaware Veterans Memorial
Cemetery-Sussex County
RD 5 Box 100
Millsboro, DE 19966
(302) 934-5653

Georgia

Georgia Veterans Memorial
Cemetery
2617 Vinson Highway
Milledgeville, Georgia 31061
(478) 445-3363

Hawaii

Director, Office of Veterans
Services
459 Patterson Road
E-Wing, Room 1-A103
Honolulu, HI 96189
(808) 433-0420

Hawaii State Veterans Cemetery
45-349 Kamehameha Highway
Kaneohe, HI 96744
(808) 233-3630

East Hawaii Veterans
Cemetery - No. I
County of Hawaii
25 Aupuni Street
Hilo, HI 96720
(Island of Hawaii)
(808) 961-8311

East Hawaii Veterans
Cemetery - No. II
County of Hawaii
25 Aupuni Street
Hilo, HI 96720
(Island of Hawaii)
(808) 961-8311

Kauai Veterans Cemetery
County of Kauai Public Works
3021 Umi Street
Lihue, HI 96766
(Island of Kauai)
(808) 241-6670

Maui Veterans Cemetery
1295 Makawao Avenue, Box 117
Makawao, HI 96768
(Island of Maui)
(808) 572-7272

Hoolehua Veterans Cemetery
(Molokai)
P. O. Box 526
Kauna Kakai, HI 96748
(Island of Molokai)
(808) 553-3204

West Hawaii State
Veterans Cemetery
(Currently under construction – located on the Island of Hawaii near town of Kona)
(808) 961-8311

Lanai Veterans Cemetery
(Currently under construction – located on the Island of Lanai)
(808) 565-6979

Idaho

Idaho Veterans Cemetery
10101 North Horseshoe Bend Road
Boise, ID 83714
(208) 334-4796

Illinois

Sunset Cemetery
Illinois Veterans Home
1707 North 12th Street
Quincy, IL 62301
(217) 222-8641

Indiana

Indiana State Soldiers Home Cemetery
3851 North River Road
West Lafayette, IN 47906-3765
(765) 463-1502

Indiana Veterans Memorial Cemetery
1415 North Gate Road
Madison, IN 47250
(812) 273-9220

Iowa

Iowa Veterans Home and Cemetery
13th & Summit Streets
Marshalltown, IA 50158
(641) 753-4309

Kansas

Kansas Veterans Cemetery
At Fort Dodge
714 Sheridan, Unit #66
Fort Dodge, KS 67801
(620) 338-8775

Kansas Veterans Cemetery
At Wakeeney
P.O. Box 185
4035 13th Street
Wakeeney, KS 67672
(785) 743-5685

Kansas Veterans Cemetery
At Winfield
1208 North College
Winfield, KS 67156
(620) 229-2287

Kentucky

Kentucky Veteran's Cemetery-West
5817 Fort Campbell Boulevard
Hopkinsville, Kentucky 42240
(270) 707-9653

Kentucky Veterans Cemetery-Central
1111 Louisville Road
Frankfort, Kentucky
(502) 564-9281

Louisiana

Northwest Louisiana Veterans Cemetery
7970 Mike Clark Road
Keithville, Louisiana 71047
(318) 925-0612

Maine

Maine Veterans Memorial Cemetery (Closed)
Civic Center Drive
Augusta, Maine

Maine Veterans Memorial Cemetery--Mt. Vernon Rd.
163 Mt. Vernon Road
Augusta, ME 04330
(207) 287-3481

Northern Maine Veterans Cemetery-Caribou
37 Lombard Road
Caribou, ME 04736
(207)-492-1173

Maryland

Maryland State Veterans Cemeteries
Federal Building-31 Hopkins Plaza
Baltimore, MD 21201
(410) 962-4700

Cheltenham Veterans Cemetery
11301 Crain Highway
P. O. Box 10
Cheltenham, MD 20623
(301) 372-6398

Crownsville Veterans Cemetery
1080 Sunrise Beach Road
Crownsville, MD 21032
(410) 987-6320 or
(301) 962-4700

Eastern Shore Veterans Cemetery
6827 East New Market
Ellwood Road
Hurlock, MD 21643
(410) 943-3420

Garrison Forest Veterans Cemetery
11501 Garrison Forest Road
Owings Mills, MD 21117
(410) 363-6090

Rocky Gap Veterans Cemetery
14205 Pleasant Valley Road, NE
Flintstone, MD 21530
(301) 777-2185

Massachusetts

Massachusetts State Veterans
Cemetery (Agawam & Winchendon)
1390 Main Street
Agawam, MA 01001
(413) 821-9500

Winchendon Veterans Cemetery
111 Glenallen Street
Winchendon, MA 01475
(978) 297-9501

Michigan

Grand Rapids Home for Veterans
Cemetery
3000 Monroe, NW
Grand Rapids, MI 49505
(616) 364-5400

Minnesota

MN State Veterans Cemetery
15550 HWY 15
Little Falls, MN 56345
(320) 616-2527

Missouri

St. James Missouri Veterans Home
Cemetery
620 North Jefferson
St. James, MO 65559
(573) 265-3271

Missouri Veterans Cemetery -
Higgensville, MO
20109 Bus. Hwy. 13
Higgensville, MO 64037
(660) 584-5252

Missouri Veterans Cemetery –
Springfield. MO
5201 South Southwood Road
Springfield, MO 65804
(417) 823-3944

Missouri State Veterans Cemetery
–Bloomfield
17357 Stars and Strips Way
Bloomfield, Missouri 63825
(573) 568-3871

Missouri State Veterans Cemetery -
Jacksonville
1479 County Road 1675
Jacksonville, Missouri 65260
(660) 295-4237

Montana

State Veterans Cemetery
Fort William H. Harrison
Box 5715
Helena, MT 59604
(406) 324-3740

State Veterans Cemetery
Miles City
Highway 59
Miles City, MT 59301
(406) 324-3740

Montana Veterans Home Cemetery
P. O. Box 250
Columbia Falls, MT 59912
(406) 892-3256

Nebraska

Nebraska Veterans
Home Cemetery
Burkett Station
Grand Island, NE 68803
(308) 385-6252, Ext. 230

Nevada

Commissioner of Veterans Affairs
1201 Terminal Way, Room 108
Reno, NV 89520
(775) 688-1155

Northern Nevada Veterans
Memorial Cemetery
14 Veterans Way
Fernley, NV 89408
(775) 575-4441

Southern Nevada Veterans
Memorial Cemetery
1900 Buchanan Boulevard
Boulder City, NV 89005
(702) 486-5920

New Hampshire

NH State Veterans Cemetery
110 Daniel Webster Hwy, Route 3
Boscawen, NH 03303
(603) 796-2026

New Jersey

Brigadier General William C. Doyle
Veterans Memorial Cemetery
350 Provenceline Road, Route #2
Wrightstown, NJ 08562
(609) 758-7250

New Jersey Memorial Home
Cemetery (Closed)
524 N.W. Boulevard
Vineland, NJ 08360
(609) 696-6350

North Carolina

Western Carolina State Veterans
Cemetery
962 Old Highway 70, West
Black Mountain, NC 28711
(828) 669-0684

Coastal Carolina State Veterans
Cemetery
P. O. Box 1486
Jacksonville, NC 28541
(910) 347-4550 or 3570

Sandhills State Veterans Cemetery
P. O. Box 39
400 Murchison Road
Spring Lake, NC 28390
(910) 436-5630 or 5635

North Dakota

North Dakota Veterans Cemetery
1825 46th Street
Mandan, ND 58554
(701) 667-1418

Ohio

Ohio Veterans Home Cemetery
3416 Columbus Avenue
Sandusky, OH 44870
(419) 625-2454, Ext. 200

Oklahoma

Oklahoma Veterans Cemetery
Military Department (OKFAC)
3501 Military Circle N.E.
Oklahoma City, OK 73111-4398
(405) 228-5334

Pennsylvania

Pennsylvania Soldiers and
Sailors Home Cemetery
P. O. Box 6239
560 East Third Street
Erie, PA 16512-6239
(814) 871-4531

Rhode Island

Rhode Island Veterans Cemetery
301 South County Trail
Exeter, RI 02822-9712
(401) 268-3088

South Dakota

SD Veterans Home Cemetery
2500 Minnekahta Avenue
Hot Springs, SD 57747
(605) 745-5127

Tennessee

East Tennessee State
Veterans Cemetery
5901 Lyons View Pike
Knoxville, TN 37919
(865) 594-6776

Middle Tennessee
Veterans Cemetery
7931 McCrory Lane
Nashville, TN 37221
(615) 532-2238

West Tennessee
Veterans Cemetery
4000 Forest Hill/Irene Road
Memphis, TN 38125
(901) 543-7005

Texas

Central Texas State Veterans
Cemetery
11463 South Highway 195
Killeen, Texas 76542
(512) 463-5977

Rio Grande Valley
State Veterans Cemetery
2520 South Inspiration Road
Mission, TX 78572
(956) 583-7227

Utah

Utah State Veterans Cemetery
Utah Parks and Recreation
17111 South Camp Williams Road
Bluffdale, UT 84065
(801) 254-9036

Vermont

Vermont Veterans Home War
Memorial Cemetery
325 North Street
Bennington, VT 05201
(802) 442-6353

Vermont Veterans Memorial
Cemetery
120 State Street
Montpelier, VT 05602-4401
(802) 828-3379

Virginia

Virginia Veterans Cemetery
10300 Pridesville Road
Amelia, VA 23002
(804) 561-1475

Albert G. Horton, Jr. Memorial
Veterans Cemetery
5310 Milner's Road
Suffolk, Virginia 23434
(757) 334-4731

Washington

Washington Soldiers Home
Colony and Cemetery
1301 Orting-Kapowsin Highway
Orting, WA 98360
(360) 893-4500

Washington Veterans Home
Cemetery
P. O. Box 698
Retsil, WA 98378
(360) 895-4700

Wisconsin

Northern Wisconsin Veterans
Memorial Cemetery
N4063 Wildcat Road QQ
Spooner, WI 54801
(715) 635-5360

Wisconsin Veterans Memorial Cemetery
Wisconsin Veterans Home
N2665 Highway QQ
King, WI 54946
(715) 258-5586

Southern Wisconsin
Veterans Memorial Cemetery
21731 Spring Street
Union Grove, WI 53182
(262) 878-5660

Wyoming

Oregon Trail Veterans Cemetery
89 Cemetery Road, Box 669
Evansville, WY 82636
(307) 235-6673

Territories

Guam Veterans Cemetery
490 Chalan Palayso
Agatna Heights, Guam 96910
(671) 475-4225

SAIPAN
CNMI Veterans Cemetery
Military/Veterans Affairs
P.O. Box 503416
Saipan, MP 96950
(670) 664-2650

NOTE:

All State cemeteries (except Nevada, Pennsylvania, Wyoming and Utah) restrict burials to State residents.

CHAPTER 11

HEALTHCARE BENEFITS

In October 1996, Congress passed Public Law 104-262, the Veterans' Healthcare Eligibility Reform Act of 1996. This legislation paved the way for the creation of a Uniform Benefits Package - a standard enhanced health benefits plan available to all enrolled veterans. The Law also simplified the process by which veterans can receive services.

Public Law 104-262 was enacted to simplify the rules for providing healthcare to veterans and to introduce improvements in the quality and timeliness of the care veterans receive.

Note: Individuals are encouraged to contact the nearest VA benefits or healthcare facility to obtain the latest information regarding healthcare benefits. Legislation often changes the specific regulations regarding healthcare and nursing home care.

VETERAN HEALTH REGISTRIES

Certain veterans can participate in a VA health registry and receive free medical examinations, including laboratory and other diagnostic tests, when determined necessary by an examining clinician.

Gulf War Registry:
For veterans who served in the Gulf War and Operation Iraqi Freedom

Depleted Uranium Registries:
VA maintains two registries for veterans possible exposed to depleted uranium. The first is for veterans who served in the Gulf War, including Operation Iraqi Freedom. The second is for veterans who served elsewhere, including Bosnia and Afghanistan.

Agent Orange Registry:
For veterans possible exposed to dioxin or other toxic substances in herbicides used during the Vietnam War, while serving in Korea in 1968 or 1969, or as a result of testing, transporting, or spraying herbicides for military purposes.

Ionizing Radiation Registry:
For veterans possibly exposed to atomic radiation during the following activities:

- Atmospheric detonation of a nuclear device;
- Occupation of Hiroshima or Nagasaki from August 6, 1945 through July 1, 1946;
- Internment as a prisoner of war in Japan during WW II

- Serving in official military duties at the gaseous diffusion plants at Paducah, KY; Portsmouth, OH; or the K-25 area at Oak Ridge, TN for at least 250 days before February 1, 1992, or in Longshot, Milrow or Cannikin underground nuclear tests at Amchitka Island, Alaska, before January 1, 1974; or
- Treatment with nasopharyngeal (NP) radium during military service.

ELIGIBILITY

The primary factor in determining a veteran's eligibility to receive VA health care benefits is "veteran status." "Veteran status" is established by active duty service in the military, naval, or air service and a discharge or release from active military service under other than dishonorable conditions.

The veteran's length of service may also matter. It depends on when he or she served. There is no length of service requirement for:

- Former enlisted persons who started active duty before September 8, 1980; or
- Former officers who first entered active duty before October 17, 1981.

All other veterans must have 24 months of continuous active duty military service or meet one of the exceptions described below.

Exceptions to the 24-month Active Duty Rule

The 24 continuous months of active duty service requirement does not apply to:

- Reservists who were called to Active Duty and who completed the term for which they were called, and who were granted an "other than dishonorable" discharge; or
- National Guard members who were called to Active Duty by federal executive order, and who completed the term for which they were called, and who were granted an "other than dishonorable" discharge; or
- Veterans requesting a benefit for, or in connection with, a service-connected condition or disability; or
- Veterans who were discharged or released from active duty under section 1171 or 1173 of title 10; or
- Veterans who were discharged or released from active duty for a disability incurred or aggravated in line of duty; or
- Veterans who have been determined by VA to have compensable service-connected conditions; or
- Veterans requesting treatment for and/or counseling of sexual trauma that occurred while on active military service, for treatment of conditions related to ionizing radiation or for head or neck cancer related to nose or throat radium treatment while in the military.

ENROLLMENT

In order to qualify for VA healthcare, a veteran must first become enrolled. Veterans must answer a few questions, and are then are then assigned by VA to one of the priority groups discussed later in this chapter.

As part of the enrollment process, a veteran may select any VA health care facility to serve as his or her primary treatment facility.

All veterans seeking VA healthcare are required to be enrolled unless they are in one of the following categories:

- VA rated the individual as having a service-connected disability of 50% or more;
- It has been less than one year since the veteran was discharged from military service for a disability that the military determined was incurred or aggravated in the line of duty, and has not yet been rated by VA;
- Veteran is seeking care from VA for a service-connected disability only.

As part of the enrollment process, a veteran may select any VA health care facility to serve as his or her primary treatment facility.

Veterans may apply for enrollment anytime during the year by completing an *Application for Benefits, VA Form 10-10 EZ*. This form may be obtained by contacting the local VA healthcare facility, County Veteran Service Office (VSO), or Veteran Service Organization.

The completed and signed form should be forwarded to the nearest VA healthcare facility. The application will be processed and forwarded to the VA Health Eligibility Center in Atlanta, GA. The Health Eligibility Center will notify the veteran of his or her status.

Once enrolled, most veterans will remain enrolled from year to year without further action on their part. However, certain veterans are required to provide income information to determine their priority level. These veterans will be mailed a *VA Form 10-10 EZ* for completion for re-enrollment on an annual basis.

A veteran may choose not to be re-enrolled, or changes in VA funding may reduce the number of priority groups VA can enroll in a given fiscal year. If VA cannot renew enrollment for another year, the veteran will be notified in writing before their enrollment period expires.

Priority Groups

The number of veterans who can be enrolled in the health care program is determined by the amount of money Congress gives VA each year. Since funds are limited, VA set up priority groups to make sure that certain groups of veterans are able to be enrolled before others.

Once a veteran applies for enrollment, his or her eligibility will be verified. Based on the individual's specific eligibility status, he or she will be assigned a priority group.

The priority groups range from 1-8 with 1 being the highest priority for enrollment. Some veterans may have to agree to pay copay to be placed in certain priority groups.

A veteran may be eligible for more than one Enrollment Priority Group. In that case, VA will always place him or her in the highest priority group that he or she is eligible for. Under the Medical Benefits Package, the same services are generally available to all enrolled veterans.

Once a veteran applies for enrollment, his or her eligibility will be verified. Based on the individual's specific eligibility status, he or she will be assigned a priority group.

The priority groups are complicated and some reference financial thresholds.

As of January 17, 2003, VA is not accepting new Priority Group 8 veterans for enrollment (veterans falling into Priority Groups 8e and 8g.).

Priority Group 1

- Veterans with service-connected disabilities rated 50% or more disabling; or
- Veterans determined by VA to be unemployable due to service-connected conditions.

Priority Group 2

- Veterans with service-connected disabilities rated 30% or 40% disabling.

Priority Group 3

- Veterans who are former POWs;
- Veterans whose discharge was for a disability that was incurred or aggravated in the line of duty;
- Veterans with service-connected disabilities rated 10% or 20% disabling;
- Veterans who are Purple Heart recipients (unless eligible for a higher Priority Group);
- Veterans awarded special eligibility classification under Title 38, U.S.C., Section 1151, "benefits for individuals disabled by treatment or vocational rehabilitation".

Priority Group 4

- Veterans who are receiving aid and attendance or housebound benefits from VA;
- Veterans who have been determined by VA to be catastrophically disabled.

Priority Group 5

- Nonservice-connected veterans and service-connected veterans rated 0% disabled whose annual income and net worth are below the established dollar threshold. (Veterans in this priority group must provide VA with information on their annual income and net worth in order to determine whether they are below the "means test" threshold; or agree to co-payment requirements. The threshold is adjusted annually, and announced in January. In making the assessment, the veteran's household income is considered.);
- Veterans receiving VA pension benefits;
- Veterans eligible for Medicaid benefits.

Priority Group 6

- Veterans with 0% service-connected conditions, but receiving VA compensation benefits
- Veterans seeking care only for disorders relating to:
- Ionizing Radiation during atmospheric testing or during the occupation of Hiroshima and Nagasaki;
- Project 112/SHAD;
- Agent Orange Exposure during service in Vietnam;
    - Environmental Contaminants / Gulf War Illness during service in the Persian Gulf;
- Veterans of World War I or the Mexican Border War;
- Veterans who served in combat in a war after the Gulf War or during a period of hostility after November 11, 1998 for 2 years following discharge or release from the military.

Priority Group 7

- Veterans who agree to pay specified copayments with income and/or net worth above the VA Means Test threshold and income below the HUD geographic index.

- **Sub-priority a:** Noncompensable 0% service-connected veterans who were enrolled in the VA Health Care System on a specified date and who have remained enrolled since that date.
- **Sub-priority c:** Nonservice-connected veterans who were enrolled in the VA Health Care System on a specified date and who have remained enrolled since that date.
- **Sub-priority e**: Noncompensable 0% service-connected veterans not included in Sub-priority a above.
- **Sub-priority g:** Nonservice-connected veterans not included in Sub-priority c above.

Priority Group 8

Veterans who agree to pay specified copayments with income and/or net worth above the VA Means Test threshold and the HUD geographic index.

(Note: Effective January 17, 2003, VA no longer enrolls new veterans in Priority Group 8)

- **Sub-priority a:** Noncompensable 0% service-connected veterans enrolled as of January 16, 2003 and who have remained enrolled since that date.
- **Sub-priority c:** Nonservice-connected veterans enrolled as of January 16, 2003 and who have remained enrolled since that date.
- **Sub-priority e:** Noncompensable 0% service-connected veterans applying for enrollment after January 16, 2003.
- **Sub-priority g:** Nonservice-connected veterans applying for enrollment after January 16, 2003.

Special Access to Care

Service Disabled Veterans:
Veterans who are 50 percent or more disabled from service-connected conditions, unemployable due to service-connected conditions, or receiving care for a service-connected disability receive priority in scheduling of hospital or outpatient medical appointments.

Combat Veterans:
Veterans who served in combat locations during active military service after Nov. 11, 1998, are eligible for free health care services for conditions potentially related to combat service for two years following separation from active duty. For additional information call 1-877-222-VETS (8387).

MEANS TEST

As described in the above priority groups, certain nonservice-connected veterans are required to fill out the financial worksheet, referred to as a "Means Test." This is the way the VA gathers financial information to determine a veteran's priority group for enrollment, and whether or not he or she is required to make copayments for services received. The means test is based on prior year income and net worth.

New veterans who apply for enrollment after January 16, 2003, and who decline to provide income information are not eligible for enrollment.

If a veterans declines to complete the financial worksheet, he or she must agree to pay the applicable co-payment, unless otherwise eligible for VA care.

New veterans who apply for enrollment after January 16, 2003, and who decline to provide income information are not eligible for enrollment.

Veterans who are required to provide their financial information generally must do so on an annual basis. To simplify this annual reporting requirement, VA recently introduced *VA Form 10-10EZR*, a new, shorter version of its application form. This new, shorter form is only to be used by previously enrolled veterans to update their previously reported information. The form can be requested toll-free from VA's Health Benefits Service Center at (877) 222-8387.

TRAVEL BENEFITS

Once enrolled in the VA health system, health care benefits become completely portable throughout the entire VA system. Enrolled veterans who are traveling or who spend time away from their primary treatment facility may obtain care at any VA health care facility across the country, without having to reapply.

EXISTING HEALTHCARE COVERAGE

Since VA health care depends primarily on annual congressional appropriations, veterans are allowed to keep their current healthcare coverage and are encouraged to do so. Veterans with private insurance or other coverage such as DoD, Medicare, or Medicaid may find these coverages to be a supplement to their VA enrollment. The use of other available healthcare coverage does not affect a veteran's enrollment status. VA does not charge the veteran for insurance company co-payments and deductibles.

When applying for medical care, all veterans will be asked to provide information pertaining to health insurance coverage, including policies held by spouses. VA is obligated to submit claims to insurance carriers for the recovery of costs for medical care provided to nonservice-connected veterans and service-connected veterans for nonservice-connected conditions.

COPAYMENT REQUIREMENTS

While some veterans qualify for cost-free health care services based on a compensable service-connected condition or other qualifying factor, most veterans are required to complete an annual financial assessment or Means Test to determine if they qualify for cost-free services.

Veterans whose income and net worth exceed the established Means Test threshold, as well as those who choose not to complete the financial assessment must agree to pay required copayments to become eligible for VA health care services. (As stated above please remember that new veterans who apply for enrollment after January 16, 2003 and who decline to provide income information are not eligible for enrollment.)

Along with their enrollment confirmation and priority group assignment, enrollees will receive information regarding their copayment requirements, if applicable.

Veterans may qualify for cost-free health care and/or medications based on

- Receiving a Purple Heart Medal, or
- Former Prisoner of War Status, or
- Compensable service-connected disabilities, or
- Low income, or
- Other qualifying factors including treatment related to their military service experience. (Some veterans are not charged a copay for health care or medications furnished for treatment of conditions related to their military service experience. This includes exposure to Agent Orange, Ionizing Radiation, Environmental Contaminants during the Gulf War, Project 112/SHAD, Nose and Throat Radium treatment, or Sexual Trauma while in the military, or care of combat-related conditions for 2 years following discharge from active duty.

Copayment Rates – Effective January 1, 2008

OUTPATIENT SERVICES	
Basic Services – Services provided by a primary care clinician	$15/visit
Specialty Care Services – services provided by a clinical specialist such as surgeon, radiologist, audiologist, optometrist, cardiologist, and specialty tests such as magnetic resonance imagery (MRI), computerized axial tomography (CAT) scan, and nuclear medicine studies	$50 /visit
Footnotes for outpatient services: • Copayment amount is limited to a single charge per visit regardless of the number of health care providers seen in a single day. The copayment amount is based on the highest level of service received. • There is no copayment requirement for preventive services such as screenings and immunizations.)	
MEDICATIONS	
Medication provided for treatment of nonservice-connected conditions	$8/prescription
The total amount paid annually by veterans in Priority Groups 2 through 6 is limited to $960.	
INPATIENT SERVICES	
Inpatient Copayment for the first 90 days of care during a 365-day period	$1,024
Inpatient copayment for each additional 90 days of care during a 365 day period	$512
Per Diem Charge	$10/day
Footnote for inpatient services: • Lower income veterans who live in high-cost areas may qualify for a reduction of inpatient copay charges.	
Long-Term Care	
Nursing Home Care / Inpatient Respite Care / Geriatric Evaluation	Maximum of $97/day Adult
Day Health Care / Outpatient Geriatric Evaluation / Outpatient Respite Care	Maximum of $15/day
Domiciliary Care	Maximum of $5/day
Footnote for inpatient services: • Copays for Long-Term Care services start on the 22nd day of care during any 12-month period—there is no copay requirement for the first 21 days. Actual copay charges will vary from veteran to veteran dependingupon financial information submitted on VA Form 10-10EC.	

HARDSHIP DETERMINATION

A Hardship Determination is a process by which a veteran may request to be placed in a different priority group based on a change in his or her financial situation from the previous year. Circumstances that may warrant hardship consideration would be the loss of employment, business bankruptcy, or out-of-pocket medical expenses.

2006 UPDATE:
INFORMATION FOR VETERANS ABOUT THE NEW MEDICARE PRESCRIPTION DRUG BENEFITS

Beginning January 1, 2006, Medicare prescription drug coverage (Medicare Part D) becomes available to everyone with Medicare Part A or B coverage. Veterans who choose to participate may sign up for Medicare's new prescription drug coverage starting November 15, 2005 through May 15, 2006. The Medicare prescription drug coverage is wholly voluntary on the part of the participant. Each individual must decide whether to participate based on his or her own circumstances.

How This Affects Veterans:

- Each veteran must decide whether to enroll in a Medicare Part D plan based on his or her own situation.
- An individual's VA prescription drug coverage will not change based on his or her decision to participate in Medicare Part D.
- VA prescription drug coverage is considered by Medicare to be at least as good as Medicare Part D coverage. (Therefore, it is considered to be ***creditable coverage***. Refer to following section for more information regarding creditable coverage.)
- If an individual's spouse is covered by Medicare, he or she must decide whether to enroll in a Medicare Part D plan regardless of the veteran's decision to participate.

Creditable Coverage

Most entities that currently provide prescription drug coverage to Medicare beneficiaries, including VA, must disclose whether the entity's coverage is "creditable prescription drug coverage."

- Enrollment in the VA health care system is creditable coverage. This means that VA prescription drug coverage is at least as good as the Medicare Part D coverage.
- Because they have creditable coverage, veterans enrolled in the VA health care program who choose not to enroll in a Medicare Part D plan before May 15, 2006 will not have to pay a higher premium on a permanent basis ("late enrollment penalty") if they enroll in a Medicare drug plan during a later enrollment period.

- However, if an individual disenrolls in VA health care or if he or she loses his or her enrollment status through no fault of his/her own (such as an enrollment decision by VA that would further restrict access to certain Priority Groups), he or she may be subject to the late enrollment penalty unless he or she enrolls in a Medicare Part D plan within 62 days of losing VA coverage.

- If a veteran becomes a patient or inmate in an institution of another government agency (for example, a state veterans home, a state institution, a jail, or a corrections facility), he or she may not have creditable coverage from VA while in that institution. For further information, individuals should contact the institution where the veteran resides, the VA Health Benefits Service Center at (877) 222-VETS, or the local VA medical facility.

COVERED SERVICES – STANDARD BENEFITS

VA's medical benefits package provides the following health care services to all enrolled veterans:

Preventive Care Services

- Immunizations
- Physical Examinations (including eye and hearing examinations)
- Health Care Assessments
- Screening Tests
- Health Education Programs

Ambulatory (Outpatient) Diagnostic and Treatment Services

- Emergency outpatient care in VA facilities
- Medical
- Surgical (including reconstructive/plastic surgery as a result of disease or trauma)
- Chiropractic Care
- Bereavement Counseling
- Mental Health
- Substance Abuse

Hospital (Inpatient) Diagnostic and Treatment

- Emergency inpatient care in VA facilities
- Medical

- Surgical (including reconstructive/plastic surgery as a result of disease or trauma)
- Mental Health
- Substance Abuse

Medications and Supplies (when prescribed by a VA physician)

Limited Benefits

The following is a partial listing of acute care services which may have limitations and special eligibility criteria:

- Ambulance Services
- Dental Care (refer to Chapter 12 of this book for additional details.)
- Durable Medical Equipment
- Eyeglasses (see footnote below)
- Hearing Aids (see footnote below)
- Home Health Care
- Homeless Programs
- Maternity and Parturition Services—usually provided in non-VA contracted hospitals at VA expense, care is limited to the mother (costs associated with the care of newborn are not covered)
- Non-VA Health Care Services
- Orthopedic, Prosthetic, and Rehabilitative Devices
- Rehabilitative Services
- Readjustment Counseling
- Sexual Trauma Counseling

Footnote: To qualify for hearing aids or eyeglasses, the individual must have a VA service-connected disability rating of 10% or more. An individual may also qualify if he or she is a former prisoner of war, Purple Heart recipient, require this benefit for treatment of a 0% service-connected condition, or are receiving increased pension based on the need for regular aid and attendance or being permanently housebound.

General Exclusions

The following is a partial listing of general exclusions:

- Abortions and abortion counseling

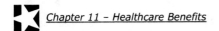

- Cosmetic surgery except where determined by VA to be medically necessary for reconstructive or psychiatric care
- Gender alteration
- Health club or spa membership, even for rehabilitation
- In-vitro fertilization
- Drugs, biological, and medical devices not approved by the Food and Drug Administration unless part of formal clinical trial under an approved research program or when prescribed under a compassionate use exemption.
- Medical care for a veteran who is either a patient or inmate in an institution of another government agency if that agency has a duty to provide the care or services.
- Services not ordered and provided by licensed/accredited professional staff
- Special private duty nursing

Non-VA Emergency Care

Veterans are eligible for emergency care at non-VA facilities only if:

- It is determined that VA health care facilities were not feasibly available; that a delay in medical attention would have endangered his or her life or health; and the veteran is personally liable for the cost of services; AND
- The care is for a service-connected condition; OR
- If enrolled, the veteran has been provided care by a VA clinician or provider within the past 24 months, and the veteran has no other health care coverage or ability to pay for the services.

If non-VA emergency care is received, notification to the nearest VA health care facility must be made within 48 hours if hospitalization is required. VA payment is limited up to the point that the veteran's condition is stable for transportation to a VA facility.

Travel Benefits

Veterans may qualify for beneficiary travel payments if they fall into one of the following categories:

- Have a service-connected rating of 30 percent or more;
- Are traveling for treatment of a service-connected condition;
- Receive a VA pension;
- Are traveling for a scheduled compensation or pension examination;

- Income does not exceed the maximum annual VA pension rate;
- If the medical condition requires an ambulance or a specially equipped van, the individual is unable to defray the cost, and the travel is pre-authorized.

LONG-TERM CARE BENEFITS

Standard Benefits

The following long-term care services are available to all enrolled veterans:

- Geriatric Evaluation
- A geriatric evaluation is the comprehensive assessment of a veteran's ability to care for him/herself, his/her physical health, and social environment, which leads to a plan of care. The plan could include treatment, rehabilitation, health promotion, and social services. These evaluations are performed by inpatient Geriatric Evaluation and Management (GEM) Units, GEM clinics, geriatric primary care clinics, and other outpatient settings.
- Adult Day Health Care
- The adult day health care (ADHC) program is a therapeutic day care program, providing medical and rehabilitation services to disabled veterans in a combined setting.
- Respite Care
- Respite care provides supportive care to veterans on a short-term basis to give the caregiver a planned period of relief from the physical and emotional demands associated with providing care. Respite care can be provided in the home or other noninstitutional settings.
- Home Care
- Skilled home care is provided by VA and contract agencies to veterans that are homebound with chronic diseases and includes nursing, physical/occupational therapy, and social services.
- Hospice/Palliative Care
- Hospice/palliative care programs offer pain management, symptom control, and other medical services to terminally ill veterans or veterans in the late stages of the chronic disease process. Services also include respite care as well as bereavement counseling to family members.

Financial Assessment for Long-Term Care Services

For veterans who are not automatically exempt from making copayments for long-term care services, a separate financial assessment must be completed to determine whether they qualify for cost-free services or to what extent they are required to make long term care copayments. For those veterans who do not qualify for cost-free services, the financial assessment for long term care services is used to determine the copayment requirement. Unlike copayments for other VA health care services, which are based on fixed charges for all, long-term care copayment charges are individually adjusted based on each veteran's financial status.

Limited Benefits

Nursing Home Care

While some veterans qualify for indefinite nursing home care services, other veterans may qualify for a limited period of time. Among those that automatically qualify for indefinite nursing home care are veterans whose service-connected condition is clinically determined to require nursing home care and veterans with a service-connected rating of 70% or more. Other veterans—with priority given to those with service-connected conditions—may be provided short-term nursing home care if space and resources are available.

Domiciliary Care

Domiciliary care provides rehabilitative and long-term, health maintenance care for veterans who require some medical care, but who do not require all the services provided in nursing homes. Domiciliary care emphasizes rehabilitation and return to the community. VA may provide domiciliary care to veterans whose annual income does not exceed the maximum annual rate of VA pension or to veterans who have no adequate means of support.

TRANSITIONAL PHARMACY BENEFIT

On July 25, 2003, VA announced a new, temporary prescription benefit called the VA Transitional Pharmacy Benefit. This new benefit began on September 22, 2003. Under this program, the VA will fill prescriptions written by non-VA physicians for veterans who have been waiting to see a VA physician.

VA will fill prescriptions written by a non-VA doctor until a veteran's first primary care appointment with VA. VA will provide all prescriptions by mail. VA may also bill veterans' health insurance. Some veterans may be required to pay a copayment based on their eligibility and financial status.

In recent years, VA has faced a large increase in demand for health care services, and has often been unable to provide all veterans with health care services in a timely manner. In many places, that means that veterans must wait a considerable length of time to receive an initial primary care visit. In an effort to ease the burden on these veterans, VA will provide this temporary benefit to veterans on waiting lists who have valid prescriptions from their non-VA physicians.

Veterans are eligible for this benefit if they meet **all** of the following requirements:

- Must be enrolled in the VA health care system prior to July 25, 2003;
- Must have requested the first primary care appointment with VA prior to July 25, 2003;

- Must be waiting more than 30 days for the initial primary care appointment as of September 22, 2003.

VA should have mailed letters to all eligible veterans by September 6, 2003. The letters should have included detailed instructions on how to use this benefit, and included a letter for veterans to give to their non-VA doctor.

For more information on the VA Transitional Pharmacy Benefit, individuals may call the VA's Health Benefits Service Center toll-free at 1-877-222-VETS (8387)

SERVICES AND AIDS FOR BLIND VETERANS

On January 8, 1944, President Franklin D. Roosevelt made an extraordinary commitment to our nation's war-blinded servicemen, when he signed an executive order declaring:

"No blinded servicemen from World War II would be returned to their homes without adequate training to meet the problems of necessity imposed upon them by their blindness."

Meeting the demands of this obligation has resulted in various programs that have evolved throughout the years.

Veterans with corrected central vision of 20/200 or less in both eyes, or field loss to 20 degrees or less in both eyes are considered to be blind.

Blind veterans may be eligible for many of the benefits detailed throughout this book, including, but not limited to: Disability Compensation, Health Insurance, Adaptive Equipment, and Training & Rehabilitation. In addition to these benefits, there are a number of miscellaneous benefits due veterans of all wars who were blinded as the result of their war service. Many individual states offer special programs and benefits for the blind.

Services are available at all VA medical facilities through Visual Impairment Services Team (VIST) coordinators.

The VIST Coordinator is a case manager who has major responsibility for the coordination of all services for legally blind veterans and their families. Duties include providing and/or arranging for appropriate treatment, identifying new cases of blindness, providing professional counseling, resolving problems, arranging annual healthcare reviews, and conducting education programs relating to blindness.

Blind veterans may be eligible for services at a VA medical center, or for admission to a VA blind rehabilitation center or clinic. In addition, blind veterans entitled to receive disability compensation may receive VA aids for the blind, which may include:

- A total health and benefits review by a VA Visual Impairment Services team;
- Adjustment to blindness training;

- Home Improvements and Structural Alterations to homes (HISA Program);
- Specially adapted housing and adaptations;
- Low-vision aids and training in their use;
- Electronic and mechanical aids for the blind, including adaptive computers and computer-assisted devices;
- Guide dogs, including the expense of training the veteran to use the dog, and the cost of the dog's medical care;
- Talking books, tapes, and Braille literature, provided from the Library of Congress.

GUIDE DOGS / SERVICE DOGS

As previously mentioned, VA may provide guide dogs to blind veterans. Additionally, Public Law 107-135 (signed by President Bush January 23, 2002) states that VA may provide:

- Service dogs trained for the aid of the hearing impaired to veterans who are hearing impaired, and are enrolled under Section 1705 of Title 38; and
- Service dogs trained for the aid of persons with spinal cord injury or dysfunction or other chronic impairment that substantially limits mobility to veterans with such injury, dysfunction, or impairment who are enrolled under section 1705 of Title 38.

VA may also pay travel and incidental expenses for the veteran to travel to and from the veteran's home while becoming adjusted to the dog.

The VA operates 9 blind rehabilitation centers in the United States and Puerto Rico. Rehabilitation centers offer comprehensive programs to guide individuals through a process that eventually leads to maximum adjustment to the disability, reorganization of the person's life, and return to a contributing place in the family and community. To achieve these goals, the rehabilitation centers offer a variety of skill courses to veterans, which are designed to help achieve a realistic level of independence. Services offered at rehabilitation centers include:

- Orientation and mobility;
- Living skills;
- Communication skills;
- Activities of daily living;
- Independent daily living program;
- Manual skills;
- Visual skills;

- Computer Access Training Section;
- Physical conditioning;
- Recreation;
- Adjustment to blindness;
- Group meetings.

The VA also employs Blind Rehabilitation Outpatient Specialists (BROS) in several areas, including:

- Albuquerque, NM
- Ann Arbor, MI
- Bay Pines / St. Petersburg, FL
- Baltimore, MD
- Boston, MA
- Cleveland, OH
- Dallas, TX
- Gainesville, FL
- Los Angeles, CA
- Phoenix, AZ
- Portland, OR
- San Antonio, TX
- San Juan, PR
- Seattle, WA
- West Haven, CT

Blind Rehabilitation Outpatient Specialists are multi-skilled, experienced, blind instructors who teach skills in the veteran's home environment, and/or local VA facility.

SPECIAL CATEGORIES FOR MEDICAL CARE

Individual chapters of this book discuss the following special categories of veterans who may qualify for medical care, as well as other benefits:

- Gulf War Veterans (See Chapter 33)
- Veterans exposed to Agent Orange during the Vietnam War (See Chapter 24)

- Veterans exposed to atomic radiation, (See Chapter 24)
- Merchant Marine Seamen (See Chapter 29)
- Allied Veterans (See Chapter 29)

HOME IMPROVEMENTS AND STRUCTURAL ALTERATIONS (HISA)

The HISA program provides funding for disabled veterans to make home improvements necessary for the continuation of treatment or for disability access to the home, essential lavatory and sanitary facilities.

Disabled veterans may be eligible for HISA when it is determined medically necessary or appropriate for the effective and economical treatment of the service-connected disability.

Lifetime home improvement benefits may not exceed $4,100.00 (U.S.). Any costs that exceed $4,100.00 (U.S.) will be the veteran's responsibility.

To apply, veterans must submit the following documentation:

- A letter from describing the physical disability and a description of the request home improvement and/or structural alteration;
- A statement from the attending physician or therapist. This statement should describe the physical condition/disability, why the home modification(s) are medically necessary or appropriate for the effective and economical treatment of the service-connected disabling condition;
- A drawing of the work to be undertaken. This drawing can be hand sketched. It should include the height, width and length dimensions. It does not have to be a formal blueprint or architectural drawing;
- A completed, signed home ownership or a rental lease form with a letter from the landlord agreeing with the modifications if required;
- A completed and signed VA Form 10-0103, Veterans Application for Assistance;
- Documentation verifying that the provider/contractor is licensed/bonded;
- An itemized cost estimate of the proposed improvement and/or structural alteration from the provider/contractor.

Preauthorization must be obtained before beginning any alterations, otherwise, HISA benefits will be denied.

For further information, contact:

The Department of Veterans Affairs Health Administration Center
Foreign Medical Program
PO Box 65021
Denver, CO 80206-9021
(303) 331-7590

LISTING OF VA HEALTHCARE FACILITIES

Alabama
Medical Centers
Birmingham
Montgomery
Tuscaloosa
Tuskegee

Clinics
Dothan
Gadsden
Huntsville
Jasper
Madison
Mobile
Oxford
Shoals Area

Alaska
Medical Center
Anchorage

Clinics
Fairbanks
Kenai

Arizona
Medical Centers
Phoenix
Prescott
Tucson

Clinics
Anthem
Bellemont
Buckeye
Casa Grande
Cottonwood
Fort Huachuca
Green Valley
Kingman
Lake Havasu
Mesa
Payson
Safford
Show Low
Sun City
Yuma

Arkansas
Medical Centers
Fayetteville
Little Rock
North Little Rock

Clinic
Paragould

California
Medical Centers
Fresno
Livermore
Loma Linda
Long Beach
Los Angeles
Menlo Park
Palo Alto
Sacramento
San Diego
San Francisco

Clinics
Anaheim
Atwater
Auburn
Bakersfield
Brawley
Capitola
Chico
Commerce
Chula Vista
Corona
Escondido
Eureka
Fairfield
French Camp
Gardena
Lancaster
Lompoc
Los Angeles
Martinez
Modesto
Oakland
Oxnard
Palm Desert
Redding
Sacramento
San Diego
San Jose
San Luis Obispo
Santa Ana
Santa Barbara

Santa Rosa
Seaside
Sepulveda
Sonora
Sun City
Tulare
Upland
Vallejo
Victorville
Vista

Colorado
Medical Centers
Denver
Grand Junction

Clinics
Alamosa
Aurora
Colorado Springs
Durango
Fort Collins
Greeley
La Junta
Lakewood
Lamar
Montrose
Pueblo

Connecticut
Medical Centers
Newington
West Haven

Clinics
Danbury
New London
Stamford
Waterbury
Willimantic
Winsted

Delaware
Medical Center
Wilmington

District of Columbia
Medical Center
Washington D.C.

Florida
Medical Centers
Bay Pines
Gainesville
Lake City
Miami
Tampa
West Palm Beach

Clinics
Avon Park
Boca Raton
Brooksville
Coral Springs
Daytona Beach
Deerfield Beach
Delray Beach
Dunedin
Ellenton
Fort Myers
Fort Pierce
Hollywood
Jacksonville
Key Largo
Key West
Kissimmee
Lakeland
Lecanto
Leesburg
Miami
Naples
New Port Richey
Oakland Park
Ocala
Okeechobee
Orlando
Panama City Beach
Pensacola
Port Charlotte
St. Augustine
St. Petersburg
Sanford
Sarasota
Sebring
Stuart
Tallahassee
The Villages
Vero Beach
Viera
Zephyrhillis

Georgia
Medical Centers
Atlanta
Augusta
Dublin

Clinics
Albany
Atlanta
Columbus
East Point
Lawrenceville
Macon
Midtown Atlanta
Oakwood
Savannah
Smyrna
Valdosta

Guam
Agana Heights

Hawaii
Medical Office
Honolulu

Idaho
Medical Center
Boise

Clinics
Pocatello
Twin Falls

Illinois
Medical Centers
Chicago
Danville
Hines
Marion
North Chicago

Clinics
Aurora
Belleville
Chicago
Chicago Heights
Decatur
Effingham
Elgin
Evanston
Freeport
Galesburg
Joliet
LaSalle
Manteno
McHenry
Mount Vernon
Oak Lawn
Oak Park
Peoria
Quincy
Rockford
Springfield

Indiana
Medical Centers
Fort Wayne
Indianapolis
Marion

Clinics
Bloomington
Crown Point
Evansville
Hagerstown
Lawrenceburg
Muncie
Richmond
South Bend
Terre Haute
West Lafayette

Iowa
Medical Centers
Des Moines
Iowa City
Knoxville

Clinics
Bettendorf
Dubuque
Fort Dodge
Mason City
Sioux City
Waterloo

Kansas
Medical Centers
Leavenworth
Topeka
Wichita

Clinics
Ft. Dodge
Ft. Scott
Hays
Kansas City
Liberal
Paola
Parsons
Salina

Kentucky
Medical Centers
Lexington
Louisville

Clinics
Bellevue
Hanson
Paducah

Louisiana
Medical Centers
Alexandria
New Orleans
Shreveport
Slidell

Clinics
Baton Rouge
Hammond
Jennings
Lafayette
LaPlace

Maine
Medical Center
Augusta

Clinics
Bangor
Calais
Caribou
Rumford
Saco

Maryland
Medical Centers
Baltimore
Perry Point

Clinics
Baltimore
Cambridge
Charlotte Hall
Cumberland
Fort Howard
Glen Burnie
Greenbelt
Hagerstown
Perry Point
Pocomoke

Massachusetts
Medical Centers
Bedford
Boston
Brockton
Leeds
West Roxbury

Clinics
Boston
Dorchester
Fitchburg
Framingham
Gloucester
Greenfield
Haverhill
Hyannis
Lowell
Lynn
Martha's Vineyard
Nantucket
New Bedford
Pittsfield
Quincy
Springfield
Worcester

Michigan
Medical Centers
Ann Arbor
Battle Creek
Detroit
Iron Mountain
Saginaw

Clinics
Benton Harbor
East Lansing
Flint
Gaylord
Grand Rapids
Hancock
Ironwood
Jackson
Lansing
Marquette
Menominee
Muskegon

Oscoda
Pontiac
Sault Ste. Marie
Traverse City
Yale

Minnesota
Medical Centers
Minneapolis
St. Cloud

Clinics
Arlington
Blue Earth
Brainerd
Bricelyn
Chisholm
Elmore
Fergus Falls
Gaylord
Hibbing
Janesville
Lake Crystal
Madelia
Maplewood
Montevideo
Mountain Iron
Nashwauk
Rochester
Springfield
St. James
Trimont
Waseca
Waterville
Winnebago
Winthrop

Mississippi
Medical Centers
Biloxi
Jackson

Missouri
Medical Centers
Columbia
Kansas City
Poplar Bluff
St. Louis

Clinics
Belton
Camdenton
Cameron
Cape Girardeau
Farmington
Ft. Leonard Wood
Kirksville
Mexico
Mt. Vernon
Nevada
Salem
St. Charles
St. James
St. Joseph
St. Louis
Warrensburg
West Plains

Montana
Medical Centers
Fort Harrison

Clinics
Anaconda
Ashland
Billings
Bozeman
Glasgow
Great Falls
Kalispell
Miles City
Missoula
Sidney

Nebraska
Medical Centers
Grand Island
Omaha

Clinics
Alliance
Lincoln
Norfolk
North Platte
Rushville
Sidney

Nevada
Medical Center
Las Vegas
Reno

Clinics
Ely
Henderson
Las Vegas
Pahrump

New Hampshire
Medical Center
Manchester

Clinics
Conway
Littleton
Portsmouth
Tilton

New Jersey
Medical Centers
East Orange
Lyons

Clinics
Brick
Cape May
Elizabeth
Ft. Dix
Ft. Monmouth
Hackensack
Jersey
Morristown
New Burnswick
Newark
Peterson
Sewell
Trenton
Ventnor
Vineland

New Mexico
Medical Center
Albuquerque

Clinics
Alamogordo
Artesia
Clovis
Espanola
Farmington
Gallup
Hobbs
Las Cruces
Las Vegas
Raton
Santa Fe
Silver City
Truth or Consequences

New York
Medical Centers
Albany
Batavia
Bath
Bronx
Brooklyn
Buffalo
Canandaigua
Castle Point
Montrose
New York City
Northport
Syracuse

Clinics
Auburn
Bainbridge
Binghamton
Bronx
Brooklyn
Carmel
Carthage
Catskill
Clifton Park
Cortland
Dunkirk
Elizabethtown
Elmira
Fonda
Glens Falls
Goshen
Ithaca
Jamestown
Kingston
Lackawanna
Lockport
Malone
Massena
Monticello
New City
New York
Niagara Falls
Olean
Oswego
Patchogue
Pine Plains
Plainview
Plattsburgh
Port Jervis
Poughkeepsie
Rochester
Rome
Schenectady
St. Albans

Staten Island
Sunnyside
Troy
Warsaw
Wellsville
Westhampton
White Plains
Yonkers

North Carolina
Medical Centers
Asheville
Durham
Fayetteville
Salisbury

Clinics
Winton-Salem

North Dakota
Medical Center
Fargo

Clinics
Bismarck
Grafton
Minot

Ohio
Medical Centers
Chillicothe
Cincinnati
Cleveland
Dayton

Clinics
Akron
Ashtabula
Athens
Canton
Cincinnati
Cleveland
Columbus
East Liverpool
Grove City
Lancaster
Lima
Lorain
Mansfiled
Marietta
Marion
Middletown
Painesville
Portsmouth
St. Clairsville
Sandusky
Springfield
Toledo
Warren
Youngstown
Zanesville

Oklahoma
Medical Centers
Muskogee
Oklahoma City

Oregon
Medical Centers
Portland
Roseburg

Clinics
Bandon
Bend
Brookings
Eugene
Klamath Falls
Salem
Warrenton

Pennsylvania
Medical Centers
Altoona
Butler
Coatesville
Erie
Lebanon
Philadelphia
Pittsburgh
Wilkes-Barre

Clinics
Aliquippa
Allentown
Bangor
Berwick
Brookville
Camp Hill
DuBois
Ellwood City
Farrell
Frackville
Greensburg
Horsham
Johnstown
Kittanning
Knox
Lancaster
Meadville

Philadelphia
Pottsville
Pottsville
Reading
Reading
Sayre
Schuylkill
Smethport
Spring City
Springfield
State College
Tobyhanna
Washington
Wilkes-Barre
Williamsport
York

Philippines
Outpatient Clinic
Pasay City

Puerto Rico
Medical Center
San Juan

Clinics
Arecibo
Guayama
Mayaguez
Ponce

Rhode Island
Medical Center
Providence

Clinics
Middletown

South Carolina
Medical Centers
Charleston
Columbia

Clinics
Anderson
Beaufort
Florence
Greenville
Myrtle Beach
Orangeburg
Rock Hill
Sumter

South Dakota
Medical Centers
Fort Meade
Hot Springs
Sioux Falls

Clinics
Aberdeen
Eagle Butte
McLaughlin
Mission
Pierre
Pine Ridge
Rapid City
Winner

Tennessee
Medical Centers
Memphis
Mountain Home
Murfreesboro
Nashville

Clinics
Chattanooga
Cookville
Knoxville

Texas
Medical Centers
Amarillo
Big Spring
Bonham
Dallas
El Paso
Houston
Kerrville
San Antonio
Temple
Waco

Clinics
Abilene
Austin
Beaumont
Brownwood
Cedar Park
Childress
College Station
Corpus Christi
Fort Worth
Fort Stockton
Harlingen
Laredo
Lubbock

Lufkin
McAllen
Marlin
Odessa
Palestine
San Angelo
San Antonio
Stamford
Stratford
Victoria

Utah
Medical Center
Salt Lake City

Clinics
Fountain Green
Nephi
Ogden
Orem
Roosevelt
St. George

Vermont
Medical Centers
White River Junction

Clinics
Bennington
Colchester
Rutland

Virginia
Medical Centers
Hampton
Richmond
Salem

Clinics
Alexandria
Harrisonburg
Stephens City

Virgin Islands
Clinics
Kings Hill
St. Thomas

Washington
Medical Centers
Seattle
Spokane
Walla Walla

Clinics
Bremerton
Longview
Richland
Seattle
Yakima

West Virginia
Medical Centers
Beckley
Clarksburg
Huntington
Martinsburg

Clinics
Franklin
Gassaway
Parkersburg
Parsons
Petersburg

Wisconsin
Medical Centers
Madison
Milwaukee
Tomah

Clinics
Appleton
Baraboo
Beaver Dam
Chippewa Falls
Cleveland
Green Bay
Janesville
Kenosha
LaCrosse
Loyal
Rhinelander
Superior
Union Grove
Wausau
Wisconsin Rapids

Wyoming
Medical Centers
Cheyenne
Sheridan

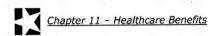

Clinics
Casper
Gillette
Green River
New Castle
Powell
Riverton
Rock Springs

CHAPTER 12

DENTAL BENEFITS

VA OUTPATIENT DENTAL BENEFITS

Outpatient dental benefits are provided by the Department of Veterans Affairs according to law. In some instances, the dental care may be extensive, while in other cases treatment may be limited.

Eligibility

Veterans are eligible for outpatient dental treatment if they are determined by VA to meet one of the following criteria:

- Those having a service-connected compensable dental disability or condition are eligible for any needed dental care.
- Those who were prisoners of war are eligible for any needed dental care.
  (Public Law 108-170, which became law December 6, 2003, eliminated the requirement that a prisoner of war have been detained or interned for a period of 90 days or more.)
- Those whose service-connected disabilities have been rated at 100 percent, or who are receiving the 100 percent rate by reason of individual unemployability are eligible for any needed dental care. (Includes veterans with temporary ratings of 100 percent for duration of that rating.)
- Those who are participating in a VA rehabilitation program are eligible for dental care necessary to complete their program.
- Recently discharged veterans with a service-connected noncompensable dental condition or disability who served on active duty 90 days or more and who apply for VA dental care within 90 days of separation from active duty, may receive one time treatment for dental conditions if the dental condition is shown to have existed at the time of discharge or release and the veteran's certificate of discharge does not indicate that the veteran received necessary dental care within a 90-day period prior to discharge or release.
- Those having a service-connected noncompensable dental condition or disability resulting from combat wounds or service trauma are eligible for repeat care for the service-connected condition(s).

- Those having a dental condition clinically determined by VA to be currently aggravating a service-connected medical condition are eligible for dental care to resolve the problem.
- Those with nonservice-connected dental conditions or disabilities for which treatment was begun while in a VA medical center, when it is clinically determined to be necessary to complete such dental treatment on an outpatient basis.
- Those receiving outpatient care or scheduled for inpatient care may receive dental care if the dental condition is clinically determined to be complicating a medical condition currently under treatment
- Certain veterans enrolled in a VA Homeless Program for 60 consecutive days or more may receive certain medically necessary outpatient dental services.

ENHANCED TRICARE RETIREE DENTAL PROGRAM

The TRICARE Retiree Dental Program (TRDP) was established February 1, 1998. It provides dental care for Uniformed Service retirees, unremarried surviving spouses, and certain other family members. Enrollment in TRDP is voluntary. The TRDP is funded solely by enrollees, and receives **no** government subsidy.

The basic Tricare Retiree Dental Program (TRDP) is available only to those who were enrolled in the TDRP program prior to September 1, 2000, and who chose to remain enrolled in the basic program.

Effective September 1, 2000, the Enhanced Tricare Retiree Dental Program took effect, and new enrollments in the basic program were discontinued.

The TRICARE Retiree Dental Program is administered by the Federal Services division of Delta Dental Plan of California. The TRICARE Retiree Dental Program is designed to provide Uniformed Services retirees and their families with optimum dental coverage at an affordable cost.

Eligibility Requirements:

Eligibility requirements for enrollment in the TRDP are set forth by the federal government in the law that established the program. Applicants may be required to submit additional information if it is needed by Delta to verify eligibility. To enroll in the enhanced program, an individual must be one of the following:

- A member of the Uniformed Services who is entitled to Uniformed Services retired pay, even if you are 65 or older;
- A current spouse of an enrolled member;
- A member of the retired Reserve/Guard, including a "gray-area" reservist, who is entitled to retired pay but does not actually begin receiving it until age 60;

- A child of an enrolled member, up to age 21 (to age 23 if a full-time student, or older if disabled before losing eligibility);
- An unremarried surviving spouse or eligible child of a deceased member who died on retired status or while on active duty;
- A Congressional Medal of Honor recipient and eligible family members, or an unremarried surviving spouse/eligible family members of a deceased recipient;
- A current spouse and/or eligible child of a non-enrolled member with documented proof the member is:
    - Eligible to receive ongoing, comprehensive dental care from the Department of Veterans Affairs;
    - Enrolled in a dental plan through employment and the plan is not available to family members; or
    - Unable to obtain benefits through the TRDP due to a current and enduring medical or dental condition.

Those who are not eligible for this program are:

- Former spouses of eligible members;
- Remarried surviving spouses of deceased members;
- Family members of non-enrolled retirees who do not meet one of the three special circumstances noted above.

Premiums

Premium rates for the enhanced TRICARE Retiree Dental Program vary depending on the retiree's location.

Coverage

This chart provides an overview of coverage under the *enhanced* TRICARE Retiree Dental Program for patients who visit a **participating network dentist**.

Benefits available during the first 12 months of enrollment:	***Delta Pays:**
Diagnostic services (such as exams)	100%
Preventive services (such as cleanings)	100%
Basic Restorative services (such as fillings)	80%
Endodontics (such as root canals)	60%
Periodontics (such as gum treatment)	60%
Oral Surgery (such as extractions)	60%
Emergency (such as treatment for minor pain)	80%
Dental Accident Coverage	100%

Additional services available after 12 months of continuous enrollment:	
Cast Crowns, Onlays & Bridges	50%
Partial/Full Dentures	50%
Orthodontics	50%
Deductibles & Maximums	
Annual Deductible (per person, limit $150 per family, per benefit year)	$50
Annual Maximum (per person, per benefit year)	$1200
Orthodontic Maximum (per person, per lifetime)	$1200
Dental Accident Maximum (per person, per benefit year)	$1000
Benefit Year: May 1- April 30	

*The percentage paid by Delta is based on the allowed amount for each procedure. Out-of-pocket costs may be higher if care is received from a non-participating provider.

Update For National Guard and Reserve Personnel

National Guard and Reserve personnel who elect to enroll in the TRICARE Retiree Dental Program (TRDP) within 120 days after retirement are now eligible to skip the 12-month waiting period normally required for certain TRDP benefits.

Effective February 1, 2005, officials authorized a waiver from requiring retired National Guard/Reserve men and women who meet the criteria to be enrolled in the TRDP for 12 months prior to gaining the maximum allowed benefits for cast crowns, cast restorations, bridges, dentures and orthodontics for both adults and children.

Additionally, this new waiver can be applied retroactively to February 1, 2004 for any Guard and Reserve enrollees who can document their enrollment in the TRDP within 120 days after their retirement effective date.

All new enrollees seeking to obtain the waiver should submit a copy of their retirement orders together with their application.

Contact Information

Covered benefits are subject to certain limitations. For more information on all covered services and detailed information on benefit levels, limitations, exclusions, program policies and payments for non-participating providers, please contact:

Delta Dental of California
Federal Services
P.O. Box 537008
Sacramento, CA 95853-7008
(888) 838-8737

BASIC TRICARE RETIREE DENTAL PROGRAM

The basic program is available **only** to those who were enrolled in the TRDP *prior to September 1, 2000*, when the enhanced program took effect, **and** who wish to remain enrolled in the basic program rather than upgrade their enrollment to the enhanced program. **Effective September 1, 2000 the basic program is no longer accepting new enrollments.**

Retirees who are enrolled in the basic program and have questions about their coverage should contact:

Delta Dental of California
Federal Services
P.O. Box 537008
Sacramento, CA 95853-7008
(888) 838-8737

TRICARE SELECTED RESERVE DENTAL PROGRAM BENEFITS

Individuals with at least one year of service commitment remaining who are serving in the Army Reserve, Naval Reserve, Air Force Reserve, Marine Corps Reserve, Coast Guard Reserve, Army National Guard or Air National Guard, may be eligible to enroll in the Tricare Selected Reserve Dental Program (TSRDP).

The Department of Defense works in conjunction with Humana Military Healthcare Services to offer and administer the TRICARE Selected Reserve Dental Program.

Coverage remains available as long as an individual maintains his or her Reserve status, and is shown as eligible on the DEERS record.

The information provided in this section is intended only as a brief overview. Humana Military Healthcare Services has a staff of trained Beneficiary Services Representatives who are available to answer your questions. They can be reached at (800) 866-8499.

CHAPTER 13

CHAMPVA AND CHAMPVA FOR LIFE

CHAMPVA

> *Under CHAMPVA, VA shares the cost of covered healthcare services and supplies with eligible beneficiaries.*

Although similar, CHAMPVA and TRICARE are completely separate programs, with totally different beneficiary populations. While the benefits provided are similar, the programs are administered separately, with significant differences in claim filing procedures and preauthorization requirements.

Under CHAMPVA, VA shares the cost of covered healthcare services and supplies with eligible beneficiaries.

The administration of CHAMPVA is centralized to the Health Administration Center in Denver, Colorado.

Eligibility Requirements

To be eligible for CHAMPVA, you cannot be eligible for TRICARE/CHAMPUS and you must be in one of these categories:

- The spouse or child of a veteran who has been rated permanently and totally disabled for a service-connected disability by a VA regional office; or
- The surviving spouse or child of a veteran who died from a VA-rated service connected disability; or
- The surviving spouse or child of a veteran who was at the time death rated permanently and totally disabled from a service connected disability; or
- The surviving spouse or child of a military member who died in the line of duty, not due to misconduct (in most of these cases, these family members are eligible for TRICARE, not CHAMPVA).

Update: An eligible CHAMPVA sponsor may be entitled to receive medical care through the VA health care system based on his or her own veteran status. Additionally, as the result of a recent policy change, if the eligible CHAMPVA sponsor is the spouse of another eligible CHAMPVA sponsor, both may now be eligible for CHAMPVA benefits. In each instance where the eligible spouse requires medical attention, he or she may choose the VA health care system or coverage under CHAMPVA for his/her health care needs. If you have been previously denied CHAMPVA benefits and you believe you would now be qualified, please call (800) 733-8387.

Benefits

In general, CHAMPVA covers most healthcare services and supplies that are medically and psychologically necessary. Upon confirmation of eligibility, applicants will receive program material that specifically addresses covered and noncovered services and supplies.

CHAMPVA General Exclusions

- Services determined by VA to be medically unnecessary;
- Care as part of a grant, study, or research program;
- Care considered experimental or investigational;
- Care for persons eligible for benefits under other government agency programs, except Medicaid and State Victims of Crime Compensation programs;
- Care for which the beneficiary is not obligated to pay, such as services obtained at a health fair;
- Care provided outside the scope of the provider's license or certification;
- Custodial, domiciliary, or rest cures;
- Dental care (except treatment related to certain covered medical conditions);
- Medications that do no require a prescription (except insulin);
- Personal comfort and convenience items;
- Services rendered by providers suspended or sanctioned by other Federal entities.

Important Update Regarding Retention Of CHAMPVA For Surviving Spouses Remarrying After Age 55

Eligibility for CHAMPVA ends at midnight on the date of your remarriage if you remarry prior to age 55. However, Public Law 107-330 (signed by President Bush on December 6, 2002) contained a provision stating that:

> *"For marriages occurring on or after February 4, 2003, the remarriage after age 55 of the surviving spouse of a veteran shall not bar the furnishing of benefits under CHAMPVA to such person as the surviving spouse of the veteran".*

(Such surviving spouses do, however, continue to lose eligibility for DIC.)

The law also contained a provision allowing those widows who remarried prior to February 4, 2003, and were over the age of 55 and lost their CHAMPVA benefits, to apply to have their medical benefits reinstated. ***However, such widows had to apply for reinstatement of benefits by February 4, 2004. (The deadline was later extended to December 16, 2004.)***

Termination of Remarriage: If a widow(er) of a qualifying sponsor remarries, and the remarriage is later terminated by death, divorce, or annulment he or she may reestablish CHAMPVA eligibility. The beginning date of re-eligibility is the first day of the month after termination of the remarriage or December 1, 1999, whichever date is later. To reestablish CHAMPVA eligibility, copies of the marriage certificate and death, divorce, or annulment documents (as appropriate) must be provided.

Applying for CHAMPVA And Filing Claims

Generally, applicants can expect to receive written notification from the Health Administration Center within 45 days from the mailing of the application.

Prospective applicants should contact the Health Administration Center at (800) 733-8387.

Applications may also be requested by FAX at (303) 331-7804

For inquiries, applications, appeals, and healthcare claims older than one year, please use:

VA Health Administration Center
CHAMPVA
PO Box 65023
Denver, CO 80206-9023

For submitting new (less than one year old) healthcare claims, please use:

VA Health Administration Center
CHAMPVA
PO Box 65024
Denver, CO 80206-9023

To streamline the process, applicants are encouraged to complete the *Application for CHAMPVA Benefits, (VA 10D)* in its entirety and to attach all required documents. As further explained on the application, required documents include a copy of each applicant's Medicare card (if Medicare eligible) and a school certification for all applicant children between the ages of 18 and 23.

Generally, applicants can expect to receive written notification from the Health Administration Center within 45 days from the mailing of the application.

CHAMPVA As Secondary Payer

CHAMPVA is intended to serve as a safety net in the event other coverage is not available—rather than being the primary carrier. While families with other health insurance are not disqualified from CHAMPVA benefits, CHAMPVA's safety net protection only kicks in after the application of all other policies—including benefits available from the enrollment in a health maintenance organization (HMO).

(Exceptions to CHAMPVA's secondary payer status are supplemental CHAMPVA policies, Medicaid, and State Victims Compensation Programs—CHAMPVA assumes primary payer in these cases.)

Beneficiaries enrolled in an HMO cannot elect to waive the HMO benefits without forfeiting their CHAMPVA benefits. CHAMPVA benefits, however, do apply to covered services that are not covered by the HMO.

Healthcare Services At VA Facilities

Under the CHAMPVA In-house Treatment Initiative (CITI for short), CHAMPVA beneficiaries may receive cost-free healthcare services at participating VA facilities.

Although some VA facilities are not CITI participants due to the volume of veterans they are responsible for serving, most are. **The CITI program is not available to beneficiaries with Medicare or with an HMO insurance plan**

Medicare Impact

CHAMPVA is always the secondary payer to Medicare.

If a person is eligible for CHAMPVA, under age 65 and enrolled in both Medicare Parts A & B, SSA documentation of enrollment in both Parts A&B is required.

CHAMPVA is always the secondary payer to Medicare.

For benefits to be extended past age 65, the individual must meet the following conditions:

- If he or she turned 65 before June 5, 2001, and only has Medicare Part A, he or she will be eligible for CHAMPVA without having to have Medicare Part B coverage.
- If he or she turned 65 on/or before June 5, 2001, and has Medicare Parts A and B, he or she must keep both Parts to be eligible.
- If he or she turned 65 on or after June 5, 2001, he or she must be enrolled in Medicare Parts A and B to be eligible.

CHAMPVA FOR LIFE

One of the provisions of "The Veterans Survival Benefits Improvement Act" (P.L. 107-14) required that CHAMPVA provide secondary coverage for those individuals who had only Medicare Part A before June 5, 2001 (the date of enactment). After that date, coverage is provided only if the individual has Medicare Parts A and B.

CHAMPVA for Life (CFL) provides benefits for CHAMPVA eligible family members who are over age 65. In summary, the law says CHAMPVA will be a second payer to Medicare, including supplemental insurance policies like MEDIGAP. CFL began on October 1, 2001.

CHAMPVA For Life is not separate from CHAMPVA; it is simply an extension of benefits to certain individuals over age 65.

If an individual is determined to be eligible for CFL, his or her benefits begin either on October 1, 2001, or on the individual's 65th birthday, if he or she turns 65 after October 1, 2001.

Application Process

If an individual is already covered by CHAMPVA, the Health Administration Center will contact him or her by mail with instructions. The individual will be asked to complete an *"Other Health Insurance Certification"* and provide a copy of his or her MEDICARE card.

To apply for CHAMPVA For Life, individuals must complete a VA form 1010D and an *"Other Health Insurance Certificate."* These two documents, along with a copy of the MEDICARE card should be mailed to:

CHAMPVA For Life - Eligibility
PO Box 469028
Denver CO 80246-9028.

Eligibility

To be eligible for CHAMPVA benefits over age 65, individuals cannot be eligible for TRICARE/CHAMPUS, and must be in one of the following categories:

- The spouse or child of a veteran who has been rated 100% permanently and totally disabled for a service connected disability by a VA regional office; or
- The surviving spouse or child of a veteran who died from a VA-rated service connected disability, or who was at the time of death rated 100% permanently and totally disabled; or
- The surviving spouse or child of a military member who died in the line of duty, not due to misconduct (in most of these cases, these family members are eligible for TRICARE, not CHAMPVA).

Individuals must also meet the following conditions:

- If the individual turned 65 before June 5, 2001, and only has MEDICARE Part A, he or she will be eligible for CHAMPVA without having to have MEDICARE Part B coverage.
- If the individual turned 65 before June 5, 2001 and has MEDICARE Parts A and B, he or she must keep both Parts to be eligible.
- If the individual turned age 65 on or after June 5, 2001, he or she must be enrolled in MEDICARE Parts A and B to be eligible.

CHAMPVA For Life And Outpatient Prescription Medications

One major benefit of CHAMPVA for Life is that it includes prescription outpatient medication coverage. If there is supplemental insurance, CHAMPVA will be the secondary payer. The normal 25% cost share applies.

CHAMPVA For Life And MEDICARE

Both CHAMPVA and MEDICARE are Federal benefits programs. CFL is always the last payer after claims are paid by MEDICARE, as well as by any other health insurance.

MEDICARE Ineligibility

If an individual is a CHAMPVA beneficiary, or otherwise meets CHAMPVA criteria, and is not eligible for MEDICARE, he or she needs to submit a "non-entitlement" letter from the Social Security Administration, and CHAMPVA will then provide coverage.

MEDICARE Part B Requirements

If an individual is eligible for MEDICARE and his or her 65th birthday is on or after June 5, 2001, he or she must have Part B to be eligible for CFL.

If an individual did not select MEDICARE Part B when he or she turned age 65 and wants to do so now, he or she should contact their local Social Security Administration office for guidance.

If an individual is eligible for MEDICARE and his or her 65th birthday was before June 5, 2001, and he or she had Parts A and B on that date the individual must keep Part B. If he or she only had Part A, the individual does not need Part B to be eligible for CFL.

If an individual did not select MEDICARE Part B when he or she turned age 65 and wants to do so now, he or she should contact their local Social Security Administration office for guidance.

CHAMPVA For Life Beneficiaries Cannot Use A VA Medical Center

CHAMPVA beneficiaries with MEDICARE cannot use a VA medical center because MEDICARE does not pay for services provided by a VA Medical Center. If an individual is currently being seen at a VA medical center, he or she will need to find a different provider before MEDICARE and CFL will cover them.

Costs Under CHAMPVA For Life

If the service is covered by MEDICARE and CHAMPVA, an individual will almost always have no out-of-pocket expense.

If the service is covered by MEDICARE and not by CHAMPVA, the individual will pay the MEDICARE co-pay.

If the service is not covered by MEDICARE, but is covered by CHAMPVA, the individual will pay the CHAMPVA co-pay (typically 25%).

CHAMPVA For Life Does Not Pay for MEDICARE Part B Premiums.

Contact Information

For additional information individuals may call a recorded, toll free line 24 hours a day. The number is (888) 289-2411. Individuals will not be able to talk to a benefits advisor on this line. To speak to a benefits advisor, individuals should call (800) 733-8387, Monday - Friday from 9:00 AM - 1:30 PM and 2:30 - 5:00 PM Eastern Time.

CHAPTER 14

TRICARE AND TRICARE FOR LIFE

TRICARE is the Department of Defense's worldwide health care program for active duty and retired uniformed services members and their families. TRICARE consists of:

- TRICARE Prime, a managed care option;
- TRICARE Extra, a preferred provider option;
- TRICARE Standard, a fee-for-service option.
- TRICARE For Life is also available for Medicare-eligible beneficiaries age 65 and over.
- TRICARE Plus, a primary care enrollment program offered at selected military treatment facilities.

Each of the above programs is discussed later in this chapter.

ELIGIBILITY

An individual's key to TRICARE eligibility depends on his or her enrollment in the Defense Enrollment Eligibility Reporting System (DEERS).

The DEERS record will indicate the dates of eligibility.

All uniformed services sponsors (active, reserve or retired) should ensure that their family status (marriage, death, divorce, new child, etc.) and residential address are current in DEERS at all times.

DEERS enrollment and/or updates are completed at uniformed services personnel offices, not TRICARE service centers.

All uniformed services sponsors (active, reserve or retired) should ensure that their family status (marriage, death, divorce, new child, etc.) and residential address are current in DEERS at all times.

For more information about DEERS, individuals should contact the Defense Manpower Data Center Support Office (DSO) Telephone Center from 6 a.m. to 5 p.m., Pacific Time, Monday through Friday, at the following toll-free number: (800) 538-9552.

The following table highlights the *basic* categories of eligible beneficiaries:

Beneficiary Category	***Description***
Active duty & retired service members	From the Army, Air Force, Navy, Marine Corps, Coast Guard, Public Health Service, or National Oceanic & Atmospheric Administration
Spouses & unmarried children (including stepchildren) of active duty or retired service members Note: Stepchildren lose eligibility after a divorce unless adopted by the sponsor.	Remain eligible even if parents divorce or remarry. Eligibility ends at age 21, unless the child is a full-time student, then eligibility ends at age 23, or when the full-time student status ends, whichever comes first. Eligibility may extend past age 21 if the child is incapable of self-support because of a mental or physical incapacity, and the condition existed prior to age 21, or the condition occurred between the ages of 21 & 23, while the child was a full-time student. Illegitimate children of current or former service members or their spouses may be eligible under certain conditions. Children placed in the custody of a service member or former member, either by a court or by a recognized adoption agency, in anticipation of legal adoption by the member.
Reserve Component members on active duty for more than 30 days - under Federal orders Note: Please be sure to read the sections titled *Early Tricare Benefit For Some Activated National Guard & Reserve Members & Family Members*, and *TRICARE Reserve Select.*	From the Army, Air Force, Navy, Marine Corps, Coast Guard, Public Health Service, or National Oceanic & Atmospheric Administration
Spouses & unmarried children of reserve component service members	Covered while reserve component sponsor is on active duty for more than 30 consecutive days. Covered if reserve sponsor was injured or dies during, or on the way to or from, active-duty training for a period of 30 days or less.

Beneficiary Category	***Description***
Retired reserve component service members & their family members	When the retired reserve component service member is eligible for retirement pay (usually at age 60), the member and his/her eligible family members become TRICARE eligible.
Widows or widowers & unmarried children of deceased active-duty or retired service members	Are eligible as family members of deceased member if sponsor was serving or was ordered to active duty for more than 30 days at time of death. Claims will be cost-shared at the active-duty family member rate for 3 years after death of active duty sponsor, and thereafter at the retiree rate. Widows or widowers remain eligible until they remarry (loss of benefits remains applicable even if remarriage ends in death or divorce). Children remain eligible until age 21, unless they meet the exceptions noted above.
Medal of Honor recipients & their family members	Any service member who has been awarded the Medal of Honor, his/her eligible family members & widows are eligible for medical & dental benefits under TRICARE.

Beneficiary Category	***Description***
Certain eligible former spouses of active duty or retired service members	Must not have remarried. Must not be covered by an employer-sponsored health plan. Must not be the former spouse of a NATO or "Partners for Peace" nation member. Must meet the requirements of one of the following three situations:

- Must have been married to the SAME military member or former member for at least 20 years, & at least 20 of those married years must have been creditable in determining the member's eligibility for retirement pay.

  (If the date of divorce is before 4/1/85, the spouse is eligible only for care received on or after the date of the decree.)

  (If the date of the final decree of divorce or annulment was on or after 2/1/83, the former spouse is eligible for TRICARE coverage for health care that is received after the date of the divorce or annulment.)

  (If the date of the final decree is before Feb. 1, 1983, the former spouse is eligible for TRICARE coverage for health care received on or after Jan. 1, 1985.)

  Eligibility continues as long as the preceding requirements continue to be met.

1. Must have been married to the SAME military member or former member for at least 20 years, and at least 15—but less than 20—of those married years must have been creditable in determining the member's eligibility for retirement pay.

   (If the date of the final decree of divorce or annulment is before April 1, 1985, the former spouse is eligible only for care received on or after Jan. 1, 1985, or the date of the decree, whichever is later.)

   (Eligibility continues as long as the preceding requirements continue to be met. However, if the date of the final divorce decree or annulment is on or after April 1, 1985, but before Sept. 29, 1988, the former spouse is eligible for care received from the date of the decree until Dec. 31, 1988, or two years from the date of the decree, whichever is later.)

2. Must have been married to the SAME military member or former member for at least 20 years, and at least 15—but less than 20—of those married years must have been creditable in determining the member's eligibility for retirement pay.

   (If the date of the final decree of divorce or annulment is on or after Sept. 29, 1988, the former spouse is eligible only for care received for one year from the date of the decree.)

TRICARE PRIME

TRICARE Prime is a managed care option similar to a civilian health maintenance organization (HMO). This option requires enrollment. Active duty service members are required to enroll in Prime. Active duty family members, retirees and their family members are encouraged, but not required, to enroll in Prime. However, to receive the TRICARE Prime benefit, they must reside where TRICARE Prime is offered. Individuals should contact their local TRICARE service center (TSC) about the TRICARE Prime availability in their area.

TRICARE Prime offers less out-of-pocket costs than any other TRICARE option.

For individuals stationed in a remote area, TPR/TRICARE Prime Remote for Active Duty Family Members (TPRADFM) may be the option available to them and their family members. This option also requires enrollment.

If enrollment for TRICARE Prime and TPR/TPRADFM is received by the 20th of the month, it is effective the first day of the next month. If an individual disenrolls from TRICARE Prime, he or she is locked out for 12 months.

TRICARE Prime offers less out-of-pocket costs than any other TRICARE option.

Active duty members and their families do not pay enrollment fees, annual deductibles or co-payments for care in the TRICARE network. Retired service members pay an annual enrollment fee of $230 for an individual or $460 for a family, and minimal co-pays apply for care in the TRICARE network. TRICARE Prime offers a "point-of-service" option for care received outside of the TRICARE Prime network, but point-of-service care requires payment of significant out of pocket costs.

TRICARE Prime enrollees receive most of their care from military providers or from civilian providers who belong to the TRICARE Prime network. Enrollees are assigned a primary care manager (PCM) who manages their care and provides referrals for specialty care. All referrals for specialty care must be arranged by the PCM to avoid point-of-service charges.

TRICARE STANDARD & TRICARE EXTRA

TRICARE Standard is a fee-for-service option. Individuals can see an authorized TRICARE provider of their choice. Having this flexibility means that care generally costs more.

TRICARE Extra is a preferred provider option (PPO) in which beneficiaries choose a doctor, hospital, or other medical provider within the TRICARE provider network. Network providers can be located by calling your local TRICARE service center

- TRICARE Extra and TRICARE Standard are available for all TRICARE-eligible beneficiaries who elect or are not able to enroll in TRICARE Prime.
- Active duty service members are not eligible for Extra or Standard.
- There is no enrollment required for TRICARE Extra or Standard—no annual enrollment fees, no enrollment forms.
- Beneficiaries are responsible for annual deductibles and cost-shares.
- Beneficiaries may see any TRICARE authorized provider they choose, and the government will share the cost with the beneficiaries after deductibles.

TRICARE FOR LIFE

When beneficiaries age 65 and over become eligible for Medicare Part A, they can use TRICARE For Life (TFL) if they purchase Medicare Part B. These beneficiaries are not eligible for TRICARE Prime but are eligible to use Medicare, network and non-network providers.

> *Under TRICARE For Life, TRICARE acts as a second payer to Medicare for benefits payable by both.*

Beneficiaries can use an authorized Medicare provider and claims will be automatically sent to TRICARE after Medicare pays its portion. There are no enrollment fees for TFL—beneficiaries are only required to pay the Medicare Part B premium. TRICARE is first payer for TRICARE benefits not covered by Medicare, such as pharmacy, which is available only under TRICARE.

Medicare Part B

Under TRICARE For Life, TRICARE acts as a second payer to Medicare for benefits payable by both.

The Department of Defense (DoD) encourages beneficiaries to purchase Medicare Part B when they are first eligible. Although beneficiaries may delay Medicare Part B sign up for up to eight months in certain circumstances, they will not be covered by TRICARE until Part B coverage begins. Beneficiaries that do not sign up for Medicare Part B when first eligible will pay a 10 percent surcharge for each 12-month period that they delayed signing up.

Beneficiaries should confirm that their Medicare status is current in the Defense Eligibility and Enrollment Reporting System (DEERS) by calling (800) 538-9552.

Beneficiaries are signed up for Medicare Part B during their *initial enrollment period*, which begins three months before the month beneficiaries turn 65 and ends seven months after the month beneficiaries turn 65.

Beneficiaries who do not sign up for Medicare Part B when first eligible may sign up for Part B during the *general enrollment period* that occurs January 1 through March 31 of each year. When beneficiaries enroll in Part B during the general enrollment period, Part B and TFL coverage begin July 1 of that year.

Beneficiaries pay a Medicare Part B premium penalty surcharge of 10 percent per year they failed to sign up when first eligible.

How TRICARE For Life Works With Medicare

- For services received from a provider that accepts Medicare, the provider first files claims with Medicare. Medicare pays its portion and electronically forwards the claim to Wisconsin Physicians Service (WPS), the TFL claims processor. TFL sends its payment for Medicare-covered services directly to the provider. Beneficiaries receive a Medicare summary notice from Medicare and a TFL explanation of benefits (EOB) from the TFL contractor indicating the amounts paid.

- For Medicare and TRICARE covered services, Medicare pays first and the remaining beneficiary liability may be paid by TFL.

- For services covered by TRICARE but not by Medicare, such as care received overseas, TFL pays first and Medicare pays nothing. Beneficiaries are responsible for the TRICARE fiscal year deductible and cost shares.

- For services covered by Medicare but not by TRICARE, such as chiropractic services, Medicare is the first payer and TFL pays nothing. Beneficiaries are responsible for Medicare deductibles and coinsurance.

- For services not covered by Medicare or TRICARE, such as cosmetic surgery, Medicare and TRICARE pay nothing. Beneficiaries are responsible for the entire bill.

Medicare Part D

Unlike Medicare Parts A and B, purchase of a Medicare Part D prescription drug plan is *not required* to retain TRICARE eligibility.

TRICARE PLUS

Some military treatment facilities will have capacity to offer a primary care affiliation program called TRICARE Plus. Enrolled beneficiaries have priority access to care at military treatment facilities; however, beneficiaries who choose to use TRICARE Extra, TRICARE Standard or TRICARE For Life may also continue to receive care in a military treatment facility on a space-available basis.

TRICARE Plus Benefits:

- Enrollees will use their designated primary care provider at the military treatment facility as their principal source of health care.

- Persons enrolled in TRICARE Plus can continue to obtain care from civilian and/or Medicare providers; TRICARE Standard/Extra or Medicare rules apply. TRICARE will be second payer to Medicare for TRICARE-covered services.

- Enrollees are not locked into a health maintenance organization (HMO)-like program.

- There are no enrollment fees.
- TRICARE Plus enrollees will receive primary care appointments with the same access standards as TRICARE Prime enrollees.
- TRICARE Plus enrollment is noted on beneficiary records in Defense Enrollment Eligibility Reporting System (DEERS).
- Eligible beneficiaries with existing relationships with primary care providers at military treatment facilities will have the first opportunity to enroll as long as the facility has the capacity (space) and capability (resources). Remaining enrollment capacity will be made available to other beneficiaries through a fair process.

TRICARE Plus Limitations:

- TRICARE Plus will not be available at all military treatment facilities. Local commanders will retain discretion to continue or discontinue TRICARE Plus at individual military treatment facilities depending on their capacities/capabilities and missions.
- TRICARE Plus is a military treatment facility primary care access program, not a health plan. For care from civilian providers, TRICARE Plus has no effect and TRICARE Standard/Extra rules will apply for most enrollees. For services payable by Medicare, Medicare rules will apply, with TRICARE as second payer for TRICARE covered services and supplies.
- TRICARE Plus does not guarantee access to specialty care at the military treatment facility where the beneficiary is enrolled.
- Prospective enrollees will apply for enrollment in TRICARE Plus. Enrollment may be determined, in part, by the specific missions and needs of each military treatment facility (for example, GME, existing TRICARE Senior Prime program, etc.).
- TRICARE Plus is not a portable benefit. Enrollment at one facility will not guarantee access at another facility.
- TRICARE Plus enrollees are discouraged from obtaining nonemergency primary care from sources outside the military treatment facility where they are enrolled.
- Beneficiaries enrolled in an HMO or similar program of another sponsor (TRICARE Prime, employer-sponsored HMO, Medicare Choice) are not eligible for TRICARE Plus because they have an established primary care relationship.
- Continued enrollment in TRICARE Plus is reviewed annually by the local military treatment facility; beneficiaries may be disenrolled if capacity is no longer available.

"EARLY" TRICARE BENEFIT FOR SOME ACTIVATED NATIONAL GUARD & RESERVE MEMBERS & FAMILY MEMBERS

Some members of the National Guard and Reserve (collectively known as the Reserve Component, or RC), who are issued delayed-effective-date active duty orders for more than 30 days in support of a contingency operation, are eligible for "early" TRICARE medical and dental benefits beginning on the later of either:

- The date their orders were issued; or
- 90 days before they report to active duty.

This early eligibility TRICARE benefit was introduced under Section 703 of the National Defense Authorization Act (NDAA) and the Emergency Supplemental Appropriations Act for Fiscal Year (FY) 2004 and made permanent by Section 703 of the NDAA for FY 2005. The Department of Defense implemented the early eligibility TRICARE benefit in July 2004.

If the RC member is issued delayed-effective-date active duty orders (for more than 30 days in support of a contingency operation) and the orders are cancelled prior to the member reporting to active duty, TRICARE coverage (eligibility) for the member and eligible family members terminates on the effective date the orders are cancelled.

Uniformed Services Employment Reemployment Rights Act (USERRA) protections for members that ensure an employer-sponsored health plan can be reinstated do not go into effect until the member actually reports for active duty. Therefore, members and their family members are strongly encouraged to consider retaining their employer's health plan coverage until the RC member actually reports for active duty, at which time the RC member and family members are fully covered by USERRA protections.

TRICARE PRIME for rESERVE COMPONENT Members

Reserve Component (RC) members will not be enrolled into TRICARE Prime until they reach their final duty station location. During the early eligibility period, RC members residing inside the 50 United States who are TRICARE-eligible in DEERS will not be enrolled in the TRICARE Prime or TRICARE Prime Remote (TPR) programs. These members will receive health services in the same manner as any non-enrolled active duty service member.

Dental Services for RC Members

If the RC member was previously enrolled in the TRICARE Dental Program (TDP) prior to receiving delayed-effective-date active duty orders, he or she will be disenrolled from the TDP and will become eligible for the same dental services provided to active duty service members.

TRICARE Benefit for reserve component Family Members

When RC sponsors become eligible for TRICARE benefits as described above, their DEERS-eligible family members become eligible for care in MTFs on a space-available basis and coverage under TRICARE Standard/Extra.

Once RC family members become eligible in DEERS, they may enroll in TRICARE Prime or the TRICARE Prime Remote for Active Duty Family Members (TPRADFM) program, depending on their residence.

There are no enrollment fees for RC family members to enroll in the TRICARE Prime or the TPRADFM program. However, to enroll in the TPRADFM program, the residential address shown in DEERS for the RC member and family members must be the same.

Also, to be eligible for TPRADFM, family members must have resided with their RC member before the member departed for his/her duty station, mobilization site or deployment location, and the family member must continue to reside in the TPR location.

Other TRICARE Options for Eligible Reserve Component Family Members

RC family members who choose not to enroll in either TRICARE Prime or TPRADFM remain eligible for TRICARE Extra and TRICARE Standard benefits. RC family members are also eligible for benefits under the TRICARE Reserve Family Member Demonstration project (see following section).

TRICARE Reserve Family Demonstration Project

The TRICARE Reserve Family Demonstration Project is a nationwide program for health care services received on or after September 14, 2001. The Department of Defense has approved this benefit through October 31, 2007.

The purpose of the demonstration project is to test approaches for the Military Health System to ensure timely access to health care during a national crisis for family members of activated reservists and members of the National Guard; and to maintain clinically appropriate continuity of health care for their family members.

The purpose of the demonstration project is to test approaches for the Military Health System to ensure timely access to health care during a national crisis for family members of activated reservists and members of the National Guard; and to maintain clinically appropriate continuity of health care for their family members.

Demonstration participants are limited to families of Reserve and National Guard members called to active duty for periods of more than 30 days in support of operations that result from the terrorist attacks of September 11, 2001. Such operations include, for example, Operation ENDURING FREEDOM and NOBLE EAGLE.

The demonstration project has three major components that remove potential barriers to health care access and limit out-of-pocket expenses.

1. Waiver of TRICARE Standard and Extra Annual Deductible:

Participants who do not or cannot enroll in TRICARE Prime are not required to pay the annual outpatient deductible under Standard or Extra (up to $300). These beneficiaries are only responsible for their cost share (20 percent for TRICARE Standard and 15 percent for TRICARE Extra). This component covers all outpatient health care received by an eligible participant through October 31, 2007.

2. Waiver of the TRICARE Maximum Allowable Charge under TRICARE Standard:

   The Department of Defense will pay up to 115 percent of the TRICARE maximum allowable charge, less the applicable cost share, for demonstration participants who are covered by TRICARE Standard and receive care from nonparticipating providers who bill in excess of the TRICARE maximum allowable charge. This component covers all health care received by an eligible participant through October 31, 2007.

3. Waiver of Nonavailability Statement (NAS) Requirement for Nonemergency Inpatient Care:

   The requirement to obtain a NAS before nonemergency inpatient care can be paid under TRICARE Standard is waived for all eligible demonstration participants. This component covers all nonemergency inpatient care received by an eligible participant through October 31, 2007.

TRICARE RESERVE SELECT

Beginning April 26, 2005, certain members and former members of the National Guard and Reserve became able to purchase premium-based health care coverage under a new TRICARE health plan called TRICARE Reserve Select (TRS) for themselves and their family members.

TRICARE Reserve Select (TRS) is available to Reserve Component (RC) members who separate from qualifying active duty service on or after April 27, 2005.

TRICARE Reserve Select (TRS) is available to Reserve Component (RC) members who separate from qualifying active duty service on or after April 27, 2005.

(The Reserve Component includes the Army National Guard, the Army Reserve, the Navy Reserve, the Marine Corps Reserve, the Air National Guard, the Air Force Reserve and the U.S. Coast Guard Reserve.)

TRS ELIGIBILITY

TRS eligibility is established with the member's Service/Reserve Component personnel offices. RC members may be eligible to purchase TRS for themselves and their immediate family members if they meet the following conditions: First, if they were called or ordered to active duty under Title 10 in support of a contingency operation for more than 30 consecutive days on or after *September 11, 2001*. Second, if they served continuously on active duty for 90 days or more under such call or order. Third, if they enter into a Service Agreement (DD Form 2895) to serve in the Selected Reserves.

> ***2006 Update:***
> ***The 2006 NDAA expanded coverage for Tricare Reserve Select to include demobilized reservists. Demobilized members who become eligible under the new legislation will pay higher premiums than mobilized members. (Specific information was not available at the time of publication.)***

period of coverage

RC members may be eligible for one whole year of TRS coverage for each whole year of service commitment in the executed Service Agreement up to a maximum of one whole year of coverage for each 90 days of continuous active duty service in support of a contingency operation. The following chart illustrates several examples:

Days Served on Active Duty	Maximum Period of Coverage
1 - 89 days	None**
90 - 179 days	1 year
180 - 269 days	2 years
270 - 359 days	3 years
360 - 449 days	4 years

(RC members who are otherwise eligible, but did not serve continuously on active duty for 90 days solely because of an injury, illness, or disease incurred or aggravated while activated may be eligible for one whole year of TRS coverage.)

Time-Limited Opportunity To Decide

Purchasing TRS coverage is a three-step process. The members' Service/Reserve Component will provide an opportunity to enter into a Service Agreement to continue service in the Selected Reserve, which is required before they are eligible to purchase TRS.

If they do not complete Steps 1 and 2 within the specified deadlines, they forfeit their opportunity to purchase TRS in Step 3, based on this period of active service. TRS coverage may not be initiated or extended later, nor may any period of eligibility be saved until a later time.

Step 1—Enter into the Service Agreement
RC members who separate from qualifying active duty service on or after April 27, 2005 must enter into a Service Agreement **before** they leave active duty.

Step 2—Execute the Service Agreement
RC members should contact their Reserve Component and execute the Service Agreement within four months after leaving active duty. The Service Agreement

does not guarantee a Selected Reserve billet. RC members must be in the Selected Reserve by the time their TRS coverage begins.

Step 3—Purchasing TRICARE Reserve Select
After the RC member has completed the Service Agreement, the Service/Reserve Component will record eligibility in the Defense Enrollment Eligibility Reporting System (DEERS).

RC members should follow the instructions on their TRS enrollment form to complete the form and submit it with a one-month premium payment to their TRICARE regional contractor. It must be received no later than 30 days before their transitional TRICARE coverage ends under the Transitional Assistance Management Program (TAMP). The initial payment may be made by check, money order or cashier's check payable to the appropriate TRICARE regional contractor. Payment can also be made by Visa or MasterCard.

premiums

When a member completes a TRS enrollment form, he/she must select a type of coverage. Monthly premiums vary, depending on the type of coverage, and the member's active-duty status.

TRANSITIONAL ASSISTANCE MANAGEMENT PROGRAM

The Transitional Assistance Management Program (TAMP) offers transitional TRICARE coverage to certain separating active duty members and their eligible family members. Care is available for a limited time.

Under the National Defense Authorization Act for Fiscal Year 2005, effective October 28, 2004, TRICARE eligibility under the TAMP has been permanently extended from 60 or 120 days to 180 days.

The four categories for TAMP are:

- Members involuntarily separated from active duty and their eligible family members;
- National Guard and Reserve members, collectively known as the Reserve Component (RC), separated from active duty after being called up or ordered in support of a contingency operation for an active duty period of more than 30 days and their family members;
- Members separated from active duty after being involuntarily retained in support of a contingency operation and their family members; and
- Members separated from active duty following a voluntary agreement to stay on active duty for less than one year in support of a contingency mission and their family members.

Active duty sponsors and family members enrolled in TRICARE Prime who desire to continue their enrollment upon the sponsor's separation from active duty status are required to reenroll. To reenroll in TRICARE Prime, the sponsor or family member must complete and submit a TRICARE Prime enrollment application. Under TAMP, former active duty sponsors, former activated reservists, and family members of both are not eligible to enroll or reenroll in TRICARE Prime Remote or in TRICARE Prime Remote for Active Duty Family Members because both programs require the sponsor to be on active duty.

Under TAMP, the sponsor is no longer on active duty and is treated as an active duty family member for benefits and cost sharing purposes.

Eligibility for TAMP for sponsors and family members is determined by the sponsor's Service branch and information in the Defense Enrollment Eligibility Reporting System. Sponsors may verify eligibility for themselves and their family members by visiting or contacting the nearest military identification card issuing facility or contacting the Defense Manpower Data Center Support Office toll free at (800) 538-9552.

Continued Health Care Benefit Program (CHCBP)

CHCBP provides a conversion health plan similar to TRICARE Standard for a specific time (18 months) to former service members and their families who pay quarterly premiums.

After TAMP eligibility expires, members and eligible family members may choose to enroll in the *Continued Health Care Benefit Program* (CHCBP).

CHCBP provides a conversion health plan similar to TRICARE Standard for a specific time (18 months) to former service members and their families who pay quarterly premiums.

Eligible persons must enroll in the CHCBP within 60 days after separation from active duty or loss of eligibility for military health care under TAMP.

Eligibility for CHCBP is determined through the military personnel offices.

For more information about CHCBP, interested parties may check with a beneficiary counseling and assistance coordinator or call the contractor that runs the program toll free at (800) 444-5445.

PHARMACY BENEFITS

TRICARE provides a pharmacy benefit to all eligible Uniformed Services members, including TRICARE for Life (TFL) beneficiaries entitled to Medicare Parts A and Parts B based on their age, disability and/or end-stage renal disease. Eligible beneficiaries may fill prescription medications:

To have a prescription filled, beneficiaries need a written prescription and a valid Uniformed Services identification card.

- At military treatment facility (MTF) pharmacies;
- Through the TRICARE Mail Order Pharmacy (TMOP);
- At TRICARE retail network pharmacies (TRRx); and

- At non-network pharmacies.

To have a prescription filled, beneficiaries need a written prescription and a valid Uniformed Services identification card.

TFL beneficiaries, who turned age 65 on April 1, 2001, or later, must be enrolled in Medicare Part B to use the pharmacy program. TFL beneficiaries who turned age 65 before April 1, 2001, are not required to be enrolled in Medicare Part B for the pharmacy program, but are required to be enrolled in Medicare Part B for all other benefits available under TFL.

TRICARE's mandatory generic drug policy requires that prescriptions be filled with a generic product, if one is available.

Copayments

Beneficiaries currently pay the pharmacy copayment based on whether the prescription medication is classified as a formulary generic (Tier 1), formulary brand name (Tier 2), or non-formulary (Tier 3) drug. The copayment depends on where the beneficiary chooses to fill their prescription.

Active duty service members do not pay copayments for prescriptions. However, if they receive medications through an overseas pharmacy or an out-of-network pharmacy, they may need to pay out-of-pocket for the total cost of the medication and then file a claim for reimbursement for the full amount.

Medicare Part D Prescription Drug Benefit

Starting January 1, 2006, the new Medicare prescription drug coverage became available to everyone with Medicare Part A and/or Part B. (Beneficiaries that live overseas or are in prison are not eligible for the Medicare pharmacy program.)

For nearly all TRICARE-Medicare beneficiaries, under most circumstances, there is no added value in purchasing Medicare prescription drug coverage if you have TRICARE. The exception to this general rule may be for those with limited incomes and assets who qualify for Medicare's extra help with prescription drug plan costs; such individuals may benefit by enrolling in a Medicare prescription drug plan.

TRICARE-Medicare eligible beneficiaries, entitled to the TRICARE Pharmacy benefit, need to consider a number of factors when deciding whether or not to enroll in a Medicare drug plan. They should consider monthly premiums, deductibles, co-pays and drug coverage under the different prescription drug plan options offered (also known as a formulary), including the TRICARE Pharmacy Program. The Medicare Part D drug plan options will vary by location.

Individuals should be aware that the above-information is GENERAL INFORMATION only! Individuals are encouraged to seek professional advice in making these decisions.

CHIROPRACTIC CARE

The National Defense Authorization Act for fiscal year 2001 established the Chiropractic Care Program, replacing the former Chiropractic Health Care Demonstration Program (CHCDP) that ended in September 1999.

Effective October 1, 2001, the Chiropractic Care Program is only available to **active duty** service members at designated military treatment facilities (MTFs).

TRICARE CATASTROPHIC CAP

The TRICARE catastrophic cap limits the amount of out-of-pocket expenses a family will have to pay for TRICARE-covered medical services. The cap applies to the allowable charges for covered services—annual deductibles, Prime enrollment fees, pharmacy co-pays, and other cost shares based on TRICARE-allowable charges. Out-of-pocket expenses paid under the TRICARE Prime point-of-service (POS) option (deductibles and cost-shares) are not applied to the annual enrollment year catastrophic cap. Additionally, any POS charges incurred after the catastrophic cap has been met are the beneficiary's financial responsibility.

Families Using TRICARE Extra and Standard

The catastrophic cap applies to the fiscal year (October 1 to September 30) for families using TRICARE Extra and TRICARE Standard.

The catastrophic cap is $1,000 for family members of active duty service members (using TRICARE Extra or TRICARE Standard) and $3,000 for all other beneficiaries.

After the catastrophic cap is met, TRICARE will pay the beneficiary's portion of the TRICARE-allowable amount for all covered services for the remainder of the fiscal year. The catastrophic cap does not apply to services not covered by TRICARE or to any amount that nonparticipating providers may charge above the TRICARE maximum allowable charge for services.

TRICARE Prime Enrollees

Active Duty (AD) and Active Duty Family Members (ADFM)

The catastrophic cap amount for AD service members and their family members is $1,000. Since AD service members and their families do not pay enrollment fees, there has never been an enrollment year catastrophic cap. Catastrophic cap amounts for AD service members and their families are tracked on a fiscal year basis, which begins October 1 and ends September 30.

Retirees, their family members and survivors enrolled in Prime

Retirees, their family members and survivors are subject to enrollment year and fiscal year catastrophic cap limits. The current enrollment year and fiscal catastrophic cap limit for retirees and their family members is $3,000.

Under the new contracts, retirees, their family members and survivors enrolled in Prime now have their enrollment year aligned to the fiscal year.

Aligning the enrollment year to the fiscal year affects these beneficiaries except for current enrollees and new enrollees whose enrollment effective date is October 1.

TRICARE REGIONS

North

TRICARE's North region includes Connecticut, Delaware, the District of Columbia, Illinois, Indiana, Kentucky, Maine, Maryland, Massachusetts, Michigan, New Hampshire, New Jersey, New York, North Carolina, Ohio, Pennsylvania, Rhode Island, Vermont, Virginia, West Virginia, and Wisconsin (and some zip code areas in Iowa, Missouri, and Tennessee). Health Net Federal Services, Inc. is the new regional contractor providing health care services and network-provider support in the TRICARE North region.

Health Net's customer service representatives are available Monday - Friday, 8 a.m. to 7 p.m. in all North region time zones, at 1-877-TRICARE (1-877-874-2273).

South

TRICARE's South region includes Alabama, Arkansas, Florida, Georgia, Louisiana, Mississippi Oklahoma, South Carolina, and Tennessee (excluding 35 Tennessee zip codes in the Fort Campbell, KY area), and Texas (excluding, only, the extreme southwestern El Paso-area). Humana-Military is the regional contractor providing health care services and network provider support in the TRICARE South region.

Humana's customer service representatives are available Monday - Friday, 8 a.m. to 6 p.m. in all South region time zones, at 1-800-444-5445.

West

TRICARE's West region includes Alaska, Arizona, California, Colorado, Hawaii, Idaho, Iowa (except 82 Iowa zip codes that are in the Rock Island, Illinois area), Kansas, Minnesota, Missouri (except the St. Louis area), Montana, Nebraska, Nevada, New Mexico, North Dakota, Oregon, South Dakota, Texas (the southwestern corner, including El Paso, only) Utah, Washington, and Wyoming. TriWest Healthcare Alliance is the regional contractor providing health care services and network-provider support in the TRICARE West region.

TriWest's customer service representatives are available Monday - Friday, 8 a.m. to 6 p.m. in the West Region time zone in which you reside, at 1-888-TRIWEST (1-888-874-9378).

CHAPTER 15

VOCATIONAL REHABILITATION AND EMPLOYMENT SERVICES FOR VETERANS WITH SERVICE-CONNECTED DISABILITIES

OVERVIEW

Vocational Rehabilitation is a program which helps eligible disabled veterans get and keep lasting, suitable jobs. It also helps seriously disabled veterans achieve independence in daily living.

The program offers a number of services to help each eligible disabled veteran reach his or her rehabilitation goal. These services include:

- Vocational and personal counseling;
- Evaluation of abilities, skill and interests;
- Assistance finding and keeping a suitable job, including special employer incentives;
- If needed, education and training such as certificate, two, or four year college programs;
- Financial aid;
- If needed, training such as on-the-job and non-paid work experiences;
- Supportive rehabilitation services and additional counseling;
- Medical and dental treatment, if needed;
- Education and training benefits for dependent children with the birth defect spina bifida, caused by a veteran-parent's service in the Vietnam theater.
- Vocational and educational guidance and counseling to certain veteran's dependents eligible for one of VA's educational benefit programs.

If entitled to Vocational Rehabilitation, the law provides for a maximum of 48 months of services. These limitations may be extended in certain circumstances.

ELIGIBILITY

Usually, a veteran must first be awarded a monthly VA Disability Compensation payment. In some cases, veterans may be eligible if they are not getting VA compensation (for example, if they are awaiting discharge from the service because of a disability, OR they are entitled to VA compensation but have decided not to reduce their military retirement or disability pay).

Eligibility is also based on meeting the following conditions:

- The veteran served on or after September 16, 1940; and
- The veteran's discharge or release from active duty was under was under other than dishonorable conditions; and
- The veteran's service-connected disabilities are rated at least 20% disabling by VA (***NOTE:*** Effective October 1, 1993, a veteran may be eligible for Vocational Rehabilitation if he or she is rated 10% disabled, and has a serious employment handicap.); and
- The veteran needs Vocational Rehabilitation to overcome an employment handicap; and
- It has been less than 12 years since VA notified the veteran of his or her eligibility. (A veteran may have longer than 12 years to use this benefit if certain conditions prevented him or her from training.)

AMOUNT OF VA PAYMENTS

If a veteran needs training, VA will pay his or her training costs, such as:

- Tuition and fees;
- Books;
- Supplies;
- Equipment; and
- Special services (such as prosthetic devices, lip-reading training, or signing for the deaf), if needed

While a veteran is in training, VA will also pay him or her a monthly benefit to help with living expenses, called a subsistence allowance. Details are provided in the next section of this chapter.

SUBSISTENCE ALLOWANCE (CHAPTER 31)

In some cases, a veteran requires additional education or training in order to become employable. A Subsistence Allowance may then be paid each month, and is based on the rate of attendance (full-time or part-time) and the number of dependents. The charts on the following page reflect the rates as of October 1, 2007.

The following Subsistence Allowance rates are paid for training in an Institution of Higher Learning:

Number Of Dependents	Full Time	Three Quarter Time	One Half Time
No Dependents	$520.74	$391.27	$261.81
One Dependent	$645.94	$485.15	$324.38
Two Dependents	$761.18	$569.09	$381.30
Each Additional Dependent	$55.49	$42.67	$28.47

Subsistence Allowance is paid for full time training only, in the following training programs:
Nonpay or nominal pay on-job training in a federal, state, local, or federally recognized Indian tribe agency; training in the home; vocational course in a rehabilitation facility or sheltered workshop; institutional non-farm cooperative.

Number Of Dependents	Full Time
No Dependents	$520.74
One Dependent	$645.94
Two Dependents	$761.18
Each Additional Dependent	$55.49

The following rates are paid for Work Experience programs:
Nonpay or nominal pay work experience in a federal, state, local or federally recognized Indian tribe agency.

Number Of Dependents	Full Time	Three Quarter Time	One Half Time
No Dependents	$520.74	$391.27	$261.81
One Dependent	$645.94	$485.15	$324.38
Two Dependents	$761.18	$569.09	$381.30
Each Additional Dependent	$55.49	$42.67	$28.47

Subsistence Allowance is paid for full time training only in the following training programs:
Farm cooperative, apprenticeship, or other on-job training.

Number of Dependents	Full Time
No Dependents	$455.25
One Dependent	$550.59
Two Dependents	$634.55
Each Additional Dependent	$41.28

Subsistence Allowance is paid at the following rates for combined training programs:
Combination of Institutional and On-Job Training (Full Time Rate Only).

Number Of Dependents	Institutional Greater than one half	On-The-Job Greater than one half
No Dependents	$520.74	$455.29
One Dependent	$645.94	$550.59
Two Dependents	$761.18	$634.55
Each Additional Dependent	$55.49	$41.28

Subsistence Allowance is paid at the following rates for Non-farm Cooperative Training:
Non-farm Cooperative Institutional Training and Non-farm Cooperative On-Job Training - Full Time Rate Only.

Number Of Dependents	FT Non-farm Coop/Institutional	FT Non-farm Coop/On-The-Job
No Dependents	$520.74	$455.29
One Dependent	$645.94	$550.59
Two Dependents	$761.18	$634.55
Each Additional Dependent	$55.49	$41.28

Subsistence Allowance is paid at the following rates for Independent Living programs:
A subsistence allowance is paid each month during the period of enrollment in a rehabilitation facility when a veteran is pursuing an approved Independent Living Program plan. Subsistence allowance paid during a period of Independent Living Services is based on rate of pursuit and number of dependents.

Number Of Dependents	Full Time	Three Quarter Time	One Half Time
No Dependents	$520.74	$391.27	$261.81
One Dependent	$645.94	$485.15	$324.38
Two Dependents	$761.18	$569.09	$381.30
Each Additional Dependent	$55.49	$42.67	$28.47

Subsistence Allowance is paid at the following rates for Extended Evaluation programs:
A subsistence allowance is paid each month during the period of enrollment in a rehabilitation facility when a veteran requires this service for the purpose of extended evaluation. Subsistence allowance during a period of extended evaluation is paid based on the rate of attendance and the number of dependents.

Number of Dependents	Full Time	Three Quarter Time	One Half Time	One Quarter Time
No Dependents	$520.74	$391.27	$261.81	$130.89
One Dependent	$645.94	$485.15	$324.38	$162.20
Two Dependents	$761.18	$569.09	$381.30	$190.64
Each Additional Dependent	$55.49	$42.67	$28.47	$14.20

PROGRAM FOR UNEMPLOYABLE VETERANS

Veterans awarded 100% disability compensation based upon unemployability may still request an evaluation, and, if found eligible, may participate in a vocational rehabilitation program and receive help in getting a job. A veteran who secures employment under the special program will continue to receive 100% disability compensation until the veteran has worked continuously for at least 12 months.

VOCATIONAL TRAINING FOR CHILDREN WITH SPINA BIFIDA

To qualify for entitlement to a vocational training program an applicant must be a child:

- To whom VA has awarded a monthly allowance for spina bifida; and
- For whom VA has determined that achievement of a vocational goal is reasonably feasible.

A vocational training program may not begin before a child's 18th birthday, or the date of completion of secondary schooling, whichever comes first. Depending on the need, a child may be provided up to 24 months of full-time training.

VOCATIONAL TRAINING FOR CHILDREN OF FEMALE VIETNAM VETERANS BORN WITH CERTAIN BIRTH DEFECTS

Section 401 of P.L. 106-416, which became law on November 1, 2000 directed the Secretary of VA to identify birth defects of children of female Vietnam veterans that: (1) are associated with service during the Vietnam era; and (2) result in the permanent physical or mental disability of such children. The law excludes from such defects familial or birth-related defects or injuries. The law further directs the Secretary to provide to such children a monthly monetary allowance, as well as necessary health care to address the defect and any associated disability. It authorizes the Secretary to provide vocational training to such a child if the achievement of a vocational goal is reasonably feasible.

INDEPENDENT LIVING SERVICES

These services can help an individual with disabilities so severe that he or she cannot work. These services can lessen the individual's need to rely on others by giving him or her the skills needed to live as independently as possible at home and in the community.

Independent living services include:

- Extended evaluation of the individual's independent living needs;
- Training in activities of daily living;
- Case management;
- Personal adjustment counseling;
- Assistive technology;
- Training to improve the individual's chances of reaching a vocational goal.

APPLYING FOR BENEFITS

Interested veterans can apply by filling out VA Form 28-1900, Disabled Veterans Application for Vocational Rehabilitation, and mailing it to the VA regional office serving his or her area. (For a complete list of VA Regional Offices, refer to Chapter 37 of this book.)

CHAPTER 16

VET CENTERS

Vet Centers serve veterans and their families by providing a continuum of quality care that adds value for veterans, families, and communities. Care includes:

- Professional readjustment counseling;
- Professional counseling for posttraumatic stress disorder;
- Marital and family counseling;
- Substance abuse information and referral;
- Community education;
- Outreach to special populations, including disenfranchised and unserved veterans;
- The brokering of services with community agencies;
- Provides a key access link between the veteran and other services in the U.S. Department of Veterans Affairs;
- Promotion of wellness activities with veterans to help them reach quality health and life goals, and diminish the need for more intensive healthcare.

ELIGIBILITY

Legislation passed by Congress and signed into law by the President changed eligibility for Vet Center services, and extended the definition of the Vietnam era for war zone veterans (P.L. 104-262 and P.L. 104-275.)

Vet Centers serve the following veterans:

War Zone Veterans- all eras, including:

- **Vietnam War** – February 28, 1961 to May 7, 1975
- **Vietnam Era Veterans Not In The War Zone** – August 5, 1964 to May 7, 1975 (Veterans must request services at a Vet Center prior to January 1, 2004, to guarantee eligibility.)
- **Korean War** – June 27, 1950 to July 27, 1954 (eligible for the Korean Service Medal)

- **World War II** – There are 3 eligible categories:

  1. European-African-Middle Eastern Campaign Medal – December 7, 1941 to November 8, 1945

  2. Asiatic-Pacific Campaign Medal – December 7, 1941 to March 2, 1946

  3. American Campaign Medal – December 7, 1941 to March 2, 1946

- **Lebanon** – August 25, 1982 to February 26, 1984

- **Grenada** – October 23, 1983 to November 21, 1983

- **Panama** – December 20, 1989 to January 31, 1990

- **Persian Gulf** – August 2, 1990 to a date to be set by law or Presidential Proclamation

- **Somalia** – September 17, 1992 to a date to be set by law or Presidential Proclamation

- **Operation Joint Endeavor, Operation Joint Guard, & Operation Joint Forge** - Vet Center eligibility has been extended to veterans who participated in one or more of the three successive operations in the former Yugoslavia (Bosnia-Herzegovina and Croatia, aboard U.S. Naval vessels operating in the Adriatic Sea, or air spaces above those areas).

- **Global War on Terrorism –** Veterans who serve or have served in military expeditions to combat terrorism on or after September 11, 2001 and before a terminal date yet to be established.

Sexual Trauma And Harassment Counseling

Veterans of both sexes, all eras. Vet Center services include individual readjustment counseling, referral for benefits assistance, group readjustment counseling, liaison with community agencies, marital and family counseling, substance abuse information and referral, job counseling and placement, sexual trauma counseling, and community education.

Bereavement Counseling

The Department of Veteran Affairs (VA) offers bereavement counseling to parents, spouses and children of Armed Forces personnel who died in the service of their country. Also eligible are family members of reservists and National Guardsmen who die while on duty.

VET CENTER LOCATIONS

Alabama
Birmingham Vet Center
1500 5th Avenue South
Birmingham, AL 35205
(205) 731-0550

Mobile Vet Center
2577 Government Boulevard
Mobile, AL 36606
(251) 478-5906

Montgomery Vet Center Outstation
Colonial Park, Bldg. 600, #603
Montgomery, AL 35233
(334) 396-1986

Alaska
Anchorage Vet Center
4201 Tudor Centre Dr, Suite 115
Anchorage, AK 99508
(907) 563-6966

Fairbanks Vet Center
542 4th Avenue
Suite 100
Fairbanks, AK 99701
(907) 456-4238

Kenai Vet Center
Building F, Suite 4
Red Diamond Center
43335 K-Beach Road
Kenai, AK 99669
(907) 260-7640

Wasilla Vet Center
851 East Westpoint Ave, Suite 109
Wasilla, AK 99654
(907) 376-4318

Arizona
Chinle Vet Center Outstation
P.O. Box 1934
Chinle, AZ 86503
(928)-674-3682

Hopi Vet Center Outstation 2
P.O. Box 267
Keams Canyon, AZ 86034
(928)-738-5166

Phoenix Vet Center
77 East Weldon Avenue, Suite 100
Phoenix, AZ 85012-2075
(602) 640-2981

Prescott Vet Center
161 South Granite Street
Prescott, AZ 86303
(928) 778-3469

Tucson Vet Center
3055 North 1st Avenue
Tucson, AZ 85719
(520) 882-0333

Arkansas
North Little Rock Vet Center
201 West Broadway
Suite A
Little Rock, AR 72114
(501) 324-6395

California
Anaheim Vet Center
859 South Harbor Boulevard
Anaheim, CA 92805
(714) 776-0161

Chico Vet Center
280 Cohasset Road
Chico, CA 95926
(530) 899-8549

Concord Vet Center
1899 Clayton Rd, Suite 140
Concord, CA 94520
(925) 680-4526

Corona Vet Center
800 Magnolia Avenue, Suite 110
Corona, CA 92879-8202
(909)-734-0525

East Los Angeles Vet Center
5400 E Olympic Blvd, #140
East Los Angeles, CA 90022
(323) 728-9966

Eureka Vet Center
2830 G Street, Suite A
Eureka, CA 95501
(707) 444-8271

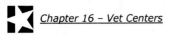

Fresno Vet Center
3636 North 1st St, Suite 112
Fresno, CA 93726
(559) 487-5660

Los Angeles Vet Center
1045 W. Redondo Beach Blvd., Suite 150
Gardena, CA 90247
(310)-767-1221

Oakland Vet Center
1504 Franklin St, Suite 200
Oakland, CA 94612
(510) 763-3904

Redwood City Vet Center
2946 Broadway Street
Redwood City, CA 94062
(650) 299-0672

Rohnert Park Vet Center
6225 State Farm Drive
Suite 101
Rohnert Park, CA 94928
(707) 586-3295

Sacramento Vet Center
1111 Howe Avenue
Suite 390
Sacramento, CA 95825
(916) 566-7430

San Bernardino Vet Center
155 West Hospitality Lane
Suite #140
San Bernardino, CA 92408
(909) 890-0797

San Diego Vet Center
2900 6th Avenue
San Diego, CA 92103
(619) 294-2040

San Francisco Vet Center
505 Polk Street
San Francisco, CA 94102
(415) 441-5051

San Jose Vet Center
278 North 2nd Street
San Jose, CA 95112
(408) 993-0729

Santa Cruz County Vet Center
1350 41st Ave, Suite 102
Capitola, CA 95010
(831)-464-4575

Sepulveda Vet Center
9737 Hascle Street
Sepulveda, CA 91343
(818) 892-9227

Ventura Vet Center
790 E. Santa Clara St., Suite 100
Ventura, CA 93001
(805)-585-1860

Vista Vet Center
1830 West Drive, Suite 103
Vista, CA 92083
(760) 643-2070

West Los Angeles Vet Center
5730 Uplander Way, Suite 100
Culver City, CA 90230
(310) 641-0326

Colorado

Boulder Vet Center
2336 Canyon Blvd, Suite 130
Boulder, CO 80302
(303) 440-7306

Colorado Springs Vet Center
416 East Colorado Avenue
Colorado Springs, CO 80903
(719) 471-9992

Denver Vet Center
7465 E Academy Boulevard
Denver, CO 80220
(303) 326-0645

Ft. Collins Vet Center Outstation
1100 Poudre River Dr. (Lower)
Ft. Collins, CO 80524
(970)-221-5176

Pueblo Vet Center Outstation
509 E. 13th St.
Pueblo, CO 81001
(719) 546-6666

Connecticut
New Haven Vet Center
141 Captain Thomas Boulevard
New Haven, CT 06516
(203) 932-9899

Norwich Vet Center
5 Cliff Street
Norwich, CT 06360
(860) 887-1755

Wethersfield Vet Center
30 Jordan Lane
Wethersfield, CT 06109
(860) 563-2320

Delaware
Wilmington Vet Center
1601 Kirkwood Highway
Wilmington, DE 19805
(302) 994-1660

District of Columbia
Washington, D.C. Vet Center
1250 Taylor Street, NW
Washington, DC 20011
(202) 726-5212

Florida
Fort Lauderdale Vet Center
713 NE 3rd Avenue
Fort Lauderdale, FL 33304
(954) 356-7926

Ft. Myers Outstation Vet Center
3691 Evans
Ft. Myers, FL 33901
(239)-938-1100

Jacksonville Vet Center
300 East State Street
Jacksonville, FL 32202
(904) 232-3621

Key Largo Vet Center Outstation
105662 Overseas Hwy.
Key Largo, FL 33037
(305)-451-0164

Miami Vet Center
2700 SW 3rd Avenue
Suite 1A
Miami, FL 33129
(305) 859-8387

Orlando Vet Center
5575 S Semoran Blvd
Suite 36
Orlando, FL 32822
(407) 857-2800

Palm Beach Vet Center
2311 10th Avenue, North #13
Palm Beach, FL 33461
(561) 585-0441

Pensacola Vet Center
4501 Twin Oaks Drive
Pensacola, FL 32506
(850) 456-5886

Sarasota Vet Center
4801 Swift Road
Sarasota, FL 34231
(941) 927-8285

St. Petersburg Vet Center
2880 1st Avenue, N.
St. Petersburg, FL 33713
(727) 893-3791

Tallahassee Vet Center
548 Bradford Road
Tallahassee, FL 32303
(850) 942-8810

Tampa Vet Center
8900N Armenia Ave, #312
Tampa, FL 33604
(813) 228-2621

Georgia
Atlanta Vet Center
1440 Dutch Valley Place
Suite G, Box 29
Atlanta, GA 30324
(404) 347-7264

Savannah Vet Center
8110A White Bluff Road
Savannah, GA 31406
(912) 652-4097

Guam
Agana Vet Center
222 Chalan Santo Papa Street
Reflection Center, Suite 102
Agana, Guam 96910
(671) 472-7160

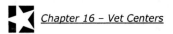

Hawaii
Hilo Vet Center
120 Keawe Street
Suite 201
Hilo, HI 96720
(808) 969-3833

Honolulu Vet Center
1680 Kapiolani Boulevard
Suite F3
Honolulu, HI 96814
(808) 973-8387

Kailua-Kona Vet Center
Pottery Terrace, Fern Building
75-5995 Kuakini Highway, #415
Kailua-Kona, HI 96470
(808) 329-0574

Lihue Vet Center
3-3367 Kuhlo Highway
Suite 101
Lihue, HI 96766
(808) 246-1163

Wailuku Vet Center
35 Lunalilo
Suite 101
Wailuku, HI 96793
(808) 242-8557

Idaho
Boise Vet Center
5440 Franklin Road, Suite 100
Boise, ID 83705
(208) 342-3612

Pocatello Vet Center
1800 Garrett Way
Pocatello, ID 83201
(208) 232-0316

Illinois
Chicago Vet Center
2038 West 95th Street
Suite 200
Chicago, IL 60643
(773) 881-9900

Chicago Heights Vet Center
1600 Halsted Street
Chicago Heights, IL 60411
(708) 754-0340

East St. Louis Vet Center
1265 North 89th Street, Suite 5
East St. Louis, IL 62203
(618) 397-6602

Evanston Vet Center
565 Howard Street
Evanston, IL 60202
(847) 332-1019

Moline Vet Center
1529 46th Avenue, #6
Moline, IL 61265
(309) 762-6954

Oak Park Vet Center
155 S Oak Park Blvd
Oak Park, IL 60302
(708) 383-3225

Peoria Vet Center
3310 North Prospect Street
Peoria, IL 61603
(309) 688-2170

Rockford Vet Center Outstation
4960 E. State St. #3
Rockford, IL 61108
(815)-395-1276

Springfield Vet Center
624 South 4th Street
Springfield, IL 62703
(217) 492-4955

Indiana
Evansville Vet Center
311 North Weinbach Avenue
Evansville, IN 47711
(812) 473-5993

Fort Wayne Vet Center
528 West Berry Street
Fort Wayne, IN 46802
(260) 460-1456

Gary Vet Center
6505 Broadway Ave.
Merrillville, IN 46410
219-736-5633

Indianapolis Vet Center
3833 Meridian, Suite 120
Indianapolis, IN 46208
(317) 927-6440

Iowa
Cedar Rapids Vet Center
1642 42nd Street, N.E.
Cedar Rapids, IA 52402
(319) 378-0016

Des Moines Vet Center
2600 Martin Luther King Jr. Parkway
Des Moines, IA 50310
(515) 284-4929

Sioux City Vet Center
1551 Indian Hills Drive
Sioux City, IA 51104
(712) 255-3808

Kansas
Wichita Vet Center
413 South Pattie
Wichita, KS 67211
(316) 265-3260

Kentucky
Lexington Vet Center
301 East Vine Street, Suite C
Lexington, KY 40507
(859) 253-0717

Louisville Vet Center
1347 South 3rd Street
Louisville, KY 40208
(502) 634-1916

Louisiana
New Orleans Vet Center
2200 Veterans Blvd, Suite 114
Kenner, LA 70062
(504) 464-4743

Shreveport Vet Center
2800 Youree Drive
Building 1, Suite 105
Shreveport, LA 71104
(318) 861-1776

Maine
Bangor Vet Center
352 Harlow Street
Bangor, ME 04401
(207) 947-3391

Caribou Vet Center
York Street Complex
Caribou, ME 04736
(207) 496-3900

Lewiston Vet Center
Parkway Complex
29 Westminster Street
Lewiston, ME 04240
(207) 783-0068

Portland Vet Center
475 Stevens Avenue
Portland, ME 04103
(207) 780-3584

Sanford Vet Center
628 Main Street
Springvale, ME 04083
(207) 490-1513

Maryland
Baltimore Vet Center
1777 Reisterstown Road
Suite 199
Baltimore, MD 21208
(410) 764-9400

Cambridge Vet Center
5510 West Shore Drive
Cambridge, MD 21613
(410) 228-6305

Elkton Vet Center
103 Chesapeake Blvd, Suite A
Elkton, MD 21921
(410) 394-4485

Harford County Vet Center Outstation
223 W. Bel Air Avenue
Aberdeen, MD 21001
(410)-272-6771

Silver Spring Vet Center
1015 Spring St, Suite 101
Silver Spring, MD 20910
(301) 589-1073

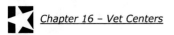

Massachusetts
Boston Vet Center
665 Beacon Street
Boston, MA 02215
(617) 424-0665

Brockton Vet Center
1041-L Pearl Street
Brockton, MA 02401
(508) 580-2730

Lowell Vet Center
73 East Merrimack Street
Lowell, MA 01852
(978) 453-1151

New Bedford Vet Center
468 North Street
New Bedford, MA 02740
(508) 999-6920

Springfield Vet Center
1985 Main Street
Northgate Plaza
Springfield, MA 01103
(413) 737-5167

Worcester Vet Center
597 Lincoln Street
Worcester, MA 01605
(508) 856-7428

Michigan
Dearborn Vet Center
2881 Monroe Street
Suite 100
Deerborn, MI 48124
(313) 277-1428

Detroit Vet Center
4161 Cass Avenue
Detroit, MI 48201
(313) 831-6509

Grand Rapids Vet Center
1940 Eastern SE
Grand Rapids, MI 48507
(616) 243-0385

Michigan Upper Peninsula Vet Center
2600 College Ave.
Escanaba, MI 49829
(906)-789-9732

Minnesota
Duluth Vet Center
405 East Superior Street
Duluth, MN 55802
(218) 722-8654

St. Paul Vet Center
2480 University Avenue
St. Paul, MN 55114
(651) 644-4022

Mississippi
Biloxi Vet Center
288 Veterans Avenue
Biloxi, MS 39531
(228) 388-9938

Jackson Vet Center
4436 North State Street
Suite A3
Jackson, MS 39206
(601) 965-5727

Missouri
Kansas City Vet Center
3931 Main Street
Kansas City, MO 64111
(816) 753-1866

St. Louis Vet Center
2345 Pine Street
St. Louis, MO 63103
(314) 231-1260

Montana
Billings Vet Center
1234 Avenue C
Billings, MT 59102
(406) 657-6071

Missoula Vet Center
500 North Higgins Avenue
Missoula, MT 59802
(406) 721-4918

Nebraska
Lincoln Vet Center
920 L Street
Lincoln, NE 68508
(402) 476-9736

Omaha Vet Center
2428 Cuming Street
Omaha, NE 68131
(402) 346-6735

Nevada
Las Vegas Vet Center
1040 East Sahara Avenue
Suite 102
Las Vegas, NV 89104
(702) 388-6368

Reno Vet Center
1155 West 4th Street
Suite 101
Reno, NV 89503
(775) 323-1294

New Hampshire
Manchester Vet Center
103 Liberty Street
Manchester, NH 03104
(603) 668-7060

New Jersey
Jersey City Vet Center
115 Christopher Columbus Drive
Room 200
Jersey City, NJ 07302
(201) 748-4467

Newark Vet Center
45 Academy Street
Suite 303
Newark, NJ 07102
(973) 645-5954

Trenton Vet Center
171 Jersey St., Building 36
Trenton, NJ 08611
(609) 989-2260

Ventnor Vet Center
6601 Ventnor Avenue, Suite 105
Ventnor, NJ 08406
(609) 487-8387

New Mexico
Albuquerque Vet Center
1600 Mountain Road, NW
Albuquerque, NM 87104
(505) 346-6562

Farmington Vet Center
4251 East Main, Suite B
Farmington, NM 87402
(505) 327-9684

Santa Fe Vet Center
2209 Brothers Road, Suite 110
Santa Fe, NM 87505
(505) 988-6562

New York
Albany Vet Center
875 Central Avenue
Albany, NY 12206
(518) 438-2505

Babylon Vet Center
116 West Main Street
Babylon, NY 11702
(631) 661-3930

Bronx Vet Center
226 East Fordham Road
Room 220
Bronx, NY 10458
(718) 367-3500

Brooklyn Vet Center
25 Chapel Street, Suite 604
Brooklyn, NY 11201
(718) 330-2825

Buffalo Vet Center
564 Franklin Street
Buffalo, NY 14202
(716) 882-0505

Harlem Vet Center
55 West 125th Street
New York, NY 10027
(212) 426-2200

Manhattan Vet Center
32 Broadway, 2nd Floor
Suite 200
New York, NY 10004
(212) 742-9591

Rochester Vet Center
1867 Mount Hope Avenue
Rochester, NY 14620
(585) 232-5040

Staten Island Vet Center
150 Richmond Terrace
Staten Island, NY 10301
(718) 816-4499

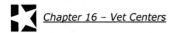

Syracuse Vet Center
716 East Washington Street
Syracuse, NY 13210
(315) 478-7127

White Plains Vet Center
300 Hamilton Avenue
White Plains, NY 10601
(914) 682-6250

Woodhaven Vet Center
75-10B 91st Avenue
Woodhaven, NY 11421
(718) 296-2871

North Carolina
Charlotte Vet Center
223 South Brevard Street
Suite 103
Charlotte, NC 28202
(704) 333-6107

Fayetteville Vet Center
4140 Ramsey St., Suite 110
Fayetteville, NC 28311
(910) 488-6252

Greensboro Vet Center
2009 South Elm-Eugene Street
Greensboro, NC 27406
(336) 333-5366

Greenville Vet Center
150 Arlington Blvd., Suite B
Greenville, NC 27858
(252) 355-7920

Raleigh Vet Center
1649 Old Louisburg Road
Raleigh, NC 27604
(919) 856-4616

North Dakota
Bismarck Vet Center
1684 Capital Way
Bismarck, ND 58501
(701) 244-9751

Fargo Vet Center
3310 Fiechtner Drive, Suite 100
Fargo. MD 58103
(701) 237-0942

Minot Vet Center
2041 3rd Street, N.W.
Minot, ND 58701
(701) 852-0177

Ohio
Cincinnati Vet Center
801-B West 8th Street
Cincinnati, OH 45203
(513) 763-3500

Cleveland Heights Center
2022 Lee Road
Cleveland Heights, OH 44118
(216) 932-8471

Columbus Vet Center
30 Spruce Street
Columbus, OH 43215
(614) 257-5550

Dayton Vet Center
6th Floor, East Medical Plaza
627 Edwin
Dayton, OH 45408
(937) 461-9150

McCafferty Outstation Vet Center
4242 Lorain Avenue, Suite 201
Cleveland, OH 44113
(216)-939-0784

Parma Vet Center
5700 Pearl Rd., Suite 102
Parma, OH 44129
(440) 845-5023

Oklahoma
Cherokee Nation Vet Center
Outstation
17675 South Muskogee
Tahlequah, OK 74465
(918) 456-8219

Oklahoma City Vet Center
3033 North Walnut, Suite 101W
Oklahoma City, OK 73105
(405) 270-5184

Tulsa Vet Center
1408 South Harvard
Tulsa, OK 74112
(918) 748-5105

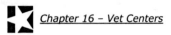

Oregon
Eugene Vet Center
1255 Pearl Street
Eugene, OR 97403
(541) 465-6918

Grants Pass Vet Center
211 S.E. 10th Street
Grants Pass, OR 97526
(541) 479-6912

Portland Vet Center
8383 N.E. Sandy Blvd, Suite 110
Portland, OR 97220
(503) 273-5370

Salem Vet Center
617 Chemeketa St., N.E.
Salem, OR 97301
(503) 362-9911

Pennsylvania
Erie Vet Center
1001 State Street
Suites 1 & 2
Erie, PA 16501
(814) 453-7955

Harrisburg Vet Center
1500 N 2nd Street, Suite 2
Harrisburg, PA 17102
(717) 782-3954

McKeesport Vet Center
2001 Lincoln Way
McKeesport, PA 15131
(412) 678-7704

Philadelphia Vet Center
801 Arch Street, Suite 102
Philadelphia, PA 19107
(215) 627-0238

Philadelphia Vet Center
101 East Olney Avenue
Philadelphia, PA 19120
(215) 924-4670

Pittsburgh Vet Center
2500 Baldwick Road
Pittsburgh, PA 15205
(412) 920-1765

Scranton Vet Center
1002 Pittston Avenue
Scranton, PA 18505
(570) 344-2676

Williamsport Vet Center
805 Penn Street
Williamsport, PA 17701
(570) 327-5281

Puerto Rico
Arecibo Vet Center
52 Gonzalo Marin Street
Arecibo, Puerto Rico 00612-4702
(787) 879-4510

Ponce Vet Center
35 Mayor Street
Ponce, Puerto Rico 00730
(787) 841-3260

San Juan Vet Center
Condominio Medical Center Plaza
Suite LC8A and LC9
Rio Piedras, Puerto Rico 00921
(787) 749-4409

Rhode Island
Warwick Vet Center
2038 Warwick Avenue
Warwick, RI 02889
(401) 739-0167

South Carolina
Columbia Vet Center
1513 Pickens Street
Columbia, SC 29201
(803) 765-9944

Greenville Vet Center
14 Lavinia Avenue
Greenville, SC 29601
(864) 271-2711

North Charleston Vet Center
5603A Rivers Avenue
North Charleston, SC 29406
(843) 747-8387

South Dakota
Pine Ridge Vet Center Outstation
P.O. Box 910, 105 E. Hwy 18
Martin, SD 57747
(605) 685-1300

Rapid City Vet Center
621 Sixth Street, Suite 101
Rapid City, SD 57701
(605) 348-0077

Sioux Falls Vet Center
601 S. Cliff Ave., Suite C
Sioux Falls, SD 57104
(605) 330-4552

Tennessee
Chattanooga Vet Center
951 Eastgate Loop Road
Building 5700, Suite 300
Chattanooga, TN 37411
(423) 855-6570

Johnson City Vet Center
1615A West Market Street
Johnson City, TN 37604
(423) 928-8387

Knoxville Vet Center
2817 East Magnolia Avenue
Knoxville, TN 37914
(865) 545-4680

Memphis Vet Center
1835 Union, Suite 100
Memphis, TN 38104
(901) 544-0173

Texas
Amarillo Vet Center
3414 Olsen Blvd., Suite E
Amarillo, TX 79109
(806) 354-9779

Austin Vet Center
1110 W William Cannon Dr
Suite 301
Austin, TX 78745
(512) 416-1314

Corpus Christi Vet Center
4646 Corona, Suite 250
Corpus Christi, TX 78411
(361) 854-9961

Dallas Vet Center
5232 Forest Lane, Suite 111
Dallas, TX 75244
(214) 361-5896

El Paso Vet Center
1155 Westmoreland
Suite 121
El Paso, TX 79925
(915) 772-0013

Fort Worth Vet Center
1305 West Magnolia, Suite B
Forth Worth, TX 76104
(817) 921-9095

Houston Vet Center
503 Westheimer
Houston, TX 77006
(713) 523-0884

Houston Vet Center
701 N. Post Oak Rd., Suite 102
Houston, TX 77024
(713) 682-2288

Laredo Vet Center
6020 McPherson Road, #1A
Laredo, TX 78041
(956) 723-4680

Lubbock Vet Center
3208 34th Street
Lubbock, TX 79410
(806) 792-9782

McAllen Vet Center
801 Nolana Loop, Suite 115
McAllen, TX 78504
(956) 631-2147

Midland Vet Center
3404 W. Illinois, Suite 1
Midland, TX 79703
(432) 697-8222

San Antonio Vet Center
231 West Cypress Street
San Antonio, TX 78212
(210) 472-4025

Utah
Provo Vet Center
750 North 200 West
Suite 105
Provo, UT 84601
(801) 377-1117

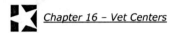

Salt Lake City Vet Center
1354 East 3300 South
Salt Lake City, UT 84106
(801) 584-1294

Vermont
South Burlington Vet Center
359 Dorset Street
South Burlington, VT 05403
(802) 862-1806

White River Junction Vet Center
222 Holiday Drive
Gilman Office Center Building #2
White River Junction, VT 05001
(802) 295-2908

Virginia
Alexandria Vet Center
8796 Sacramento Drive
Suites D & E
Alexandria, VA 22309
(703) 360-8633

Norfolk Vet Center
2200 Colonial Avenue, Suite 3
Norfolk, VA 23517
(757) 623-7584

Richmond Vet Center
4202 Fitzhugh Avenue
Richmond, VA 23230
(804) 353-8958

Roanoke Vet Center
350 Albemarle Avenue, S.W.
Roanoke, VA 24016
(540) 342-9726

Virgin Islands
St. Croix Vet Center
The Village Mall
Rural Route 2
Box 10553, Kingshill
St. Croix, Virgin Islands 00850
(340) 778-5553

St. Thomas Vet Center
9800 Buccaneer Mall, Suite 8
St. Thomas, Virgin Islands 00802
(340) 774-6674

Washington
Bellingham Vet Center
3800 Byron Avenue, Suite 124
Bellingham, WA 98229
(360) 733-9226

Seattle Vet Center
2030 9th Avenue, Suite 210
Seattle, WA 98121
(206) 553-2706

Spokane Vet Center
100 North Mullan Road, Suite 102
Spokane, WA 99206
(509) 444-8387

Tacoma Vet Center
4916 Center Street, Suite E
Tacoma, WA 98409
(253) 565-7038

Yakima Valley Vet Center
1111 North 1st Street
Suite 1
Yakima, WA 98901
(509) 457-2736

West Virginia
Beckley Vet Center
101 Ellison Avenue
Beckley, WV 25801
(304) 252-8220

Charleston Vet Center
521 Central Avenue
Charleston, WV 25302
(304) 343-3825

Huntington Vet Center
3135 16th Street Road
Suite 11
Huntington, WV 25701
(304) 523-8387

Logan Vet Center Outstation
21 Main Street West
Henlawson, WV 25624
(304)-752-4453

Martinsburg Vet Center
900 Winchester Avenue
Martinsburg, WV 25401
(304) 263-6776

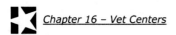

Morgantown Vet Center
1083 Greenbag Road
Morgantown, WV 26508
(304) 291-4303

Princeton Vet Center
905 Mercer Street
Princeton, WV 24740
(304) 425-5653

Wheeling Vet Center
1206 Chapline Street
Wheeling, WV 26003
(304) 232-0587

Wisconsin
Madison Vet Center
147 South Butler Street
Madison, WI 53703
(608) 264-5342

Milwaukee Vet Center
5401 North 76th Street
Milwaukee, WI 53218
(414) 536-1301

Wyoming
Casper Vet Center
111 South Jefferson
Casper, WY 82601
(307) 261-5355

Cheyenne Vet Center
2424 Pioneer Avenue, Suite 103
Cheyenne, WY 82001
(307) 778-7370

CHAPTER 17

EDUCATION BENEFITS

The Veterans' Administration administers ten educational assistance programs, each with different eligibility criteria. Typically, a veteran's eligibility is based on his or her dates of active duty. Generally, only the VA can determine an applicant's eligibility. Specific information regarding educational benefits can be obtained from the Education Service of the VA (1-888-GI-BILL-1) or any VA regional office.

The basic categories of VA educational assistance programs are:

- Montgomery G.I. Bill - Active Duty (MGIB - Chapter 30)
- Montgomery G.I. Bill - Selected Reserve (Chapter 1606)
- Reserve Educational Assistance Program (REAP – Chapter 1607)
- Veterans' Educational Assistance Program (VEAP - Chapter 32)
- Educational Assistance Test Program (Section 901)
- Educational Assistance Pilot Program (Section 903)
- Survivors' and Dependents' Educational Assistance Program (Chapter 35)
- Restored Entitlement Program for Survivors (REPS)
- Vocational Rehabilitation (Chapter 31) (This topic is discussed in detail in Chapter 15 of this book.)
- Omnibus Diplomatic Security and Antiterrorism Act

MGIB, REAP, & MGIB-SR are discussed in the following three chapters. This chapter discusses the remaining seven educational assistance programs.

An individual can be eligible for more than one of the above education benefits. If so, he or she must elect which benefit to receive. Payments for more than one benefit at a time may not be made. *The VA strongly encourages individuals who qualify for more than one type of education benefit to discuss their education plans with a Veterans Benefits Counselor so that all options can be explored, and maximum benefits can be paid.*

VETERANS EDUCATIONAL ASSISTANCE PROGRAM (VEAP) - CHAPTER 32

Veterans who first entered active duty between January 1, 1977 and June 30, 1985 were able to voluntarily contribute to an education account to establish eligibility for this program.

The Post-Vietnam Veterans' Educational Assistance Program is also known as VEAP or Chapter 32.

Veterans who first entered active duty between January 1, 1977 and June 30, 1985 were able to voluntarily contribute to an education account to establish eligibility for this program.

VEAP provides education and training opportunities to eligible persons who contributed to the program while on active duty. If an individual did not contribute, or received a refund of contributions, he or she is not eligible for VEAP benefits. The initial contribution must have been made by March 31, 1987. The maximum contribution by any individual participant is $2,700. A participating member's contributions are matched on a $2 for $1 basis by the Government.

VEAP Eligibility

To qualify for VEAP benefits, individuals must have:

- Entered active duty for the first time between January 1, 1977 and June 30, 1985; and

Benefits are generally payable for 10 years following a veteran's release from active duty.

- Enrolled in and contributed to VEAP before April 1, 1987; and
- Served for a continuous period of 181 days or more (Individuals may be eligible if discharged from a shorter period of active duty for a service-connected disability.); and
- Been discharged or released from service under conditions other than dishonorable; and
- Completed 24 continuous months of active duty if enlisted for the first time after September 7, 1980, or entered active duty as an officer or enlistee after October 16, 1981. (Individuals meet this requirement if they completed a shorter period of active duty to which the service department called or ordered the individual.)

Individuals may be eligible for VEAP benefits if they did not complete 24 continuous months of active duty if they:

- Received VA disability compensation or military disability retirement; or
- Served a period of at least 24 continuous months of active duty before October 17, 1981; or

- Were discharged or released for early out, hardship, or service-connected disability.

Individuals may be eligible for VEAP benefits while still on active duty if they:

- Entered active duty for the first time after December 31, 1976, and before July 1, 1985; and
- Enrolled in and contributed to VEAP before April 1, 1987, and have at least three months of contributions available (For an elementary or high school program, at least one month of contributions must be available.); and
- Served for a continuous period of 181 days or more; and
- Completed their first active duty commitment.

The following types of active duty do not establish eligibility:

- Time assigned by the military to a civilian institution for the same course provided to civilians;
- Time served as a cadet or midshipman at a service academy;
- Time spent on active duty for training in the National Guard or Reserve.

NOTE: Individuals are not eligible for VEAP if they are eligible for the Montgomery GI Bill-Active Duty based on prior eligibility for Vietnam Ear Veterans' Educational Assistance.

Approved Courses

VEAP benefits may be received for a wide variety of training, including:

- Training for a high school diploma or the equivalent
- Undergraduate or graduate degrees from a college or university
- Cooperative training programs
- Accredited independent study programs leading to standard college degrees
- Courses leading to certificates or diplomas from business, technical or vocational schools
- Vocational flight training (Individuals must have a private pilot's license and meet the medical requirements for a desired license before beginning training, and throughout the flight training program)
- Apprenticeship or job training programs offered by a company or union
- Correspondence courses
- VA may approve programs offered by institutions outside of the United States, when they are pursued at educational institutions of higher

learning, and lead to a college degree. Individuals must receive VA approval prior to attending or enrolling in any foreign programs.

- **Effective March 1, 2001**, benefits may be payable for licensing or certification tests. The tests are those needed to enter, maintain, or advance into employment in a civilian vocation or profession. The eligible veteran or family member may receive payment of the fee charged for the test or $2,000, whichever is less. *The tests must be approved for VA benefits.*

If an individual is seeking a college degree, the school must admit him or her to a degree program by the start of the third term.

Restrictions on Training

- Bartending and personality development courses
- Non-accredited independent study courses
- Any course given by radio
- Self-improvement courses such as reading, speaking, woodworking, basic seamanship, and English as a second language
- Any course which is avocational or recreational in character
- Farm cooperative courses
- Audited courses
- Courses not leading to an educational, professional, or vocational objective
- Courses an individual has previously taken and successfully completed
- Courses taken by a Federal government employee under the Government Employees' Training Act
- Courses paid for in whole or in part by the Armed Forces while on active duty
- Courses taken while in receipt of benefits for the same program from the Office of Workers' Compensation Programs

The VA must reduce benefits for individuals in Federal, State or local prisons after being convicted of a felony.

An individual may not receive benefits for a program at a proprietary school if he or she is an owner or official of the school.

Part-Time Training

Individuals unable to attend school full-time should consider going part-time. Benefit rates and entitlement charges are less than the full-time rates. For example, if a student receives full-time benefits for 12 months, the entitlement charge is 12 months. However, if the student receives ½ time benefits for 12 months, the charge is 6 months. VA will pay for less than ½ time training if the student is not receiving Tuition Assistance for those courses.

Remedial, Deficiency And Refresher Training

Remedial and deficiency courses are intended to assist a student in overcoming a deficiency in a particular area of study. In order for such courses to be approved, the courses must be deemed necessary for pursuit of a program of education.

Refresher training is for technological advances that occurred in a field of employment. The advance must have occurred while the student was on active duty, or after release.

There is an entitlement charge for these courses.

Tutorial Assistance

Students may receive a special allowance for individual tutoring if they entered school at one-half time or more. To qualify, the student must have a deficiency in a subject. The school must certify the tutor's qualifications, and the hours of tutoring. Eligible students may receive a maximum monthly payment of $100.00. The maximum total benefit payable is $1,200.00.

There is no entitlement charge for the first $600.00 of tutorial assistance.

To apply for tutorial assistance, students must submit VA Form 22-1990t, Application and Enrollment Certification for Individualized Tutorial Assistance. The form should be given to the certifying official in the office handling VA paperwork at the school for completion.

Months of Benefits / Entitlement Charged

Individuals are charged one full day of entitlement for each day of full-time benefits paid.

Eligible members may be entitled to receive up to 36 months of VEAP benefits. Usually, the number of monthly payments for full-time training is the same as the number of months an individual contributed to VEAP.

Benefits are generally payable for 10 years following a veteran's release from active duty.

Individuals qualifying for more than one VA education program may receive a maximum of 48 months of benefits. For example, if a student used 30 months of Dependents' Educational Assistance, and is eligible for chapter 1606 benefits, he or she could have a maximum of 18 months of entitlement remaining.

Individuals are charged one full day of entitlement for each day of full-time benefits paid.

For correspondence and flight training, one month of entitlement is charged each time VA pays one month of benefits. For cooperative programs, one month of entitlement is used for each month of benefits paid.

For apprenticeship and job training programs, the entitlement charge changes every 6 months. During the first 6 months, the charge is 75% of full time. For the second 6 months, the charge is 55% of full time. For the remainder of the program, the charge is 35% of full time.

Rates of Educational Assistance Pay

The total dollar amount of VEAP benefits is:

- An individual's total contributions, plus
- Matching funds equal to 2 times the individual's contributions, plus
- Any additional contributions or kickers made by the Department of Defense

The amount of money an individual receives each month depends on the type of training and the training time.

Institutional Training:

The monthly benefit payment will vary depending on the amount and number of contributions. Divide the total contributions by the number of months contributed, and this equals the full-time institutional rate.

Example:

Step 1:
$1,800 individual contributions
+3,600 matching funds (2 times individual contribution)
+ -0- kicker
______
$5,400 TOTAL ENTITLEMENT

Step 2:
$5,400 divided by 36 months of contributions = $150 monthly full-time institutional rate

(No amount in excess of an individual's total entitlement can be paid.)

Correspondence Training

An individual can be reimbursed for the entire established charges paid for a correspondence course. However, no amount in excess of an individual's total entitlement can be paid.

Flight Training

Individuals taking flight training will receive 60% of the approved charges for the course, including solo hours. (VA does not pay for solo hours before October 1, 1992.) No amount in excess of an individual's total entitlement can be paid.

Apprenticeship or Job Training

The monthly benefit amount is:

- 75% of the full-time rate for the first 6 months of training;
- 55% of the full-time rate for the second 6 months of training;
- 35% of the full-time rate for the rest of the training.

Monthly payments are reduced if an individual works less than 120 hours a month.

Cooperative Training

Individuals may receive payment at 80% of the rate to which he or she is entitled for institutional training.

Eligibility Periods

Benefits end 10 years from the date of the individual's last discharge or release from active duty.

VA can extend the 10-year period by the amount of time a service member was prevented from training during the period due to a disability or being held by a foreign government or power.

VA may extend the 10-year period if the individual reenters active duty for 90 days or more after becoming eligible. The extension ends 10 years from the date of discharge or release from the later period. Periods of active duty of less than 90 days can qualify for extensions only if discharge or release was due to:

Benefits end 10 years from the date of the individual's last discharge or release from active duty.

- A service-connected disability; or
- A medical condition existing before active duty; or
- Hardship; or
- A reduction in force.

If a discharge is upgraded by the military, the 10-year period begins on the date of the upgrade.

Miscellaneous Information

- Any change in educational, professional or vocational objectives is considered a "*change of program.*" The law permits one change of program without prior VA approval, provided an individual's attendance, conduct and progress in the last program were satisfactory. Additional "*changes of program*" require prior VA approval. VA will not charge a *change of program* if the individual enrolls in a new program after successful completion of the immediately preceding program.

- Once an individual starts receiving benefits, he must maintain satisfactory attendance, conduct and progress. The VA may stop benefits if an individual does not meet the standards set by the school. VA may later resume benefits if the individual reenters the same program at the same school, and the school approves the reentry, and certifies it to VA.

- If the individual does not reenter the same program at the same school, VA may resume benefits if the cause of unsatisfactory attendance, conduct or progress has been removed; and the program that the student intends to pursue is suitable to his or her abilities, aptitudes and interests.

- **Effective November 1, 2000,** VA education benefits can be paid (with some exceptions) for school breaks, if the breaks do not exceed 8 weeks; and the terms before and after the breaks are not shorter than the break. Prior to November 1 2000, VA education benefits could be paid only if the breaks did not exceed a calendar month.

Application For Benefits

When the individual finds a school, program, company, apprenticeship or job-training program, there are two important steps that must be followed:

1. Make sure the program is approved for VA training. Contact the local VA regional office if there are any questions.
2. Compete VA Form 22-1990, Application for Education Benefits. The completed form should be sent to the VA regional office with jurisdiction over the State where training will occur. (See the following section for Areas of VA jurisdiction.) Individuals not on active duty should send copy 4 of Form DD-214 along with the completed VA Form 22-1990.

Following receipt of an application, VA will review it and advise if anything else is needed.

If an individual has started training, the application and Notice of Basic Eligibility should be taken to the school, employer or union. The certifying official should complete VA Form 22-1999, Enrollment Certification, and send all the forms to VA.

Areas Of VA Jurisdiction

Eastern VA
Regional Office
PO Box 4616
Buffalo, NY
14240-4616

Connecticut
Delaware
District of Columbia
Maine
Maryland
Massachusetts
New Hampshire
New Jersey
New York
Ohio
Pennsylvania
Rhode Island
Vermont
Virginia
West Virginia
Foreign Schools

Southern VA
Regional Office
PO Box 100022
Decatur, GA 30031-7022

Alabama
Florida
Georgia
Mississippi
North Carolina
Puerto Rico
South Carolina
U.S. Virgin Islands

Western VA
Regional Office
PO Box 8888
Muskogee, OK
74402-8888

Alaska
Arizona
Arkansas
California
Hawaii
Idaho
Louisiana
New Mexico
Nevada
Oklahoma
Oregon
Philippines
Texas
Utah
Washington
American Samoa
Guam
Midway
Wake Island
Any of the islands in the Federated States of the Marshall Islands, the Republic of Micronesia, or the Republic of Palau

Central VA
Regional Office
PO Box 66830
St. Louis, MO
63166-6830

Colorado
Illinois
Indiana
Iowa
Kansas
Kentucky
Michigan
Minnesota
Missouri
Montana
Nebraska
North Dakota
South Dakota
Tennessee
Wisconsin
Wyoming

Procedures For Receipt of Monthly Payments

After selecting a school and submitting an application to VA, the school official must complete an enrollment certification, and submit it to the appropriate VA regional office. If a student meets the basic eligibility requirements for benefits, and the program or course is approved, VA will process the enrollment based on certified training time.

If a student is enrolled in a degree program at a college or university, he or she will receive payment after the first of each month for the training during the preceding month. If a student is enrolled in a certificate or diploma program at a business, technical, or vocational school, he or she will not receive payment until they have verified their attendance. Students will receive a *Student Verification of Enrollment Form 22-8979* each month, and must complete and return it to the appropriate VA regional office. After processing, VA will release a check.

If an individual is in an apprenticeship or job-training program, he or she will receive a form to report the hours worked each month. The form must be signed and given to the certifying official for the company or union. The certifying official must complete the form and send it to the appropriate VA regional office. After processing, VA will release a check.

If an individual is taking a correspondence course, he or she will receive a form each quarter, on which the student must show the number of lessons completed that quarter. The completed form should be sent to the school for certification of the number of lessons serviced during the quarter. The school will send the form to the appropriate VA regional office. After processing, VA will release a check. Payments are based on the number of lessons serviced by the school.

VA will send flight schools a supply of blank monthly certification of flight training forms. The school must complete the form by entering the number of hours, the hourly rate, and the total charges for flight training received during the month. The student should review and sign the completed form, and send it to the appropriate VA regional office. After processing, VA will release a check.

NOTE: It is against the law for schools to cash VA checks under a Power of Attorney Agreement.

Timely Receipt of Verification Forms And Checks

Once a completed verification form has been submitted, the student should receive a check within 2 weeks. If a check is not received by then, the VA should immediately be contacted so that appropriate action can be taken.

Once a completed verification form has been submitted, the student should receive a check within 2 weeks. If a check is not received by then, the VA should immediately be contacted so that appropriate action can be taken.

Students taking courses leading to a degree at a college or university should receive their checks for each month by the fifth of the next month. If it is not received by then, the VA should be immediately contacted so that appropriate action can be taken.

Students taking courses leading to a certificate or diploma from a business, technical, or vocational school should receive their verification forms for each month by the fifth of the following month. If it is not received by then, the VA should be immediately contacted so that another form can be issued.

Advance Payments

An advance payment for the initial month, or partial month and the following month may be made, if:

- The school agrees to handle advance payments; and
- Training is one-half time or more; and
- A request is made by the individual in writing; and
- The VA receives the enrollment certification at least 30 days prior to the start of classes.

Advance payments are made out to the individual, and sent to the applicable school for delivery to the individual registration. VA cannot issue a check more than 30 days before classes start. Before requesting an advance payment, students should verify with the school certifying official that the school has agreed to process advance payments.

Requests for advance payments must be on VA Form 22-1999, Enrollment Certification, or a sheet of paper attached to the enrollment certification.

Once a student receives an advance payment at registration, the school must certify to VA that the student received the check. If a student reduces enrollment, or withdraws from all courses during the period covered by an advance payment, he or she must repay the overpayment to VA.

If an individual believes that the amount of a VA check is incorrect, the VA should be contacted before the check is cashed.

Direct Deposit

Payments can be sent directly to a student's savings or checking account through Direct Deposit (Electronic Funds Transfer). To sign up for direct deposit by phone, students must call 1-877-838-2778.

Student Responsibilities

To ensure timely receipt of correct payments, students should be sure to promptly notify the VA of:

- Any change in enrollment
- Any change in address

In addition, students should use reasonable judgment when accepting and cashing a check. All letters from VA about monthly rates and effective dates should be read carefully. If a student thinks the amount of a VA check is wrong, VA should be contacted *before* cashing the check. Any incorrect checks should be returned to VA.

If a student cashes a check for the wrong amount, he or she will be liable for repayment of any resulting overpayment.

Recovery of Overpayments

VA must take prompt and aggressive action to recover overpayments. Students have the right to request a waiver of the overpayment, or verification that the amount is correct. If an overpayment is not repaid or waived, VA may add interest and collection fees to the debt. VA may also take one or more of the following actions to collect the debt:

- Withhold future benefits to apply to the debt;
- Refer the debt to a private collection agency;
- Recover the debt from any Federal income tax refund;
- Recover the debt from the salary (if student is a Federal employee);
- File a lawsuit in Federal court to collect the debt;
- Withhold approval of a VA home loan guarantee.

An individual's reserve component will act to collect penalties caused by unsatisfactory participation in the reserve.

Changes in Enrollment

If a student withdraws from one or more courses after the end of the school's drop period, VA will reduce or stop benefits on the date of reduction or withdrawal. Unless the student can show that the change was due to *mitigating circumstances*, the student may have to repay **all** benefits for the course.

VA defines *mitigating circumstances* as "unavoidable and unexpected events that directly interfere with the pursuit of a course, and which are beyond the student's control.

Examples of reasons VA may accept include:

- Extended illness;
- Severe illness or death in immediate family;
- Unscheduled changes in employment; and
- Lack of child care.

Examples of reasons VA may not accept include:

- Withdrawal to avoid a failing grade;
- Dislike of the instructor; and
- Too many courses attempted.

(VA may ask the student to furnish evidence to support the reason for change, such as physician or employer written statements.)

The first time a student withdraws from up to 6 credit hours, VA will "excuse" the withdrawal, and pay benefits for the period attended.

If a student receives a grade that does not count toward graduation, all benefits for the course may have to be repaid.

If a student receives a non-punitive grade, the school will notify VA, and VA may reduce or stop benefits. The student may not have to repay the benefits if he or she can show that the grades were due to mitigating circumstances.

Work-Study Programs

Students may be eligible for an additional allowance under a work-study program that allows students to perform work for VA in return for an hourly wage. Students may perform outreach services under VA supervision, prepare and process VA paperwork, work at a VA medical facility or National Cemetery, or perform other approved activities.

Students must attend school at the three-quarter of full-time rate.

VA will select students for the work-study program based on different factors. Such factors include:

- Disability of the student;
- Ability of the student to complete the work-study contract before the end of his or her eligibility for education benefits;
- Job availability within normal commuting distance to the student.

VA will give the highest priority to a veteran who has a service-connected disability or disabilities rated by VA at 30% or more

The number of applicants selected will depend on the availability of VA-related work at the school or at VA facilities in the area.

Students may work during or between periods of enrollment, and can arrange with VA to work any number of hours during his or her enrollment. However, the maximum number of hours a student may work is 25 times the number of weeks in the enrollment period.

Students will earn an hourly wage equal to the Federal or State minimum wage, whichever is greater. If a student works at a college or university, the school *may* pay the difference between the amount VA pays and the amount the school normally pays other work-study students doing the same job.

Students interested in taking part in a work-study program must complete VA Form 22,8691, Application for Work-Study Allowance. Completed forms should be sent to the nearest VA regional office.

Educational Counseling

VA can provide services to help eligible individuals understand their educational and vocational strengths and weaknesses and to plan:

- An educational or training goal, and the means by which the goal can be reached; or
- An employment goal for which an individual qualifies on the basis of present training or experience.

VA can also help plan an effective job search.

Counseling is available for:

- Service members eligible for VA educational assistance; or
- Service members on active duty and within 180 days of discharge; or
- Veterans with discharges that are not dishonorable, who are within one year from date of discharge.

Vocational Rehabilitation

Vocational rehabilitation helps disabled veterans become independent in daily living. Veterans may also receive assistance in selecting, preparing for, and securing employment that is compatible with their interests, talents, skills, physical capabilities, and goals.

Veterans may qualify for Training and Rehabilitation under Chapter 31 of Title 38, United States Code, if:

Vocational rehabilitation helps disabled veterans become independent in daily living. Veterans may also receive assistance in selecting, preparing for, and securing employment that is compatible with their interests, talents, skills, physical capabilities, and goals.

- The veteran has a service-connected disability or disabilities rated by VA at 20% or more; and
- The veteran received a discharge from active duty that was not dishonorable; and
- The veteran has an employment handicap.

Veterans may also qualify with a service-connected disability or disabilities rated by VA at 10%, and:

- The veteran has a serious employment handicap; or
- The veteran first applied for vocational rehabilitation benefits before November 1, 1990, reapplied after that date, and has an employment handicap.

To apply for vocational rehabilitation, VA for 28-1900, Disabled Veterans Application for Vocational Rehabilitation, must be completed and sent to the nearest VA regional office.

For detailed information on vocational rehabilitation, refer to Chapter 15 of this book.

Refund of VEAP Benefits

If a service member does not wish to use his or her VEAP benefits, he or she must apply to the nearest VA regional office for a refund of his or her contributions.

Appeal of VA Decision

VA decisions on education benefits may be appealed within one year of the date an individual receives notice of a VA decision.

For detailed information on filing an appeal, please refer to Chapter 36 of this book.

EDUCATIONAL AND ASSISTANCE TEST PROGRAM (SECTION 901)

This program was included as part of the "Department of Defense Authorization Act of 1981". The test program is funded by the Department of Defense, and administered by the VA. "Section 901" has been used to identify the program since its inception. However, the title "chapter 107" may also be used.

Section 901 is a noncontributory program in which an eligible participant, or in some cases his or her dependent(s), may receive an educational assistance and subsistence allowance while training at an accredited institution.

Basic eligibility to section 901 benefits was limited to a small group of servicepersons who enlisted between September 30, 1980 and October 1, 1981, met strict guidelines and were selected by the Department of Defense. The Waco Regional Office processes all section 901 payments.

EDUCATIONAL ASSISTANCE PILOT PROGRAM (SECTION 903)

Section 903 is a modified Chapter 32 (VEAP) program, in which the Service Department makes the individual's monthly contributions. Eligibility was limited to a small group of participants, selected by the service department, who enlisted between November 30, 1980 and October 1, 1981. Individuals must have been selected for the pilot program.

SURVIVORS' AND DEPENDENTS EDUCATIONAL ASSISTANCE PROGRAM (DEA) – CHAPTER 35

The Survivors' and Dependents Educational Assistance Program (DEA) was enacted by Congress to provide education and training opportunities to eligible dependents of certain veterans. The program offers up to 45 months of education benefits.

ELIGIBILITY REQUIREMENTS

To qualify, one must be the son, daughter or spouse of:

- A veteran who died, or is permanently and totally disabled as the result of a service-connected disability, which arose out of active service in the Armed Forces.
- A veteran who died from any cause while such service-connected disability was in existence.
- A service member who is missing in action or captured in the line of duty by a hostile force.
- A service member who is being forcibly detained or interned in the line of duty by a foreign power.
- A service member who is hospitalized or receiving outpatient treatment for a service connected permanent and total disability and is likely to be discharged for that disability. This change is effective December 23, 2006.

Important update for service members who are hospitalized or receiving outpatient medical care <u>before their discharge for a total and permanent service-connected disability.</u>

Section 301 of Public Law 109-461 adds a new category to the definition of "eligible person" for DEA benefits . The new category includes the spouse or child of a person who:

- VA determines has a service-connected permanent and total disability; and
- at the time of VA's determination is a member of the Armed Forces who is hospitalized or receiving outpatient medical care, services, or treatment; and
- is likely to be discharged or released from service for this service-connected disability.
-

Persons eligible under this new provision may be eligible for DEA benefits

Eligibility Period: Son Or Daughter

As a son or daughter (including stepchild or adopted child), as long as the individual has entitlement left, he or she may generally receive benefits under this program from age 18 to 26 (8 years).

However, in certain instances, benefits may begin before age 18 and continue after age 26. In some instances, the individual may choose among possible beginning dates.

Effect of Active Duty on Eligibility

Following are the effects of active duty on an individual's period of eligibility. (See also **Effect of Active Duty on Entitlement.**)

- Individuals may not receive DEA benefits while on active duty in the Armed Forces.

- To receive DEA benefits after military service, discharge must not be under dishonorable conditions.

- The eligibility period can generally extend for eight years from the date of the individual's first unconditional release from active duty, if his or her service was between ages 18 and 26. But this extension can't go beyond the individual's 31st birthday.

- If, on or after September 11, 2001, an individual is called to active duty under title 10, or if he or she was involuntarily ordered to full-time National Guard duty under section 502 (f) of title 32 (State authority), in most cases VA can extend the eligibility period for DEA by the number of months and days spent on active duty plus four months. This extension may go beyond the 31st birthday, depending on the facts in the claim.

Other Extensions of The Eligibility Period

Circumstances Beyond An Individual's Control

If evidence is provided that training had to stop because of conditions beyond an individual's control, in some cases VA can extend eligibility for the period he or she had to stop training.

Circumstances that may be considered beyond control (if verified by evidence) include:

- Service in an official missionary capacity;
- Immediate family or financial obligations that require the individual to stop training, for example, to take employment;
- Unavoidable conditions of employment that require the individual to stop training;
- The individual's illness or death; or illness in his or her immediate family.

In Training When Eligibility Ends

If an individual is enrolled in training when eligibility ends, in most cases VA can extend his or her eligibility to the end of the semester or quarter, or to the end of twelve weeks if the course isn't operated on a semester or quarter basis.

Marriage

As a son or daughter, marriage doesn't affect the period of eligibility.

ELIGIBILITY PERIOD: SPOUSE

If a spouse is eligible because the veteran has a permanent and total service-connected disability, benefits generally end 10 years from one of the following dates:

- Effective date of the veteran's permanent and total disability evaluation;
- Date VA notifies the veteran of the permanent and total disability evaluation;
- Beginning date chosen by the spouse, between the date the spouse become eligible and the date VA notifies the veteran of the permanent and total disability evaluation.

Service member held captive or missing

If a spouse is eligible because the veteran or service member is being held or is missing, as:

- A prisoner of war;
- Missing in action; or
- Forcibly held by a foreign government or power;

His or her 10-year period of eligibility begins on the 91st day after the date the service member was listed as a captive or missing.

If the veteran or service member is released from captivity, or is determined to be alive and no longer missing, the spouse's period of eligibility ends on that date. If the spouse is enrolled in training on that date, his or her eligibility may be extended to the end of the term or course.

Veteran Died on Active Duty

If a spouse is eligible because the veteran died on active duty, his or her eligibility period is 20 years from the date of death.

Effect of Active Duty on Eligibility

Following are the effects of active duty on the eligibility period:

- Individuals may not receive DEA benefits while on active duty in the Armed Forces.
- To receive DEA benefits after military service, his or her discharge must not be under dishonorable conditions.
- If, on or after September 11, 2001, the individual was called to active duty under title 10, or involuntarily ordered to full-time National Guard duty under section 502 (f) of title 32 (State authority), in most cases VA can extend the eligibility period for DEA by the number of months and days spent on active duty plus four months.

Effect of Divorce on Eligibility

If marriage to the veteran ends in divorce, the spouse's eligibility for DEA benefits ends on that date. But if he or she is in training, and the divorce occurs through no fault of him or her, VA can extend the eligibility as explained in the next section under ***While in Training.***

Extensions of Eligibility Period

Disability

VA may be able to extend the 10-year eligibility period by the amount of time the spouse was prevented from training during that period because of a disability he or she incurred.

While in Training

If the spouse is enrolled in training when his or her eligibility ends, in most cases VA can extend eligibility to the end of the semester or quarter, or to the end of twelve weeks if the course isn't operated on a semester or quarter basis.

Effect of Remarriage

Before age 57:

- If a surviving spouse remarries before age 57, his or her eligibility ends on the date of remarriage.
- If an individual remarried after November 30, 1999, and the remarriage ends, VA may reinstate eligibility to DEA. The remarriage must be ended by death, divorce, or because the individual stopped living with his or her spouse and stopped holding him or herself out to the public as the person's spouse.
- If a surviving spouse remarried after October 31, 1990, but before November 30, 1999, VA can't reinstate eligibility, even if remarriage ends.

After age 57:

- If a surviving spouse remarries on or after January 1, 2004, and is 57 or older, he or she can still be eligible for DEA benefits.
- (If the surviving spouse remarried after age 57 and before December 16, 2003, ***he or she must have applied in writing before December 16, 2004,*** for eligibility to be reinstated.)

  Note: Remarrying after age 57 doesn't extend the 10-year period of eligibility that was established before remarriage.

  Example: A surviving spouse established eligibility for a 10-year period ending on November 15, 2005, which is 10 years from the date of the veteran's death. She remarried in April

2004 at age 58. She will keep her eligibility for DEA through November 15, 2005.

MONTHS OF BENEFITS PAYABLE

The following applies to sons and daughters (including stepchildren and adopted children), spouses and surviving spouses.

Individuals may be entitled to receive up to 45 months of DEA benefits. They may receive a maximum of 48 months of benefits combined if they are eligible under more than one VA education program.

Individuals are charged one full day for each day of full-time benefits paid. Entitlement is charged in months and days. Each month is counted as 30 days. If he or she trains part-time, VA adjusts the entitlement charge according to the training time

Effect of Active Duty on Available Months of Benefits

- If an individual is called up to active duty under title 10 (federal authority) while he or she is receiving benefits, and has to drop out of school without receiving credit, VA will restore (give back) the months of benefits used for that period of training.

- If called up under title 32 (State authority), VA can't restore the months of benefits used.

Pension, Compensation, and DIC Programs

A son or daughter who is eligible for Chapter 35 benefits, as well as pension, compensation, or Dependency & Indemnity Compensation (DIC) based on school attendance, must elect which benefit to receive. An election of Chapter 35 benefits is a bar to further payment of pension, compensation, or DIC after the age of 18.

NOTE: If a program will last longer than 45 months, the son or daughter may find it to his or her advantage to defer Chapter 35 benefits. He or she could continue to receive pension, compensation, or DIC benefits which are payable as a result of school attendance. *The VA strongly encourages individuals who qualify for more than one type of education benefit to discuss their education plans with a Veterans Benefits Counselor so that all options can be explored, and maximum benefits can be paid.*

Approved Courses

A State agency or VA must approve each program offered by a school or company.

Individuals may receive benefits for a wide variety of training, including:

- Undergraduate degrees from a college or university

- Graduate degrees from a college or university

- Cooperative training programs
- Accredited independent study programs leading to a college degree
- Courses leading to a certificate or diploma from business, technical, or vocational schools
- Apprenticeship or job training program offered by a company or union
- Correspondence courses (spouses only)
- Farm cooperative courses
- Secondary school programs for individuals who are not high school graduates
- Secondary school deficiency or remedial courses to qualify for admission to an educational institution
- Effective November 1, 2000, persons eligible for DEA can receive benefits for VA-approved preparation courses for college and graduate school entrance exams. (The law also allows children to pursue these courses before age 18.)
- Effective March 1, 2001, benefits may be payable for licensing or certification tests. The tests are those needed to enter, maintain, or advance into employment in a civilian vocation or profession. The eligible veteran or family member may receive payment of the fee charged for the test or $2,000, whichever is less. *The tests must be approved for VA benefits.* Contact the VA for a complete list of approved certification tests.

VA may approve programs offered by institutions outside of the United States, when they are pursued at educational institutions of higher learning, and lead to a college degree. Individuals must receive VA approval prior to attending or enrolling in any foreign programs.

An eligible son or daughter who is handicapped by a physical or mental disability that prevents pursuit of an educational program may receive Special Restorative Training. This may involve speech and voice correction, language retraining, lip reading, auditory training, Braille reading and writing, etc.

An eligible spouse or son or daughter over age 14 who is handicapped by a physical or mental disability that prevents pursuit of an educational program may receive Specialized Vocational Training. This includes specialized courses, alone or in combination with other courses, leading to a vocational objective that is suitable for the person and required by reason of physical or mental handicap.

A State agency or VA must approve each program offered by a school or company.

If an individual is seeking a college degree, the school must admit the individual to a degree program by the start of the individual's third term.

Restrictions on Training

Benefits are not payable for the following courses:

- Non-accredited independent study courses
- Bartending and personality development courses
- Correspondence courses (if you are a dependent or surviving child)
- Any course given by radio
- Vocational flight training
- Self-improvement courses such as reading, speaking, woodworking, basic seamanship, and English as a 2nd language
- Any course which is avocational or recreational in character
- Audited courses
- Courses not leading to an educational, professional, or vocational objective
- Courses previously taken and successfully completed
- Courses taken by a Federal government employee under the Government Employee's Training Act
- Courses taken while in receipt of benefits for the same program from the Office of Workers' Compensation Programs

VA must reduce benefits for individuals in Federal, State, or local prisons after being convicted of a felony.

An individual may not receive benefits for a program at a proprietary school if her or she is an owner or official of the school.

An individual may not receive benefits under this program while serving on active duty in the Armed Forces.

Part-Time Training

Individuals unable to attend school full-time should consider going part-time. Benefit rates and entitlement charges are less than the full-time rates. For example, if a student receives full-time benefits for 12 months, the entitlement charge is 12 months. However, if the student receives ½ time benefits for 12 months, the charge is 6 months. VA will pay for less than ½ time training if the student is not receiving Tuition Assistance for those courses.

Remedial, Deficiency and Refresher Training

Remedial and deficiency courses are intended to assist a student in overcoming a deficiency in a particular area of study.

Refresher training is available only at the elementary or secondary level. It is for reviewing or updating material previously covered in a course satisfactorily completed.

There is no entitlement charge for these courses for the first 5 months of training.

Tutorial Assistance

Students may receive a special allowance for individual tutoring performed after September 30, 1992, if they entered school at one-half time or more. To qualify, the student must have a deficiency in a subject. The school must certify the tutor's qualifications, and the hours of tutoring. Eligible students may receive a maximum monthly payment of $100.00. The maximum total benefit payable is $1,200.00.

There is no entitlement charge for the first $600.00 of tutorial assistance.

To apply for tutorial assistance, students must submit VA Form 22-1990t, Application and Enrollment Certification for Individualized Tutorial Assistance. The form should be given to the certifying official in the office handling VA paperwork at the school for completion.

Rates of Educational Assistance

The following basic monthly rates are effective October 1, 2007:

Basic Monthly Rates Survivors' And Dependents Educational Assistance Program (DEA)					
Type of Training	Full-Time	Three-Quarter Time	One-Half Time	Less than ½ Time, But More Than ¼ Time	One-Quarter Time
Institutional	$881.00	$661.00	$439.00	Tuition & Fees, not to exceed $439.00	Tuition & Fees, not to exceed $220.25
Farm Cooperative Training	$710.00	$533.00	$355.00		
Correspondence Training	Entitlement charged at the rate of one month for each $881.00 paid.				
Apprenticeship On-The-Job Training - *10-1-2007 thru 12-31-2007*	First six months: $692.00 Second six months: $540.00 Third six months: $389.00 Remainder of program: $160.00				
Apprenticeship On-The-Job Training - *Effective 1-1-2008*	First six months: $641.00 Second six months: $480.00 Third six months: $317.00 Remainder of program: $160.00				
Special Restorative Training:	$881.00				
Accelerated Charges: Cost of Tuition & Fees in Excess of:	$274.00				
Entitlement Reduced 1 Day For Each	$29.37 (1/30th of Full-Time Rate)				

IMPORTANT UPDATE -

OJT & Apprenticeship Rates to Change January 1, 2008

Effective October 1, 2005 Public Law 108-454, Section 103 temporarily increased the reimbursement rates for On the Job Training & Apprenticeship training. This temporary rate increase was effective from October 1, 2005 to December 31, 2007. Congress has not extended this temporary increase, therefore effective January 1, 2008 reimbursement rates will decrease.

Change of Program

Any change in educational, professional or vocational objectives is considered a "*change of program.*" VA will not charge a change of program when a student enrolls in a new program, provided he or she successfully completed the immediately preceding program.

Spouse, Widow or Widower of Veteran

A spouse, widow, or widower of a veteran may make one change of program without prior VA approval if attendance, conduct, and progress in the last program were satisfactory. VA may approve additional changes if the proposed programs are suitable to the student's abilities, aptitudes, and interests.

Child of Veteran

VA may approve a change of program for sons or daughters if it finds that the new program is suitable to the student's abilities, aptitudes, and interests.

Attendance, Conduct and Progress

Once an individual starts receiving benefits, he must maintain satisfactory attendance, conduct and progress. The VA may stop benefits if an individual does not meet the standards set by the school. VA may later resume benefits if the individual reenters the same program at the same school, and the school approves the reentry, and certifies it to VA.

If the individual does not reenter the same program at the same school, VA may resume benefits if the cause of unsatisfactory attendance, conduct or progress has been removed; and the program that the student intends to pursue is suitable to his or her abilities, aptitudes and interests.

Application For Benefits

When the individual finds a school, company or apprenticeship, there are two important steps that must be followed:

1. Make sure the program is approved for VA training. Contact the local VA regional office if there are any questions.
2. Compete VA Form 22-5490, Application for Survivors' and Dependents' Educational Assistance. The completed form should be sent to the VA regional office with jurisdiction over the State where training will occur. Sons or daughters under legal age must have the application signed by a parent or guardian. Sons or daughters of age can apply alone.

Following receipt of an application, VA will review it and advise if anything else is needed.

If an individual has started training, the application and Notice of Basic Eligibility should be taken to the school, employer or union. The certifying official should complete VA Form 22-1999, Enrollment Certification, and send all the forms to VA.

Procedures For Receipt of Monthly Payments

After selecting a school and submitting an application to VA, the school official must complete an enrollment certification, and submit it to the appropriate VA regional office. If a student meets the basic eligibility requirements for benefits, and the program or course is approved, VA will process the enrollment based on certified training time.

If a student is enrolled in a degree program at a college or university, he or she will receive payment after the first of each month for the training during the preceding month. If a student is enrolled in a certificate or diploma program at a business, technical, or vocational school, he or she will not receive payment until they have verified their attendance. Students will receive a *Student Verification of Enrollment Form 22-8979* each month, and must complete and return it to the appropriate VA regional office. After processing, VA will release a check.

If an individual is in an apprenticeship or job-training program, he or she will receive a form to report the hours worked each month. The form must be signed and given to the certifying official for the company or union. The certifying official must complete the form and send it to the appropriate VA regional office. After processing, VA will release a check.

If an individual is taking a correspondence course, he or she will receive a form each quarter, on which the student must show the number of lessons completed that quarter. The completed form should be sent to the school for certification of the number of lessons serviced during the quarter. The school will send the form to the appropriate VA regional office. After processing, VA will release a check. Payments are based on the number of lessons serviced by the school.

NOTE: It is against the law for schools to cash VA checks under a Power of Attorney Agreement.

Effective November 1, 2000, VA education benefits can be paid (with some exceptions) for school breaks, if the breaks do not exceed 8 weeks; and the terms before and after the breaks are not shorter than the break. Prior to November 1 2000, VA education benefits could be paid only if the breaks did not exceed a calendar month.

Timely Receipt of Verification Forms And Checks

Students taking courses leading to a degree at a college or university should receive their checks for each month by the fifth of the next month. If it is not received by then, the VA should be immediately contacted so that appropriate action can be taken.

Students taking courses leading to a certificate or diploma from a business, technical, or vocational school should receive their verification forms for each month by the fifth of the following month. If it is not received by then, the VA should be immediately contacted so that another form can be issued.

One a completed verification form has been submitted, the student should receive a check within 2 weeks. If a check is not received by then, the VA should immediately be contacted so that appropriate action can be taken.

Advance Payments

An advance payment for the initial month, or partial month and the following month may be made, if:

- The school agrees to handle advance payments; and
- Training is one-half time or more; and
- A request is made by the individual in writing; and
- The VA receives the enrollment certification at least 30 days prior to the start of classes.

Requests for advance payments must be on VA Form 22-1999, Enrollment Certification, or a sheet of paper attached to the enrollment certification.

Advance payments are made out to the individual, and sent to the applicable school for delivery to the individual registration. VA cannot issue a check more than 30 days before classes start. Before requesting an advance payment, students should verify with the school certifying official that the school has agreed to process advance payments.

Requests for advance payments must be on VA Form 22-1999, Enrollment Certification, or a sheet of paper attached to the enrollment certification.

Once a student receives an advance payment at registration, the school must certify to VA that the student received the check. If a student reduces enrollment, or withdraws from all courses during the period covered by an advance payment, he or she must repay the overpayment to VA.

If an individual believes that the amount of a VA check is incorrect, the VA should be contacted before the check is cashed.

Direct Deposit

Payments can be sent directly to a student's savings or checking account through Direct Deposit (Electronic Funds Transfer). To sign up for direct deposit by phone, students must call 1-877-838-2778.

Student Responsibilities

To ensure timely receipt of correct payments, students should be sure to promptly notify the VA of:

- Any change in enrollment;
- Any change in address;
- Any change in marital status (separation from the veteran, divorce from the veteran, or remarriage following the death of the veteran).

In addition, students should use reasonable judgment when accepting and cashing a check. All letters from VA about monthly rates and effective dates should be read carefully. If a student thinks the amount of a VA check is wrong,

VA should be contacted **before** cashing the check. Any incorrect checks should be returned to VA.

If a student cashes a check for the wrong amount, he or she will be liable for repayment of any resulting overpayment.

Recovery of Overpayments

VA must take prompt and aggressive action to recover overpayments. Students have the right to request a waiver of the overpayment, or verification that the amount is correct. If an overpayment is not repaid or waived, VA may add interest and collection fees to the debt. VA may also take one or more of the following actions to collect the debt:

- Withhold future benefits to apply to the debt;
- Refer the debt to a private collection agency;
- Recover the debt from any Federal income tax refund;
- Recover the debt from the salary (if student is a Federal employee);
- File a lawsuit in Federal court to collect the debt;
- Withhold approval of a VA home loan guarantee.

Changes in Enrollment

If a student withdraws from one or more courses after the end of the school's drop period, VA will reduce or stop benefits on the date of reduction or withdrawal. Unless the student can show that the change was due to *mitigating circumstances*, the student may have to repay **all** benefits for the course.

VA defines *mitigating circumstances* as "unavoidable and unexpected events that directly interfere with the pursuit of a course, and which are beyond the student's control.

Examples of reasons VA may accept include:

- Extended illness;
- Severe illness or death in immediate family;
- Unscheduled changes in employment; and
- Lack of child care.

Examples of reasons VA may not accept include:

- Withdrawal to avoid a failing grade;
- Dislike of the instructor; and
- Too many courses attempted.

(VA may ask the student to furnish evidence to support the reason for change, such as physician or employer written statements.)

The first time a student withdraws from up to 6 credit hours, VA will "excuse" the withdrawal, and pay benefits for the period attended.

If a student receives a grade that does not count toward graduation, all benefits for the course may have to be repaid.

If a student receives a non-punitive grade, the school will notify VA, and VA may reduce or stop benefits. The student may not have to repay the benefits if he or she can show that the grades were due to mitigating circumstances.

Work-Study Programs

Students may be eligible for an additional allowance under a work-study program that allows students to perform work for VA in return for an hourly wage. Students may perform outreach services under VA supervision, prepare and process VA paperwork, work at a VA medical facility or National Cemetery, or perform other approved activities.

Students must attend school at the three-quarter of full-time rate.

VA will select students for the work-study program based on different factors. Such factors include:

- Disability of the student;
- Ability of the student to complete the work-study contract before the end of his or her eligibility for education benefits;
- Job availability within normal commuting distance to the student;
- VA will give the highest priority to a veteran who has a service-connected disability or disabilities rated by VA at 30% or more.

The number of applicants selected will depend on the availability of VA-related work at the school or at VA facilities in the area.

Students may work during or between periods of enrollment, and can arrange with VA to work any number of hours during his or her enrollment. However, the maximum number of hours a student may work is 25 times the number of weeks in the enrollment period.

Students will earn an hourly wage equal to the Federal or State minimum wage, whichever is greater. If a student works at a college or university, the school **may** pay the difference between the amount VA pays and the amount the school normally pays other work-study students doing the same job.

Students interested in taking part in a work-study program must complete VA Form 22,8691, Application for Work-Study Allowance. Completed forms should be sent to the nearest VA regional office.

Educational Counseling

Upon request, VA will provide counseling services, including testing, to help qualified individuals:

- Select an educational, vocational, or professional objective;
- Develop a plan to achieve the above objective;
- Overcome any personal or academic problems that may interfere with the successful achievement of the stated objective.

Qualified VA personnel are available to provide counseling services free of charge to qualified individuals. Individuals must pay the cost of any travel to and from the place at which VA provides counseling.

VA requires and provides counseling for each disabled child who needs special services to pursue a program of education and for certain other eligible children.

VA requires and provides counseling for disabled spouses and those who need specialized programs of vocational training as a result of the handicapping effects of their disabilities.

Individuals should contact the nearest VA regional office to make counseling appointments.

Appeal of VA Decision

VA decisions on education benefits may be appealed within one year of the date an individual receives notice of a VA decision.

For detailed information on filing an appeal, please refer to Chapter 36 of this book.

RESTORED ENTITLEMENT PROGRAM FOR SURVIVORS (REPS)

The Restored Entitlement Program for Survivors (REPS) is authorized by Section 156 of Public Law 97-377. This program restores social security benefits that were reduced or terminated by Public Law 97-35, the Omnibus Budget Reconciliation Act of 1981. This act eliminated the "parent with child in care" benefit when a surviving spouse's last child in care attained age 16. REPS restores the benefit until the youngest child in care attains 18, unless entitled to another Social Security benefit of equal or greater value.

The REPS program is funded by the Department of Defense, based on Social Security rules, and administered by the VA.

REPS benefits are payable to certain spouses and children of veterans who died while on active duty before August 13, 1981, or died from disabilities incurred in active duty before August 13, 1981. If a surviving spouse remarries, his or her benefits are terminated. If the child in care leaves the parent's custody, marries or dies, REPS entitlement ends. REPS benefits are reduced by $1 for each $2 of earned income over the exempt amount for Social Security (announced by Social Security Administration at the beginning of each calendar year).

REPS benefits are payable to unmarried children between the ages of 18 and 22 who are full-time students at approved schools beyond the high school level. Benefits are awarded on a school year basis. Each year verification must be received before any additional benefits can be awarded. If the child marries or reduces to less than full-time attendance, benefits will be discontinued. If the child has earned income or wages, REPS benefits are reduced.
REPS benefits are not payable based on service in the commissioned corps of the National Oceanic and Atmospheric Administration, or the Public Health Service.

To apply for REPS benefits, VA Form 21-8924, Application of Surviving Spouse or Child for REPS Benefits must be completed and sent to the local VA regional VA office for basic eligibility determination.

Once completed, the application will be forwarded to the St. Louis office for processing. A *Student Beneficiary Report* is mailed to each student receiving REPS benefits each March. The report confirms enrollment, and allows students to report any earnings.

For specific information, contact the nearest regional VA office.

VOCATIONAL REHABILITATION (CHAPTER 31)

This topic is discussed in detail in Chapter 15 of this book.

OMNIBUS DIPLOMATIC SECURITY AND ANTITERRORISM ACT

Public Law 99-399, The Omnibus Diplomatic Security and Antiterrorism Act of 91986 (the Antiterrorism Act) became effective January 21, 1981. This program is designed to provide educational assistance for persons held as captives, and their dependents.

Under this Act, VA may provide education benefits to:

- Former captives who were employees of the United States Government. Individuals providing personal services to the United States similar to that provided by civil service employees may also be eligible. This includes foreign nationals and resident aliens of the United States.
- Former captives taken during hostile action resulting from their relationship with the United States.
- Family members of individuals in captivity or individuals who die while in captivity.

VA will provide educational benefits to persons eligible under the Antiterrorism Act that are identical to those provided to eligible persons under Chapter 35 of title 38, U.S. Code (Survivors' and Dependents' Educational Assistance Program).

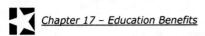

All inquiries regarding this Act should be directed to the nearest VA regional office.

CHAPTER 18

EDUCATION BENEFITS - MONTGOMERY G.I. BILL (MGIB), CHAPTER 30

ELIGIBILITY REQUIREMENTS

The Montgomery G.I. Bill (MGIB) establishes education benefits for four categories of individuals, based on active duty service. The benefits available under each category may vary depending on individual situations and lengths of active duty service. The eligibility requirements for each category are described below. However, the following two requirements must be met by all individuals, no matter which category his or her eligibility falls under:

1. **Character Of Discharge:**

   To use MGIB after an individual is separated from active duty, an individual's discharge must be fully honorable. Discharges "under honorable conditions" and "general" discharges don't establish eligibility for MGIB.

2. **Completed High School:**

   To use MGIB as an active duty member, or after separation from active duty, an individual must obtain a high school diploma or equivalency certificate before applying for benefits.

   Completing 12 hours toward a college degree before applying for benefits also meets this requirement. This is a change in eligibility rules that became effective November 1, 2000. If an individual wasn't previously eligible because he or she did not meet the high school requirement, the change provides a second chance.

In addition to the above requirements, individuals must meet requirements from one of the four following categories. (Individuals who entered active duty before July 1, 1985 may only qualify under Categories 2, 3, or 4.

Category I

- The veteran must have entered active duty for the first time on or after July 1, 1985.
- The veteran must have enrolled in MGIB (didn't decline MGIB in writing upon entry into active duty).

Exception: If an individual declined MGIB in writing, he or she may not change this decision at a later date unless:

- The individual qualifies under Category 3; or
- The individual withdrew his or her election not to participate during the "open period" for withdrawal (December 1, 1988 through June 30, 1989).
- Individuals who graduated from a service academy and received a commission are not eligible.
- Individuals who became commissioned upon completing an ROTC scholarship program are not eligible, unless one of the following exceptions applies:
- The individual received a commission after becoming eligible for MGIB.
- The individual received a commission after September 30, 1996, and received less than $3,400 during any one year of his or her ROTC program.
- Individuals who received loan repayment from the military for their education are not eligible. (Note: Individuals who received loan repayment for one period of active duty, may still be eligible based on another period of active duty, as long as they did not decline MGIB when they first entered active duty.
- To use MGIB while on active duty, an individual must serve two continuous years of active duty.
- To use MGIB after separation from active duty, the individual must have served 3 continuous years of active duty, unless discharged early for one of the following reasons:
- Convenience of the government (veteran must have served 30 months if he had a 3-year obligation)
- Service-connected disability
- Hardship
- A medical condition the individual had before service
- A condition that interfered with performance of duty
- Certain reductions in force (RIF)

Exception: To use MGIB after separation from active duty, the individual may only need 2 years of active duty if:

- He or she first enlisted for 2 years of active duty; or
- The individual has an obligation to serve 4 years in the Selected Reserve (the 2 X 4 program). The individual must enter the Selected Reserve within one year of release from active duty; or

- The individual was separated early for one of the following reasons:
- Convenience of the government (veteran must have served 20 months if he had a 2-year obligation)
- Service-connected disability
- Hardship
- A medical condition the individual had before service
- A condition that interfered with performance of duty
- Certain reductions in force (RIF)

Note: Until November 1, 2000, the above "length of service" requirements had to be met during an individual's *initial* period of active duty.

Effective November 1, 2000, the above "length of service" requirements are no longer based on the *initial* period of active duty - any period of active duty may establish eligibility. Veterans still have to serve their obligated period of service, but that time does not have to be only from their first period of service. They can now serve the required number of years in a later period of service.

Likewise, veterans who were discharged for convenience of the government still have to serve 20 months, if they had a 2-year obligation, or 30 months, if they had an obligation of 3 years or more. However, effective November 1, 2000, that time can now be from a later period of service.

Service In The National Guard Or Reserve

Service in the National Guard or reserve is qualifying as active duty for MGIB benefits only under the following conditions:

1. Full-time National Guard or Reserve service authorized under title 10, U.S. Code (Active Guard/Reserve, or AGR) is considered active duty for purposes of qualifying for VA education benefits, unless the service is active duty for training.
2. Full-time National Guard service under title 32, U.S. Code (State authority) is considered active duty for purposes of qualifying for VA education benefits, provided the service was first performed after November 29, 1989 (with no previous active duty); and is for the purpose of organizing, administering, recruiting, instructing, or training the National Guard. Duty for the purpose of performing operations (such as drug interdiction, for example) is not considered active duty for MGIB benefits.

Category II

- The veteran had remaining entitlement under the Vietnam Era Veterans' Educational Assistance Program (chapter 34 of Title 38, U.S. Code) on December 31, 1989; and
- The veteran served on active duty for any number of days during the period October 19, 1984 to June 30, 1985, and then continued on active duty without a break from July 1, 1985 through:

- June 30, 1988, or
- June 30, 1987, and then served four years in the Selected Reserve after release from active duty. The individual must have entered the Selected Reserve within one year of his or her release from active duty.

  (This option became effective December 27, 2001.)

- The individual wasn't on active duty on October 19, 1984, but reentered active duty after that date, and served three continuous years on active duty on or after July 1, 1985, or two years on active duty followed by four years in the Selected Reserve on or after July 1, 1985. *(This option became effective December 27, 2001.)*
- Individuals who graduated from a service academy and received a commission after December 31, 1976 are not eligible.
- Individuals who received a commission after September 30, 1996 upon completing an ROTC scholarship program are not eligible, unless one of the following exceptions applies:
- The individual received a commission after becoming eligible for MGIB.
- The individual completed ROTC without a full scholarship.
- The individual received a commission after September 30, 1996, and received less than $3,400 during any one year of his or her ROTC program.

Category III

Effective February 3, 1991, the law was amended to allow certain individuals who were involuntarily separated from service as a result of reduction in personnel, who would not otherwise be eligible, to have the opportunity to elect MGIB benefits before separation. A veteran may qualify if:

- The veteran was on active duty on September 30, 1990, and was involuntarily separated after February 2, 1991; or
- The veteran was involuntarily separated on or after November 30, 1993.
- Effective October 23, 1992, the law was expanded to allow the same opportunity to elect MGIB benefits before separation to members voluntarily separated under either the Voluntary Separation Incentive (VSI) or Special Separation Benefit (SSB) program.
- If the member was eligible for the Post Vietnam Era Veterans' Educational Assistance Program (VEAP), he must elect to receive MGIB benefits, and apply for a refund of contributions to Chapter 32.
- The member must have had his military pay reduced by $1,200 before discharge.

Members qualifying under Category III based on a voluntary or involuntary separation are not eligible for MGIB benefits until the day following discharge.

(If a veteran eligible under Category 3 had a chapter 32 *kicker,* VA will pay the basic chapter 30 rate and an additional amount based upon the amount of the remaining kicker.)

Category IV

Individuals may qualify under Category IV if they were on active duty on October 9, 1996, and were VEAP participants with money in the VEAP fund. These individuals must have elected MGIB, and paid $1,200 by October 9, 1997.

Individuals may also be eligible if they served on full time active duty in the National Guard between June 10, 1985 and November 29, 1989, and elected to have their National Guard service count toward establishing eligibility for MGIB benefits by July 9, 1997.

Effective November 1, 2000, VEAP participants, whether they had contributions in their accounts or not, could become eligible for MGIB if they:

- Made an irrevocable election to receive MGIB; and
- Were VEAP participants on or before October 9, 1996; and
- Continuously served on active duty from October 9, 1996 through April 1, 2000; and
- Made a payment of $2,700. The payment will be made by reducing their basic pay before their discharge from service. If $2,700 is not collected before discharge from pay reductions, veterans must make payments to the military service in the amount needed to bring the total to $2,700. DoD can also collect the additional amount by reducing retired or retainer pay.
  (NOTE: This payment, unlike earlier contributions to VEAP is *not refundable.* The payment does not go into the VEAP account, it is deposited into the Treasury of the United States as miscellaneous receipts; and
- Met other VEAP eligibility requirements.
- VEAP participants must have made this election on or before October 31, 2001.

Important Information Regarding Eligibility For Increased Payments:

The Floyd D. Spence National Defense Authorization Act for Fiscal Year 2001 (Public Law 106-398), which was signed into law on October 30, 2000, gives many members of the Armed Forces a chance to receive increased payment for off-duty training and education.

- **Before this law—**the military services in most cases could pay up to 75% of the tuition or expenses charged by the school. This program is known as Tuition Assistance. Eligible service members had to find additional financing, or pay the remaining expenses, from their own pockets. A service member eligible for the Montgomery GI Bill (MGIB), a VA education benefit, wasn't allowed to receive both Tuition Assistance and the MGIB for the same course.

- **Now, with this law**—the military services can pay up to 100% of the tuition and expenses charged by the school, up to limits determined by the Department of Defense. If the tuition and expenses are more than the amount a service department will pay, a service member eligible for MGIB can elect to receive MGIB benefits for all or a part of the remaining expenses. This add-on payment is referred to as a "Top-up" benefit by VA. Top-up benefits are limited to 36 months.

A service member who receives MGIB benefits as a result of the provision will receive a lower rate once he or she is discharged. The full-time monthly rate will be the rate that would have been payable to him or her had he or she not used the MGIB in service for tuition assistance, reduced by the amount of payments received in service, divided by 36.

IMPORTANT UPDATE EFFECTIVE NOVEMBER 1, 2007 -

Army Makes Changes to its Program offering Transferability of GI Bill to Dependents

Effective November 1, 2007 the ***Army*** has made changes to its GI Bill transferability program. Eligible soldiers may now transfer up to 18 months of their GI Bill to spouses or children.

This pilot program is authorized under Title 38, U.S. Code, Chapter 30 (amended by PL 107-107), the Montgomery GI Bill (MGIB).

ELIGIBILITY REQUIREMENTS

Participants must ensure they meet the following eligibility requirements and take the following actions to participate in the program:

- MGIB-era Soldiers who are eligible for MGIB must have enrolled in the MGIB upon initial entry to active duty and paid the $1,200 for MGIB enrollment. (Not eligible are Vietnam Ear-Rollover, VEAP conversion, and Involuntary Separation.)
- Completed at least 6 years of service in the Armed Forces at the time of reenlistment.
- Reenlist for a period of at least 4 years and complete DD Form 2366-2 with their servicing Army Retention Career Counselor.
- Qualify for a MOS Specific Selective Reenlistment Bonus (SRB) and entitled to a Zone B or Zone C bonus at the time of reenlistment.

The following individuals may receive transfer of entitlement:

- The spouse of the individual making the transfer;
- One or more of the children of the individual making the transfer; or

- A combination of the individuals referred above.

A dependent to whom the entitlement is transferred may not begin using the entitlement until:

Spouse:
The Soldier has completed at least six years of service in the Armed Forces.

Child:
The Soldier has completed at least 10 years of service in the Armed Forces, and either:

- The completion by the child of the requirement of a secondary school diploma (or equivalency certificate); or
- The attainment by the child of 18 years of age.

DISCHARGES AND SEPARATIONS

As previously mentioned, if the veteran is separated from active duty, the character of discharge must specifically be listed as "Honorable." "Under Honorable Conditions," or a "General" discharge do not establish eligibility. A discharge for one of the following reasons may result in a reduction of the required length of active duty to qualify for benefits under the MGIB:

- Convenience of the Government; or
- Disability; or
- Hardship; or
- Medical conditions existing before entry into Service; or
- Force reductions; or
- Medical condition which is not a disability due to misconduct, but which prevents satisfactory performance of duty.

CERTAIN TYPES OF ACTIVE DUTY WHICH DO NOT ESTABLISH ELIGIBILITY

The following types of active duty do not establish eligibility for MGIB benefits:

- Time assigned by the military to a civilian institution to take the same course provided to civilians.
- Time served as a cadet or a midshipman at a service academy.
- Time spent on active duty for training in the National Guard or Reserve.

(Please note: Time assigned by the military to a civilian institution, and time served at a service academy does not break the continuity of active duty required to establish eligibility for MGIB benefits. Active duty for training does count toward the four years in the Selected Reserve under the 2 by 4 program.)

APPROVED COURSES

This program provides veterans up to 36 months of education benefits. The benefits may be used for:

- Undergraduate or graduate degrees from a college or university;
- Cooperative training programs;
- Accredited independent study programs leading to standard college degrees;
- Courses leading to certificates or diplomas from business, technical or vocational schools;
- Vocational flight training (from September 30, 1990 only – Individuals must have a private pilot's license and meet the medical requirements for a desired license before beginning training, and throughout the flight training program);
- Apprenticeship / job training programs offered by a company or union;
- Correspondence courses;
- VA may approve programs offered by institutions outside of the United States, when they are pursued at educational institutions of higher learning, and lead to an associate or higher degree, or the equivalent. Individuals must receive VA approval prior to attending or enrolling in any foreign programs;
- Effective March 1, 2001, benefits can be payable for licensing or certification tests. The tests are those needed to enter, maintain, or advance into employment in a civilian vocation or profession. The eligible veteran or family member may receive payment of the fee charged for the test or $2,000, whichever is less. Individuals may take as many tests as needed. They do not have to pass the test to receive benefits. Individuals can receive benefits to retake a failed test, and to renew or update a license or certificate. *The tests must be approved for VA benefits*. Contact the VA for a complete list of approved certification tests.

UPDATE – Public Law 108-183, The Veterans Benefits Act of 2003, expands, effective June 16, 2004, the MGIB program to cover self-employment training programs of less than six months, and entrepreneurship courses at approved institutions.

If an individual is seeking a college degree, the school must admit the individual to a degree program by the start of the individual's third term.

Under certain circumstances, remedial, deficiency and refresher courses may be approved. A special allowance for tutorial assistance, vocational counseling, and work-study programs may also be payable to individuals.

RESTRICTIONS ON TRAINING

- Bartending and personality development courses;
- Non-accredited independent study courses;
- Any course given by radio;
- Self-improvement courses such as reading, speaking, woodworking, basic seamanship, and English as a second language;
- Any course which is avocational or recreational in character;
- Farm cooperative courses;
- Audited courses;
- Courses not leading to an educational, professional, or vocational objective;
- Courses an individual has previously completed;
- Courses taken by a Federal government employee under the Government Employees' Training Act;
- Courses paid for in whole or in part by the Armed Forces while on active duty;
- Courses taken while in receipt of benefits for the same program from the Office of Workers' Compensation Programs.

The VA must reduce benefits for individuals in Federal, State or local prisons after being convicted of a felony.

An individual may not receive benefits for a program at a proprietary school if he or she is an owner or official of the school.

Benefits are generally payable for 10 years following a veteran's release from active duty.

PART-TIME TRAINING

Individuals unable to attend school full-time should consider going part-time. Benefit rates and entitlement charges are pro-rated as follows:

- Individuals who are on active duty or training at less than one-half time, will receive the lesser of:
    - The monthly rate based on tuition and fees for the course(s); or
    - The maximum monthly rate based on training time.
- Individuals training at less than one-half time will receive payment in one sum for the whole enrollment period.

REMEDIAL, DEFICIENCY AND REFRESHER TRAINING

Remedial and deficiency courses are intended to assist a student in overcoming a deficiency in a particular area of study. In order for such courses to be approved, the courses must be deemed necessary for pursuit of a program of education.

Refresher training is for technological advances that occurred in a field of employment. The advance must have occurred while the student was on active duty, or after release.

There is an entitlement charge for these courses.

TUTORIAL ASSISTANCE

Students may receive a special allowance for individual tutoring, if attending school at one-half time or more. To qualify, the student must have a deficiency in a subject. The school must certify the tutor's qualifications, and the hours of tutoring. Eligible students may receive a maximum monthly payment of $100.00. The maximum total benefit payable is $1,200.00.

There is no entitlement charge for the first $600.00 of tutorial assistance.

To apply for tutorial assistance, students must submit VA Form 22-1990t, Application and Enrollment Certification for Individualized Tutorial Assistance. The form should be given to the certifying official in the office handling VA paperwork at the school for completion.

MONTHS OF BENEFITS / ENTITLEMENT CHARGED

Individuals who complete their full period of enlistment may receive up to 36 months of MGIB benefits.

Individuals are considered to have completed their full enlistment period if they are discharged for the convenience of the government after completing 20 months of an enlistment of less than three years; or 30 months of an enlistment of three years or more.

Individuals will earn only one month of entitlement for each month of active duty after June 39, 1985, if they are discharged for other specific reasons (i.e. service-connected disability, reduction in force, hardship, etc.) before completing the enlistment period.

Individuals will earn one month of entitlement for each four months in the Selected Reserve after June 30, 1985.

Individuals qualifying for more than one VA education program may receive a maximum of 48 months of benefits. For example, if a student used 30 months of Dependents' Educational Assistance, and is eligible for chapter 1606 benefits, he or she could have a maximum of 18 months of entitlement remaining.

Individuals are charged one full day of entitlement for each day of full-time benefits paid. For correspondence and flight training, individuals use one month of entitlement each time the VA pays the equivalent of one month of full-time benefits. Individuals pursuing a cooperative program use one month for each month of benefits paid.

For apprenticeship and job-training programs, the entitlement charge during the first 6 months is 75% of full-time. For the second six months, the charge is 55% of full-time. For the rest of the program, the charge is 35% of full-time.

VA can extend entitlement to the end of a term, quarter, or semester if the ending date of an individual's entitlement falls within such period. If a school does not operate on a term basis, entitlement can be extended for 12 weeks.

RATES OF EDUCATIONAL ASSISTANCE AFTER SEPARATION FROM ACTIVE DUTY

The basic monthly rates increase October 1 every year with the Consumer Price Index (CPI) increase. While in training, students receive a letter with the current rates when the increase goes into effect each year. The rates may increase at other times by an act of Congress.

Basic Monthly Rates for College and Vocational School

For approved programs in college and vocational or technical schools, basic payments are monthly and the rates are based on training time. When students train at less than half time, they will be paid tuition and fees. But if tuition and fees amount to more than would be paid at the half-time rate (or the quarter-time rate if training at quarter-time or less), payments will be limited to the half time (or the quarter-time rate).

For on-the-job training (OJT) and apprenticeship programs, rates are monthly and based on the length of time in the program. MGIB rates decrease as the student's wages increase according to an approved wage schedule.

Rates For Other Types of Training

For correspondence courses, students receive 55% of the approved charges for the course.

For flight training, students receive 60% of the approved charges for the course. For reimbursement of tests for licenses or certifications, students receive 100% of the charges up to a maximum of $2,000 per test.

RATES OF EDUCATIONAL ASSISTANCE *WHILE ON ACTIVE DUTY*

If a service member goes to school while on active duty, he or she may have two options for using MGIB benefits. The may be eligible to receive:

- "Regular" MGIB; or
- Tuition Assistance plus MGIB, or Tuition Assistance "Top-Up"

Using "Regular" MGIB on Active Duty

If a service member uses "regular" MGIB while on active duty, VA can pay whichever is less:

- The monthly rate based on tuition and fees for your course(s); or
- The maximum monthly MGIB rate (basic rate plus any increases he or she may qualify for).

The basic monthly rates increase October 1 every year with the Consumer Price Index (CPI) increase. While in training, students receive a letter with the current rates when the increase goes into effect each year. The rates may increase at other times by an act of Congress.

Using Tuition Assistance "Top-Up"

If a student is on active duty, he or she may be eligible to receive Tuition Assistance (TA) from his or her branch of service. If the student has been on active duty for two years, he or she may also be eligible to use MGIB to supplement, or "top up," the TA. Top-up covers the remaining percentage of costs approved for TA that TA alone doesn't' cover—***up to specified limits***. For example, if a student's service authorizes 75% of costs, top-up can pay the remaining 25% of costs approved for TA.

Following are some questions and answers provided by VA regarding the "Top-Up" program.

(From the Floyd D. Spence National Defense Authorization Act for Fiscal Year 2001 - Public Law 106-398)

Question: What does this provision change?
Answer: Before this law, the military services, through their Tuition Assistance program, generally could pay up to 75% of the tuition or expenses charged by the school. Eligible service members had to find additional financing, or pay the remaining expenses from their own pockets. A service member eligible for the Montgomery GI Bill (MGIB), a VA education benefit, wasn't allowed to receive both Tuition Assistance and the MGIB for the same course.

Because of the new law, the military services can now pay up to 100% of the tuition and expenses charged by the school up to limits established by DOD. If the tuition and expenses are more than the amount a service department will pay, a service member eligible for MGIB can elect to receive MGIB benefits for all or a part of the remaining expenses. VA is calling this add-on payment "Top-up."

Question: What does this provision mean to me?
Answer: If you're eligible for MGIB, and plan to use Tuition Assistance (TA), and your service will not pay 100% of tuition and fees, you can use MGIB Top-up to pay the balance.

Question: Can VEAP converters and service members eligible for MGIB based on Vietnam Era service receive the Top-up?
Answer: Yes, anyone who is eligible for MGIB - Active Duty (not MGIB - Selected Reserves) can receive the Top-up benefits.

Question: Is this a good deal for me?
Answer: Using Top-up is a good deal if you plan to use TA to complete a degree program while on active duty, and don't plan to continue your education

after service. Top-up can also be helpful for just taking a few courses with TA while on active duty. Then you can save most of your MGIB to use after service to complete your education program.

You need to consider carefully your own situations, and check with your education officer or counselor, before applying for Top-up. For example, if you plan to take expensive courses using Top-up, you need to consider whether you'll take additional training after you're discharged from active duty. If so, you need to understand the effect of using the Top-up. You can then calculate whether your remaining benefits will cover the additional training you might need.

Question: Is there a limit to the amount of Top-up I can use?
Answer: Yes, Top-up is limited to 36 months of payments. For example, if you are paid Top-up for a 3-month course, you use 3 of the 36 months.

Question: Does this mean if I use 36 months of Top-up, I've used up all my MGIB benefits?
Answer: Probably not. The 36-month limit for Top-up is based on 1 month used for each month of Top-up paid no matter how much is paid. Your regular MGIB entitlement is based on your full-time monthly rate. For example, if your full-time rate is $600 and you are paid $300 Top-up, you only use 1/2 month of your MGIB ($300 is 1/2 of $600).

Question: Can the Top-up apply retroactively, to training already received?
Answer: Yes, the Top-up can apply retroactively, **but** you must be eligible for the Montgomery GI Bill, **and** we can only go back one year from the date your claim was/is received in VA **and** only for training in terms that began on or after October 30, 2000, which is the effective date of the law.

Question: Will DoD pay 100% tuition assistance?
Answer: DoD will encourage services to pay 100% TA if their budgets permit, but this could vary from service to service. Of course, if DoD does pay 100%, you won't need to use MGIB Top-up.

Question: What should I do to apply for Top-up?
Answer: If you want to use Top-up for winter term 2001 or later, go ahead and file the claim following the instructions below.

If you haven't previously filed a claim for MGIB, you should do the following:

Request TA from your branch of service. See your education services officer or education counselor.

Complete an application for VA education benefits, VA Form 22-1990. Indicate "Top-up" on the VA application in item 1A under the MGIB–Active Duty block. Send your TA approval form, along with the application for VA education benefits, to the VA Regional Processing Office that handles your claim. The address is on the form.

If you've previously filed a claim for MGIB and weren't denied benefits, simply submit your signed TA approval form to the VA Regional Processing Office that handles your claim.

Important: These claims are handled differently from claims for MGIB without TA. For Top-up claims, you **won't** need to check in with the school official who certifies VA benefits. VA won't need an enrollment certification on VA Form 22-1999. You won't need to check for approval of the program for VA benefits; approval isn't an issue. That's because Top-up is payable for any course for which TA is payable under DOD criteria.

VA determines your eligibility for MGIB. If you're eligible for MGIB, the TA approval form establishes your eligibility for Top-up. No certifications from the school are needed.

What about the signatures on the TA approval form? The TA approval form must be signed by the approving DoD officials. Some branches of service require the commanding officer's signature; some require the education service officer's signature.

DETAILED RATES OF EDUCATIONAL ASSISTANCE

The rates, effective October 1, 2007, are detailed in the following charts.

BASIC MONTHLY RATES EFFECTIVE OCTOBER 1, 2007
Montgomery G.I. Bill - Active Duty (MGIB), Chapter 30

Type of Training	Full-Time	Three-Quarter Time	One-Half Time	Less than ½ Time, But More Than ¼ Time	One-Quarter Time
Institutional	$1101.00	$825.75	$550.50	Tuition & Fees, not to exceed $550.50	$275.25
Cooperative Training	$1101.00 (Full-Time Only)				
Correspondence Training	Entitlement charged at the rate of one month for each $1101.00 paid				
Apprenticeship On-The-Job Training - *10-1-2007 thru 12-31-2007*	First six months: $935.85 Second six months: $715.65 Remainder of program: $495.45				
Apprenticeship On-The-Job Training - *Effective 1-1-2008*	First six months: $825.75 Second six months: $605.55 Remainder of program: $385.35				
Flight Training	Entitlement charged at the rate of one month for each $1101.00 paid				

BASIC MONTHLY RATES EFFECTIVE OCTOBER 1, 2007 FOR PERSONS WHOSE INITIAL ACTIVE DUTY OBLIGATION WAS LESS THAN THREE YEARS, AND WHO SERVED LESS THAN THREE YEARS (EXCLUDING 2 X 4 PARTICIPANTS)					
Type of Training	**Full-Time**	**Three-Quarter Time**	**One-Half Time**	**Less than ½ Time, But More Than ¼ Time**	**One-Quarter Time**
Institutional	$894.00	$670.50	$447.00	Tuition & Fees, not to exceed $447.00	$223.50
Cooperative Training	$894.00 (Full-Time Only)				
Correspondence Training	Entitlement charged at the rate of one month for each $894.00 paid				
Apprenticeship On-The-Job Training - *10-1-2007 thru 12-31-2007*	First six months: $759.90 Second six months: $581.10 Remainder of program: $402.30				
Apprenticeship On-The-Job Training - *Effective 1-1-2008*	First six months: $670.50 Second six months: $491.70 Remainder of program: $312.90				
Flight Training	Entitlement charged at the rate of one month for each $894.00 paid				

BASIC INSTITUTIONAL RATES EFFECTIVE OCTOBER 1, 2007 FOR PERSONS WITH REMAINING ENTITLEMENT UNDER CHAPTER 34 OF TITLE 38, U.S.C.				
Time	**No Dependents**	**One Dependent**	**Two Dependents**	**Each Add'l Dependent**
Full	$1289.00	$1325.00	$1356.00	$16.00
Three-Quarter	$967.25	$993.75	$1017.25	$12.00
One-Half	$644.50	$662.50	$678.00	$8.50
Less Than 1/2, But More Than 1/4	Tuition and fees, not to exceed the rate of $644.50			
One-Quarter	Tuition and fees, not to exceed the rate of $322.25			
Cooperative	$1289.00	$1325.00	$1356.00	$16.00

BASIC JOB TRAINING RATES EFFECTIVE
OCTOBER 1, 2007 THRU DECEMBER 31, 2007
FOR PERSONS WITH REMAINING ENTITLEMENT
UNDER CHAPTER 34 OF TITLE 38, U.S.C.

Apprenticeship and On-The-Job Training

Time	No Dependents	One Dependent	Two Dependents	Each Add'l Dependent
First six months	$1052.30	$1066.33	$1078.65	$5.95
Second six months	$782.28	$793.33	$802.43	$4.55
Third six months	$526.05	$533.93	$540.00	$3.15
Remainder	$510.75	$518.18	$524.93	$3.15

BASIC JOB TRAINING RATES EFFECTIVE
JANUARY 1, 2008
FOR PERSONS WITH REMAINING ENTITLEMENT
UNDER CHAPTER 34 OF TITLE 38, U.S.C.

Apprenticeship and On-The-Job Training

Time	No Dependents	One Dependent	Two Dependents	Each Add'l Dependent
First six months	$928.50	$940.88	$951.75	$5.25
Second six months	$661.93	$671.28	$678.98	$3.85
Third six months	$409.15	$415.28	$420.00	$2.45
Remainder	$397.25	$403.03	$408.28	$2.45

SPECIAL NOTES:

- Cooperative Training is full time only.
- Individuals taking correspondence courses will receive 55% of the approved charges for the course.
- Individuals taking flight training will receive 60% of the approved charges for the course, including solo hours.

Increases Above Basic Rates

Individuals may qualify for the following increases above their basic monthly rates. These increases don't apply to correspondence courses, the test for a license or certification, or flight training.

College Fund
Certain branches of service may offer the College Fund. The College Fund money, or "kicker," is an additional amount of money that increases the basic MGIB monthly benefit and is included in the VA payment.

Important: Students can't receive College Fund money without receiving MGIB. A common misunderstanding is that the College Fund is a separate benefit from MGIB. The College Fund is an add-on to the MGIB benefit.

VEAP "KICKER."
VA pays an additional amount, commonly known as a "kicker," if directed by the Department of Defense (DoD). If an individual is eligible under Category 3 or Category 4 and has a VEAP kicker, he or she can receive the amount of the VEAP kicker contributed by the service department divided by the total months of MGIB eligibility.

Increase based on contributions made up to $600.
Individuals may be eligible to make these contributions if they are eligible for MGIB under Category 1, and on active duty, or were separated from active duty during the period November 1, 2000, to May 1, 2001.

Important: If an individual was separated during this period, **he or she must have made these contributions by July 31. 2001.**

Unfortunately, the law doesn't allow these contributions from individuals who are eligible for MGIB under Categories 2, 3, or 4.

If a service member was originally eligible under Category 1 and made contributions, but later become eligible under Category 3 because of the type of separation, he or she can still use the contributions to increase the MGIB rate.

Caution: Unless a student takes expensive courses, he or she won't receive the increases while training on active duty (or while training at less than half time after discharged) because VA can't pay more than the tuition and fees charged for the course.

ACCELERATED PAYMENTS FOR EDUCATION LEADING TO EMPLOYMENT IN HIGH TECHNOLOGY

One of the provisions contained in the Veterans Education and Benefits Expansion Act of 2001 (Public Law 107-103) called for accelerated payments for education leading to employment in high technology, effective October 1, 2002. Following are questions and answers provided by the VA regarding this provision.

What is an Accelerated Payment?

An accelerated payment is a lump sum payment of 60% of tuition and fees for certain high cost, high tech programs. If a participant does not have sufficient entitlement to cover 60% of tuition and fees, he or she will receive pay based on the actual remaining entitlement.

VA will make accelerated payments for one term, quarter, or semester at a time. However, if the program is not offered on a term, quarter or semester basis, the accelerated payment is paid for the entire program. To qualify, a participant must be enrolled in a high tech program and must certify that he or she intends to seek employment in a high tech industry as defined by VA. Accelerated payment is paid instead of Montgomery GI Bill benefits that would otherwise have been received.

Who qualifies for accelerated payments?

Only individuals eligible for the Montgomery GI Bill - Active Duty (Chapter 30) qualify for accelerated payments.

How high do the tuition and fees have to be?

To receive accelerated payment, the tuition and fees must be more than double the Montgomery GI Bill benefits that a participant would otherwise receive for that term. For example, if the full-time rate is $732 and a participant is enrolled in a 4-month semester, the tuition and fees must be over $5,856 (4 months x $732=$2,928; $5,856=2 x $2,928) before he or she could receive an accelerated payment.

If a participant receives $900 in monthly benefits, the tuition and fees must be over $7,200 (4 months x $900=$3,600; $7,200= 2 x $3,600).

If a participant receives $1,050 in monthly benefits, the tuition and fees must be over $8,400 (4 months x $1,050 = $4,200; 2 x $4,200 = $8,400).

What programs qualify for accelerated payment?

Both degree and non-degree programs qualify. A participant must be enrolled in a program in one of the following categories:

Life science or physical science (but not social science);
Engineering (all fields);
Mathematics;
Engineering and science technology;
Computer specialties; and·
Engineering, science, and computer management

What industries qualify for accelerated payments?

A participant must intend to seek employment in one of the following industries:

Biotechnology;
Life Science Technologies;
Opto-electronics;
Computers and telecommunications;
Electronics;
Computer-integrated manufacturing;
Material Design;
Aerospace;
Weapons;
Nuclear technology

How does a participant apply for accelerated payments?

The individual must ask the school to include his or her request for accelerated payment to VA when it sends the enrollment information to VA for processing. The individual's request must include his or her certification of intent to seek employment in a high technology industry.

How is the education entitlement charged?

VA will divide the accelerated payment by the amount of the individual's full-time monthly rate (including kickers and additional contributions) and will reduce the entitlement by the resulting number of months and days.

Example: Jill received an accelerated payment of $3,600. Her full-time rate is $900. VA will charge her entitlement as follows: $3,600/$900 = 4 months.

When can accelerated payments be made?

Accelerated payments may only be made for terms or other enrollment periods that begin on or after October 1, 2002.

Can school related expenses (such as books, supplies, and living expenses) be counted as tuition and fees for accelerated payments?

No. Only the school's tuition and fees can be considered for accelerated payment.

Can an individual receive accelerated payments for short, non-degree course?

Yes, as long as they are approved for VA benefits. Short, expensive, IT courses offered by businesses typically are <u>not</u> approved for VA benefits.

Can an individual receive accelerated payments for non-technical courses (such as English, history, etc.) when taking those courses as part of a high technology program?

Yes. However, the degree or certificate must require the completion of these other non-technical courses.

Is it possible to receive an accelerated payment check before a school term begins?

No. VA needs to verify that the individual has enrolled before sending out the large payment. VA will pay the student as soon after the start of the term as possible. Individuals will receive payment faster if they receive direct deposit.

Does a student have to verify enrollment each month if he or she receives an accelerated payment?

No. After the individual completes his or her enrollment, VA will ask the student to verify that he or she have received the accelerated payment. VA will also ask the individual to indicate how he or she used the accelerated payment (such as toward tuition, fees and books and supplies). VA is asking the latter question for statistical purposes only because the law requires them to collect this information. A student's answer will have no bearing on his or her entitlement to the accelerated payment. The student must respond to these questions within 60 days from the end of the enrollment period or VA will create an overpayment equal to the accelerated payment. As with any course, the student must notify VA of any change in his or her enrollment. The student's school must report any changes as well.

Is there any financial risk with accelerated payment?

Yes. If a student receives a grade, which does not count toward graduation requirements, he or she may have to repay all or part of the accelerated payment, depending on the circumstances. This could be a large amount of money.

Do the accelerated payments have to be paid back if the individual fails to find employment in a high technology industry?

No. The fact that he or she intended to find employment in a high technology industry is sufficient.

List Of Approved High Technology Programs

1.09 Animal Sciences
01.0901 Animal Sciences, General
01.0902 Agricultural Animal Breeding
01.0903 Animal Health
01.0904 Animal Nutrition
01.0905 Dairy Science
01.0906 Livestock Management
01.0907 Poultry Science

01.10 Food Science and Technology
01.1001 Food Science
01.1002 Food Technology and Processing
01.1099 Food Science and Technology
01.1101 Plant Sciences General
01.1102 Agronomy and Crop Science
01.1103 Horticultural Science
01.1104 Agricultural and Horticultural Plant Breeding
01.1105 Plant Protection and Integrated Pest Management
01.1106 Range Science Management

01.12 Soil Sciences
01.1201 Soil Science and Agronomy General
01.1202 Soil Chemistry and Physics
01.1203 Soil Microbiology
01.1299 Soil Sciences

03.01 Natural Resources Conservation and Research
03.0104 Environmental Science

03.03 Fishing and Fisheries Sciences and Management

03.05 Forestry
03.0501 Forestry, General

03.0502 Forest Sciences and Biology
03.0506 Forest Management/Forest Resources Management
03.0508 Urban Forestry
03.0509 Wood Science and Wood Products/Pulp and Paper Technology
03.0510 Forest Resources Production and Management
03.0511 Forest Technology/Technician

03.06 Wildlife and Wildlands Science and Management

09.07 Radio, Television, and Digital Communication
09.0702 Digital Communication and Media/Multimedia

11.0101 Computer and Information Sciences, General
11.0102 Artificial Intelligence and Robotics
11.0103 Information Technology
11.0199 Computer and Information Sciences

11.02 Computer Programming
11.0201 Computer Programming/Programmer General
11.0202 Computer Programming Specific Applications

11.03 Data Processing
11.0301 Data Process and Data Processing Technology/Technician

11.04 Information Science/Studies

11.05 Computer Systems Analysis

11.07 Computer Science

11.08 Computer Software and Media Application
11.0801 Web Page, Digital/Multimedia and Information Resources Design
11.0802 Data Modeling/Warehousing and Database Administration
11.0803 Computer Graphics
11.0899 Computer Software and Media Applications, Other.

11.09 Computer System Networking and Telecommunications

11.10 Computer/Information Technology Administration and Management
11.1001 System Administration/Administrator
11.1002 System, Networking and LAN/WAN Management/Manager
11.1003 Computer and Information Systems Security
11.1004 Web/Multimedia Management and Webmaster

***14. Engineering**.
Instructional program that prepare individuals to apply mathematical and scientific principles to the solution of practical problems.

***15. Engineering Technologies/Technicians**.
Instructional programs that prepare individuals to apply basic engineering principles and technical skills in support of engineering and related projects.

***26. Biological and Biomedical Sciences.**

Instructional programs that focus on the biological sciences and the non-clinical biomedical sciences, and that prepare individuals for research and professional careers as biologist and biomedical scientist.

***27. Mathematics and Statistics.**
Instructional programs that focus on the systematic study of logical symbolic language and its applications.

***29. Military Technologies.**
A program that prepares individuals to undertake advanced and specialized leadership and technical responsibilities for the armed services and related national security organizations. Includes instruction in such areas as weapons systems and technology, communications, intelligence, management, logistics and strategy.

30.01 Biological and Physical Sciences

30.06 System Science and Theory

30.08 Mathematics and Computer Science

30.10 Biopsychology

30.11 Gerontology

30.16 Accounting and Computer Science

30.17 Behavioral Sciences

30.18 Natural Sciences

30.19 Nutrition Sciences

30.24 Neuroscience

30.25 Cognitive Science

***40. Physical Sciences.**
Instructional programs that focus on the scientific study of inanimate objects, processes of matter and energy, and associated phenomena.

***41. Science Technologies/Technicians.**
Instructional programs that prepare individuals to apply scientific principles and technical skills in support of scientific research and development.

42.11 Physiological Psychology/Psychobiology

42.19 Psychometrics and Quantitative Psychology

42. 24 Psychopharmacology

42.26 Forensic Psychology

***51.14 Medical Clinical Sciences/Graduate Medical Studies**
51.1401 Medical Scientist (MS, PhD)

NOTE: "*" means all programs are considered high technology programs within that discipline.

ELIGIBILITY PERIODS

Benefits generally end 10 years from the date of an individual's last discharge or release from active duty. The VA may extend the 10-year period by the amount of time an individual is prevented from training due to a disability, or the individual is being held by a foreign government or power.

The VA may extend the 10-year period if an individual reenters active duty for 90 days or more after becoming eligible. The extension ends 10 years from the date of discharge or release from the later period. Periods of active duty of less than 90 days may qualify for extensions, only if the discharge or release was for:

- A service-connected disability; or
- A medical condition existing before active duty; or
- Hardship; or
- A reduction in force.

If an individual's discharge is upgraded by the military, the 10-year period begins on the date of the upgrade.

Special Note For Individuals Eligible Under Category II:

If an individual is eligible under Category II, and discharge was before December 31, 1989,he had until January 1, 2000 to use his entitlement. In most cases, the VA will subtract periods an individual was not on active duty between January 1, 1977 and June 30, 1985, from the individual's 10-year period.

Special Note For Individuals Eligible Under The 2 By 4 Program

If an individual is eligible based upon two years of active duty followed by four years in the Selected Reserve, the individual may have 10 years from release from active duty, or 10 years from the completion of the four-year Selected Reserve obligation to use benefits, whichever is later.

Miscellaneous Information

- Any change in educational, professional or vocational objectives is considered a "*change of program.*" The law permits one change of program without prior VA approval, provided an individual's attendance, conduct and progress in the last program were satisfactory. Additional "*changes of program*" require prior VA approval. VA will not charge a *change of program* if the individual enrolls in a new program after successful completion of the immediately preceding program.
- Once an individual starts receiving benefits, he must maintain satisfactory attendance, conduct and progress. The VA may stop

benefits if an individual does not meet the standards set by the school. VA may later resume benefits if the individual reenters the same program at the same school, and the school approves the reentry, and certifies it to VA.

- If the individual does not reenter the same program at the same school, VA may resume benefits if the cause of unsatisfactory attendance, conduct or progress has been removed; and the program that the student intends to pursue is suitable to his or her abilities, aptitudes and interests.

- **Update: Effective November 1, 2000,** VA education benefits can be paid (with some exceptions) for school breaks, if the breaks do not exceed 8 weeks; and the terms before and after the breaks are not shorter than the break. Prior to November 1 2000, VA education benefits could be paid only if the breaks did not exceed a calendar month.

APPLICATION FOR BENEFITS

VA Form 22-1990, "Application for Education Benefits" must be completed. The form may be obtained from individual schools, from any VA regional office, or by calling 1-888-GIBILL-1.

The completed form should be sent to the VA regional office with jurisdiction over the state in which the individual will train.

If an individual is not on active duty, copy 4 of DD Form 214 (Certificate of Release or Discharge from Active Duty), must also be sent to the VA. If an individual is on active duty, enrollment must be approved by the Base Education Services Officer, and service must be verified by the Commanding Officer.

If training has already started, the school, employer, or union should complete VA Form 22-1999 (Enrollment Certification) and submit it along with the application.

PROCEDURES FOR RECEIPT OF MONTHLY PAYMENTS

Students will receive a Student Verification of Enrollment Form 22-8979 each month, and must complete and return it to the appropriate VA regional office. After processing, VA will release a check.

After selecting a school and submitting an application to VA, the school official must complete an enrollment certification, and submit it to the appropriate VA regional office. If a student meets the basic eligibility requirements for benefits, and the program or course is approved, VA will process the enrollment based on certified training time.

If a student is enrolled in a degree program at a college or university, or a certificate or diploma program at a business, technical, or vocational school, they will not receive payment until they have verified their attendance. Students will receive a *Student Verification of Enrollment Form 22-8979* each month, and must complete and return it to the appropriate VA regional office. After processing, VA will release a check.

Beginning in the Fall of 2000, VA announced a new way to verify enrollment. **All students who are receiving MGIB Active Duty (chapter 30) education benefits are now able to certify their monthly Verification of Enrollment (VAF 22-8979) over the by using a toll free phone system (Interactive Voice Response - IVR) or the internet (Web Automated Verification of Enrollment (WAVE).** Use of these systems eliminates the need for the student to sign and return the VA Form 22-8979 every month.

Once the IVR or WAVE system tells the student that he or she is certified, it is not necessary to return the Verification of Enrollment form.

If an individual is in an apprenticeship or job-training program, he or she will receive a form to report the hours worked each month. The form must be signed and given to the certifying official for the company or union. The certifying official must complete the form and send it to the appropriate VA regional office. After processing, VA will release a check.

If an individual is taking a correspondence course, he or she will receive a form each quarter, on which the student must show the number of lessons completed that quarter. The completed form should be sent to the school for certification of the number of lessons serviced during the quarter. The school will send the form to the appropriate VA regional office. After processing, VA will release a check. Payments are based on the number of lessons serviced by the school.

VA will send flight schools a supply of blank monthly certification of flight training forms. The school must complete the form by entering the number of hours, the hourly rate, and the total charges for flight training received during the month. The student should review and sign the completed form, and send it to the appropriate VA regional office. After processing, VA will release a check.

NOTE: It is against the law for schools to cash VA checks under a Power of Attorney Agreement.

TIMELY RECEIPT OF VERIFICATION FORMS AND CHECKS

Students should receive their verification forms for each month by the fifth of the following month. If it is not received by then, the VA should be immediately contacted so that another form can be issued.

One a completed verification form has been submitted, the student should receive a check within 2 weeks. If a check is not received by then, the VA should immediately be contacted so that appropriate action can be taken.

ADVANCE PAYMENTS

An advance payment for the initial month, or partial month and the following month may be made, if:

1. The school agrees to handle advance payments; and
2. Training is one-half time or more; and
3. A request is made by the individual in writing; and

4. The VA receives the enrollment certification at least 30 days prior to the start of classes.

Advance payments are made out to the individual, and sent to the applicable school for delivery to the individual registration. VA cannot issue a check more than 30 days before classes start. Before requesting an advance payment, students should verify with the school certifying official that the school has agreed to process advance payments.

Requests for advance payments must be on VA Form 22-1999, Enrollment Certification, or a sheet of paper attached to the enrollment certification.

Once a student receives an advance payment at registration, the school must certify to VA that the student received the check. If a student reduces enrollment, or withdraws from all courses during the period covered by an advance payment, he or she must repay the overpayment to VA.

If an individual believes that the amount of a VA check is incorrect, the VA should be contacted before the check is cashed.

DIRECT DEPOSIT

Chapter 30 payments can be sent directly to a student's savings or checking account through Direct Deposit (Electronic Funds Transfer). To sign up for direct deposit by phone, students must call 1-877-838-2778.

STUDENT RESPONSIBILITIES

To ensure timely receipt of correct payments, students should be sure to promptly notify the VA of:

- Any change in enrollment;
- Any change in address;
- Any change in selected reserve status;
- Any changes affecting a student's dependents (if a student is receiving an allowance which includes an additional amount for dependents).

In addition, students should use reasonable judgment when accepting and cashing a check. All letters from VA about monthly rates and effective dates should be read carefully. If a student thinks the amount of a VA check is wrong, VA should be contacted **before** cashing the check. Any incorrect checks should be returned to VA.

If a student cashes a check for the wrong amount, he or she will be liable for repayment of any resulting overpayment.

RECOVERY OF OVERPAYMENTS

VA must take prompt and aggressive action to recover overpayments. Students have the right to request a waiver of the overpayment, or verification that the amount is correct. If an overpayment is not repaid or waived, VA may add interest and collection fees to the debt. VA may also take one or more of the following actions to collect the debt:

- Withhold future benefits to apply to the debt;
- Refer the debt to a private collection agency;
- Recover the debt from any Federal income tax refund;
- Recover the debt from the salary (if student is a Federal employee);
- File a lawsuit in Federal court to collect the debt;
- Withhold approval of a VA home loan guarantee.

CHANGES IN ENROLLMENT

If a student withdraws from one or more courses after the end of the school's drop period, VA will reduce or stop benefits on the date of reduction or withdrawal. Unless the student can show that the change was due to *mitigating circumstances*, the student may have to repay **all** benefits for the course.

VA defines *mitigating circumstances* as "unavoidable and unexpected events that directly interfere with the pursuit of a course, and which are beyond the student's control.

Examples of reasons VA may accept include:

- Extended illness;
- Severe illness or death in immediate family;
- Unscheduled changes in employment; and
- Lack of child care.

Examples of reasons VA may not accept include:

- Withdrawal to avoid a failing grade;
- Dislike of the instructor; and
- Too many courses attempted.

(VA may ask the student to furnish evidence to support the reason for change, such as physician or employer written statements.)

The first time a student withdraws from up to 6 credit hours, VA will "excuse" the withdrawal, and pay benefits for the period attended.

If a student receives a grade that does not count toward graduation, all benefits for the course may have to be repaid. Affected students should check the school's grading policy with the office handling VA paperwork.

If a student receives a non-punitive grade, the school will notify VA, and VA may reduce or stop benefits. The student may not have to repay the benefits if he or she can show that the grades were due to mitigating circumstances.

WORK-STUDY PROGRAMS

Students may be eligible for an additional allowance under a work-study program that allows students to perform work for VA in return for an hourly wage. Students may perform outreach services under VA supervision, prepare and process VA paperwork, work at a VA medical facility or National Cemetery, or perform other approved activities.

Students must attend school at the three-quarter of full-time rate.

VA will select students for the work study program based on different factors. Such factors include:

- Disability of the student;
- Ability of the student to complete the work-study contract before the end of his or her eligibility for education benefits;
- Job availability within normal commuting distance to the student;
- VA will give the highest priority to a veteran who has a service-connected disability or disabilities rated by VA at 30% or more.

The number of applicants selected will depend on the availability of VA-related work at the school or at VA facilities in the area.

Students may work during or between periods of enrollment, and can arrange with VA to work any number of hours during his or her enrollment. However, the maximum number of hours a student may work is 25 times the number of weeks in the enrollment period.

Students will earn an hourly wage equal to the Federal or State minimum wage, whichever is greater. If a student works at a college or university, the school **may** pay the difference between the amount VA pays and the amount the school normally pays other work-study students doing the same job.

Students may elect to be paid in advance for 40% of the number of hours in the work-study agreement, or for 50 hours, whichever is less. After completion of the hours covered by the first payment, VA will pay the student after completion of each 50 hours of service.

Students interested in taking part in a work-study program must complete VA Form 22,8691, Application for Work-Study Allowance. Completed forms should be sent to the nearest VA regional office.

EDUCATIONAL COUNSELING

VA can provide services to help eligible individuals understand their educational and vocational strengths and weaknesses and to plan:

- An educational or training goal, and the means by which the goal can be reached; or
- An employment goal for which an individual qualifies on the basis of present training or experience.

VA can also help plan an effective job search.

Counseling is available for:

- Service members who are on active duty, and are within 180 days of discharge, and are stationed in the United States; or
- Veterans with discharges that are not dishonorable, who are within one year from date of discharge.

VOCATIONAL REHABILITATION

Veterans may qualify for Training and Rehabilitation under Chapter 31 of Title 38, United States Code, if:

- The veteran has a service-connected disability or disabilities rated by VA at 20% or more; and
- The veteran received a discharge from active duty that was not dishonorable; and
- The veteran has an employment handicap.

Veterans may also qualify with a service-connected disability or disabilities rated by VA at 10%, and:

- The veteran has a serious employment handicap; or
- The veteran first applied for vocational rehabilitation benefits before November 1, 1990, reapplied after that date, and has an employment handicap.

Vocational rehabilitation helps disabled veterans become independent in daily living. Veterans may also receive assistance in selecting, preparing for, and securing employment that is compatible with their interests, talents, skills, physical capabilities, and goals.

To apply for vocational rehabilitation, VA for 28-1900, Disabled Veterans Application for Vocational Rehabilitation, must be completed and sent to the nearest VA regional office.

For detailed information on vocational rehabilitation refer to Chapter 15 of this book.

APPEAL OF VA DECISION

VA decisions on education benefits may be appealed within one year of the date an individual receives notice of a VA decision.

For detailed information on filing an appeal, please refer to Chapter 36 of this book.

CHAPTER 19

EDUCATION BENEFITS – RESERVE EDUCATIONAL ASSISTANCE PROGRAM (REAP) CHAPTER 1607

H.R. 4200 created a new education benefit called the **"Reserve Educational Assistance Program" (REAP)** or Chapter 1607. This new program makes certain individuals who were activated after September 11, 2001 either eligible for education benefits or eligible for increased benefits.

Purpose

Chapter 1607 was established as a part of the Ronald W. Reagan National Defense Authorization Act for Fiscal Year 2005. It is a new Department of Defense education benefit program designed to provide educational assistance to members of the Reserve components called or ordered to active duty in response to a war or national emergency (contingency operation) as declared by the President or Congress. The Department of Defense and the Department of Homeland Security will determine who is eligible for this program. The Department of Veterans Affairs will administer the program and pay benefits from funds contributed by DOD.

Chapter 1607 provides educational assistance to members of the reserve components called or ordered to active duty in response to a war or national emergency (contingency operations) as declared by the President or Congress.

Note: "Contingency operations" as defined in title 10 U.S. Code means "military operations that are designated by the Secretary of Defense as an operation in which members of the armed forces are or may become involved in military actions, operations or hostilities against an enemy of the United States or against opposing military force; or results in the call or order to, or retention on active duty of members of the uniformed services...."

Eligibility

The Secretaries of each military service, Department of Defense, and Department of Homeland Security (Coast Guard) will determine eligibility.

The law requires DoD to give individuals written notification of eligibility for REAP.

- Unlike the MGIB-Active Duty, service members do not have to pay anything to participate in Chapter 1607.

- A member of a reserve component who serves on active duty on or after September 11, 2001 under title 10 U.S. Code for a contingency operation and who serves at least 90 consecutive days or more is eligible for chapter 1607.

- National Guard members also are eligible if their active duty is under section 502(f), title 32 U.S.C. and they serve for 90 consecutive days when authorized by the President or Secretary of Defense for a national emergency and is supported by federal funds. Individuals are eligible as soon as they reach the 90-day point whether or not they are currently on active duty. DoD will fully identify contingency operations that qualify for benefits under chapter 1607.

- Disabled members who are injured or have an illness or disease incurred or aggravated in the line of duty and are released from active duty before completing 90 consecutive days are also eligible.

  (Members released early for disability incurred or aggravated in the line of duty may receive Chapter 1607 benefits at the 40% rate. The member is entitled to Chapter 1607 benefits for 10 years from the date of eligibility.)

Payment Rates

The benefit amount payable under Chapter 1607 is a percentage of the MGIB (Chapter 30) 3-year rate, based on the number of continuous days served on active duty.

Time Reserve Member Serves on Active Duty	Percentage of Ch 30 (3-Year Rate)
90 days but less than one year	40%
One year but less than two years	60%
Two years or more	80%

IMPORTANT UPDATE -

OJT & Apprenticeship Rates to Change January 1, 2008

Effective October 1, 2005 Public Law 108-454, Section 103 temporarily increased the reimbursement rates for On the Job Training & Apprenticeship training. This temporary rate increase was effective from October 1, 2005 to December 31, 2007. Congress has not extended this temporary increase, therefore effective January 1, 2008 reimbursement rates for OJT and Apprenticeships will decrease.

The following basic monthly rates are effective October 1, 2007:

INSTITUTIONAL TRAINING			
Training Time	Consecutive service of 90 days but less than one year	Consecutive service of 1 year or more	Consecutive service of 2 years or more
Full Time	$440.40	$660.60	$880.80
¾ Time	330.30	495.45	660.60
½ Time	220.20	330.30	430.00
Less than ½ time, but more than ¼ time	220.20 (tuition & fees only)	330.30 (tuition & fees only)	440.40 (tuition & fees only)
¼ time or less	110.10 (tuition & fees only)	165.15 (tuition & fees only)	220.20 (tuition & fees only)

CORRESPONDENCE TRAINING	
40% Level	22% of the approved cost of course
60% Level	33% of the approved cost of course
80% Level	44% of the approved cost of course

FLIGHT TRAINING	
40% Level	24% of the approved cost of course
60% Level	36% of the approved cost of course
80% Level	48% of the approved cost of course

APPRENTICESHIP AND ON-THE-JOB TRAINING ***Rates Effective October 1, 2007 – December 31, 2007***			
Training Period	Consecutive service of 90 days, but less than one year	Consecutive service of 1 year or more	Consecutive service of 2 years or more
First six months of training	$374.34	$561.51	$748.68
Second six months of training	286.26	429.39	572.52
Remaining pursuit of training	198.18	290.27	396.36

APPRENTICESHIP AND ON-THE-JOB TRAINING ***Rates Effective January 1, 2008***			
Training Period	Consecutive service of 90 days, but less than one year	Consecutive service of 1 year or more	Consecutive service of 2 years or more
First six months of training	$330.30	$495.45	$660.60
Second six months of training	242.22	363.33	484.44
Remaining pursuit of training	154.14	231.21	308.28

COOPERATIVE TRAINING			
Training Time	Service of 90 days, but less than one year	Service of 1 year or more	Service of 2 years or more
Monthly Rate	$440.40	$660.60	$880.80

Applying For Benefits

VA Regional Processing Offices in Atlanta, St. Louis, Buffalo, and Muskogee will accept applications and supporting documents for Chapter 1607 claims. VA will take action on your claim at this time.

Individuals who have never submitted an Education Claim to VA:

Submit an ***Application for VA Education Benefits (VA Form 22-1990)*** and submit any available documents such as Discharge from Military Service (DD Form 214), copies of orders to active duty and anything else available as evidence of qualifying service.

Annotate "Chapter 1607" prominently on all correspondence and documents.

Individuals who have previously filed a claim for Education benefits:

A new application form is not required. However, individuals should submit any available documents such as Discharge from Military Service (DD Form 214), copies of orders to active duty and anything else available as evidence of qualifying service to help establish eligibility for this program. Individuals should also submit a ***Request For Change of Program or Place of Training (VA form 22-1995)*** which should be annotated "1607."

Annotate "Chapter 1607" prominently on all correspondence and documents.

Earliest Eligibility Date

Chapter 1607 benefits may be paid before the date of enactment the law, which was October 28, 2004. Chapter 1607 benefits are **potentially** payable from December 9, 2001 (90 days after September 11, 2001) for persons who were serving on a contingency operation on September 11, 2001 and who were in school on December 9, 2001.

Months of Benefits Payable

Individuals may receive 36 months of full time entitlement at his or her given rate. A Chapter 1607 participant may not use more than 48 months of entitlement under any combination of VA Educational programs. For example, if he or she has already used 20 months of Chapter 1606, he or she will only receive 28 months of Chapter 1607.

Benefit Ending Date

Individuals may use benefits under Chapter 1607 as long as they remain within their component. Benefits must be terminated if an individual leaves the Reserves or participates in a ROTC program under Title 10 Section 2107.

Note: There is no fixed delimiting period (ending date) for persons eligible under chapter 1607, as there is for all of the other VA education programs so long as an individual does not leave his or her Reserve component. There is one exception: If an individual is separated from the Ready Reserve for a disability which was not the result of his or her own willful misconduct, he or she is entitled to chapter 1607 benefits for 10-years after the date of entitlement.

Receipt of Other VA Education Benefits

Individuals must make an irrevocable election choosing which program they want their military service to count towards. Individuals also cannot receive assistance under more than one VA Education program at one time.

If an individual is eligible for a Chapter 1606 kicker, he or she can still be paid that kicker while receiving Chapter 1607.

Approved Courses

The following programs are available:

- College or University Degree Programs
- Vocational Programs
- Independent Study or Distance Learning Programs
- Correspondence Courses
- Flight Training
- On-the-Job Training and Apprenticeship Programs
- Tuition Assistance Top-Up Program
- Entrepreneurship Courses

(NOTE: VA does not approve schools or programs for benefits. Each individual state approves schools and courses. To find out if your school or program is approved for VA Educational Benefits under REAP, contact your school's VA Certifying Official, or call VA at 1-888-442-4551.)

CHAPTER 20

EDUCATION BENEFITS - MONTGOMERY G.I. BILL – SELECTED RESERVE (MGIB-SR), CHAPTER 1606

Please be sure to review Chapter 19 of this book, which highlights a new education benefit, "Reserve Educational Assistance Program" (REAP) or Chapter 1607, established to provide increased educational assistance to members of the reserve components called or ordered to active duty in response to a war or national emergency (contingency operations) as declared by the President or Congress.

The Montgomery GI Bill-Selected Reserve Program is for members of the Selected Reserve, including the Army Reserve, Navy Reserve, Air Force Reserve, Marine Corps Reserve, Coast Guard Reserve, Army National Guard and Air National Guard. While the reserve components decide who is eligible for the program, VA makes the payments for the program. Chapter 1606 is the first educational program that does not require service in the *active* Armed Forces in order to qualify.

ELIGIBILITY REQUIREMENTS

- Member must have signed a 6-year obligation to serve in the Selected Reserve after June 30, 1985. (Officers must have agreed to serve 6 years in addition to his or her original obligation.) For some types of training, it is necessary to have a 6-year commitment that began after September 30, 1990. Call 1-888-GIBILL-1 for more information;

- Member must have completed his or her Initial Active Duty for Training (IADT);

- Member must maintain *Selected Reserve Status* - Serve in a drilling Selected Reserve unit and remain in good standing;

- Member must meet the requirement to receive a high school diploma or equivalency certificate before completing IADT. Member must remain in good standing while serving in an active Selected Reserve Unit;

- Effective November 1, 2000, veterans and reservists can apply for MGIB-SR benefits *any time* after receiving their high school diploma or equivalency certificate. It no longer has to be received prior to the end of the individual's first period of active duty.

Beginning on October 1, 1990, a member of the Selected Reserve with a bachelor's degree can become eligible by signing a new contract that will result in a 6 year reserve obligation. Beginning on November 30, 1993, a member of the Selected Reserve can become eligible for graduate degree training. A new 6 year contract is not required in order to pursue graduate training.

If an individual enters active duty in the Selected Reserve (AGR, TAR, FTS) after November 29, 1989, he or she must have been eligible *before* November 29, 1989 in order to remain eligible.

ELIGIBILITY RESTRICTIONS

MGIB – AD:
An individual can't be eligible for MGIB - SR if he or she elected to have his or her service in the Selected Reserve credited toward establishing eligibility under the Montgomery GI Bill - Active Duty

ROTC (Reserve Officers' Training Corps) scholarship under section 2107 of title 10, U.S. Code:
An individual can't be eligible for MGIB - SR if he or she is receiving financial assistance through the Senior ROTC program under this section of the law.

Note: However, an individual may still be eligible for MGIB - SR if he or she receives financial assistance under ***Section 2107a*** of title 10, U.S. Code. This financial assistance program is for specially selected members of the Army Reserve and National Guard only. Individuals should check with their ROTC advisor for more information.

Note: There's no restriction on service academy graduates receiving MGIB - SR. Service academy graduates who received a commission aren't eligible under MGIB - AD.

If an individual enters Active Guard and Reserve (AGR) status, his or her eligibility for MGIB - SR will be suspended. He or she may be eligible for MGIB - AD. The individual may resume MGIB - SR eligibility after AGR status ends.

APPROVED COURSES

Individuals may receive benefits for a wide variety of training, including:

- Undergraduate degrees from a college or university;
- Beginning November 30, 1993, graduate degrees from a college or university;
- Accredited independent study programs leading to standard college degrees;
- Technical courses for a certificate at a college or university.

Individuals with 6-year commitments beginning after September 30, 1990 may take the following types of training:

- Courses leading to a certificate or diploma from business, technical, or vocational schools;

- Cooperative training;
- Apprenticeship or job training programs offered by companies;
- Correspondence training;
- Independent study programs;
- Flight training (Individuals must have a private pilot's license, and must meet the medical requirements for the desired license program before beginning training, and throughout the flight training program.)

VA may approve programs offered by institutions outside of the United States, when they are pursued at educational institutions of higher learning, and lead to a college degree. Individuals must receive VA approval prior to attending or enrolling in any foreign programs.

Eligibility for this program is determined by the Selected Reserve components. Payments for the program are made by the VA.

A State agency or VA must approve each program offered by a school or company.

If an individual is seeking a college degree, the school must admit the individual to a degree program by the start of the individual's third term.

RESTRICTIONS ON TRAINING

Benefits are not payable for the following courses:

- Courses paid by the military Tuition Assistance program, if student is enrolled at less than ½ time;
- Courses taken while student is receiving a Reserve Officers' Training Corps scholarship;
- Non-accredited independent study courses;
- Bartending and personality development courses;
- Any course given by radio;
- Self-improvement courses such as reading, speaking, woodworking, basic seamanship, and English as a 2nd language;
- Any course which is avocational or recreational in character;
- Farm-cooperative courses;
- Audited courses;
- Courses not leading to an educational, professional, or vocational objective;
- Courses previously taken and successfully completed;

- Courses taken by a Federal government employee under the Government Employee's Training Act;
- Courses taken while in receipt of benefits for the same program from the Office of Workers' Compensation Programs.

VA must reduce benefits for individuals in Federal, State, or local prisons after being convicted of a felony.
An individual may not receive benefits for a program at a proprietary school if her or she is an owner or official of the school.

PART-TIME TRAINING

Individuals unable to attend school full-time should consider going part-time. Benefit rates and entitlement charges are less than the full-time rates. For example, if a student receives full-time benefits for 12 months, the entitlement charge is 12 months. However, if the student receives ½ time benefits for 12 months, the charge is 6 months. VA will pay for less than ½ time training if the student is not receiving Tuition Assistance for those courses.

REMEDIAL, DEFICIENCY AND REFRESHER TRAINING

Remedial and deficiency courses are intended to assist a student in overcoming a deficiency in a particular area of study. Individuals may qualify for benefits for remedial, deficiency, and refresher courses if they have a 6-year commitment that began after September 30, 1990. In order for such courses to be approved, the courses must be deemed necessary for pursuit of a program of education.

Refresher training is for technological advances that occurred in a field of employment. The advance must have occurred while the student was on active duty, or after release.

There is an entitlement charge for these courses.

TUTORIAL ASSISTANCE

Students may receive a special allowance for individual tutoring performed after September 30, 1992, if they entered school at one-half time or more. To qualify, the student must have a deficiency in a subject. The school must certify the tutor's qualifications, and the hours of tutoring. Eligible students may receive a maximum monthly payment of $100.00. The maximum total benefit payable is $1,200.00.

There is no entitlement charge for the first $600.00 of tutorial assistance.

To apply for tutorial assistance, students must submit VA Form 22-1990t, Application and Enrollment Certification for Individualized Tutorial Assistance. The form should be given to the certifying official in the office handling VA paperwork at the school for completion.

MONTHS OF BENEFITS / ENTITLEMENT CHARGED

Eligible members may be entitled to receive up to 36 months of education benefits. Benefit entitlement ends 10 years from the date the member becomes eligible for the program, or on the day the member leaves the Selected Reserve. (If a member's Reserve or National Guard unit was deactivated during the period October 1, 1991 through September 30, 1999, or if the member was involuntarily separated from service during this same period, eligibility for MGIB-SR benefits is retained for the full 10-year eligibility period. Eligibility for MGIB-SR benefits is also retained if a member is discharged due to a disability that was not caused by misconduct. Eligibility periods may be extended if a member is ordered to active duty.)

Individuals qualifying for more than one VA education program may receive a maximum of 48 months of benefits. For example, if a student used 30 months of Dependents' Educational Assistance, and is eligible for chapter 1606 benefits, he or she could have a maximum of 18 months of entitlement remaining.

Individuals are charged one full day of entitlement for each day of full-time benefits paid. For correspondence and flight training, one month of entitlement is charged each time VA pays one month of benefits. For cooperative programs, one month of entitlement is used for each month of benefits paid.

For apprenticeship and job training programs, the entitlement charge changes every 6 months. During the first 6 months, the charge is 75% of full time. For the second 6 months, the charge is 55% of full time. For the remainder of the program, the charge is 35% of full time.

RATES OF EDUCATIONAL ASSISTANCE PAY

IMPORTANT UPDATE -

OJT & Apprenticeship Rates to Change January 1, 2008

Effective October 1, 2005 Public Law 108-454, Section 103 temporarily increased the reimbursement rates for On the Job Training & Apprenticeship training. This temporary rate increase was effective from October 1, 2005 to December 31, 2007. Congress has not extended this temporary increase, therefore effective January 1, 2008 reimbursement rates for OJT and Apprenticeships will decrease.

The following basic monthly rates are effective October 1, 2007:

BASIC MONTHLY RATES *MONTGOMERY G.I. BILL – SELECTED RESERVE (MGIB-SR), CHAPTER 1606*				
Type of Training	**Full-Time**	**Three-Quarter Time**	**One-Half Time**	**Less than ½ Time**
Institutional	$317.00	$237.00	$157.00	$79.25
Cooperative Training	$317.00 (Full-Time Only)			
Correspondence Training	Entitlement charged at the rate of one month for each $317.00 paid *(Payment for correspondence courses is made at 55% of the approved charges for the course.)*			
Apprenticeship On-The-Job Training - *Effective 10-1-07 thru 12-31-07*	First six months: $269.45 Second six months: $206.05 Remainder of program: $142.65			
Apprenticeship On-The-Job Training - *Effective 10-1-07 thru 12-31-07*	First six months: $237.75 Second six months: $174.35 Remainder of program: $110.95			
Flight Training	Entitlement charged at the rate of one month for each $317.00 paid *(Payment for flight training is made at 60% of the approved charges for the course, including solo hours.)*			

ELIGIBILITY PERIODS

For individuals who separate from the Selected Reserve, generally benefits end the day of separation.

For individuals who stay in the Selected Reserve, generally benefits end 14 years from the date the individual became eligible for the program.

Exceptions: *If an individual stays in the Selected Reserve,* VA can generally extend the 14-year period if:

- The individual couldn't train due to a disability caused by Selected Reserve service; or
- The individual was activated for service in the Persian Gulf Era (which hasn't ended for purposes of VA education benefits); or
- The individual's eligibility expired during a period of his or her enrollment in training.

If an individual leaves the Selected Reserve, he or she can generally still use the full 14 years if:

- The individual was separated because of a disability that wasn't caused by misconduct; or
- The individual's unit was inactivated or the individual was otherwise involuntarily separated during the period from October 1, 1991, through September 30, 2001.

In all other cases, if an individual leaves the Selected Reserve before completion of his or her obligation, benefits will stop.

MISCELLANEOUS INFORMATION

- Any change in educational, professional or vocational objectives is considered a *"change of program."* The law permits one change of program without prior VA approval, provided an individual's attendance, conduct and progress in the last program were satisfactory. Additional *"changes of program"* require prior VA approval. VA will not charge a *change of program* if the individual enrolls in a new program after successful completion of the immediately preceding program.

- Once an individual starts receiving benefits, he must maintain satisfactory attendance, conduct and progress. The VA may stop benefits if an individual does not meet the standards set by the school. VA may later resume benefits if the individual reenters the same program at the same school, and the school approves the reentry, and certifies it to VA.

- If the individual does not reenter the same program at the same school, VA may resume benefits if the cause of unsatisfactory attendance, conduct or progress has been removed; and the program that the student intends to pursue is suitable to his or her abilities, aptitudes and interests.

- Effective November 1, 2000, VA education benefits can be paid (with some exceptions) for school breaks, if the breaks do not exceed 8 weeks; and the terms before and after the breaks are not shorter than the break. Prior to November 1 2000, VA education benefits could be paid only if the breaks did not exceed a calendar month.

APPLICATION FOR BENEFITS

When an individual becomes eligible for the program, his or her unit will provide the individual with a Notice of Basic Eligibility, DD Form 2384, or DD Form 2384-1 (for persons who establish eligibility on or after October 1, 1990). The unit will also code the eligibility into the Department of Defense personnel system.

When the individual finds a school, program, company, apprenticeship or job-training program, there are two important steps that must be followed:

- Make sure the program is approved for VA training. Contact the local VA regional office if there are any questions.

- Compete VA Form 22-1990, Application for Education Benefits. The completed form should be sent to the VA regional office with jurisdiction over the State where training will occur.

Following receipt of an application, VA will review it and advise if anything else is needed.

If an individual has started training, the application and Notice of Basic Eligibility should be taken to the school, employer or union. The certifying official should complete VA Form 22-1999, Enrollment Certification, and send all the forms to VA.

PROCEDURES FOR RECEIPT OF MONTHLY PAYMENTS

After selecting a school and submitting an application to VA, the school official must complete an enrollment certification, and submit it to the appropriate VA regional office. If a student meets the basic eligibility requirements for benefits, and the program or course is approved, VA will process the enrollment based on certified training time.

VA will accept the Notice of Basic Eligibility to pay benefits for 120 days after an individual's eligibility date. If the eligibility date is more than 120 days before the training program starts, VA will not approve the claim unless the Department of Defense personnel system shows that the individual is eligible. Only a student's reserve component can update the DoD personnel system. VA cannot change an individual's eligibility record.

When VA approves a claim, it will issue a letter with the details of the benefits payable. The first payment should be received within a few days of receipt of the letter.

If a student is enrolled in a degree program at a college or university, he or she will receive payment after the first of each month for the training during the preceding month. If a student is enrolled in a certificate or diploma program at a business, technical, or vocational school, he or she will not receive payment until they have verified their attendance. Students will receive a *Student Verification of Enrollment Form 22-8979* each month, and must complete and return it to the appropriate VA regional office. After processing, VA will release a check.

If an individual is in an apprenticeship or job-training program, he or she will receive a form to report the hours worked each month. The form must be signed and given to the certifying official for the company or union. The certifying official must complete the form and send it to the appropriate VA regional office. After processing, VA will release a check.

If an individual is taking a correspondence course, he or she will receive a form each quarter, on which the student must show the number of lessons completed that quarter. The completed form should be sent to the school for certification of the number of lessons serviced during the quarter. The school will send the form to the appropriate VA regional office. After processing, VA will release a check. Payments are based on the number of lessons serviced by the school.

VA will send flight schools a supply of blank monthly certification of flight training forms. The school must complete the form by entering the number of hours, the hourly rate, and the total charges for flight training received during the month. The student should review and sign the completed form, and send it to the appropriate VA regional office. After processing, VA will release a check.

NOTE: It is against the law for schools to cash VA checks under a Power of Attorney Agreement.

TIMELY RECEIPT OF VERIFICATION FORMS AND CHECKS

Students taking courses leading to a degree at a college or university should receive their checks for each month by the fifth of the next month. If it is not received by then, the VA should be immediately contacted so that appropriate action can be taken.

Students taking courses leading to a certificate or diploma from a business, technical, or vocational school should receive their verification forms for each month by the fifth of the following month. If it is not received by then, the VA should be immediately contacted so that another form can be issued.

One a completed verification form has been submitted, the student should receive a check within 2 weeks. If a check is not received by then, the VA should immediately be contacted so that appropriate action can be taken.

ADVANCE PAYMENTS

An advance payment for the initial month, or partial month and the following month may be made, if:

- The school agrees to handle advance payments; and
- Training is one-half time or more; and
- A request is made by the individual in writing; and
- The VA receives the enrollment certification at least 30 days prior to the start of classes.

Advance payments are made out to the individual, and sent to the applicable school for delivery to the individual registration. VA cannot issue a check more than 30 days before classes start. Before requesting an advance payment, students should verify with the school certifying official that the school has agreed to process advance payments.

Requests for advance payments must be on VA Form 22-1999, Enrollment Certification, or a sheet of paper attached to the enrollment certification.

Once a student receives an advance payment at registration, the school must certify to VA that the student received the check. If a student reduces enrollment, or withdraws from all courses during the period covered by an advance payment, he or she must repay the overpayment to VA.

If an individual believes that the amount of a VA check is incorrect, the VA should be contacted before the check is cashed.

DIRECT DEPOSIT

Payments can be sent directly to a student's savings or checking account through Direct Deposit (Electronic Funds Transfer). To sign up for direct deposit by phone, students must call (877) 838-2778.

STUDENT RESPONSIBILITIES

To ensure timely receipt of correct payments, students should be sure to promptly notify the VA of:

- Any change in enrollment;
- Any change in address;
- Any change in selected reserve status (If an individual changes units or components, both the old and new units must report the change to VA through the components' eligibility data systems.)

In addition, students should use reasonable judgment when accepting and cashing a check. All letters from VA about monthly rates and effective dates should be read carefully. If a student thinks the amount of a VA check is wrong, VA should be contacted **before** cashing the check. Any incorrect checks should be returned to VA.

If a student cashes a check for the wrong amount, he or she will be liable for repayment of any resulting overpayment.

If an individual does not participate satisfactorily in the Selected Reserve, his or her eligibility ends. His or her component can require that a penalty be paid, based on a portion of payments received.

RECOVERY OF OVERPAYMENTS

VA must take prompt and aggressive action to recover overpayments. Students have the right to request a waiver of the overpayment, or verification that the amount is correct. If an overpayment is not repaid or waived, VA may add interest and collection fees to the debt. VA may also take one or more of the following actions to collect the debt:

- Withhold future benefits to apply to the debt;
- Refer the debt to a private collection agency;
- Recover the debt from any Federal income tax refund;
- Recover the debt from the salary (if student is a Federal employee);
- File a lawsuit in Federal court to collect the debt;
- Withhold approval of a VA home loan guarantee.

An individual's reserve component will act to collect penalties caused by unsatisfactory participation in the reserve.

CHANGES IN ENROLLMENT

If a student withdraws from one or more courses after the end of the school's drop period, VA will reduce or stop benefits on the date of reduction or withdrawal. Unless the student can show that the change was due to *mitigating circumstances*, the student may have to repay **all** benefits for the course.

VA defines *mitigating circumstances* as "unavoidable and unexpected events that directly interfere with the pursuit of a course, and which are beyond the student's control.

Examples of reasons VA may accept include:

- Extended illness;
- Severe illness or death in immediate family;
- Unscheduled changes in employment; and
- Lack of child care.

Examples of reasons VA may not accept include:

- Withdrawal to avoid a failing grade;
- Dislike of the instructor; and
- Too many courses attempted.

(VA may ask the student to furnish evidence to support the reason for change, such as physician or employer written statements.)

The first time a student withdraws from up to 6 credit hours, VA will "excuse" the withdrawal, and pay benefits for the period attended.

If a student receives a grade that does not count toward graduation, all benefits for the course may have to be repaid.

If a student receives a non-punitive grade, the school will notify VA, and VA may reduce or stop benefits. The student may not have to repay the benefits if he or she can show that the grades were due to mitigating circumstances.

WORK-STUDY PROGRAMS

Students may be eligible for an additional allowance under a work-study program that allows students to perform work for VA in return for an hourly wage. Students may perform outreach services under VA supervision, prepare and process VA paperwork, work at a VA medical facility or National Cemetery, or perform other approved activities.

Students must attend school at the three-quarter of full-time rate.

VA will select students for the work-study program based on different factors. Such factors include:

- Disability of the student;
- Ability of the student to complete the work-study contract before the end of his or her eligibility for education benefits;
- Job availability within normal commuting distance to the student;
- VA will give the highest priority to a veteran who has a service-connected disability or disabilities rated by VA at 30% or more.

The number of applicants selected will depend on the availability of VA-related work at the school or at VA facilities in the area.

Students may work during or between periods of enrollment, and can arrange with VA to work any number of hours during his or her enrollment. However, the maximum number of hours a student may work is 25 times the number of weeks in the enrollment period.

Students will earn an hourly wage equal to the Federal or State minimum wage, whichever is greater. If a student works at a college or university, the school **may** pay the difference between the amount VA pays and the amount the school normally pays other work-study students doing the same job.

Students interested in taking part in a work-study program must complete VA Form 22,8691, Application for Work-Study Allowance. Completed forms should be sent to the nearest VA regional office.

EDUCATIONAL COUNSELING

VA can provide services to help eligible individuals understand their educational and vocational strengths and weaknesses and to plan:

- An educational or training goal, and the means by which the goal can be reached; or
- An employment goal for which an individual qualifies on the basis of present training or experience.

VA can also help plan an effective job search.

Counseling is available for:

- Service members eligible for VA educational assistance; and
- Service members on active duty and within 180 days of discharge; or
- Veterans with discharges that are not dishonorable, who are within one year from date of discharge.

VOCATIONAL REHABILITATION

Veterans may qualify for Training and Rehabilitation under Chapter 31 of Title 38, United States Code, if:

- The veteran has a service-connected disability or disabilities rated by VA at 20% or more; and
- The veteran received a discharge from active duty that was not dishonorable; and
- The veteran has an employment handicap.

Veterans may also qualify with a service-connected disability or disabilities rated by VA at 10%, and:

- The veteran has a serious employment handicap; or
- The veteran first applied for vocational rehabilitation benefits before November 1, 1990, reapplied after that date, and has an employment handicap.

Vocational rehabilitation helps disabled veterans become independent in daily living. Veterans may also receive assistance in selecting, preparing for, and securing employment that is compatible with their interests, talents, skills, physical capabilities, and goals.

To apply for vocational rehabilitation, VA for 28-1900, Disabled Veterans Application for Vocational Rehabilitation, must be completed and sent to the nearest VA regional office.

For detailed information on vocational rehabilitation, refer to Chapter 15 of this book.

APPEAL OF VA DECISION

VA decisions on education benefits may be appealed within one year of the date an individual receives notice of a VA decision. Examples of *VA decisions* include:

- Training time,
- Change of program,
- School or course approval.

If a service member disagrees with a decision about his or her basic eligibility, he or she must contact the unit, National Guard Education Officer, or Army Reserve Education Services Officer. VA does not have authority under the law to reverse eligibility determinations. If the eligibility status is corrected, VA will pay benefits for periods during which the individual was eligible.

For detailed information on filing an appeal, please refer to Chapter 36 of this book.

CHAPTER 21

LIFE INSURANCE

VA insurance programs were developed to provide insurance benefits for veterans and servicemembers who may not be able to get insurance from private companies because of a service connected disability or because of the extra risks involved in military service.

VA has responsibility for veterans' and servicemembers' life insurance programs. Listed below are the eight life insurance programs managed by VA. The first four programs listed are closed to new issues. The last four are still issuing new policies.

WAR RISK INSURANCE ACT (1914)

The United States Government first became involved in the insurance business when war broke out in Europe in 1914. Although President Wilson declared America neutral, commercial merchant ships supplied war materials to the allies in the war against Germany. Owners of these merchant ships could not get marine insurance from commercial companies. Congress passed the War Risk Insurance Act on September 2, 1914, providing marine insurance protection for merchant ships supplying the allies.

America entered the war against Germany in April 1917. Life insurance issued by commercial life insurers either excluded protection against the extra hazards of war, or if such protection was included, the premium rates were much higher than the normal rate. The War Risk Insurance Act was amended on June 12, 1917, to cover merchant marine personnel. The act was again amended on October 6, 1917, authorizing, for the first time, issuance of government life insurance to members of the armed forces. Over 4 million policies were issued during World War I.

UNITED STATES GOVERNMENT LIFE INSURANCE – USGLI (1919-1940) POLICY PREFIX – K

The United States Government Life Insurance program (USGLI) was established in 1919 and replaced War Risk policies. Individuals could keep this coverage after separation from service.

The program was established to meet the needs of World War I veterans, but remained open to servicemembers and veterans with service before October 8, 1940. The government became a self-insurer, since private insurance companies were unwilling to assume the unpredictable risks associated with a war.

Premiums No Longer Paid

Because of the strong financial position of this program, all USGLI policies were declared paid-up as of January 1, 1983. *Premiums are no longer collected from policyholders in this program.*

Dividends Paid To USGLI Policyholders

Dividends are paid on all but a few USGLI policies.

Reserves set aside in the trust funds continue to earn interest each year in excess of what is needed to pay future claims allowing VA to pay dividends.

Disability Provisions

USGLI policies (except Special Endowment at Age 96) contain a provision that matures the policy upon the insured's total permanent disability. Under this provision:

- Proceeds are payable in installments of $5.75 monthly per $1,000 of insurance, as long as the insured remains totally and permanently disabled, with 240 payments guaranteed.
- If the insured dies before all guaranteed installments have been paid, the balance is payable to his or her named beneficiary.
- No additional premium is charged.
- There is no limit as to the age at which a disability may occur.

Filing a Death Claim

To file a death claim, the beneficiary should complete *VA Form 29-4125, Claim for One Sum Payment*. The completed form should be mailed or faxed, along with a death certificate to:

Department of Veterans Affairs
Regional Office and Insurance Center
PO Box 7208
Philadelphia, PA 19101
Fax: (215) 381-3561

If the beneficiary desires monthly payments instead of one lump sum, additional information is needed. The beneficiary should call the Insurance Center at (800) 669-8477 for instructions.

Customer Service

Any questions regarding USGLI should be directed to the VA Life Insurance Program at (800) 669-8477.

NATIONAL SERVICE LIFE INSURANCE (1940-1951) POLICY PREFIX - V, H, N OR AN

The National Service Life Insurance program (NSLI) was established on October 8, 1940 to meet the insurance needs of World War II military personnel and veterans. Like USGLI coverage, insureds could keep their NSLI coverage after discharge from service.

Any questions regarding NSLI should be directed to the VA Life Insurance Program at (800) 669-8477.

Over 22 million policies were issued under the NSLI program. The majority of policies VA administers directly are NSLI policies. This program remained open until April 25, 1951, when two new programs were established for Korean War servicemembers and veterans.

The NSLI program provides for:

- A maximum amount of $10,000 insurance coverage. (However, this limit does not include *paid-up additional insurance* which can be purchased with the annual dividends.);
- Individual policies issued to each policyholder;
- Certain contractual rights whereby a policyholder can bring a suit against VA in a US District Court. Administrative decisions of the Board of Veterans Appeals can be appealed to the Court of Veterans Appeals.

Premium Rates "Capped" For Term Policies

NSLI "V" term policies can be renewed indefinitely. At the older ages, premium rates increase significantly to cover the higher death rates at those ages.

In 1984, the VA "capped" premium rates at the age 70 rate. This means that a term policyholder's premium will never increase over the age 70 -premium rate.

Effective September 11, 2000, "capped" NSLI term policies receive a termination dividend if a policy lapses, or if the policyholder voluntarily cancels their policy. The termination dividend will be used to purchase paid-up additional whole life insurance.

Dividends Paid To NSLI Policyholders

After the reserve level requirements are determined by the Insurance Actuarial Staff, any surplus funds are returned to policyholders as a dividend.

Disability Provisions

All NSLI policies provide for

- A waiver of premiums at no extra cost if the insured becomes totally disabled for six months or longer prior to age 65.
- An optional "Total Disability Income Provision" covering disability before age 65, providing a monthly income of up to $100 per month, as long as total disability continues.

"H" Insurance

"H" policies were issued between August 1, 1946, and December 31, 1949, to veterans with service-incurred disabilities.

On November 11, 1998, the President signed into law the 'Veterans Programs Enhancement Act of 1998' (Public Law 105-368), which contained provisions affecting VA benefits. Included in the legislation was the merger of "H" policies into the regular NSLI "V" policies. Under the new law:

- All "H" policies were to be converted to "V" policies by January 1999.
- Converted policies now have the same premium rates and policy provisions as "V" policies.
- "H" policyholders now receive dividends.

Filing a Death Claim

To file a death claim, the beneficiary should complete *VA Form 29-4125, Claim for One Sum Payment*. The completed form should be mailed or faxed, along with a death certificate to:

Department of Veterans Affairs
Regional Office and Insurance Center
PO Box 7208
Philadelphia, PA 19101
Fax: (215) 381-3561

If the beneficiary desires monthly payments instead of one lump sum, additional information is needed. The beneficiary should call the Insurance Center at 1-800-669-8477 for instructions.

Customer Service

Any questions regarding NSLI should be directed to the VA Life Insurance Program at (800) 669-8477.

SERVICEMEN'S INDEMNITY INSURANCE (1951-1956)

In 1951, NSLI was replaced by Servicemen's Indemnity Insurance, which automatically covered active duty servicemembers for $10,000 at no cost to the individual. Servicemembers remained covered for 120 days after their discharge.

VETERANS' SPECIAL LIFE INSURANCE - VSLI (1951-1956) POLICY PREFIX - RS OR W

Discharged servicemembers who had Servicemen's Indemnity Insurance could replace their coverage with Veterans' Special Life Insurance (VSLI). VSLI was established in 1951 to meet the insurance needs of veterans who served during the Korean Conflict, and the post Korean period through January 1, 1957. The VSLI program allowed these newly discharged servicemembers to apply for $10,000 of contract term insurance. Application had to be made during the 120-day period during which they remained covered by Servicemen's Indemnity Insurance. (The $10,000 policy limit does not include *paid-up additional insurance*, which can be purchased with the annual dividends.)

The Veterans' Special Life Insurance program was closed to new issues at the end of 1956.

In the early 1950's, commercial life insurance companies began to view the government's life insurance programs for veterans as competition for their business and began lobbying Congress to remove the government from the life insurance business. As a result, the Veterans' Special Life Insurance program was closed to new issues at the end of 1956.

Features Of "RS" And "W" Policies:

There are two types of VSLI policies:

"RS" - five-year level premium term policies:

- These were the original policies available in this program.
- "RS" policies could remain in force as 5 Year Level Premium Term beyond the age of 50.
- To provide financial relief from the high premium rates at advanced ages, "RS" term premiums were capped at the age 70-renewal rate effective May 1, 1989. This meant that the annual premium for these policies would not exceed $69.73 per $1,000 of coverage.

Effective September 11, 2000, "capped" VSLI term policies receive a termination dividend if a policy lapses, or if the policyholder voluntarily cancels their policy. The termination dividend will be used to purchase paid-up additional whole life insurance.

"W" - five-year level premium term policies:

- A 1959 legislative change permitted "RS" policyholders to convert to permanent plans or to exchange their policies for a special lower premium term policy. These newer policies are identified by the prefix "W."

- To avoid "W" term policyholders from keeping their policies into advanced ages (when premiums are very high), these policies had to be converted to permanent plans before age 50, or coverage ceased. There are no longer any "W" term policyholders eligible for this conversion.

Disability Provisions

All VSLI policies provide for:

- A waiver of premiums at no extra cost based on the insured's total disability lasting six months or longer and starting before age 65.

- An optional Total Disability Income Provision covering disability before age 65, providing a monthly income of $10 per $1,000 of insurance, is available at an extra cost.

Filing a Death Claim

To file a death claim, the beneficiary should complete *VA Form 29-4125, Claim for One Sum Payment.*

The completed form should be mailed or faxed, along with a death certificate to:

Department of Veterans Affairs
Regional Office and Insurance Center
PO Box 7208
Philadelphia, PA 19101
Fax: (215) 381-3561

If the beneficiary desires monthly payments instead of one lump sum, additional information is needed. The beneficiary should call the Insurance Center at (800) 669-8477 for instructions.

Customer Service

Any questions regarding VSLI should be directed to the VA Life Insurance Program at (800) 669-8477.

SERVICE-DISABLED VETERANS INSURANCE-S-DVI (1951-PRESENT) (POLICY PREFIX - RH OR ARH)

The only new insurance issued between 1957 and 1965 to either servicemembers or veterans was Service-Disabled Veterans Insurance. This insurance was (and still is) available to veterans with a service-connected disability.

S-DVI, also called "RH Insurance" is available in a variety of permanent plans, as well as term insurance. Policies are issued for a maximum face amount of $10,000.

S-DVI is open to veterans separated from the service on or after April 25, 1951, who receive a service-connected disability rating of 0% or greater. New policies are still being issued under this program.

Eligibility For S-DVI Insurance ("RH")

Veterans are eligible to apply for S-DVI if:

- They have received a rating for a service-connected disability.
- They apply for the insurance within two years from the date service-connection is established. (Public Law 102-86 extended the initial one-year limit for service-connection grants made on or after September 1, 1991.)

Eligibility For Supplemental S-DVI ("Supplemental RH")

The Veterans' Benefits Act of 1992, provided for $20,000 of supplemental coverage to S-DVI policyholders. ***Premiums may not be waived on this supplemental coverage.***

S-DVI policyholders are eligible for this supplemental coverage if:

- They are eligible for a waiver of premiums.
- They apply for the coverage within one year from notice of the grant of waiver.

Gratuitous S-DVI ("ARH")

Congress enacted legislation in 1959 to protect veterans who become incompetent from a service-connected disability while eligible to apply for S-DVI, but who die before an application is filed. "ARH" insurance is:

- Issued posthumously;
- Payable to a preferred class of the veteran's relatives;
- Payable in a lump sum only.

Premiums For S-DVI Insurance

The premiums charged for this coverage are:

- Based on the rates a healthy individual would have been charged when the program began in 1951.

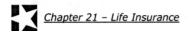

- Insufficient to pay all of the claims because the program insures many veterans with severe disabilities.
- Waived for totally disabled veterans (27% of S-DVI policyholders).
- Supplemented on an annual basis by Congressional appropriations.

Effective November 1, 2000, the VA "capped" premium rates at the age 70 rate. This means that a term policyholder's premium will never increase over the age 70 -premium rate.

There are no reserves or surplus funds in this program. Therefore, dividends are *not* paid.

Disability Provisions

S-DVI policies (except supplemental coverage) provide for the following disability benefits:

- A waiver of premiums at no extra premium based on the insured's total disability lasting six months or longer and starting before age 65;
- A total disability premium waiver in cases where the disability commenced prior to the effective date of the policy, providing the disability is service-connected.

The optional Total Disability Income Provision is not available under this program.

Filing a Death Claim

To file a death claim, the beneficiary should complete *VA Form 29-4125, Claim for One Sum Payment*. The completed form should be mailed or faxed, along with a death certificate to:

Department of Veterans Affairs
Regional Office and Insurance Center
PO Box 7208
Philadelphia, PA 19101
Fax: (215) 381-3561

If the beneficiary desires monthly payments instead of one lump sum, additional information is needed. The beneficiary should call the Insurance Center at (800) 669-8477 for instructions.

Customer Service

Any questions regarding USGLI should be directed to the VA Life Insurance Program at (800) 669-8477.

VETERANS' REOPENED INSURANCE - VRI (1965-1966) POLICY PREFIX - J, JR, OR JS

In 1964, Congress enacted legislation providing for a limited reopening of NSLI and VSLI. Beginning May 1, 1965, veterans who had been eligible to obtain insurance between October 8, 1940 and January l, 1957, could once again apply for government life insurance. They had one year to apply for this "reopened" insurance, which was available *only* to disabled veterans. Approximately 228,000 VRI policies were issued. No term insurance policies were issued in this program.

The maximum face amount of a policy is $10,000. However, this limit does not include *paid-up additional insurance*, which can be purchased with the dividends that are paid annually on these policies.

Premium Rates

Premium rates for this insurance depend on the nature and severity of the disability.

Disability Provisions

VRI policies provide for:

- A waiver of premium at no extra premium based on the insured's total disability lasting six months or longer, and starting prior to age 65.
- An optional total disability income benefit covering disability occurring before age 65 for "J" policyholders. (This is ***not*** available on policies prefixed by "JR" or "JS".) Payments are made at the rate of $10 monthly per $1,000 of coverage, as long as the insured remains totally disabled.

Dividends Paid To VRI Policyholders

The VRI program began paying dividends in 1980 in order to more equitably distribute the surplus earnings of the program.

Filing a Death Claim

To file a death claim, the beneficiary should complete *VA Form 29-4125, Claim for One Sum Payment*. The completed form should be mailed or faxed, along with a death certificate to:

Department of Veterans Affairs
Regional Office and Insurance Center
PO Box 7208
Philadelphia, PA 19101
Fax: (215) 381-3561

If the beneficiary desires monthly payments instead of one lump sum, additional information is needed. The beneficiary should call the Insurance Center at (800) 669-8477 for instructions.

Customer Service

Any questions regarding VRI should be directed to the VA Life Insurance Program at (800) 669-8477.

SERVICEMEMBERS' GROUP LIFE INSURANCE - SGLI (1965-PRESENT)

To meet the insurance needs of Vietnam Era servicemembers, the government entered into a cooperative effort with the private insurance industry. In 1965, the Servicemembers' Group Life Insurance (SGLI) program was established. This program provides low-cost term insurance protection to servicemembers through a group policy issued by a commercial life insurance company. Under this policy, the government agrees to pay the claim costs resulting from of the extra hazards of service. All other costs of the program are covered by the premiums deducted from the service member's pay.

SGLI is supervised by the Department of Veterans Affairs and is administered by the Office of Servicemembers' Group Life Insurance (OSGLI) under terms of a group insurance contract.

2006 Update:

Effective December 1, 2005, a new program of insurance was created under SGLI, called Traumatic Servicemembers' Group Life Insurance (TSGLI). This coverage provides servicemembers protection against loss due to traumatic injuries and is designed to provide financial assistance to members so their loved ones can be with them during their recovery from their injuries. The coverage ranges from $25,000 to $100,000 depending on the nature of the injury.

(See following section for further information regarding Traumatic Injury Coverage.)

Eligibility For SGLI

Full-time coverage is available for:

- Commissioned, warrant and enlisted members of the Army, Navy, Air Force, Marine Corps and Coast Guard;
- Commissioned members of the National Oceanic and Atmospheric Administration and the Public Health Service;
- Cadets or midshipmen of the four United States Service Academies;
- Ready Reservists scheduled to perform at least 12 periods of inactive training per year.

- Members of the Individual Ready Reserves who volunteer for assignment to a mobilization category.
- Part-time coverage is available for eligible members of the Reserves who do not qualify for full-time coverage.

Coverage Amounts

2006 Update:

- Effective September 1, 2005 coverage in the SGLI Program increased from $250,000 to $400,000. As of September 1, 2005, coverage must be elected in $50,000 increments. (Prior to September 1, 2005, coverage could be elected in $10,000 increments.)
- A special death gratuity of $150,000 was approved for survivors of servicemembers who:
- Died from October 7, 2001 to September 1, 2005, and
- Died while on active duty.

SGLI coverage is:

- Automatic at the time of entry into a period of active duty or reserve status.
- Available in $50,000 increments up to the maximum of $400,000 of insurance.

Members may decline coverage or may elect reduced coverage by contacting their personnel officer and completing Form 8286, SGLI Election and Certificate. If such a member later wishes to obtain or increase coverage, proof of good health will be required.

NOTE: *Reservists called to active duty, are* ***automatically*** *insured for$400,000 regardless of whether or not they had previously declined coverage, or elected a lesser amount of coverage while on reserve duty.*

Coverage Periods

Full-time SGLI coverage for members on active duty or active duty for training and members of the Ready Reserve will terminate:

1. The 120th day after separation or release from duty, or separation or release from assignment to a unit or position of the Ready Reserve;
2. For members who are totally disabled on the date of separation or release, at the end of the last day of one year following separation or release or at the end of the day on which the insured ceases to be totally disabled, whichever is earlier, but in no event earlier than 120 days following separation or release from such duty; **(NOTE: Refer to important updated information following #4, below.)**
3. At the end of the 31st day of a continuous period of:

a. Absence without leave;
b. Confinement by military authorities under a court-martial sentence involving total forfeiture of pay and allowances; or
c. Confinement by civilian authorities under sentence adjudged by a civilian court. Note: Any insurance terminated as the result of the absence or confinement, together with any beneficiary designation in effect at the time the insurance was terminated, will be automatically restored as of the date the member returns to duty with pay.

4. The last day of the month in which the member files with the uniformed service, written notice of an election not to be insured.

UPDATE - SGLI Disability Extension Increased to Two Years

On June 15, 2006, the President signed P.L. 109- 233, the Veterans' Housing Opportunity & Benefits Improvement Act of 2006. The Law extends the period of Servicemembers' Group Life Insurance (SGLI) coverage for totally disabled veterans following separation from active duty or active duty for training to the earlier of:

1. The date on which the insured ceases to be totally disabled;
2. The date that is:
   - Two years after separation or release, in the case of a separation or release during the period beginning one year before the enactment of this Act and ending on September 30, 2011; and
   - 18 months after separation or release, in the case of a separation or release on or after October 1, 2011.

The Law makes identical changes with respect to certain reserve assignments in which the individual performs active duty or volunteers for assignment to a mobilization category.

The SGLI Disability Extension is available to you if you are totally disabled at time of discharge. To be considered totally disabled, you must have a disability that prevents you from being gainfully employed OR have one of the following conditions, regardless of your employment status:

- Permanent loss of use of both hands
- Permanent loss of use of both feet
- Permanent loss of use of both eyes
- Permanent loss of use of one hand and one foot
- Permanent loss of use of one foot and one eye
- Permanent loss of use of one hand and one eye
- Total loss of hearing in both ears
- Organic loss of speech (lost ability to express oneself, both by voice and whisper, through normal organs for speech - being able to speak with an artificial appliance is disregarded in determination of total disability)

Part-time coverage terminates as follows:

1. Part-time coverage is in effect only on the days of active duty or active duty for training, and the hours of inactive duty training, including period of

travel to and from duty. A temporary termination of coverage occurs at the end of each such period of duty, including travel time, and coverage is resumed at the commencement of the next period of covered duty or travel.

2. When part-time coverage is extended for 120 days as the result of a disability, the extended coverage terminates at the end of the 120th day following the Reservist active or inactive period during which the disability was incurred or aggravated.
3. Unless extended for 120 days because of disability as referred to above, eligibility for part-time coverage terminates at the end of the last day of the member's obligation to perform such duty.
4. If a member files with the uniformed service a written notice of an election not to be insured, coverage terminates on the last day of the period of active duty or active duty for training, or at the end of the period of inactive duty training, including travel time while returning from such duty during which the election is filed. If the election is filed with a member's uniformed service other than during a period of active duty, active duty for training, or inactive duty the coverage is terminated immediately.

Beneficiary Selection

Any beneficiary can be named. If none is selected, the insurance is distributed, by law, in the following order:

- Spouse; or
- Children; or
- Parents; or
- Executor of estate; or
- Other next of kin.

An insured should designate a beneficiary by completing *Form SGVL 8286, Servicemembers' Group Life Insurance Election and Certificate.* The completed form should be submit to the individual's uniformed service.

Options For Payment Of Policy Proceeds

SGLI proceeds can be paid in a lump sum ***or*** over a 36-month period.

Alliance Account

If the proceeds are to be paid in a lump sum then beneficiaries of SGLI and VGLI will receive the payment of their insurance proceeds via an "*Alliance Account*". Rather than the traditional single check for the full amount of insurance proceeds, the beneficiary receives a checkbook for an interest bearing account from which the beneficiary can write a check for any amount from $250 up to the full amount of the proceeds. The Alliance Account :

- Earns interest at a competitive rate;
- Is guaranteed by Prudential;

- Gives the beneficiary time to make important financial decisions while their funds are secure and earning interest ;

- Gives them instant access to their money at all times.

Accelerated Benefits

On November 11, 1998, the President signed legislation authorizing the payment of "Accelerated Benefits" in the SGLI and VGLI programs subject to the following:

- Terminally ill insureds will have access of up to 50% of the face amount of their coverage during their lifetime.

- This money will be available in increments of $5,000.

- An insured must have a medical prognosis of life expectancy of 9 months or less.

Insurance Options After Separation From Service

When released from active duty or the Reserve, members with full-time SGLI coverage can convert their coverage to Veterans Group Life Insurance ***or*** to an individual commercial life insurance policy with any one of 99 participating commercial insurance companies.

Filing Death Claims

A beneficiary may file a claim for VGLI proceeds by submitting *Form SGLV 8283, Claim For Death Benefits*, to:

Office of Servicemembers' Group Life Insurance
213 Washington Avenue
Newark, NJ 07102-2999

Taxation

SGLI proceeds that are payable at the death of the insured are excluded from gross income for tax purposes. (The value of the proceeds, however, may be included in determining the value of an estate, and that estate may ultimately be subject to tax.)

If SGLI proceeds are paid to a beneficiary in 36 equal installments, the interest portion included in these installments is also exempt from taxation. In addition, delayed settlement interest (interest accrued from the date of the insured's death to the date of settlement) is also exempt from taxation.

A beneficiary is not required to report to the Internal Revenue Service any installment interest or delayed settlement interest received in addition to the proceeds.

Customer Service

Any questions regarding SGLI should be directed to the office of Servicemembers' Group Life Insurance (OSGLI) at (800) 419-1473.

TRAUMATIC INJURY PROTECTION UNDER SERVICEMEMBERS' GROUP LIFE INSURANCE (TSGLI)

TSGLI is a program that provides automatic traumatic injury coverage to all servicemembers covered under the Servicemembers' Group Life Insurance (SGLI) program.

Every member who has SGLI also has TSGLI effective December 1, 2005. This coverage applies to active duty members, reservists, funeral honors duty and one-day muster duty. The premium for TSGLI is a flat rate of $1 per month for most service members.

This benefit is also provided retroactively for members who incur severe losses as a result of traumatic a injury between October 7, 2001 and December 1, 2005 if the loss was the direct result of injuries incurred in Operations Enduring Freedom or Iraqi Freedom. For the purposes of TSGLI only, "incurred in Operation Enduring Freedom or Operation Iraqi Freedom" means that the member must have been deployed outside the United States on orders in support of OEF or OIF or serving in a geographic location that qualified the service member for the Combat Zone Tax Exclusion under the Internal Revenue Service Code.

Effective December 1, 2005 every member who has SGLI also has TSGLI.

The service member is the beneficiary of TSGLI. The member cannot name someone other than himself or herself as the TSGLI beneficiary. If the member is incompetent, the benefit will be paid to his or her guardian or attorney-in-fact. If the service member is deceased, the TSGLI payment will be made to the beneficiary or beneficiaries of the member's basic SGLI.

TSGLI coverage will pay a benefit of between $25,000 and $100,000 depending on the loss directly resulting from the traumatic injury.

TSGLI Schedule of Payments for Traumatic Losses

If the loss is--		Then the amount that will be paid is--
1	Total and permanent loss of sight in both eyes.	$100,000
2	Total and permanent loss of hearing in both ears.	$100,000
3	Loss of both hands at or above wrist.	$100,000
4	Loss of both feet at or above ankle.	$100,000
5	Quadriplegia.	$100,000
6	Hemiplegia.	$100,000
7	Paraplegia.	$100,000
8	3rd degree or worse burns, covering 30% of the body or 30% of the face.	$100,000
9	Loss of one hand at or above wrist and one foot at or above ankle.	$100,000
10	Loss of one hand at or above wrist and total and permanent loss of sight in one eye.	$100,000
11	Loss of one foot at or above ankle and total and permanent loss of sight in one eye.	$100,000
12	Total and permanent loss of speech and total and permanent loss of hearing in one ear	$75,000
13	Loss of one hand at or above wrist and total and permanent loss of speech.	$100,000
14	Loss of one hand at or above wrist and total and permanent loss of hearing in one ear.	$75,000
15	Loss of one hand at or above wrist and loss of thumb and index finger of other hand.	$100,000
16	Loss of one foot at or above ankle and total and permanent loss of speech.	$100,000

If the loss is--		Then the amount that will be paid is--
17	Loss of one foot at or above ankle and total and permanent loss of hearing in one ear.	$75,000
18	Loss of one foot at or above ankle and loss of thumb and index finger of same hand.	$100,000
19	Total and permanent loss of sight in one eye and total and permanent loss of speech.	$100,000
20	Total and permanent loss of sight in one eye and total and permanent loss of hearing in one ear.	$75,000
21	Total and permanent loss of sight in one eye and loss of thumb and index finger of same hand.	$100,000
22	Total and permanent loss of thumb of both hands, regardless of the loss of any other digits.	$100,000
23	Total and permanent loss of speech and loss of thumb and index finger of same hand.	$100,000
24	Total and permanent loss of hearing in one ear and loss of thumb and index finger of same hand.	$75,000
25	Loss of one hand at or above wrist and coma.	$50,000 for loss of hand
26	Loss of one foot at or above ankle and coma.	$50,000 for loss of foot
27	Total and permanent loss of speech and coma.	$50,000 for total and permanent loss of speech plus the amount paid for coma as noted in Item 37 of this schedule up to a combined maximum of $100,000.
28	Total and permanent loss of sight in one eye and coma.	$50,000 for total and permanent loss of sight in one eye plus the amount paid for coma as noted in Item 37 of this schedule up to a combined maximum of $100,000.

If the loss is--		Then the amount that will be paid is--
29	Total and permanent loss of hearing in one ear and coma.	$25,000 for total and permanent loss of hearing in one ear plus the amount paid for coma as noted in Item 37 of this schedule up to a combined maximum of $100,000.
30	Loss of thumb and index finger of same hand and coma.	$50,000 for loss of thumb and index finger of the same hand plus the amount paid for coma as noted in Item 37 of this schedule up to a combined maximum of $100,000.
31	Total and permanent loss of sight in one eye and inability to carry out activities of daily living due to traumatic brain injury.	$50,000 for loss of sight in one eye plus the amount paid for the inability to carry out activities of daily living due to traumatic brain injury as noted in Item 37 of this schedule up to a combined maximum of $100,000.
32	Loss of one hand at or above wrist and inability to carry out activities of daily living due to traumatic brain injury.	$50,000 for loss of hand plus the amount paid for the inability to carry out activities of daily living due to traumatic brain injury as noted in Item 37 of this schedule up to a combined maximum of $100,000.
33	Loss of one foot at or above ankle and inability to carry out activities of daily living due to traumatic brain injury.	$50,000 for loss of foot plus the amount paid for the inability to carry out activities of daily living due to traumatic brain injury as noted in Item 37 of this schedule up to a combined maximum of $100,000.
34	Loss of thumb and index finger of same hand and inability to carry out activities of daily living due to traumatic brain injury.	$50,000 for loss of thumb and index finger plus the amount paid for the inability to carry out activities of daily living due to traumatic brain injury as noted in Item 37 of this schedule up to a combined maximum of $100,000.
35	Total and permanent loss of hearing in one ear and inability to carry out activities of daily living due to traumatic brain injury.	$25,000 for total and permanent loss of hearing in one ear plus the amount paid for the inability to carry out activities of daily living due to traumatic brain injury as noted in Item 37 of this schedule up to a combined maximum of $100,000.

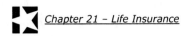

If the loss is--		Then the amount that will be paid is--
36	Total and permanent loss of speech and inability to carry out activities of daily living due to traumatic brain injury.	$50,000 for total and permanent loss of speech plus the amount paid for the inability to carry out activities of daily living due to traumatic brain injury as noted in Item 37of this schedule up to a combined maximum of $100,000.
37	Coma from traumatic injury and/or the inability to carry out activities of daily living due to traumatic brain injury. Note 1: Benefits will not be paid under this schedule for concurrent conditions of coma and traumatic brain injury. Note 2: Duration of coma includes the day of onset of the coma and the day when the member recovers from coma. Note 3: Duration of the inability to carry out activities of daily living due to traumatic brain injury includes the day of the onset of the inability to carry out activities of daily living and the day the member once again can carry out activities of daily living.	At 15th consecutive day in a coma, and/or the inability to carry out activities of daily living - $25,000 At 30th consecutive day in a coma, and/or the inability to carry out activities of daily living - Additional $25,000 At 60th consecutive day in a coma, and/or the inability to carry out activities of daily living - Additional $25,000 At 90th consecutive day in a coma, and/or the inability to carry out activities of daily living - Additional $25,000 (Benefits can be paid for both conditions only if experienced consecutively, not concurrently.)
38	Total and permanent loss of speech.	$50,000
39	Loss of one hand at or above wrist.	$50,000
40	Loss of one foot at or above ankle.	$50,000
41	Total and permanent loss of sight in one eye.	$50,000
42	Loss of thumb and index finger of same hand.	$50,000
43	Total and permanent loss of hearing in one ear.	$25,000

If the loss is--		Then the amount that will be paid is--
44	The inability to carry out activities of daily living due to loss directly resulting from a traumatic injury other than an injury to the brain. Note: Duration of the inability to carry out activities of daily living includes the day of onset of the inability to carry out activities of daily living and the day when the member can once again carry out activities of daily living.	At 30th consecutive day of the inability to carry out activities of daily living - $25,000 At 60th consecutive day of the inability to carry out of activities of daily living - Additional $25,000 At 90th consecutive day of the inability to carry out activities of daily living - Additional $25,000 At 120th consecutive day of the inability to carry out activities of daily living - Additional $25,000

SERVICEMEMBERS' GROUP LIFE INSURANCE FAMILY COVERAGE

The Veterans' Opportunities Act of 2001 extended life insurance coverage to spouses and children of members insured under the SGLI program, **effective November 1, 2001.**

Amount of Coverage

Eligible individuals may purchase up to $100,000 of SGLI coverage for a spouse, in increments of $10,000. However, individuals may not purchase more SGLI coverage for a spouse than he or she has for him/herself.

Each dependent child of every active duty servicemember or reservist who is insured under SGLI is automatically insured for $10,000.

Eligibility

Family coverage is available for the spouses and children of:

- Active duty servicemembers; and
- Members of the Ready Reserve of a uniformed service.

Note: *Family coverage is available only for members insured under the SGLI program. Family coverage is not available for those insured under the VGLI program.*

Premiums

SGLI coverage for children is free. For monthly premiums for spouses, individuals should call (800) 419-1473.

Declining Coverage

If an individual does not want insurance coverage for a spouse, or wants a reduced amount of coverage, he or she must complete *form SGLV-82861, Family Coverage Election,* and submit it to his or her personnel officer.

Termination of Coverage

Coverage for a spouse ends 120 days after any of the following events:

- The date elected in writing to terminate a spouse's coverage;
- The date elected in writing to terminate the service member's own coverage;
- The date of the service member's death;
- The date the service member's coverage terminates;
- The date of divorce.

A spouse can covert his or her coverage to a policy with a commercial company within 120 days following one of the events listed above. He or she should contact the Office of Servicemembers' Group Life Insurance at (800) 419-1473.

Coverage for a service member's children ends 120 days after any of the following events:

- The date elected in writing to terminate the service member's own coverage;
- The date the service member separates from service;
- The date of the service member's death;
- The date the child is no longer the service member's dependent.

No conversion options are available to children.

Payment of Proceeds

The service member is paid the proceeds due to the death of a spouse or child. If the service member were to die before payment could be made, the proceeds of a spouse or child claim would be paid to the member's beneficiary, as designated by the member.

VETERANS' GROUP LIFE INSURANCE – VGLI (1974-PRESENT)

In 1974, the Veterans' Group Life Insurance (VGLI) program became available to veterans, providing term insurance protection after separation from service.

VGLI, like SGLI, is supervised by the Department of Veterans Affairs, but is administered by the Office of Servicemembers' Group Life Insurance (OSGLI). VGLI provides for the conversion of Servicemembers' Group Life Insurance to a five-year renewable term policy of insurance protection after a service member's separation from service.

Eligibility For VGLI

Full-time coverage is available for the following members:

- Full-time SGLI insureds that are released from active duty or the Reserves.
- Ready Reservists who have part-time SGLI coverage, and who, while performing active duty or inactive duty for training for a period of less than 31 days, incur a disability or aggravate a preexisting disability that makes them uninsurable at standard premium rates.
- Members of the Individual Ready Reserve (IRR) and Inactive National Guard (ING).

Coverage Amounts

2006 Update:
Effective September 1, 2005, the maximum amount of SGLI and VGLI coverage increased from $250,000 to $400,000.

VGLI is issued in multiples of $10,000 up to a maximum of $400,000, but not for more than the amount of SGLI coverage the member had in force at the time of separation from active duty or the reserves.

VGLI Renewal

Members may renew their VGLI coverage under the following conditions:

- Members who have separated from service may renew their VGLI coverage for life in 5-year term periods.
- Members of the IRR or ING may renew their VGLI for additional 5-year term periods, as long as they remain in the IRR or ING.
- Rather than renew, a member also has the right at any time to ***convert*** VGLI to an individual commercial life insurance policy with any one of 99 participating commercial insurance companies.

How To Apply For VGLI

VGLI applications are mailed to eligible members, generally within 60 days after separation, and again shortly before the end of the 16-month application period. Applications are mailed to the address shown on the member's DD-Form 214 or equivalent separation orders. ***It is the member's responsibility, however, to apply within the time limits, even if they do not receive an application in the mail.***

Applications should be mailed to:

Office Of Servicemembers' Group Life Insurance
P.O. Box 5000
Millville, New Jersey 08332-9928.

Time Limits To Apply For VGLI

To be eligible, a member must apply for VGLI within the following time limits:

- Ordinarily, a member must submit an application to the OSGLI with the required premium within 120 days following separation from service.
- If a member is *totally disabled* at the time of separation from active duty *and* is granted extended free SGLI coverage, he or she may apply for VGLI anytime during the one-year period of extension.
- Individuals who are assigned to the IRR and ING have 120 days after assignment to apply, without evidence of good health, and one year after that with evidence of good health.
- If an application or the initial premium has not been submitted within the time limits above, VGLI may still be granted if an application, the initial premium and ***evidence of insurability*** (good health) are submitted to OSGLI within 1 year and 120 days following termination of SGLI. ***Applications will not be accepted after one year and 120 days.***
- An application for an incompetent member may be made by a guardian, committee, conservator or curator. In the absence of a court appointed representative, the application may be submitted by a family member or anyone acting on the member's behalf.

VGLI Premiums Rates

VGLI premium rates are determined by age group and amount of insurance. To lessen the high cost of term insurance at the older ages, a Decreasing Term Option is available, starting at age group 60 to 64. Under this option an insured pays a level premium for life, while the insurance amount declines by 25% for three subsequent five-year renewals. At that point, coverage remains level at 25% of the original insurance amount.

Payment Of Premiums

Once the VGLI application is approved, the OSGLI will send the insured a certificate and a supply of monthly premium payment coupons.

Premiums may be paid:

- Monthly;
- Quarterly;
- Semiannually;
- Annually;
- By monthly allotment from military retirement pay;
- By monthly deduction from VA compensation payments.

If the insured does not pay the premium when it is due, or within a grace period of 60 days, the VGLI coverage will lapse. If VGLI lapsed due to failure to pay the premiums on time, the insured will receive a notification of the lapse and a reinstatement form. The insured may apply to reinstate coverage at any time within 5 years of the date of the unpaid premium. If the insured applies for reinstatement within 6 months from the date of lapse, the individual only needs to provide evidence that he or she is in the same state of health on the date of reinstatement as on the date of lapse. Otherwise, the individual may need to provide proof of good health.

Beneficiary Selection

Any beneficiary can be named. If none is selected, the insurance is distributed, by law, in the following order:

- Spouse, or
- Children, or
- Parents, or
- Executor of estate, or
- Other next of kin.

To name a beneficiary, the insured must submit *Form SGLV 8712, Beneficiary Designation-Veterans' Group Life Insurance.* The completed form should be sent to:

Office of Servicemembers' Group Life Insurance
213 Washington Avenue
Newark, NJ 07102-2999

When an insured converts SGLI to VGLI following separation from service, a new beneficiary designation form must be completed. If a new form is not filed, the SGLI beneficiary designation will be considered the VGLI designation for up to 60 days after the effective date of the VGLI. If a new beneficiary is not designated after this 60-day period, the proceeds would be paid "By Law" under the order of precedence in the law.

Options For Payment Of Policy Proceeds

Alliance Account

VGLI proceeds can be paid in a lump sum or over a 36-month period.
If the proceeds are to be paid in a lump sum then beneficiaries of SGLI and VGLI will receive the payment of their insurance proceeds via an "*Alliance Account*".

Rather than the traditional single check for the full amount of insurance proceeds, the beneficiary receives a checkbook for an interest bearing account from which the beneficiary can write a check for any amount from $250 up to the full amount of the proceeds. The Alliance Account:

- Earns interest at a competitive rate;
- Is guaranteed by Prudential;
- Gives the beneficiary time to make important financial decisions while their funds are secure and earning interest;
- Gives them instant access to their money at all times.

Accelerated Benefits

On November 11, 1998, the President signed legislation authorizing the payment of *"Accelerated Benefits"* in the SGLI and VGLI programs subject to the following:

- Terminally ill insureds will have access of up to 50 percent of the face amount of their coverage during their lifetime.
- This money will be available in increments of $5,000.
- An insured must have a medical prognosis of life expectancy of 9 months or less.

Filing Death Claims

A beneficiary may file a claim for VGLI proceeds by submitting *Form SGLV 8283, Claim For Death Benefits*, to:

Office of Servicemembers' Group Life Insurance
213 Washington Avenue
Newark, NJ 07102-2999

Taxation

VGLI proceeds are exempt from taxation. Any installment interest or delayed settlement interest that a beneficiary receives in addition to the proceed is also exempt from taxation, and does not need to be reported to the IRS.

Customer Service

Any questions regarding VGLI should be directed to the office of Servicemembers' Group Life Insurance (OSGLI) at (800) 419-1473.

VETERANS' MORTGAGE LIFE INSURANCE – VMLI (1971-PRESENT)

The Veterans' Mortgage Life Insurance (VMLI) program began in 1971, and is designed to provide financial protection to cover eligible veterans' home mortgages in the event of death. VMLI is issued to those severely disabled veterans, under age 70, who have received grants for Specially Adapted Housing from VA. (Refer to Chapter 5 of this book for information regarding Specially Adapted Housing.)

The maximum amount of VMLI allowed an eligible veteran is $90,000. The insurance is payable if the veteran dies before the mortgage is paid off. VA will pay the amount of money still owed on the mortgage up to $90,000. ***The insurance is payable only to the mortgage lender.*** The day-to-day operations of the program are handled by the Philadelphia VAROIC.

Coverage Amounts

VMLI coverage decreases as the insured's mortgage falls below $90,000. This reduced coverage cannot be reinstated. However, if the home is sold and a new home is purchased the veteran becomes eligible once again for the maximum amount of coverage.

Payment Of VMLI Proceeds

Certain conditions apply to the payment of VMLI benefits:

- The insurance is payable at the death of the veteran only to the mortgage holder.
- If the title of the property is shared with anyone other than the veteran's spouse, the insurance coverage is only for the percentage of the title that is in the veteran's name.
- No insurance is payable if the mortgage is paid off before the death of the insured or if it was paid off by other mortgage insurance before the VMLI payment is made.

The insurance will be canceled for any of the following conditions:

- The mortgage is paid in full.

- Termination of the veteran's ownership of the property securing the loan.
- The request of the veteran.
- Failure of the veteran to submit timely statements or other required information.

Premiums

Premiums are determined by the insurance age of the veteran, the outstanding balance of the mortgage at the time of application, and the remaining length of time the mortgage has to run. Veterans who desire insurance will be advised of the correct premium when it is determined.

Premiums ***must*** be paid by deduction from the veteran's monthly compensation or pension payments, if the veteran is receiving such payments. If such payments are not being received the veteran may make direct payments, on a monthly, quarterly, semiannual, or annual basis, to the VA Insurance Center in Philadelphia, Pennsylvania.

DIVIDEND OPTIONS

If a policyholder is eligible for a dividend, he or she may choose from several dividend options that are available:

- ***Cash***, paid to policyholder by US Treasury check.
- ***Credit***, held in account for the insured with interest. Can be used to prevent policy lapse. Will be refunded upon the insured's request, or will be included in the award to the beneficiary(ies) at the time of the insured's death.
- ***Paid-Up Additions (PUA'S)***, used as a net single premium to purchase additional paid-up insurance. Available only on "V," "RS," "W," "J," "JR," and "JS" policies. PUA's will be whole life insurance if the basic insurance is an endowment policy.
- ***Deposit***, held in account for insured with interest. Available only on permanent plan policies. Considered part of the policy's cash value for the purpose of purchasing reduced paid-up insurance, or if the policy lapses, extended insurance (except for "K" or "JS" policies). Will be refunded upon the insured's request. Will be included in the award to the beneficiary(ies) at the time of the insured's death.
- ***Premium***, applied to pay premiums in advance.
- ***Indebtedness***, applied toward a loan or lien on a policy.
- ***Net Cash***, used to pay an annual premium with any remainder paid to the policyholder under the cash option.
- ***Net PUA***, used to pan an annual premium with any remainder used to purchase paid-up additional insurance.

- ***Net Loan-Lien***, used to pay an annual premium with any remainder used to reduce an outstanding loan or lien.

To change the method in which dividends are paid, individuals should speak with an Insurance Specialist at (800) 669-8477.

MISCELLANEOUS INFORMATION ABOUT GOVERNMENT LIFE INSURANCE POLICIES

Power of Attorney is not acceptable for executing a change of beneficiary for government life insurance, even if certain state statutes allow it. Only a court appointed guardian that is recognized by state statutes can execute a beneficiary designation. If the state statute does not give the guardian broad powers to authorize a beneficiary change, a specific court order is needed to effectuate a change.

Assignment of government life insurance is not allowed, for any reason, nor can ownership of a policy be transferred. Only the insured can exercise the rights and privileges inherent in the ownership of the policy.

Policy Loans are available on permanent plans of insurance. The policyholder can take up to 94% of the reserve value of the policy, less any indebtedness. The policy cannot be lapsed, and premiums must be paid or waived at least one year before a policy has a loan value. Changes in interest rates are made on October 1 of each year, if warranted. Rate changes are tied to the "ten year constant maturities", U.S. Treasury securities index.

A policyholder can apply for a loan by filing *VA Form 29-1546, Application for Policy Loan.* The completed form can be faxed to (215) 381-3580, or mailed to:

Department of Veterans Affairs
Regional Office and Insurance Center
PO Box 7327
Philadelphia, PA 19101

An Annual Insurance Policy Statement is mailed to the insured on the policy anniversary date of each policy. The statement provides the insured with information about his or her VA insurance. The statement should be reviewed for accuracy each year, and the VA should be contacted immediately if there are any discrepancies.

Dividend Hoax - Rumors that Congress approved a "Special Dividend" for veterans who do or do not have Government life insurance have been spread for over 30 years. These rumors are false. The only dividends being paid by VA are on active Government life insurance policies. Dividends on active policies have been paid annually for many years and policyholders do not need to apply for them.

"Special Dividend" rumors are spread by well-meaning people who want to help veterans but fail to check out their sources before passing the information along to others. Notices have appeared in veterans' magazines, union newspapers, fraternal publications, newspapers and every other publication imaginable. The hoax has appeared in many forms and seems to change to fit the times. It started in the 1960's as a rumor about veterans with WW II insurance. More recently, it has been adapted to state that a dividend is being paid on Servicemembers' Group Life Insurance (SGLI) or Veterans' Group Life Insurance (VGLI) coverage.

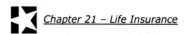

Unfortunately, this misinformation unnecessarily raises the expectations of veterans and service personnel. There has been no recent legislation authorizing any "special" dividends.

If you have any questions regarding this issue, feel free to contact the VA Insurance Center at (800) 669-8477.

CHAPTER 22

HOME LOAN GUARANTIES

GENERAL INFORMATION

> *The VA does not actually lend the money to veterans. The VA guaranty means the lender is protected against loss if the veteran fails to repay the loan.*

The purpose of the VA loan guaranty program is to help veterans and active duty personnel finance the purchase of homes with competitive loan terms and interest rates. The VA does not actually lend the money to veterans. VA guaranteed loans are made by private lenders, such as banks, savings & loans, or mortgage companies. The VA guaranty means the lender is protected against loss if the veteran fails to repay the loan.

The VA Loan Guaranty Service is the organization within the VA that has the responsibility of administering the home loan program.

VA guaranteed loans offer the following important features:

- Equal opportunity for all qualified veterans to obtain a VA guaranteed loan.
- No downpayment (unless required by the lender or the purchase price is more than the reasonable value of the property).
- Buyer is informed of reasonable value.
- Buyer's interest rate is negotiable.
- Buyer has the ability to finance the VA funding fee (plus reduced funding fees with a downpayment of at least 5%, and exemption for veterans receiving VA compensation).
- Closing costs are comparable with other financing types (and may be lower).
- No mortgage insurance premiums are necessary.
- An assumable mortgage may be available.
- Buyer has the right to prepay without penalty.
- A warranty from the builder, and assistance from VA to obtain cooperation of builder is offered for homes inspected by VA during construction.

- VA may offer assistance to a veteran borrow who is in default due to temporary financial difficulty.

VA guaranteed loans do not do the following:

- Guarantee that a home is free of defects (VA only guarantees the loan. It is the veteran's responsibility to assure that he or she is satisfied with the property being purchased. Veterans should seek expert advice as necessary, *before* legally committing to a purchase agreement.)
- If a veteran has a home built, VA cannot compel the builder to correct construction defects, although VA does have the authority to suspend a builder from further participation in the VA home loan program.
- VA cannot guarantee the veteran is making a good investment.
- VA cannot provide a veteran with legal service.

Uses For VA Loan Guaranties

Veterans must certify that they plan to live in the home they are buying or building in order to qualify for a VA loan guaranty.

VA loan guaranties can be used for the following:

- To purchase, construct, or improve a home.
- To purchase and improve a home concurrently.
- To purchase a residential condominium or townhouse unit in a VA approved project. (If one veteran is purchasing the property, the total number of separate units cannot be more than 4.)
- To purchase a manufactured home or a manufactured home and manufactured home lot.
- To purchase and improve a manufactured home lot on which to place a manufactured home which the veteran already owns and occupies.
- To refinance an existing home loan.
- To refinance an existing VA loan to reduce the interest rate, and make energy-efficient improvements.
- To refinance an existing manufactured home loan in order to acquire a lot.
- To improve a home by installing a solar heating and/or cooling system, or other energy efficient improvements.

Veterans must certify that they plan to live in the home they are buying or building in order to qualify for a VA loan guaranty.

VA loan guaranties are available only for property located in the United States, its territories, or possessions (Puerto Rico, Guam, Virgin Islands, American Samoa, and Northern Mariana Islands).

VA loan guaranties are not available for farm loans, unless there is a home on the property, which will be personally occupied by the veteran. Non-realty loans for the purchase of equipment, livestock, machinery, etc. are not made. Other loan programs for farm financing may be available through the Farmers Home Administration, which gives preference to veteran applicants. (Interested veterans should refer to the local telephone directory for the phone number of a local office.)

Although business loans are not available through VA, the Small Business Administration (SBA) has a number of programs designed to help foster and encourage small business enterprises, including financial and management assistance. Each SBA office has a veteran's affairs officer available to speak with. (Interested veterans should refer to the local telephone directory for the phone number of a local SBA office, or call (800) 827-5722.)

ELIGIBILITY REQUIREMENTS

Individuals may qualify for VA home loan guaranties if their service falls within any of the following categories:

World War II Eligibility Requirements:

- Active duty on or after September 16, 1940 and prior to July 26, 1947; and
- Discharge or separation under other than dishonorable conditions; and
- At least 90 days of total service, unless discharged earlier for a service-connected disability.
- Unremarried widows of above-described eligible individuals who died as a result of service.
- Widows of above-described eligible individuals who died as a result of service ***who remarried after age 57***. (This provision is effective January 1, 2004.)

Post World War II Eligibility Requirements:

- Active duty on or after July 26, 1947 and prior to June 27, 1950; and
- Discharge or separation under other than dishonorable conditions; and
- At least 181 days continuous service, unless discharged earlier for a service-connected disability.
- Unremarried widows of above-described eligible individuals who died as a result of service.
- Widows of above-described eligible individuals who died as a result of service ***who remarried after age 57***. (This provision is effective January 1, 2004.)

Korean Conflict Eligibility Requirements:

- Active duty on or after June 27, 1950 and prior to February 1, 1955; and
- Discharge or separation under other than dishonorable conditions; and
- At least 90 days of total service, unless discharged earlier for a service-connected disability.
- Unremarried widows of above-described eligible individuals who died as a result of service.
- Widows of above-described eligible individuals who died as a result of service ***who remarried after age 57***. (This provision is effective January 1, 2004.)

Post-Korean Conflict Eligibility Requirements:

- Active duty on or after February 1, 1955 and prior to August 5, 1964; and
- Discharge or separation under other than dishonorable conditions; and
- At least 181 days continuous service, unless discharged earlier for a service-connected disability.
- Unremarried widows of above-described eligible individuals who died as a result of service.
- Widows of above-described eligible individuals who died as a result of service ***who remarried after age 57***. (This provision is effective January 1, 2004.)

Vietnam Eligibility Requirements:

- Active duty on or after August 5, 1964, and prior to May 8, 1975. (For those serving in the Republic of Vietnam, the beginning date is February 28, 1961.); and
- Discharge or separation under other than dishonorable conditions; and
- At least 90 days of total service, unless discharged earlier for a service-connected disability.
- Unremarried widows of above-described eligible individuals who died as a result of service.
- Widows of above-described eligible individuals who died as a result of service ***who remarried after age 57***. (This provision is effective January 1, 2004.)

Post-Vietnam Eligibility Requirements for Veterans With Enlisted Service Between May 8, 1975 and September 7, 1980 (if enlisted) or October 16, 1981 (if officer):

- At least 181 days of continuous service, all of which occurred on or after May 8, 1975, unless discharged earlier for a service-connected disability; and
- Discharge or separation under other than dishonorable conditions.
- Unremarried widows of above-described eligible individuals who died as a result of service.
- Widows of above-described eligible individuals who died as a result of service ***who remarried after age 57***. (This provision is effective January 1, 2004.)

Post-Vietnam Eligibility Requirements for Veterans Separated from Enlisted Service Between September 7, 1980 (October 17, 1981 for Officers) and August 1, 1990:

- At least 24 months of continuous active duty, or the full period (at least 181 days) for which individual was called or ordered to active duty, and discharged or separated under other than dishonorable conditions; or
- At least 181 days of continuous active duty, and discharged due to:
- a hardship; or
- a service-connected, compensable disability; or
- a medical condition which preexisted service, and has not been determined to be service-connected; or
- the convenience of the government as a result of a reduction in force; or
- a physical or mental condition not characterized as a disability, and not the result of misconduct, but which did interfere with the performance of duty.
- Early discharge for a service-connected disability.
- Unremarried widows of above-described eligible persons who died as the result of service.
- Widows of above-described eligible individuals who died as a result of service ***who remarried after age 57***. (This provision is effective January 1, 2004.)

Persian Gulf War Eligibility Requirements:

- At least 24 months of continuous active duty on or after August 2, 1990, or the full period for which the individual was called or ordered to active duty, and discharged or separated under other than dishonorable conditions; or
- At least 90 days of continuous active duty, and discharged due to:
- A hardship; or
- A service-connected, compensable disability; or
- A medical condition which preexisted service, and has not been determined to be service-connected; or
- The convenience of the government as a result of a reduction in force; or
- A physical or mental condition not characterized as a disability, and not the result of misconduct, but which did interfere with the performance of duty.
- Early discharge for a service-connected disability.
- Unremarried widows of above-described eligible individuals who died as the result of service.
- Widows of above-described eligible individuals who died as a result of service ***who remarried after age 57***. (This provision is effective January 1, 2004.)

(When law or Presidential Proclamation ends the Persian Gulf War, a minimum of 181 days of continuous active duty will be required for those who did not serve during wartime.)

Members of the Reserve and National Guard are eligible if activated after August 1, 1990, served at least 90 days, and discharged or separated under other than dishonorable conditions.)

Active Duty Personnel Eligibility Requirements

- Individuals currently on active duty are eligible after serving on continuous active duty for at least 90 days.
- (Individuals who are six-month enlistees, and serve six months active duty for training only are not eligible for VA guaranteed loans. However, these individuals may be eligible for FHA home mortgage insurance for veterans.

Eligibility Requirements for Members of the Selected Reserve:

- At least 6 years in the Reserves or National Guard, or discharged earlier due to a service-connected disability; and
- Discharged or separated under other than dishonorable conditions; or
- Placed on the retired list; or
- Transferred to an element of the Ready Reserve other than the Selected Reserve; or
- Continue to serve in the Selected Reserve.
- Unremarried widows of above-described eligible persons who died as the result of service.
- Widows of above-described eligible individuals who died as a result of service ***who remarried after age 57***. (This provision is effective January 1, 2004.)

Eligibility Requirements for Other Types of Service:

- Certain U.S. citizens who served in the armed forces of a U.S. ally in World War II.
- Members of organizations with recognized contributions to the U.S. during World War II. (Questions about this type of service eligibility can be answered at any VA regional office.)
- Spouses of American servicemen who are listed as missing-in-action, or prisoners-of-war for a total of 90 days or more.

CERTIFICATE OF ELIGIBILITY

The Certificate of Eligibility is the medium by which VA certifies eligibility for A VA loan guaranty.

Individuals may request a Certificate of Eligibility by completing VA Form 26-1880, Request for a Certificate of Eligibility for VA Home Loan Benefits. The completed form should be submitted to a VA Eligibility Center along with acceptable proof of service.

Veterans separated after January 1, 1950 should submit DD Form 214, Certificate of Release or Discharge from active Duty.

Veterans separated after October 1, 1979 should submit copy 4 of DD Form 214.

Since there is no uniform document similar to the DD Form 214 for proof of service in the Selected Reserve a number of different forms may be accepted as documentation of service in the Selected Reserve:

- For those who served in the Army or Air National Guard and were discharged after at least 6 years of such service, NGB Form 22 may be sufficient.
- Those who served in the Army, Navy, Air Force, Marine Corps or Coast Guard Reserves may need to rely on a variety of forms that document at least 6 years of participation in paid training periods, or have paid active duty for training.
- Often it will be necessary to submit a combination of documents, such as an Honorable Discharge certificate together with a Retirement Points Statement. It is the reservist's responsibility to obtain and submit documentation of 6 years of honorable service.

In addition, if an individual is now on active duty, and has not been previously discharged from active duty service, he or she must submit a statement of service that includes the name of the issuing authority (base or command), and is signed by or at the direction of an appropriate official. The statement must identify the individual, include the social security number, provide the date of entry on active duty and the duration of any lost time.

The Certificate of Eligibility should be presented to the lender when completing the loan application. (However, if an individual does not have a Certificate, the lender may have the forms necessary to apply for the Certificate of Eligibility.)

VA Eligibility Centers

Specific questions regarding VA home loan eligibility, and all requests for Certificates of Eligibility should be sent to the appropriate Eligibility Center:

Los Angeles Eligibility Center
P.O. Box 240097
Los Angeles, CA 90024
1-888-487-1970

Alaska
Arizona
Arkansas
California
Colorado
Hawaii
Idaho
Illinois
Iowa
Kansas
Louisiana
Minnesota
Missouri
Montana
Nebraska
Nevada
New Mexico
North Dakota
Oklahoma
Oregon
South Dakota
Texas
Utah
Washington
Wisconsin
Wyoming

Winston-Salem Eligibility Center
P.O. Box 20729
Winston-Salem, NC 27120
1-888-244-6711

Alabama
Connecticut
District of Columbia
Delaware
Florida
Georgia
Indiana
Kentucky
Maine
Maryland
Massachusetts
Michigan

Mississippi
New Hampshire
New Jersey
New York
North Carolina
Ohio
Pennsylvania
Puerto Rico
Rhode Island
South Carolina
Tennessee
Vermont
Virginia
West Virginia

PROCEDURES FOR OBTAINING LOANS

- Apply for a Certificate of Eligibility.
- Decide on a home the buyer wants to purchase, and sign a purchase agreement.
- Order an appraisal from VA. (Usually this is done by the lender.) Most VA regional offices offer a "speed-up" telephone appraisal system. Call the local VA office for details.
- Apply to a mortgage lender for the loan. While the appraisal is being done, the lender (mortgage company, savings and loan, bank, etc.) can be gathering credit and income information. If the lender is authorized by VA to do automatic processing, upon receipt of the VA or LAPP appraised value determination, the loan can be approved and closed without waiting for VA's review of the credit application. For loans that must first be approved by VA, the lender will send the application to the local VA office, which will notify the lender of its decision.
- Close the loan and the buyer moves in.

If a lender cannot be located, the local VA regional office can provide a list of lenders active in the VA program.

A VA loan guaranty does not guarantee approval of a loan. The veteran must still meet the financial institution's income and credit requirements. If a loan is approved, the VA guarantees the loan when it's closed.

GUARANTY OR ENTITLEMENT AMOUNT

The amount of the VA guaranty available to a veteran is called the entitlement. The lender may use the entitlement amount in place of a down payment. The amount of entitlement varies with the loan amount, as detailed in the following table:

Loan Amount	VA Guaranty	Maximum Guaranty
Up to $45,000	50%	$22,500
$45,001 - $144,000	40% - 50%	$36,000
Greater than $144,000	25%	$60,000* (see footnote)
Manufactured Home or Lot	40%	$20,000

**One of the provisions of The Veterans Benefits Act of 2004 changed the maximum guaranty amount of $60,000, for certain loans in excess of $144,000 to an amount equal to 25% of the Freddie Mac conforming loan limit determined under section 305(a)(2) of the Federal Home Loan Mortgage Corporation Act for a single family residence, as adjusted for the year involved. For example, the maximum guaranty for 2006 was $104,250, which is 25% of the 2006 Freddie Mac conforming loan limit for a single family residence of $417,000.*

The VA does not establish a maximum loan amount, although lenders generally limit the maximum VA loan to $203,000, because most VA loans are sold in the secondary market, which limits VA loans to that amount.

No loan, however, may exceed the reasonable value of the property. When refinancing certain loans, the maximum loan is 90% of the value of the property, plus the funding fee, if required. When purchasing a manufactured home or lot, the maximum loan is 95% of the amount that would be subject to finance charges.

Home loan entitlement is generally good until used. However, the eligibility of service personnel is only available as long as they remain on active duty. If an individual is discharged or released from active duty before using his or her entitlement, a new determination of eligibility must be made, based on the length of service and the type of discharge received.

HYBRID ADJUSTABLE RATE MORTGAGES

The Veterans Benefits Act of 2002 authorizes VA to carry out a demonstration project to guarantee Hybrid Adjustable Rate Mortgages (Hybrid ARMs or HARM loans) during Fiscal Years 2004 and 2005. **(The Veterans Benefits Act of 2005 extends the VA's authority to guarantee hybrid ARM loans to September 30, 2008.)**

DOWN PAYMENTS

The VA does not require a down payment be made, provided that:

- The loan is not for a manufactured home or lot (a 5% down payment is required for manufactured home or lot loans); and
- The purchase price or cost does not exceed the reasonable value of the property, as determined by VA; and
- The loan does not have graduated payment features. (Because with a graduated payment mortgage, the loan balance will be increasing

during the first years of the loan, a down payment is required to keep the loan balance from going over the reasonable value or the purchase price.)

Even though the VA may not require a down payment, the lender may require one.

CLOSING COSTS AND FEES

The VA regulates the closing costs that a veteran may be charged in connection with closing a VA loan. The closing costs and origination fees must be paid in cash, and cannot be included in the loan itself, except in the case of refinancing loans.

Although some additional costs are unique to certain localities, the closing costs generally include:

- VA appraisal
- Credit report
- Survey
- Title evidence
- Recording fees
- A 1% loan origination fee
- Discount points

A veteran is charged the customary fees for title search, credit report, appraisal and transfer fees, etc., the same as any other borrower, but he is not required to pay commission or brokerage fees for obtaining the loan. In home loans, the lender may also charge a reasonable flat charge, called a funding fee, to cover the costs of originating the loan.

FUNDING FEES

A VA funding fee is payable at the time of loan closing. This fee may be included in the loan and paid from the loan proceeds. The funding fee does not have to be paid by veterans receiving VA compensation for service-connected disabilities, or who but for the receipt of retirement pay, would be entitled to receive compensation for service-connected disabilities, or surviving spouses of veterans who died in service or from a service-connected disability.

The funding fee rates are as follows (Unless otherwise specified, the following rates are effective January 1, 2004:

Loan Purpose	**Percent Of Loan For Veterans**	**Percent Of Loan For Reservists**
Purchase or construction loan with down payment of less than 5%; or Refinancing loan; or Home improvement loan	2.15% (10/1/04 - 9/30/2011)	2.4%
Purchase or construction loan with down payment between 5% and 10%	1.5	1.75
Purchase or construction loan with down payment of 10% or more	1.25	1.5
Manufactured home loan	1.0	1.0
Interest rate reduction loan	0.5	0.5
Assumption of VA guaranteed loan	0.5	0.5
Second or subsequent use without a down payment	3.3	3.3

FLOOD INSURANCE

If the dwelling is in an area identified by the Department of Housing and Urban Development as having special flood hazards, and the sale of flood insurance under the national program is available, such insurance is required on loans made since March 1, 1974. The amount of insurance must be equal to the outstanding loan balance, or the maximum limit of coverage available, whichever is less.

INTEREST RATES

The interest rate on VA loans varies due to changes in the prevailing rates in the mortgage market. One a loan is made, the interest rate set in the note remains the same for the life of the loan. However, if interest rates decrease, a veteran may apply for a new VA loan to refinance the previous loan at a lower interest rate.

REPAYMENT PERIOD

The maximum repayment period for VA home loans is 30 years and 32 days. However, the exact amortization period depends upon the contract between the lender and the borrower.

The VA will guarantee loans with the following repayment terms:

- Traditional Fixed Payment Mortgage
- (equal monthly payments for the life of the loan)

- Graduated Payment Mortgage - GPM
- (Smaller than normal monthly payments for the first few years - usually 5 years, which gradually increase each year, and then level off after the end of the "graduation period" to larger than normal payments for the remaining term of the loan. The reduction in the monthly payment in the early years of the loan is accomplished by delaying a portion of the interest due on the loan each month, and by adding that interest to the principal balance.)
- Buydown
- (The builder of a new home or seller of an existing home may "buy down" the veteran's mortgage payments by making a large lump sum payment up front at closing that will be used to supplement the monthly payments for a certain period, usually 1 to 3 years.)
- Growing Equity Mortgage (GEM)
- (Provides for a gradual annual increase in monthly payments, with all of the increase applied to the principal balance, resulting in early payoff of the loan.)

Prepayment of Loan

A veteran or serviceman may pay off his entire loan at any time without penalty or fee, or make advance payments equal to one monthly installment or $100, whichever is the lesser amount. Individuals should check with the mortgage holder for the proper procedure.

Loan Defaults

If a veteran fails to make payments as agreed, the lender may foreclose on the property.. If the lender takes a loss, the VA must pay the guaranty to the lender, and the individual must repay this amount to the VA. If the loan closed on or after January 1, 1990, the veteran will owe the VA in the event of default, only if there was fraud, misrepresentation, or bad faith on the veteran's part.

RELEASE OF LIABILITY

Any veteran who sells or has sold a home purchased with a VA loan guaranty may request release from liability to the VA. (If the VA loan closed prior to March 1, 1988, the application forms for a release of liability must be requested from the VA office that guaranteed the loan. If the VA loan closed on or after March 1, 1988, then the application forms must be requested from the lender to whom the payments are made.) The loan must be current, the purchaser must assume full liability for the loan, and the purchaser must sign an Assumption of Liability Agreement. The VA must approve the purchaser from a credit standpoint.

For loans closed on or after March 1, 1988, release of liability is not automatic. To approve the assumer and grant the veteran release from liability, the lender or VA must be notified, and release of liability must be requested.

If the loan was closed prior to March 1, 1988, the purchaser may assume the loan without approval from VA or the lender. However, the veteran is encouraged to request a release of liability from VA, regardless of the loan's closing date. If a veteran does not obtain a release of liability, and VA suffers a loss on account of a default by the assumer, or some future assumer, a debt may be established against the veteran. Also, strenuous collection efforts will be made against the veteran if a debt is established.

The release of a veteran from liability to the VA does not change the fact that the VA continues to be liable on the guaranty.

RESTORATION OF ENTITLEMENT

Veterans who have used all or part of their entitlement may restore their entitlement amount to purchase another home, provided:

- The property has been sold, and the loan has been paid in full; or
- A qualified veteran buyer has agreed to assume the outstanding balance on the loan, and agreed to substitute his entitlement for the same amount of entitlement the original veteran owner used to get the loan. (The veteran buyer must also meet the occupancy, income, and credit requirements of the VA and the lender.)
- If the veteran has repaid the VA loan in full, but has not disposed of the property securing that loan, the entitlement may be restored ONE TIME ONLY.

Restoration of entitlement does not occur automatically. The veteran must apply for restoration by completing Form 26, 1880. Completed forms may be returned to any VA regional office or center (A copy of the HUD-1, Closing Statement, or other appropriate evidence of payment in full should also be submitted with the completed Form 26, 1880.) Application forms for substitution of entitlement can be requested from the VA office that guaranteed the loan.

If the requirements for restoration of entitlement cannot be met, veterans who had a VA loan before may still have remaining entitlement to use for another VA loan. The current amount of entitlement available to eligible veterans has been increased over time by changes in the law.

For example, in 1974 the maximum guaranty entitlement was $12,500. Today the maximum guaranty entitlement is $36,000 (for most loans under $144,000). So, if a veteran used the $12,500 guaranty in 1974, even if that loan is not paid off, the veteran could use the $23,500 difference between the $12,500 entitlement originally used and the current maximum of $36,000 to buy another home with a VA loan guaranty.

DIRECT HOME LOANS

VA direct home loans are only available to:

- Native American veterans who plan to buy, build, or improve a home on Native American trust land; or
- Certain eligible veterans who have a permanent and total service-connected disability, for specially adapted homes.

Native American Veterans Living on Trust Lands

A VA direct loan can be used to purchase, construct, or improve a home on Native American trust land. These loans may also be used to simultaneously purchase and improve a home, or to refinance another VA direct loan made under this program in order to lower the interest rate. VA direct loans are generally limited to the cost of the home or $80,000, whichever is less.

UPDATE:

On June 15, 2006, the President signed P. L. 109233, the Veterans Housing Opportunity and Benefits Act of 2006. The Law affects VA direct loans to Native Americans Veterans living on Trust Lands in the following ways:

1. The $80,000 maximum loan amount is eliminated. Instead, the new limit is the same as the Federal Home Loan Mortgage Corporation (also known as "Freddie Mac") single-family conventional conforming loan limit.
2. The law extends eligibility for Native American Direct Loan to a veteran who is not a Native American, but who is married to a Native American nonveteran. To be eligible for such a loan, the qualified nonnative American veteran and the Native American spouse must reside on trust land, and both the veteran and spouse must have a meaningful interest in the dwelling or lot.

To qualify for a VA direct loan, the tribal organization or other appropriate Native American group must be participating in the VA direct loan program. The tribal organization must have signed a *Memorandum of Understanding* with the Secretary of Veterans Affairs that includes the conditions governing its participation in the program.

Veterans should contact their regional VA office for specific information regarding direct home loans.

RESALE OF REPOSSESSED VA HOMES

The VA sells homes that it acquires after foreclosure of a VA guaranteed loan. These home are available to veterans and non-veterans.

The properties are available for sale to the general public through the services of private sector real estate brokers. The VA cannot deal directly with purchasers. Real estate brokers receive the keys to the properties and assist prospective purchasers in finding, viewing, and offering to purchase them.

Participating brokers receive instructional material regarding the sales program, and are familiar with VA sales procedures. VA pays the sales commission.
Offers to purchase VA acquired properties must be submitted on VA forms. Offers cannot be submitted on offer forms generally used in the real estate industry.

VA financing is available for most, but not all, property sales. The downpayment requirements are usually very reasonable, the interest rate is established by VA based on market conditions. Any prospective purchaser who requests VA financing to purchase a VA-owned property must have sufficient income to meet the loan payments, maintain the property, and pay all other obligation. The purchaser must have acceptable credit, and must also have enough funds remaining for family support.

Anyone interested should consult a local real estate agent to find out about VA-acquired properties listed for sale in the area.

HUD / FHA LOANS

Veterans are not eligible for VA financing based on service in World War I, Active Duty for Training in the Reserves, or Active Duty for Training in the National Guard (unless "activated" under the authority of Title 10, U.S. Code). However, these veterans may qualify for a HUD / FHA veteran's loan.

The VA's only role in the HUD / FHA program is to determine the eligibility of the veteran, and issue a *Certificate of Veteran Status*, if qualified. Under this program, financing is available for veterans at terms slightly more favorable than those available to non-veterans.

A veteran may request a *Certificate of Veteran Status* by completing VA form 26-8261a. The completed form and required attachments should be submitted to the veteran's regional VA office for a determination of eligibility.

CHAPTER 23

OVERSEAS BENEFITS

MEDICAL BENEFITS

The Foreign Medical Program (FMP) is a healthcare benefits program for U.S. veterans with VA-rated service-connected conditions who are residing or traveling abroad (except Canada and the Philippines). Services provided in Canada and the Philippines are under separate jurisdictions, as indicated later in this chapter.

Under the FMP, VA assumes payment responsibility for certain necessary medical services associated with the treatment of service-connected conditions.

Under the FMP, VA assumes payment responsibility for *certain necessary medical services associated with the treatment of* ***service-connected conditions***.

The Foreign Medical Program Office in Denver, Colorado has jurisdiction over all foreign provided services, with the exception of medical services received in Canada and the Philippines. It is responsible for all aspects of the program, including application processing, verification of eligibility, authorization of benefits, and payments of claims.

Individuals who are traveling to or reside in one of the following countries should use the following number to contact the FMP Office in Denver, Colorado: (877) 345-8179

- Germany
- Panama
- Australia
- Italy
- England
- UK
- Japan
- Spain.

For individuals who are in Mexico or Costa Rica, first dial the U.S.A code and then (877) 345-8179. The number also works from the United States.

Generally, as long as the service is medically necessary for the treatment of a VA rated service-connected condition, it will be covered by the FMP. Additionally, the services must be accepted by VA and / or the U.S. Medical community (such as the American Medical Association and the U.S. Food and Drug Administration.)

Exclusions to Medical Benefits

The following services are not covered by the Foreign Medical Program:

- Procedures, treatments, drugs, or devices that are experimental or investigational;
- Family planning services and sterilization;
- Infertility services;
- Plastic surgery primarily for cosmetic purposes;
- Chiropractic services;
- Procedures, services, and supplies related to sex transformations;
- Non-acute institutional care such as long-term inpatient psychiatric care and nursing home care;
- Day care and day hospitalization;
- Non-medical home care (aid and attendance);
- Abortions, except when the life of the mother would be endangered if the fetus were carried to term;
- Travel, meals, and lodging (including transportation costs to return to the United States)

Prosthesis

If an individual residing in a foreign country requires a prosthesis for a VA rated service-connected condition, and the cost of the prosthetic appliance is less than $300 (U.S. currency), the individual may purchase the prosthetic appliance from a local healthcare provider, and send the invoice to the FMP Office for reimbursement, or the healthcare provider may bill the VA.

If the cost of the prosthetic appliance exceeds $300 (U.S. currency), the individual must obtain preauthorization for the VA Foreign Medical Program Office (see address below).

Application Process – Registration

Although pre-registration for eligible veterans is not necessary, veterans who are permanently relocating to a country under the FMP's jurisdiction are encouraged to notify the FMP once a permanent foreign address is established. At that time, FMP will provide detailed program material, such as benefit coverage, benefit limitations, selecting healthcare providers, and claim filing instructions.

Veterans who are simply traveling, and are not planning a permanent relocation do not need to notify the FMP of their travel plans. Program materials are available, however, upon request.

The FMP can be contacted at:

VA Health Administration Center
Foreign Medical Program (FMP)
P.O. Box 65021
Denver, CO 80206-9021
Phone: (303) 331-7590
Fax: (303) 331-7803

Medical Services in Canada

The VA Medical and Regional Office Center in White River Junction, Vermont, is responsible for determining eligibility of U.S. veterans for reimbursement of medical treatment while traveling or residing in Canada. The local offices of Veterans' Affairs-Canada assists veterans in obtaining authorizations for treatment, arranging for treatment (if necessary), and providing information about the medical treatment program.

The same exclusions listed earlier in this chapter also apply to medical services in Canada, and VA assumes payment responsibility only for *certain necessary medical services associated with the treatment of* ***service-connected conditions.***

To receive reimbursed medical treatment, an authorization must be obtained from the White River Junction office **prior to treatment** (unless an emergency situation exists).

When required by the VA to support a claim for disability benefits, Veterans' Affairs-Canada will make arrangement for disability examinations for veterans residing in Canada. In some instances, arrangements will be made locally in Canada. In other instances, arrangements will be made at bordering VA medical facilities.

Information on how to obtain medical services in Canada, including procedures for filing claims, can be obtained by contacting the following office:

VAM & RO Center (136FC)
North Hartland Road
White River Junction, VT 05009-0001
Fax: (802) 296-5174

Or

Veterans Affairs-Canada
Foreign Countries Operations
Room 1055
264 Wellington Street
Ottawa, Ontario, Canada K1A 0P4
(613) 943-7461

Medical Services in the Philippines

The Republic of the Philippines is the only foreign country in which the VA operates a regional office and outpatient clinic.

The same exclusions listed earlier in this chapter also apply to medical services in the Philippines, and VA assumes payment responsibility only for *certain necessary medical services associated with the treatment of* ***service-connected conditions.***

To receive reimbursed medical treatment, an authorization must be obtained **prior to treatment** (unless an emergency situation exists).

Information on how to obtain medical services in the Philippines, including procedures for filing claims, can be obtained by contacting the following office:

VA Outpatient Clinic (358/00)
2201 Roxas Boulevard
Pasay City 1300
Republic of the Philippines
011-632-838-4566 or (632) 833-4566

OTHER OVERSEAS BENEFITS

Virtually all VA monetary benefits, including compensation, pension, educational assistance, and burial allowances, are payable regardless of an individual's place of residence.

However, there are some program limitations in foreign jurisdictions, including:

- Home-loan guaranties are available only in the United States and selected territories and possessions.
- Educational benefits are limited to approved degree-granting programs in institutions of higher learning

Information and assistance are available to U.S. veterans worldwide at American embassies and consulates. In Canada, the local offices of Veterans Affairs-Canada provide information and assistance. Individuals may call toll-free within Canada, 1-888-996-2242.

In the Philippines, service is available at the VA Regional Office and Outpatient Clinic in Manila:

VA Regional Office
1131 Roxas Boulevard
Manila, Philippines
011-632-521-7521

Direct Deposit

The conventional method of direct deposit is not available outside of the U.S. However, there are foreign banks with branches in the United States, through which direct deposit can be established. Once the funds are received in the U.S.

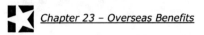

branch through electronic funds transfer, the U.S. branch transfers the money to the foreign branch.

While this process may take a few days longer than direct deposit within the United States, it is still quicker than having checks mailed overseas through the Department of State or International Priority Airmail.

CHAPTER 24

AGENT ORANGE, MUSTARD GAS, RADIATION AND PROJECT 112 / SHAD

AGENT ORANGE

Agent Orange was an herbicide used in Vietnam to defoliate trees and remove cover for the enemy. Agent Orange spraying missions were flown in Vietnam between January 1965 and April 1970.

VA has offered special access to health services and studies since 1978, when it initiated a medical surveillance program for Vietnam veterans with health concerns. By 1981, VA offered priority medical care to Vietnam veterans with any health problems, which may have resulted from Agent Orange exposure. That program continues today.

Toll-Free Agent Orange Helpline

In the Spring of 2000, VA established a national toll-free helpline to answer questions about Agent Orange exposure, health care, and benefits.

The toll-free telephone number for the helpline is (800) 749-8387.

Callers can speak directly to VA representatives Monday through Friday from 8:00 a.m. to 4:00 p.m., Central Standard Time, or access a 24-hour automated system.

Determination of Service-Connected Diseases

A disease specified below, becoming manifest in a veteran, who, during active military, naval, or air service, served in the Republic of Vietnam during the period beginning on January 9, 1962, and ending on May 7, 1975 shall be considered to have been incurred in or aggravated by such service, notwithstanding that there is no record of evidence of such disease during the period of such service.

The diseases referred to above are:

- Non-Hodgkin's lymphoma becoming manifest to a degree of disability of 10% or more.
- Each soft-tissue sarcoma becoming manifest to a degree of disability of 10% ore more other than osteosarcoma, chondrosarcoma, Kaposi's sarcoma, or mesothelioma.

- Chloracne or another acne form disease consistent with chloracne becoming manifest to a degree of disability of 10% or more within one year after the last date on which the veteran performed active military, naval, or air service in the Republic of Vietnam during the period beginning on January 9, 1962, and ending on May 7, 1975.

- Hodgkin's disease becoming manifest to a degree of disability of 10% ore more.

- Porphyria cutanea tarda becoming manifest to a degree of disability of 10% ore more within a year after the last date on which the veteran performed active military, naval, or air service in the Republic of Vietnam during the period beginning on January 9, 1962, and ending on May 7, 1975.

- Respiratory cancers (cancer of the lung, bronchus, larynx, or trachea) becoming manifest to a degree of 10% or more within 30 years after the last date on which the veteran performed active military, naval, or air service in the Republic of Vietnam during the period beginning on January 9, 1962, and ending on May 7, 1975.

- Multiple myeloma becoming manifest to a degree of disability of 10% or more.

- Acute and subacute peripheral neuropathy.

- Prostate cancer.

- Diabetes Mellitus (Type-II, adult onset diabetes)

- Chronic Lymphocytic Leukemia (CLL)

- Each additional disease (if any) that the Secretary of the VA determines warrants a presumption of service-connection by reason of having positive association with exposure to an herbicide agent, becomes manifest within the period (if any) prescribed in such regulations in a veteran who, during active military, naval, or air service, served in the Republic of Vietnam during the period beginning on January 9, 1962 and ending on May 7, 1975, and while so serving was exposed to that herbicide agent.

Veterans having a disease referred to above, shall be presumed to have been exposed during such service to an herbicide agent containing dioxin or 2,4-dichlorophenoxyacetic acid, and may be presumed to have been exposed during such service to any other chemical compound in an herbicide agent, unless there is affirmative evidence to establish that the veteran was not exposed to any such agent during that service.

If the Secretary of the VA later determines that a previously established presumption of service-connection for one of the above diseases is no longer warranted, all veterans currently awarded compensation on the basis of the presumption shall continue to be entitled to receive compensation. Additionally, all survivors of any such veterans who were awarded dependency and indemnity compensation shall continue to be entitled to receive dependency and indemnity compensation on that basis.

Rates of Disability Compensation

Rates of compensation depend upon the degree of disability, and follow a payment schedule that is adjusted annually and applies to all veterans. Please refer to the charts in Chapter 4 of this book.

Agent Orange Registry

VA developed the Agent Orange Registry Examination Program in 1978 to identify Vietnam veterans concerned about Agent Orange exposure. Nearly 300,000 Vietnam veterans have been provided examinations under the Registry program as of December 1999. VA maintains a computerized registry of data from these examinations. Registrants receive periodic updates on Agent Orange studies and VA policy.

VA's Advisory Committees on Health-Related Effects of Herbicides & Environmental Hazards

The VA's Advisory Committee on Health-Related Effects Of Herbicides was established in 1979 to examine issues surrounding the possible health effects of herbicides on Vietnam veterans.

VA also established the Veterans' Advisory Committee on Environmental Hazards, consisting of non-VA experts in dioxin and radiation exposure as well as several lay members, to advise the Secretary on the results of Agent Orange-related research, and regulatory, administrative and legislative initiatives.

Since passage of a 1991 law (PL 102-4), which directs VA to request that the National Academy of Sciences (NAS) review diseases associated with herbicide exposure, the committee's work has been superseded by the NAS review.

National Academy of Sciences (NAS)

The NAS reviews and evaluates scientific literature about Agent Orange. NAS reviewed more than 6,000 abstracts of scientific or medical articles and analyzed 230 epidemiological studies before its initial July 1993 report, which led to the inclusion of additional diseases on the list for presumptive service-connection. The NAS review has been continuing, with acute and subacute peripheral neuropathy and prostate cancer added to VA's presumptive list after the NAS issued an updated report in March 1996. Also based on that report's findings of new "limited or suggestive evidence" of an association between herbicides and Spina Bifida in the children of Vietnam veterans, VA proposed legislation to aid children of Vietnam veterans who suffer from that disorder, and established a reproductive outcomes research center to investigate potential environmental hazards of military service.

A separate VA study led Secretary of Veterans Affairs Togo D. West Jr. to call for legislation to benefit children who suffer from birth defects that may have been caused by their mothers' Vietnam service, not necessarily by herbicide exposure. Secretary West also asked NAS to review a study by the National Institute of Occupational Safety and Health of dioxin-exposed production workers at two U.S. plants that revealed elevated rates of diabetes among workers. A decision whether to establish a presumption of service-connection for diabetes will be made once the additional review is completed.

MUSTARD GAS EXPOSURE AND LONG-TERM HEALTH EFFECTS

In 1991, the Department of Veterans Affairs (VA) relaxed requirements for evaluating mustard gas-related compensation claims because of the confidentiality of some of the World War II testing and a lack of military medical records and follow-up. At that time, a review of studies of the effects of mustard gas exposure led VA to publish regulations authorizing service-connection and disability compensation payments to veterans who were exposed to significant levels of mustard gas and who suffer from chronic forms of certain diseases.

An estimated 4,000 servicemen participated in tests using significant concentrations of mustard gas either in chambers or field exercises in contaminated areas during World War II. This secret testing was conducted in order to develop better protective clothing, masks and skin ointments. There is no central roster of World War II participants in either the laboratory or field tests. The Army conducted tests on Army personnel in the laboratory and in the field. The test sites included:

- Edgewood Arsenal, Maryland;
- Camp Sibert, Alabama;
- Bushnell, Florida;
- Dugway Proving Ground, Utah; and
- San Jose Island, Panama Canal Zone

Military personnel from the U.S. Navy Training Center, Bainbridge, Maryland., also were sent to the Naval Research Lab in Washington, D.C., to participate in tests. Gas testing facilities also were located at Great Lakes Naval Training Center in Illinois and Camp Lejeune, North Carolina.

Institute of Medicine Study

Also in 1991, VA contracted with the Institute of Medicine to conduct a study of medical and scientific literature worldwide to determine the long-term health effects of mustard gas and Lewisite. The $600,000 VA-funded study, entitled "Veterans at Risk: The Health Effects of Mustard Gas and Lewisite," was released Jan. 6, 1993. The study found a relationship between exposure and the subsequent development of certain diseases.

Veterans Who May Be Eligible for Compensation

VA policies generally authorize service-connection and compensation payments to veterans who were exposed to mustard gas and/or Lewisite and who suffer from a number of diseases or conditions, including:

- Full-body exposure to nitrogen or sulfur mustard together with the subsequent development of chronic conjunctivitis, keratitis, corneal opacities, scar formation, or the following cancers: nasopharyngeal; laryngeal; lung (except mesothelioma); or squamous cell carcinoma of the skin;

- Full-body exposure to nitrogen or sulfur mustard -- or exposure to Lewisite -- and the subsequent development of a chronic form of laryngitis, bronchitis, emphysema, asthma or chronic obstructive pulmonary disease;

- Full-body exposure to nitrogen mustard with the subsequent development of acute nonlymphocytic leukemia.

Service-connection is not allowed if the claimed condition is due to the veteran's own willful misconduct or if there is affirmative evidence that establishes some other nonservice-related condition or event as the cause of the claimed disability.

Veterans who were exposed to significant amounts of mustard gas and have health problems that may be compensable (or their survivors) may contact the nearest VA regional office at 1-800-827-1000 for more information about benefits.

VA PROGRAMS FOR VETERANS EXPOSED TO RADIATION

VA provides special priority for enrollment for health-care services to any veteran exposed to ionizing radiation in connection with:

- Onsite participation in a test involving the atmospheric detonation of a nuclear device (without regard to whether the nation conducting the test was the United States or another nation).

- The American occupation of Hiroshima and Nagasaki, Japan, during the period beginning August 6, 1945, and ending July 1, 1946.

- Internment as a prisoner of war in Japan (or service on active duty in Japan immediately following such internment) during World War II which (as determined by the Secretary of the VA) resulted in an opportunity for exposure to ionizing radiation comparable to that of veterans described above.

IMPORTANT UPDATE:

- The definition of radiation-risk activities was expanded in March 2002 to include service at Amchitka Island, Alaska, prior to January 1, 1974, if a veteran was exposed while performing duties related to certain underground nuclear tests.
- The new definition also includes service at gaseous diffusion plants located in Paducah, Ky., Portsmouth, Ohio and an area known as K25 at Oak Ridge, Tenn.

In addition, these veterans are eligible to participate in the VA ionizing radiation registry examination program. VA also pays compensation to veterans and their survivors if the veteran is determined to have a disability due to radiation exposure while in service.

Radiation Statistics

Some 195,000 service members have been identified as participants in the post-World War II occupation of Hiroshima and Nagasaki, Japan. In addition, approximately 210,000 mostly military members are confirmed as participants in U.S. atmospheric nuclear tests between 1945 and 1962 in the United States and the Pacific and Atlantic oceans prior to the 1963 Limited Test Ban Treaty. The Defense Threat Reduction Agency's Nuclear Test Personnel Review program since 1978 has maintained a database of participants in atmospheric nuclear test activities. About one-fourth of the participants received no measurable dose of ionizing radiation, with fewer than one per cent of the nuclear test participants identified as having a dose of 5 rem or higher. (The current federal guideline for U.S. workplace exposure is 5 rem per year.)

Determination of Service-Connected Diseases

VA may pay compensation for radiogenic diseases under two programs specific to radiation-exposed veterans and their survivors:

Statutory List

Veterans who participated in nuclear tests by the U.S. or its allies, who served with the U.S. occupation forces in Hiroshima or Nagasaki, Japan, between August 1945 and July 1946, or who were similarly exposed to ionizing radiation while a prisoner of war in Japan, are eligible for compensation for cancers specified in legislation.

The types of cancer covered by these laws are:

- All forms of leukemia except chronic lymphocytic leukemia;
- Cancer of the thyroid,
- Cancer of the breast,
- Cancer of the pharynx,
- Cancer of the esophagus,
- Cancer of the stomach,
- Cancer of the small intestine,
- Cancer of the pancreas,
- Cancer of the bile ducts,
- Cancer of the gall bladder,
- Cancer of the salivary gland
- Cancer of the urinary tract;
- Lymphomas (except Hodgkin's disease);
- Multiple myeloma;

- Primary liver cancer.

In March 2002, VA announced the addition of five new cancers to the list of diseases presumed to be connected to the exposure of veterans to radiation during their military service:

- Bone Cancer
- Brain Cancer
- Colon Cancer
- Lung Cancer
- Ovary Cancer

The new rules apply to those veterans who participated in "radiation-risk activities" while on active duty, during active duty for training or inactive duty training as a member of a reserve component.

Regulatory List

Disability compensation claims of veterans who were exposed to radiation in service and who develop a disease within specified time periods not specified in the statutory list are governed by regulation. Under the regulations, various additional factors must be considered in determining service-connection, including amount of radiation exposure, duration of exposure, and elapsed time between exposure and onset of the disease. VA regulations identify all cancers as potentially radiogenic, as well as certain other non-malignant conditions: posterior subcapsular cataracts; non-malignant thyroid nodular disease; parathyroid adenoma; and tumors of the brain and central nervous system.

A final rule that expanded the regulatory list from more than a dozen specific cancers to add "any other cancer" (any malignancy) was published Sept. 24, 1998. The rulemaking began following a 1995 review of the radiogenicity of cancer generally by the Veterans Advisory Committee on Environmental Hazards. It concluded that, on the basis of current scientific knowledge, exposure to ionizing radiation can be a contributing factor in the development of any malignancy. VA also will consider evidence that diseases other those specified in regulation may be caused by radiation exposure.

Rates of Disability Compensation

Rates of compensation depend upon the degree of disability and follow a payment schedule that is adjusted annually and applies to all veterans. Please refer to the charts in Chapter 4 of this book.

Ionizing Radiation Registry Program

In addition to special eligibility to enroll for VA healthcare for radiation-related conditions, atomic veterans are eligible to participate in VA's Ionizing Radiation Registry examination. Under the Ionizing Radiation Registry program, VA will perform a complete physical examination, including all necessary tests, for each veteran who requests it if the veteran was exposed to ionizing radiation while participating in the nuclear weapons testing program, or if he or she served with the U.S. occupation forces in Hiroshima or Nagasaki. Veterans need not be enrolled for general VA care to be eligible for the Ionizing Radiation Registry.

PROJECT 112 / PROJECT SHAD VETERANS

Veterans who believe their health may have been affected by these tests should contact the SHAD helpline at (800) 749-8387.

Project SHAD, an acronym for Shipboard Hazard and Defense, was part of a larger effort called Project 112, which was a comprehensive program initiated in 1962 by the Department of Defense (DoD) to protect and defend against potential chemical and biological warfare threats. Project SHAD encompassed a series of tests by DoD to determine the vulnerability of U.S. warships to attacks with chemical and biological warfare agents, and the potential risk to American forces posed by these agents.

Project 112 tests involved similar tests conducted on land rather than aboard ships.

Project SHAD involved service members from the Navy and Army and may have involved a small number of personnel from the Marine Corps and Air Force. Service members were not test subjects, but rather were involved in conducting the tests. Animals were used in some, but not most, tests.

DoD continues to release declassified reports about sea- and land- based tests of chemical and biological materials known collectively as "Project 112." The Department of Veterans Affairs (VA) is working with DoD to obtain information as to the nature and availability of the tests, who participated, duration and agents used.

Veterans who believe their health may have been affected by these tests should contact the SHAD helpline at (800) 749-8387

Public Law 108-170, the Veterans Health Care, Capital Asset, and Business Improvement Act of 2003, enacted December 6, 2003, provides for veterans who participated in Project 112/SHAD to be enrolled in priority enrollment category 6 and as such, to be eligible for VA health care at no cost for any illness possibly related to their participation in that project.

Following is a table provided by the DoD regarding specific ships, tests, and current information available.

(FS = FACT SHEET PR = PERSONNEL ROSTER)

#	*Test Name*	Date	Location	Agent/Simulant	Investigation Status	Information at VA
1	63-1 Eager Belle I [SHAD]	Jan - Mar 1963	Pacific Ocean	BG	Fact Sheet Released 1/31/2002	FS, PR
	Eager Belle II [SHAD]	Jan, Mar, Jun 1963	Pacific Ocean	BG	Fact Sheet Released 1/31/2002	FS, PR
2	63-2 Autumn Gold [SHAD]	May 1963	Pacific Ocean	BG	Fact Sheet Released 9/13/2001	FS, PR
3	63-3 Whistle Down	Dec 1962 - Feb 1963	Ft. Greely, AK	GB, VX	Fact Sheet Released 10/09/2002	FS
4	63-4 Big Jack A	Feb - Mar 1963	Ft. Sherman, Panama Canal Zone	BG, FP	Fact Sheet Released 10/31/2002	FS
	Big Jack B	Feb - Mar 1963	Ft. Sherman, Panama Canal Zone	TOF	Fact Sheet Released 10/31/2002	FS
5	64-1 Errand Boy [SHAD]	September 1963	Oahu, HI	BG	Fact Sheet Released 6/30/2003	FS, PR
6	64-2 Flower Drum I [SHAD]	Feb - Apr 1964 Aug - Sep 1964	Pacific Ocean	GB, SO2, MAA	Fact Sheet Released 5/23/2002	FS, PR
	Flower Drum II [SHAD]	Nov - Dec 1964	Pacific Ocean	VX, P32, Bis	Fact Sheet Released 5/23/2002	FS
7	64-3 Little Mo [SHAD]	NA	NA	NA	Test Cancelled	NA
8	64-4 [Red Beva] Shady Grove [SHAD]	Jan - Apr 1965	Pacific Ocean	BG, OU, UL	Fact Sheet Released 9/13/2001	FS, PR
9	64-5 Night Train	Nov 1963 - Jan 1964	Ft. Greely, AK	BG, FP	Fact Sheet Released 10/09/2002	FS
10	64-6 Yellow Leaf	Feb 1964, Apr - May 1966	Ft. Sherman, Panama Canal Zone, Island of Hawaii	BG, Tiara	Fact Sheet Released 10/31/2002	FS
11	64-7 Big Thunder	NA	NA	NA	Test Cancelled	NA
12	64-8 Tall Timber	Apr - Jun 1966	Island of Hawaii	BZ	Fact Sheet Released 10/09/2002	FS
13	64-9 Big Piney	NA	NA	NA	Test Cancelled	NA
14	64-10 [65-18] Black Label	NA	NA	NA	Test Deferred/Renumbered	NA
15	64-11 [65-19] Laurel Grove	NA	NA	NA	Test Deferred/Renumbered	NA
16	65-1 Copper Head [SHAD]	Jan - Feb 1965	Atlantic Ocean off Newfoundland, Canada	BG, FP, Beta-propiolactone	Fact Sheet Released 9/13/2001	FS, PR
17	65-2 Chain Saw	NA	NA	NA	Test Cancelled	NA

#	Test Name	Date	Location	Agent/Simulant	Investigation Status	Information at VA
18	65-3 West Side I	Jan - Feb 1965	Ft. Greely, AK	BG, FP	Fact Sheet Released 10/09/2002	FS
19	65-4 Magic Sword [SHAD]	May 1965	Baker Island	mosquitoes (Aedes aegypti)	Fact Sheet Released 10/09/2002	FS, PR
20	65-5 Iron Clad [SHAD]	NA	NA	NA	Test Cancelled	NA
21	65-6 Big Tom [SHAD]	May - Jun 1965	Pacific Ocean, off Oahu, HI & surrounding water & airspace	BG, FP	Updated Fact Sheet Released 6/30/2003	FS, PR
22	65-7 Great Sole [SHAD]	NA	NA	NA	Test Cancelled	NA
23	65-8 Lone Wolf [SHAD]	NA	NA	NA	Test Cancelled	NA
24	65-9 Silver Star	NA	NA	NA	Test Cancelled	NA
25	65-10 Little Egypt	NA	NA	NA	Test Cancelled	NA
26	65-11 [Bear River] Sun Down	Feb, Apr 1966	Ft. Greely, AK	GB, MAA, Tiara	Fact Sheet Released 10/09/2002	FS
27	65-12 Devil Hole I	Summer 1965	Ft. Greely, AK	GB, FP	Fact Sheet Released 10/09/2002	FS
28	65-13 High Low [SHAD]	Jan - Feb 1966	Pacific Ocean off San Diego, CA	MAA	Corrected Fact Sheet Released 12/31/2002	FS
29	65-14 Elk Hunt I	Jul - Aug 1964	Ft. Greely, AK	VX	Fact Sheet Released 10/09/2002	FS, PR
	Elk Hunt II	Jun - Jul 1965 Oct - Dec 1965	Ft. Greely, AK & Edgewood Arsenal, MD, & Canada	VX	Fact Sheet Released 10/09/2002	FS, PR
30	65-15 Little Corporal	NA	NA	NA	Test Cancelled	NA
31	65-16 Pine Ridge	May - Jun 1966	Island of Hawaii	GB, BZ	Fact Sheet Released 10/09/2002	FS
32	65-17 Fearless Johnny [SHAD]	Aug - Sep 1965	Pacific Ocean southwest of Oahu, HI	VX, Diethylphthlate	Fact Sheet Released 5/23/2002	FS, PR
33	65-18 [64-10] Black Label	NA	NA	NA	Test Cancelled	NA
34	65-19 [64-11] Laurel Grove	NA	NA	NA	Test Cancelled	NA
35	66-1 Devil Hole II	Jul - Aug 1966	Ft. Greely, AK	VX	Fact Sheet Released 10/09/2002	FS
36	66-2 Red Oak I	Apr - May 1967	Island of Hawaii, Ft. Sherman, Panama Canal Zone	GB	Fact Sheet Released 10/31/2002	FS
37	66-3 Swamp Oak I	Mar - Apr 1966	Ft. Greely, AK	GB	Fact Sheet Released 10/09/2002	FS

#	Test Name	Date	Location	Agent/Simulant	Investigation Status	Information at VA
38	66-4 Green Mist	Mar - Apr 1967	Island of Hawaii	GB, MAA	Fact Sheet Released 10/09/2002	FS
39	66-5 Purple Sage [SHAD]	Jan - Feb 1966	Pacific Ocean off San Diego, CA	MAA	Fact Sheet Released 5/23/2002	FS, PR
40	66-6 Scarlet Sage [SHAD]	Feb - Mar 1966	Pacific Ocean off San Diego, CA	BG	Fact Sheet Released 1/31/2002	FS, PR
41	66-7 Clay Pigeon I	NA	NA	NA	Test Cancelled	NA
42	66-8 West Side II	Jan - Mar 1965	Southwestern Canada	BG, FP	Fact Sheet Released 10/09/2002	FS
43	66-9 Magic Sword II [SHAD]	NA	NA	NA	Test Cancelled	NA
44	66-10 Pin Point	1966	Unspecified	CS	Fact Sheet Released 10/31/2002	FS
45	66-11 Ebony Sun [SHAD]	NA	NA	NA	Test Cancelled	NA
46	66-12 [Bald Eagle I] Bold Captain [SHAD]	NA	NA	NA	Test Cancelled	NA
47	66-13 Half Note [SHAD]	Aug - Sep 1966	Pacific Ocean, off Hawaii	BG, E.coli, FP SM, calcaflour	Updated Fact Sheet Released 6/30/2003	FS, PR
48	66-14 Sandy Point [SHAD]	NA	NA	NA	Test Cancelled	NA
49	67-1 [68-15] Red Oak II	NA	NA	NA	Test Deferred/Renumbered	NA
50	67-2 Dew Point	Jun - Jul 1967	Ft. Greely, AK	GB	Fact Sheet Released 10/09/2002	FS
51	67-3 [68-11] [69-13] Tiny Doll	NA	NA	NA	Test Deferred/Renumbered	NA
52	67-4 Blue Note [SHAD]	NA	NA	NA	Test Cancelled	NA
53	67-5 Work Horse [SHAD]	NA	NA	NA	Test Cancelled	NA
54	67-6 Blue Tango	Jan - Feb 1967	Hawaii	BG, E.coli, SM	Fact Sheet Released 6/30/2003	FS, PR
55	67-7 [Coincidence] Red Cloud	Nov 1966 - Feb 1967	Ft. Greely, AK	BG, E.coli, SM, TT, ZZ	Fact Sheet Released 10/09/2002	FS
56	67-8 [Autobiography] Watch Dog	Summer 1967	Ft. Greely, AK	BG, E.coli, SM, TT, ZZ	Fact Sheet Released 10/09/2002	FS
57	67-9 [Key Fruit] Gray Fox [SHAD]	NA	NA	NA	Test Cancelled	NA
58	67-10 [Meddled] Night Fire [SHAD]	NA	NA	NA	Test Cancelled	NA
59	67-11 [Expunge] Slow Waltz [SHAD]	NA	NA	NA	Test Cancelled	NA

#	*Test Name*	Date	Location	Agent/Simulant	Investigation Status	Information at VA
60	67-12 [68-72] [69-30] [69-70] [69-73] [Expulsion] Sharp Nail [SHAD]	NA	NA	NA	Test Deferred/Renumbered	NA
61	67-13 Steel Point	NA	NA	NA	Test Cancelled	NA
62	68-10 [68-2] Sharp Ravine	NA	NA	NA	Test Cancelled	NA
63	68-11 [67-3] [69-13] Tiny Doll	NA	NA	NA	Test Deferred/Renumbered	NA
64	68-12 [68-1] Narrow Trail	NA	NA	NA	Test Cancelled	NA
65	68-13 [68-4] Rapid Tan	Jul - Aug 1967 May - Jun 1968 Aug - Sep 1968	Phase I & III - Porton Down, England, Phase II - Ralston, Canada	GA, GB, GD, VX	Fact Sheet Released 10/09/2002	FS
66	68-14 [68-3] Channel Crab	NA	NA	NA	Test Cancelled	NA
67	68-15 [67-1] Red Oak II	NA	NA	NA	Test Cancelled	NA
68	68-30 [68-5] [69-74] Prairie Carpet	NA	NA	NA	Test Deferred/Renumbered	NA
69	68-31 [68-6] [69-33] Exit Line	NA	NA	NA	Test Deferred/Renumbered	NA
70	68-33 [68-7] Wicked Slice	NA	NA	NA	Test Cancelled	NA
71	68-50 [68-11] Speckled Start [SHAD]	Sep - Oct 1968	Eniwetok Atoll, Marshall Islands	BG, PG2, uranine dye	Fact Sheet Released 5/23/2002	FS, PR
72	68-51 [68-9] Strange Fruit	NA	NA	NA	Test Cancelled	NA
73	68-52 Cliff Rose	Sep 27, 1967 - Jan 18, 1968	Ft Stewart Georgia and Panama Canal Zone	CS	Fact Sheet Released 12/9/2002*	FS
74	68-53	Apr - Dec 1969	DPG, UT	CS	Fact Sheet Released 10/09/2002	FS
75	68-70 [68-12] Shining Pond	NA	NA	NA	Test Cancelled	NA
76	68-71 [68-13] Folded Arrow [SHAD]	Apr – May 1968	Oahu, HI and surrounding waters	BG	Fact Sheet Released 6/30/2003	FS, PR
77	68-72 [67-12] [69-70] Sharp Nail	NA	NA	NA	Test Deferred/Renumbered	NA
78	68-73 [68-8] [69-73] Leaning Shoe	NA	NA	NA	Test Deferred/Renumbered	NA

#	Test Name	Date	Location	Agent/Simulant	Investigation Status	Information at VA
79	[68-10] Maple Board	NA	NA	NA	Test Cancelled	NA
80	69-10 [SHAD]	May 1969	Vieques, PR	TOF	Fact Sheet Released 10/09/2002	FS, PR
81	69-12	Spring 1969	Edgewood Arsenal, MD	GB, GD, GA, VX	Test Suspended Fact Sheet Released 10/09/2002	FS
82	69-13 [67-3] [68-11] Tiny Doll	NA	NA	NA	Test Cancelled	NA
83	69-14	Jul - Nov 1971	DPG, UT	DEHP	Fact Sheet Released 10/09/2002	FS
84	69-15 [SHAD]	NA	NA	NA	Test Cancelled	NA
85	69-16	NA	NA	NA	Test Cancelled	NA
86	69-30	NA	NA	NA	Test Cancelled	NA
87	69-31 [SHAD]	Aug - Sep 1968	Pacific Ocean off San Diego, CA	BG, MAA	Fact Sheet Released 10/09/2002	FS, PR
88	69-32 [SHAD]	Apr - Jun 1969	Pacific Ocean, southwest of Hawaii	BG, E.coli, SM, Calcaflour	Fact Sheet Released 5/23/2002	FS, PR
89	69-33 [68-6] [68-31] Exit Line [SHAD]	NA	NA	NA	Test Cancelled	NA
90	69-34	NA	NA	NA	Test Cancelled	NA
91	69-35	NA	NA	NA	Test Cancelled	NA
92	69-36 [SHAD]	NA	NA	NA	Test Cancelled	NA
93	69-37	NA	NA	NA	Test Cancelled	NA
94	69-70 [67-12] [68-72] Sharp Nail	NA	NA	NA	Test Cancelled	NA
95	69-71	NA	NA	NA	Test Cancelled	NA
96	69-72 [SHAD]	NA	NA	NA	Test Cancelled	NA
97	69-73 [68-73] [68-8] Leaning Shoe	NA	NA	NA	Test Cancelled	NA
98	69-74 [68-5] [68-30] Prairie Carpet	NA	NA	NA	Test Cancelled	NA
99	69-75	Oct - Dec 1968	Yeehaw Junction, FL	TX	Fact Sheet Released 10/09/2002	FS
100	70-A	NA	NA	NA	Test Cancelled	NA
101	70-B	NA	NA	NA	Test Cancelled	NA
102	70-C (SHAD)	Oct 1972, Feb - Mar 1973	Pacific Ocean, from San Diego CA to Babloa, Panama	NA	Fact Sheet Released 6/30/2003	FS
103	70-D	NA	NA	NA	Test Cancelled	NA
104	70-10	NA	NA	NA	Test Deferred	NA

#	Test Name	Date	Location	Agent/Simulant	Investigation Status	Information at VA
105	70-11 Ph I, Subtest 3	June 1972 – Nov 1973	Dugway PG, UT	Bis, TOP, FP	Fact Sheet Released 6/30/2003	FS
	70-11 Ph I, Subtest 4	May 1974	Dugway PG, UT	Bis	Fact Sheet Released 6/30/2003	FS
106	70-12	NA	NA	NA	Test Cancelled	NA
107	70-30	NA	NA	NA	Test Deferred	NA
108	70-31	NA	NA	NA	Test Cancelled	NA
109	70-50	NA	NA	NA	Test Cancelled	NA
110	70-70 [SHAD]	NA	NA	NA	Test Cancelled	NA
111	70-71 [SHAD]	NA	NA	NA	Test Cancelled	NA
112	70-72	NA	NA	NA	Test Cancelled	NA
113	70-73	Jul - Dec 1970	DPG, UT	BG, FP	Fact Sheet Released 10/09/2002	FS
114	70-74	Au 1972 – Jan 1973	Dugway PG, UT	BG, SM	Fact Sheet Released 6/30/2003	FS
115	71-10	NA	NA	NA	Test Cancelled	NA
116	71-11	NA	NA	NA	Test Cancelled	NA
117	71-12	NA	NA	NA	Test Cancelled	NA
118	71-13	NA	NA	NA	Test Cancelled	NA
119	71-30	NA	NA	NA	Test Cancelled	NA
120	71-31	NA	NA	NA	Test Cancelled	NA
121	71-32	NA	NA	NA	Test Cancelled	NA
122	71-33	NA	NA	NA	Test Cancelled	NA
123	71-34	NA	NA	NA	Test Cancelled	NA
124	71-35	NA	NA	NA	Test Cancelled	NA
125	71-70	NA	NA	NA	Test Cancelled	NA
126	71-75	NA	NA	NA	Test Cancelled	NA
127	72-30 [SHAD]	NA	NA	NA	Test Cancelled	NA
128	72-70 [SHAD]	NA	NA	NA	Test Cancelled	NA
129	73-10	NA	NA	NA	Test Cancelled	NA
130	73-11	NA	NA	NA	Test Cancelled	NA
131	73-12	NA	NA	NA	Test Cancelled	NA
132	73-30	Jan – Feb 1973	Dugway PG, UT	BG, SM, P	Fact Sheet Released 6/30/2003	FS
133	74-10 PH I	Sep – Oct 1973	Dugway PG, UT	DMMP, Bis, Trichloropropane	Fact Sheet Released 6/30/2003	FS
	74-10 PH II	Apr – May 1974	Dugway PG, Ut	DMMP	Fact Sheet Released 6/30/2003	FS
134	74-030	NA	NA	NA	Test Cancelled	NA

CHAPTER 25

SPINA BIFIDA PROGRAM

Spina bifida is the most frequently occurring permanently disabling birth defect. It affects approximately one of every 1,000 newborns in the United States. Neural tube defects (NTD) are birth defects that involve incomplete development of the brain, spinal cord, and/or protective coverings for these organs. Spina bifida, the most common NTD, results from the failure of the spine to close properly during the first month of pregnancy. (Anencephaly and encephalocele are less common types of NTDs). In severe cases, the spinal cord protrudes through the back of and may be covered by skin or a thin membrane.

> *VA provides monetary benefits, vocational training, rehabilitation, and certain healthcare benefits to children of Vietnam veterans and certain veterans who served in Korea near the demilitarized zone for disabilities resulting from spina bifida.*

Some Vietnam veterans, and certain other veterans have children with spina bifida. While Vietnam veterans and their mates are now moving out of the age category usually associated with childbirth, it is anticipated that some future births will occur and that some of these children may have birth defects, including spina bifida. Some research efforts have suggested that there may be a relationship between exposure by Vietnam veterans to Agent Orange and/or other herbicides used in Vietnam and the subsequent development of spina bifida in some of their children

Effective October 1, 1997, Public Law Number 104-204 authorized the VA to provide monetary benefits, vocational training, rehabilitation, and certain healthcare benefits to children of Vietnam veterans for disability resulting from spina bifida.

For the purpose of the Spina Bifida Program, the term ***Vietnam Veteran*** means an individual who performed active military, naval, or air service in the Republic of Vietnam during the period beginning on January 9, 1962, and ending May 7, 1975, without regard to the characterization of the individual's service. Service in the Republic of Vietnam includes service in the waters offshore and service in other locations if the conditions of service involved duty or visitation in the Republic of Vietnam.

UPDATE - Public Law 108-183, The Veterans Benefits Act of 2003, expanded benefit eligibility to children with spina bifida who were born to certain veterans who served in Korea near the demilitarized zone.

For purposes of this law, a veteran of covered service in Korea is any individual, without regard to the characterization of that individual's service, who:

- Served in the active military, naval, or air service in or near the Korean demilitarized zone (DMZ), during the period beginning on September 1, 1967, and ending on August 31, 1971; and

- Is determined by the VA to have been exposed to a herbicide agent during such service in or near the Korean demilitarized zone.

The term "herbicide agent" means a chemical in a herbicide used in support of United States and allied military operations in or near the Korean demilitarized zone, during the period beginning on September 1, 1967, and ending on August 31, 1971.

TOLL-FREE SPINA BIFIDA HOT LINE

In June 2001, VA opened a hot line for Vietnam veterans with questions about health care benefits for their children who have spina bifida.

The number for the hot line is (888) 820-1756.

Callers can speak to a benefits advisor Monday through Friday, from 10:00 a.m. to 1:30 p.m., and from 2:30 p.m. to 4:30 p.m., Eastern time. An after-hours phone message will allow callers to leave their names and telephone numbers for a return call the next business day.

The hot line is managed by VA's Health Administration Center in Denver, Colorado.

MONETARY BENEFITS

VA shall pay a monthly allowance based upon the level of disability to or for a child who is suffering from spina bifida, and who is a child of a Vietnam veteran. Receipt of this allowance shall not affect the right of the child, or the right of any individual based on the child's relationship to that individual, to receive any other benefit to which the child, or that individual, may be entitled under any law administered by VA. If a child suffering from spina bifida is the natural child of two Vietnam veterans, he or she is entitled to only one monthly allowance.

The monthly allowance is set at three levels, depending upon the degree of disability suffered by the child. VA shall determine the level of disability suffered by the child in accordance with the following criteria:

Level I

- The child is able to walk without braces or other external support (although gait may be impaired); and

- Has no sensory or motor impairment of upper extremities; and

- Has an IQ of 90 or higher; and

- Is continent of urine and feces.

Level II

Provided that none of the child's disabilities are severe enough to be evaluated at Level III, and the child is:

- Ambulatory, but only with braces or other external support; or
- Has sensory or motor impairment of upper extremities, but is able to grasp pen, feed self, and perform self care; or
- Has an IQ of at least 70 but less than 90; or
- Requires drugs or intermittent catheterization or other mechanical means to maintain proper urinary bladder function, or mechanisms for proper bowel function.

Level III

- The child is unable to ambulate; or
- Has sensory or motor impairment of upper extremities severe enough to prevent grasping a pen, feeding self, and performing self care; or
- Has an IQ of 69 or less; or
- Has complete urinary or fecal incontinence.

SPINA BIFIDA BENEFIT RATE TABLE
(Effective 12-01-2007)

Disability Level	*Monthly Allowance*
Level I	$270.00
Level II	$930.00
Level III	$1,585.00

VOCATIONAL TRAINING FOR CHILDREN WITH SPINA BIFIDA

To qualify for entitlement to a vocational training program an applicant must be a child:

- To whom VA has awarded a monthly allowance for spina bifida; and
- For whom VA has determined that achievement of a vocational goal is reasonably feasible.

A vocational training program may not begin before a child's 18th birthday, or the date of completion of secondary schooling, whichever comes first. Depending on the need, a child may be provided up to 24 months of full-time training.

HEALTHCARE BENEFITS

In addition to monetary allowances, vocational training and rehabilitation, the Department of Veterans Affairs (VA) also provides VA-financed healthcare benefits to Vietnam veterans' birth children diagnosed with spina bifida. For the purpose of this program, spina bifida is defined as all forms or manifestations of spina bifida (except spina bifida occulta), including complications or associated medical conditions related to spina bifida according to the scientific literature.

Eligibility for VA spina bifida healthcare benefits is limited to birth children of Vietnam veterans who have been diagnosed with spina bifida. Since benefits are based upon eligibility determinations made by VA regional offices, prospective beneficiaries must first contact a regional office to initiate the application process. The local VA regional office can be contacted at (800) 827-1000.

Healthcare benefits available under this program are limited to those necessary for the treatment of spina bifida and related medical conditions. Beneficiaries should be aware that this program is not a comprehensive healthcare plan and does not cover care that is unrelated to spina bifida.

Administration of the program is centralized to VA's Health Administration Center (HAC) in Denver, Colorado. HAC is responsible for all aspects of the spina bifida healthcare program, including the authorization of benefits and the subsequent processing and payment of claims. All inquiries regarding healthcare benefits should be made directly to HAC.

Healthcare benefits may be claimed for services and supplies starting on the effective date specified in the VA regional office award letter.

Beneficiaries in receipt of a VA regional office spina bifida award will receive an identification card from the Health Administration Center.

In general, the program covers most healthcare services and supplies that are medically or psychologically necessary for the treatment of conditions related to spina bifida. While some services require specific advance approval or preauthorization, the following services are specifically excluded from coverage:

- Care unrelated to spina bifida;
- Care as part of a grant study or research program;
- Care considered experimental or investigational;
- Drugs not approved by the U.S. food and drug administration for commercial marketing;
- Services, procedures or supplies for which the beneficiary has no legal obligation to pay, such as services obtained at a health fair;
- Services provided outside the scope of the provider's license or certification;
- Services rendered by providers suspended or sanctioned by a federal agency.

Covered Benefits

The following services are covered and paid by VA providing they are determined to be medically necessary for the treatment of spina bifida and related conditions, and accepted by the U.S./VA medical community. (See also preauthorization requirements above.)

- Inpatient services;
- Outpatient services;
- Pharmacy services to include supplies and over-the-counter items;
- Mental health and substance abuse services;
- Dental services;
- Emergency services;
- Durable medical equipment (furnished through VA sources unless specifically approved for private purchase);
- Preventative care;
- Rehabilitative care;
- Home care;
- Nursing home care;
- Respite care;
- Training family members;
- Travel expenses to include meals, lodging, commercial travel tickets, ambulance or special mode travel, and attendant * from the beneficiary's residence to the place of medical treatment (includes travel to and from Shriners hospitals for children);
- Travel benefits for an attendant may be covered when it has been determined that the beneficiary's physical or mental condition requires the presence of an attendant. All requests for attendant travel benefits require preauthorization.

Selecting Healthcare Providers

Beneficiaries may select the provider of their choice as long as the provider is an approved healthcare provider. Regardless of the providers selected, please be sure that they are aware of the program's benefit limitations, preauthorization requirements, claim filing instructions, as well as how to reach us for assistance.

In addition to approved healthcare providers, some services may also be obtained from VA healthcare facilities. An alternative source to VA-financed healthcare is cost-free healthcare available through the Shriners Hospitals for Children-a nonprofit charitable corporation offering comprehensive services to children under the age of 18.

CLAIMS

Claims are to be mailed directly to VA's Health Administration Center at the following address.

VA Health Administration Center
PO Box 65025
Denver CO 80206-9025

As a safeguard against claims getting lost in the mail, beneficiaries should keep copies of all claim documents submitted.

Filing Deadlines

Claims must be filed with the Health Administration Center no later than:

- One year after the date of service; or
- In the case of inpatient care, one year after the date of discharge; or
- In the case of a VA regional office award for retroactive eligibility, 180 days following beneficiary notification of the award.

Payments

Approved healthcare providers will be paid 100% of the VA-determined allowable charge for covered services. VA payment for covered services constitutes payment in full. Federal regulations prohibit providers from seeking any additional monies from beneficiaries and third party payers such as private insurers, for services paid by VA.

Note: If the beneficiary pays for care and subsequently files a claim for reimbursement, VA payment to the beneficiary will be limited to the VA-allowed amount. For this reason, beneficiaries are advised not to pay their providers- but instead, have the providers bill HAC directly.

Other Health Insurance

While VA assumes full responsibility for the cost of services related to the treatment of spina bifida and associated conditions, third-party insurers including Medicare and Medicaid, assume payment responsibility for services unrelated to the VA-covered conditions.

Explanation of Benefits

Upon completion of claim processing, an EOB will be mailed to the beneficiary. If a provider files the claim, an EOB will be mailed to them also. The EOB is a summarization of the action taken on the claim and contains, at a minimum, the following information.

- Beneficiary name;
- Description of services and/or supplies provided;
- Dates of service or supplies provided;

- Amount billed;
- VA-allowed amount;
- To whom payment, if any, was made;
- Reasons for denial (if applicable).

Reconsideration of Claims / Appeals

If a healthcare provider, beneficiary or beneficiary's representative disagrees with a claim determination, including the VA-allowed amount, a request for reconsideration of the disputed determination may be made. To do so, the request must:

- Be in writing;
- Be accompanied by a copy of the EOB in question; and
- State the specific issue that is being disputed, why the VA determination is considered to be in error, and include any new and relevant information not previously considered.

To meet the filing deadline, requests for reconsideration are to be mailed to the following address within one year of the date of the initial EOB:

Chief, Administrative Division
VA Health Administration Center
PO Box 65025
Denver CO 80206-9025

Upon complete review of the request and all the relevant documentation and evidence, a written determination will be mailed to the claimant.

CHAPTER 26

BENEFITS FOR POST-TRAUMATIC STRESS DISORDER AND SEXUAL TRAUMA

POST-TRAUMATIC STRESS DISORDER (PTSD)

Studies show that PTSD affects 30 percent of war zone veterans, including those who saw combat in World War II, Korea, Vietnam, the Persian Gulf and Bosnia.

PTSD is an anxiety disorder resulting from a psychologically stressful event beyond the scope of "normal" human experience. The trauma may be experienced alone (rape or assault) or in the company of groups of people (military combat). Stressors producing PTSD include natural disasters (floods, earthquakes), accidental man-made disasters (car accidents, airplane crashes, large fires) or deliberate man-made disasters (bombing, torture, death camps). Symptoms include recurrent thoughts of a traumatic event, reduced involvement in work or outside interests, hyper alertness, anxiety and irritability. The disorder apparently is more severe and longer lasting when the stress is of human design. Studies show that PTSD affects 30 percent of war zone veterans, including those who saw combat in World War II, Korea, Vietnam, the Persian Gulf and Bosnia.

Vet Centers

A nationwide system of community-based counseling centers, known as Vet Centers, provides counseling for psychological war trauma. Readjustment counseling features a non-medical setting, a mix of social services, community outreach activities, psychological counseling for war-related experiences, and family counseling. These services are designed to assist combat-affected and other veterans attain a well-adjusted post-war work and family life. Implemented by VA in 1979, Vet Centers were initially designed for Vietnam veterans. Current law has extended eligibility for the program to any veteran who has served in the military in combat operations during any period of armed hostility. VA operates more than 200 Vet Centers in all 50 states, Puerto Rico, the Virgin Islands, the District of Columbia and Guam. Interdisciplinary teams including psychologists, social workers, nurses and paraprofessionals staff the centers.

For a complete listing of Vet Centers, please refer to Chapter 16 of this book.

VA Medical Center Programs

While PTSD treatment is available through all of VA's 171 medical centers, a VA network of 124 facilities offers specialized inpatient and outpatient treatment. One notable program consists of PTSD clinical teams that provide outpatient treatment but also work closely with other VA treatment programs, including Vet Centers, to coordinate services and provide information on PTSD throughout the medical center and the community.

In addition to 83 PTSD clinical teams, VA operates 22 specialized inpatient units around the country, plus 13 brief-treatment units, 11 residential rehabilitation programs, and four PTSD day hospitals. There also are four outpatient Women's Stress Disorder and Treatment Teams and eight outpatient-based PTSD Teams Substance Use Disorder demonstration projects. A special focus in the program expansions has included underserved and minority populations, such as African Americans, Hispanics and Native Americans. A specialized PTSD inpatient treatment unit serves women veterans at the Palo Alto, Calif., VA Medical Center's Menlo Park Division.

National PTSD Center

In 1989, VA established the National Center for Post-Traumatic Stress Disorder -- a center for clinical research, training and information on PTSD. The center initially consisted of five divisions with distinct, but complementary responsibilities:

- Behavioral Science;
- Clinical Neurosciences;
- Education;
- Evaluation; and
- Executive and Resource Center Divisions.

Growing recognition of the dimensions of PTSD has brought new programs, such as the Women's Health Sciences Division, located at the Boston VA Medical Center, and the Pacific Islands Division in Honolulu.

Disability Compensation

PTSD can be a service-connected disability.

The process of applying for a VA disability for PTSD can take several months, and can be both complicated and quite stressful. The Veterans Service Organizations provide Service Officers at no cost to help veterans and family members pursue VA disability claims.

Service Officers are familiar with every step in the application and interview process, and can provide both technical guidance and moral support. In addition, some Service Officers particularly specialize in assisting veterans with PTSD disability claims. Even if a veteran has not been a member of a specific Veterans Service Organization, the veteran still can request the assistance of a Service Officer working for that organization. In order to get representation by a qualified and helpful Service Officer, you can directly contact the local office of any Veterans Service Organization -- or ask for recommendations from other veterans who have applied for VA disability, or from a PTSD specialist at a VA PTSD clinic or a Vet Center.

SEXUAL TRAUMA

Some veterans (women and men) suffered personal assault and/or sexual trauma while serving on active military duty. They might still struggle with fear, anxiety, embarrassment, or profound anger as a result of these experiences.

VA defines sexual trauma as any lingering physical, emotional, or psychological symptoms resulting from a physical assault of a sexual nature, or battery of a sexual nature. Examples of this are:

- Rape;
- Physical assault;
- Domestic Battering; and
- Stalking.

Compensation for Disabilities

Disability Compensation is a monthly payment to a veteran disabled by an injury or a disease incurred or aggravated on active service. The veteran must have been discharged under other than dishonorable conditions to be eligible. The individual must currently be suffering from disabling symptoms to receive compensation. Refer to Chapter 4 of this book for information regarding Disability Compensation.

CHAPTER 27

BENEFITS FOR FORMER PRISONERS OF WAR (POWS)

Former American POWs are eligible for special veterans benefits from the VA, including medical care in VA hospitals and disability compensation for injuries and disease presumed to be caused by internment. Studies have shown that the physical deprivation and psychological stress endured as a captive have life-long effects on subsequent health, social adjustment, and vocational adjustment.

In 1981, Congress passed Public Law 97-37 entitled, "Former Prisoners of War Benefit Act." This law accomplished several things. It established an Advisory Committee on Former Prisoners of War and mandated medical and dental care. It also identified certain diagnoses as presumptive service-connected conditions for former POWs. Other public laws passed since then, and a policy decision by the Secretary of Veterans Affairs in 1993, have added additional diagnoses to the list of presumptive conditions.

On November 30, 1999, the President signed into law the Veterans Millennium Healthcare and Benefits Act, Pub. L. 106-117. Section 501, a provision of the law, authorizes VA to pay DIC under 38 U.S.C. 1318 to the survivors of former Prisoners of War who died after September 30, 1999, and who were rated totally disabled continuously for a period of not less than one year immediately preceding death for a service-connected disability. This provision is effective November 30, 1999.

A POW Coordinator has been designated at each VA regional office. The POW Coordinator can furnish former POWs with information about the benefits and services available to them.

HEALTHCARE

Former POWs are recognized as a special category of veterans, and will be placed on one of the top three Priority Groups established for VA healthcare by Congress.

Veterans who were POWs may receive complete dental care.

Former POWs are eligible for any prosthetic item, including eyeglasses and hearing aids. A VA physician must order the prosthetic items, when medically indicated, for eligible veterans.

Veterans may enroll in VA healthcare by completing VA Form 10-10, Application for Medical Benefits.

Update - Public Law 108-170, which became law December 6, 2003, eliminated ***prescription drug co-payments*** for former POWs.

DISABILITY COMPENSATION

Veterans are encouraged to apply for VA disability Compensation for any disabilities related to service, whether they were a POW or not. Some disabilities are *presumptive*, which means that if a veteran is diagnosed with certain conditions, and the veteran was a POW for at least 30 days (certain conditions do not include the 30-day requirement), the VA presumes the captivity caused the disability.

Presumptions Of Service-Connection Relating To Certain Diseases And Disabilities For Former Prisoners Of War

Public Law 108-183, The Veterans Benefits Act of 2003, eliminated the requirement that a veteran was a POW for at least 30 days for certain conditions. Therefore, there are now two categories of presumptive conditions – those that include the 30-day requirement, and those that do not.

On October 7, 2004 VA expanded benefits to all former POWs with strokes and common heart diseases. Affected veterans are automatically eligible for disability compensation for those common ailments, and their spouses and dependents are eligible for service-connected survivors' benefits if these diseases contribute to the death of a former POW.

In the case of any veteran who is a former prisoner of war, and **who was detained or interned for thirty days or more,** any of the following which became manifest to a degree of 10% or more after active military, naval or air service, shall be considered to have been incurred in or aggravated by such service, notwithstanding that there is no record of such disease during the period of service:

- Avitaminosis
- Beriberi (including beriberi heart disease, which includes Ischemic Heart Disease-coronary artery disease-for former POWs who suffered during captivity from edema-swelling of the legs or feet- also known as "wet" beriberi)
- Chronic dysentery
- Helminthiasis
- Malnutrition (including optic atrophy associated with malnutrition)
- Pellagra
- Any other nutritional deficiency

- Peripheral neuropathy, except where directly related to infectious causes
- Irritable bowel syndrome
- Peptic ulcer disease
- Cirrhosis of the liver (This condition was added as part of Public Law 108-183.)
- Atherosclerotic heart disease or hypertensive vascular disease (including hypertensive heart disease) and their complications (including myocardial infarction, congestive heart failure and arrhythmia) (These conditions were added as part of Public Law 109-233.)
- Stroke and its complications (This condition was added as part of Public Law 109-233.)

In the case of any veteran who is a former prisoner of war, and **who was detained or interned for any period of time,** any of the following which became manifest to a degree of 10% or more after active military, naval or air service, shall be considered to have been incurred in or aggravated by such service, notwithstanding that there is no record of such disease during the period of service:

- Psychosis
- Dysthymic disorder, or depressive neurosis
- Post-traumatic osteoarthritis
- Any of the Anxiety States
- Cold Injury
- Stroke and complications
- Heart Disease and complications

Update:
On October 7, 2004 VA expanded benefits to all former POWs with strokes and common heart diseases. Affected veterans are automatically eligible for disability compensation for those common ailments, and their spouses and dependents are eligible for service-connected survivors' benefits if these diseases contribute to the death of a former POW.

Former POWs should file a claim by completing VA Form 21-526, Application for Compensation or Pension. The VA also offers a POW protocol exam. This is a one-time exam available to all former POWs, and is conducted at a VA medical facility to help determine if any presumptive disabilities exist.

PRISONER OF WAR MEDAL

A Prisoner of War Medal is available to any member of the U.S. Armed Forces taken prisoner during any armed conflict dating from World War I. Please refer to Chapter 42 of this book for detailed information on how to obtain medals.

CHAPTER 28

BENEFITS FOR FILIPINO VETERANS

FOUR CATEGORIES

For purposes of VA benefits and services, the service of members of the Philippine armed forces can be categorized as service in one of four groups:

Regular Philippine Scouts (also called Old Philippine Scouts)

These veterans were members of a small, regular component of the U.S. Army that was considered to be in regular active service. Originally formed in 1901, long before any formal plan for Philippine independence, the Regular Philippine Scouts were part of the U.S. Army throughout their existence.

Special Philippine Scouts (also called New Philippine Scouts)

These individuals were Philippine citizens who served with the U.S. Armed Forces with the consent of the Philippine government, and served between October 6, 1945 and June 30, 1947, inclusive.

Commonwealth Army of the Philippines (also called the Philippine Commonwealth Army)

These individuals were called into the service of the United States Armed Forces of the Far East (USAFFE), its members serving between July 26, 1941 and June 30, 1946, inclusive.

Recognized Guerillas

People in this group served as guerrillas in USAFFE in resistance units recognized by, and cooperating with U.S. forces between April 20, 1942, through June 30, 1946, inclusive.

ELIGIBILITY FOR VA BENEFITS

Regular Philippine Scouts

Regular Philippine Scouts who served with U.S. forces before October 6, 1945, are entitled to all VA benefits, under the same criteria as veterans of the U.S. Armed Forces.

Monetary benefits are payable in Dollars, at the full rate authorized, and their dependents and survivors are entitled to benefits under the eligibility rules common to the survivors of all U.S. veterans.

Special Philippine Scouts (New Philippine Scouts)

These veterans and eligible dependents are entitled to:

- Disability Compensation;
- Clothing Allowance;
- Dependency & Indemnity Compensation (DIC);
- Health care benefits in the U.S. on the same basis as U.S. veterans, provided they reside in the United States, and are citizens or lawfully admitted for permanent residence;
- Burial benefits, at the full-dollar rate, if the veterans were lawfully living in the United States on the date of death, and were U. S. citizens or lawfully admitted permanent resident aliens. Eligibility applies to death on or after December 16, 2003, based on legislation enacted in 2003.

Note: Monetary benefits are payable at a rate of $.50 of each Dollar authorized. (Commissioned officers are paid at the full rate authorized.) However, those veterans who live in the United States receive full-dollar rate compensation payments if they are either U.S. citizens or lawfully admitted permanent resident aliens.

Benefit Programs Not Available:

- Non-service connected pension benefits for veterans and dependents;
- Death pension;
- Hospital care and outpatient treatment for service-connected or non-service-connected conditions, if the care is provided outside of the U.S., or at facilities outside of the U.S. over which the VA has no jurisdiction, or has not contracted;
- Dental care;
- VA loans such as home loan guarantees;
- Specially adapted homes;
- Automobile or other conveyances;
- Service-disabled veterans insurance (RH);
- Gravemarker or headstone;
- Burial flag;
- Burial in a national cemetery.

Commonwealth Army (Philippine Commonwealth Army):

These veterans and eligible dependents are entitled to:

- Disability Compensation;
- Clothing Allowance;
- Dependency & Indemnity Compensation (DIC);
- Health care benefits in the U.S. on the same basis as U.S. veterans, provided they reside in the United States, and are citizens or lawfully admitted for permanent residence;
- Burial benefits, at the full-dollar rate, if the veterans were lawfully living in the United States on the date of death, and were U. S. citizens or lawfully admitted permanent resident aliens. Eligibility applies to death on or after November 1, 2000, based on legislation enacted in 2000;
- Burial in national cemeteries (for deaths on or after November 1, 2000);
- Headstones and markers (for deaths on or after November 1, 2000);
- Burial Flag(for deaths on or after November 1, 2000).

Note: Monetary benefits are payable at a rate of $.50 of each Dollar authorized. (Commissioned officers are paid at the full rate authorized.) However, those veterans who live in the United States receive full-dollar rate compensation payments if they are either U.S. citizens or lawfully admitted permanent resident aliens.

Benefit Programs Not Available:

- Non-service connected pension benefits for veterans and dependents;
- Death pension;
- Dental care;
- VA loans such as home loan guarantees;
- Specially adapted homes;
- Automobile or other conveyances;
- Service-disabled veterans insurance (RH).

Recognized Guerillas

These veterans and eligible dependents are entitled to:

- Disability Compensation;
- Clothing Allowance;

- Dependency & Indemnity Compensation (DIC);
- Health care benefits in the U.S. on the same basis as U.S. veterans, provided they reside in the United States, and are citizens or lawfully admitted for permanent residence;
- Burial benefits, at the full-dollar rate, if the veterans were lawfully living in the United States on the date of death, and were U. S. citizens or lawfully admitted permanent resident aliens. Eligibility applies to death on or after November 1, 2000, based on legislation enacted in 2000;
- Burial in national cemeteries (for deaths on or after November 1, 2000);
- Headstones and markers (for deaths on or after November 1, 2000);
- Burial Flag (for deaths on or after November 1, 2000).

Note: Monetary benefits are payable at a rate of $.50 of each Dollar authorized. (Commissioned officers are paid at the full rate authorized.) However, those veterans who live in the United States receive full-dollar rate compensation payments if they are either U.S. citizens or lawfully admitted permanent resident aliens.

Benefit Programs Not Available:

- Non-service connected pension benefits for veterans and dependents;
- Death pension;
- Dental care;
- VA loans such as home loan guarantees;
- Specially adapted homes;
- Automobile or other conveyances;
- Service-disabled veterans insurance (RH).

Note: Veterans may be eligible for additional healthcare services at the Veteran's Memorial Medical Center, a facility in Manila operated by the Philippine government.

CHAPTER 29

BENEFITS FOR ALLIED VETERANS AND CERTAIN NON-MILITARY GROUPS

ALLIED VETERANS

VA is authorized to provide medical care to certain veterans of nations allied or associated with the United States during World War I or World War II. Such treatment is available at any VA Medical Center if authorized and reimbursed by the foreign government. Necessary paperwork is obtained through the veteran's country in order to receive services for service connected conditions only.

MERCHANT MARINE SEAMEN

The Department of Defense announced January 19, 1988, that certain Merchant Marine seamen now qualify as veterans.

Merchant seamen who engaged in active, ocean-going service from December 7, 1941 to August 15, 1945 are eligible to apply for a certificate of release or discharge from the DoD. This certificate will then entitle the holder to apply for VA benefits currently available to World War II veterans. (Civil Service crewmembers aboard U.S. Army Transport Service and Naval Transportation vessels in ocean-going service or foreign waters were included in the DoD action.)

Generally, the newly designated veterans and their survivors are eligible to apply for the same benefits that are available to other World War II veterans. These benefits include:

- Medical care;
- Disability compensation;
- Disability pension;
- DIC;
- Dental treatment;
- GI Insurance;
- Vocational rehabilitation;
- VA-guaranteed home loans;
- Burial benefits (see following Special Note Regarding Burial Benefits).

These veterans are not eligible for VA-administered education programs, although in certain limited circumstances they may establish eligibility for vocational rehabilitation.

Special Note Regarding Burial Benefits:

The "Veterans Programs Enhancement Act of 1998", extended the ending qualifying date from August 15, 1945 to December 31, 1946 for eligibility for

- Burial flags;
- Headstones and markers;
- Internment in national cemeteries;
- Burial allowance for certain indigent wartime veterans;
- Markers in memorial areas of national cemeteries;
- Markers in memorial areas of Arlington National Cemetery; and
- Plot allowance payable to a State for burial in certain "state owned" cemeteries or cemetery sections.

Depending on the type of merchant marine service, certification of "qualified service" must come from the Department of Transportation or the Department of Defense. In general, benefits may be provided only for deaths occurring after November 11, 1998. However, in the case of an initial burial or columbarium placement in a national cemetery after November 11, 1998, benefits incident to burial and the provision of a headstone or marker are authorized regardless of the date of death.

Applying for Certificate of Release (Obtaining Veteran Status or Extension of Veteran Status)

Interested mariners or survivors should complete the following steps and mail to the proper address:

1. Compete Form DD2168 (available from all VA regional offices). Supply as much information as possible.
2. Include photocopies of discharges, identification, and any other supporting documents.
3. Survivors need to include a certified death certificate. (The Coast Guard will issue documents for a person listed as an official casualty list without a death certificate.)
4. Send to:

   The National Maritime Center (NMC-4A)

   4200 Wilson Blvd., Suite 630
   Arlington, VA 22203-1804
   (202) 493-1000

OTHER NON-MILITARY GROUPS

Through the years, a number of non-military groups have provided military-related service to the United States. Many of these groups have been formally recognized by the Department of Defense, and granted VA benefits.

Service in the following groups has been certified as active military service for benefits purposes:

- Women's Air Force Service Pilots (WASPs);
- Signal Corps Female Telephone Operators Unit of World I;
- Engineer Field Clerks;
- Women's Army Auxiliary Corps (WAAC);
- Quartermaster Corps female clerical employees serving with the American Expeditionary Forces in World War I;
- Civilian employees of Pacific naval air bases who actively participated in defense of Wake Island during World War II;
- Reconstruction aides and dietitians in World War I;
- Male civilian ferry pilots;
- Wake Island defenders from Guam;
- Civilian personnel assigned to OSS secret intelligence;
- Guam Combat Patrol;
- Quartermaster Corps members of the Keswick crew on Corregidor during World War II;
- U.S. civilians who participated in the defense of Bataan;
- U.S. merchant seamen who served on blockships in support of Operation Mulberry in the World War II invasion of Normandy;
- American merchant marines in oceangoing service during WW II;
- Civilian Navy IFF radar technicians who served in combat areas of the Pacific during World War II;
- U.S. civilians of the American Field Service who served overseas in World War I;
- U.S. civilians of the American Field Service who served overseas under U.S. armies and U.S. army groups in World War II;
- U.S. civilian employees of American Airlines who served overseas in a contract with the Air Transport Command between Dec. 14, 1941, and Aug. 14, 1945;

- Civilian crewmen of U.S. Coast and Geodetic Survey vessels who served in areas of immediate military hazard while conducting cooperative operations with and for the U.S. Armed Forces between Dec. 7, 1941, and Aug. 15, 1945;

- Members of the American Volunteer Group (Flying Tigers) serving between Dec. 7, 1941, and July 18, 1942;

- U.S. civilian flight crew and aviation ground support employees of United Air Lines who served overseas in a contract with Air Transport Command between Dec. 14, 1941, and Aug. 14, 1945;

- U.S. civilian flight crew and aviation ground support employees of Transcontinental and Western Air, Inc. (TWA), who served overseas in a contract with the Air Transport Command between Dec. 14, 1941, and Aug. 14, 1945;

- U.S. civilian flight crew and aviation ground support employees of Consolidated Vultee Aircraft Corp. (Consairway Division) who served overseas in a contract with Air Transport Command between Dec. 14, 1941, and Aug. 14, 1945;

- U.S. civilian flight crew and aviation ground support employees of Pan American World Airways and its subsidiaries and affiliates, who served overseas in a contract with the Air Transport Command and Naval Air Transport Service between Dec. 14, 1941, and Aug. 14, 1945;

- Honorably discharged members of the American Volunteer Guard, Eritrea Service Command, between June 21, 1942, and March 31, 1943;

- U.S. civilian flight crew and aviation ground support employees of Northwest Airlines who served overseas under the airline's contract with Air Transport Command from Dec. 14, 1941, through Aug. 14, 1945;

- U.S. civilian female employees of the U.S. Army Nurse Corps who served in the defense of Bataan and Corregidor during the period January 2, 1942 to February 3, 1945;

- U.S. Flight crew and aviation ground support employees of Northeast Airlines Atlantic Division, who served overseas as a result of Northeast Airlines' contract with the Air Transport Command during the period December 7, 1941 through August 14, 1945;

- U.S. civilian flight crew and aviation ground support employees of Braniff Airways, who served overseas in the North Atlantic or under the jurisdiction of the North Atlantic Wing, Air Transport Command, as a result of a contract with the Air Transport Command during the period February 26, 1942 through August 14, 1945.

For the service to qualify as military-related service, the Defense Secretary must certify that the group has provided active military service. Individual members must be issued a discharge by the Defense Secretary, which can then be used to qualify for VA benefits.

CHAPTER 30

NATURALIZATION PREFERENCE

On July 3, 2002, the president issued Executive Order 13269 providing naturalization for aliens and non-citizen nationals serving on active duty status in the U.S. armed forces from September 11, 2001, to a date not yet determined. In addition, if a person dies as a result of injury or disease incurred or aggravated by such service, their survivor(s) can apply for posthumous citizenship at any time within two years of the death of the alien or non-citizen national.

Aliens and non-citizen nationals with honorable service in the U.S. armed forces during specified periods of hostilities may be naturalized without having to comply with the general requirements for naturalization.

Veterans who served prior to September 11, 2001, are eligible to file for naturalization based on their U.S. military service. An applicant who served three years in the U.S. military and is a lawful permanent resident is excused from any specific period of required residence, period of residence in any specific place, or physical presence within the United States if the application for naturalization is filed while the applicant is still serving in the military or within six months of honorable discharge. Applicants who file for naturalization more than six months after termination of three years of U.S. military service may count any periods of honorable service as residence and physical presence in the United States.

Aliens and non-citizen nationals with honorable service in the U.S. armed forces during specified periods of hostilities may be naturalized without having to comply with the general requirements for naturalization. This is the only section of the Immigration and Nationality Act, as amended, which allows persons who have not been lawfully admitted for permanent residence to file an application for naturalization.

Any person who has served honorably during qualifying time may file an application at any time in his or her life if, at the time of enlistment, reenlistment, extension of enlistment or induction, such person shall have been in the United States, the Canal Zone, American Samoa or Swain's Island, or, on or after November 18, 1997, aboard a public vessel owned or operated by the United States for non-commercial service, whether or not lawful admittance to the United States for permanent residence has been granted.

Certain applicants who have served in the U.S. Armed Forces are eligible to file for naturalization based on current or prior U.S. military service. Such applicants should file the N-400 Military Naturalization Packet.

CHAPTER 31

HOMELESS VETERANS

Approximately one-third of the adult homeless population living on the streets or in shelters have served their country in the armed services. Many other veterans are considered at risk because of poverty, lack of support from family and friends and precarious living conditions in overcrowded or substandard housing.

VA has many benefits and services to assist homeless veterans, including:

Homeless Providers Grant and Per Diem Program

VA's Homeless Providers Grant and Per Diem Program is offered annually (as funding permits) by the Department of Veterans Affairs Health Care for Homeless Veterans (HCHV) Programs to fund community agencies providing services to homeless veterans. The purpose is to promote the development and provision of supportive housing and/or supportive services with the goal of helping homeless veterans achieve residential stability, increase their skill levels and/or income, and obtain greater self-determination.

Only programs with supportive housing (up to 24 months) or service centers (offering services such as case management, education, crisis intervention, counseling, etc.) are eligible for these funds. The program has two levels of funding: the Grant Component and the Per Diem Component.

***Grants*:**
Limit is 65% of the costs of construction, renovation, or acquisition of a building for use as service centers or transitional housing for homeless vets. Renovation of VA properties is allowed, acquiring VA properties is not. Recipients must obtain the matching 35% share from other sources. Grants may not be used for operational costs, including salaries.

Per Diem:
Priority in awarding the Per Diem funds goes to the recipients of Grants. Non-Grant programs may apply for Per Diem under a separate announcement, when published in the Federal Register, announcing the funding for "Per Diem Only."

Applications are not accepted for Capital Grants or "Per Diem Only" funding until the Notice of Funding Availability (NOFA) is published in the Federal Register. Funds will be awarded to programs determined to be the most qualified. For further information, call (877) 332-0334.

AmeriCorps

As part of the national VA effort to help homeless veterans, helping homeless veterans may benefit selected students. Working with VA staff, eligible VA beneficiary-students may receive funds to help defray school and living expenses. If you are a veteran or a VA eligible beneficiary, attending school and receiving VA education assistance, you may be entitled to participate in this work-for-pay program authorized through the VA Work-Study Allowance Program and the AmeriCorps Education Awards.

Loan Guarantee Program For Homeless Veterans Multifamily Housing

This initiative authorizes VA to guarantee no more than 15 loans with an aggregate value of $100 million within 5 years for construction, renovation of existing property, and refinancing of existing loans, facility furnishing or working capital. No more than 5 loans could be guaranteed under this program prior to November 11, 2001. The amount financed is a maximum of 90% of project costs. Legislation allows the Secretary to issue a loan guarantee for large-scale self-sustaining multifamily loans. Eligible transitional project are those that: 1) Provide supportive services including job counseling; 2) Require veteran to seek and maintain employment; 3) Require veteran to pay reasonable rent; 4) Require sobriety as a condition of occupancy; and, 5) Serves other veterans in need of housing on a space available basis.

Stand Downs

Stand Downs are one part of the Department of Veterans Affairs' efforts to provide services to homeless veterans. Stand Downs are typically one to three day events providing services to homeless veterans such as food, shelter, clothing, health screenings, VA and Social Security benefits counseling, and referrals to a variety of other necessary services, such as housing, employment and substance abuse treatment. Stand Downs are collaborative events, coordinated between local VAs, other government agencies, and community agencies who serve the homeless.

The first Stand Down was organized in 1988 by a group of Vietnam veterans in San Diego. Since then, Stand Downs have been used as an effective tool in reaching out to homeless veterans, reaching more than 200,000 veterans and their family members between 1994-2000.

For additional information on Stand Down dates and locations, please contact the Homeless Veterans Programs Office at (202) 273-5764.

Compensated Work Therapy/Transitional Residence (CWT/TR) Program

In VA's Compensated Work Therapy/Transitional Residence (CWT/TR) Program, disadvantaged, at-risk, and homeless veterans live in CWT/TR community-based supervised group homes while working for pay in VA's Compensated Work Therapy Program (also known as Veterans Industries). Veterans in the CWT/TR program work about 33 hours per week, with approximate earnings of $732 per month, and pay an average of $186 per month toward maintenance and up-keep of the residence. The average length of stay is about 174 days. VA contracts with private industry and the public sector for work done by these veterans, who learn new job skills, relearn successful work habits, and regain a sense of self-esteem and self-worth.

CHALENG

The Community Homelessness Assessment, Local Education, and Networking Groups (CHALENG) for veterans is a nationwide initiative in which VA medical center and regional office directors work with other federal, state, and local agencies and nonprofit organizations to assess the needs of homeless veterans, develop action plans to meet identified needs, and develop directories that contain local community resources to be used by homeless veterans.

More than 10,000 representatives from non-VA organizations have participated in Project CHALENG initiatives, which include holding conferences at VA medical centers to raise awareness of the needs of homeless veterans, creating new partnerships in the fight against homelessness, and developing new strategies for future action.

For more information, please contact CHALENG at (404) 327-4033.

DCHV

The Domiciliary Care for Homeless Veterans (DCHV) Program provides biopsychosocial treatment and rehabilitation to homeless veterans. The program provides residential treatment to approximately 5,000 homeless veterans with health problems each year and the average length of stay in the program is 4 months. The domiciliaries conduct outreach and referral; vocational counseling and rehabilitation; and post-discharge community support.

HUD-VASH

This joint Supported Housing Program with the Department of Housing and Urban Development provides permanent housing and ongoing treatment services to the harder-to-serve homeless mentally ill veterans and those suffering from substance abuse disorders. HUD's Section 8 Voucher Program has designated 1,780 vouchers worth $44.5 million for homeless chronically mentally ill veterans. VA staff at 35 sites provide outreach, clinical care and ongoing case management services. Rigorous evaluation of this program indicates that this approach significantly reduces days of homelessness for veterans plagued by serious mental illness and substance abuse disorders.

SUPPORTED HOUSING

Like the HUD-VASH program identified above, staff in VA's Supported Housing Program provides ongoing case management services to homeless veterans. Emphasis is placed on helping veterans find permanent housing and providing clinical support needed to keep veterans in permanent housing. Staff in these programs operate without benefit of the specially dedicated Section 8 housing vouchers available in the HUD-VASH program but are often successful in locating transitional or permanent housing through local means, especially by collaborating with Veterans Service Organizations.

Comprehensive Homeless Centers

VA's Comprehensive Homeless Centers (CHCs) place the full range of VA homeless efforts in a single medical center's catchment area and coordinate administration within a centralized framework. With extensive collaboration among non-VA service providers, VA's CHCs in Anchorage, AK; Brooklyn, NY; Cleveland, OH; Dallas, TX; Little Rock, AR; Pittsburgh, PA; San Francisco, CA; and West Los Angles, CA, provide a comprehensive continuum of care that reaches out to homeless veterans and helps them escape homelessness.

VBA-VHA SPECIAL OUTREACH AND BENEFITS ASSISTANCE

VHA has provided specialized funding to support twelve Veterans Benefits Counselors as members of HCMI and Homeless Domiciliary Programs as authorized by Public Law 102-590. These specially funded staff provide dedicated outreach, benefits counseling, referral, and additional assistance to eligible veterans applying for VA benefits. This specially funded initiative complements VBA's ongoing efforts to target homeless veterans for special attention. To reach more homeless veterans, designated homeless veterans coordinators at VBA's 58 regional offices annually make over 4,700 visits to homeless facilities and over 9,000 contacts with non-VA agencies working with the homeless and provide over 24,000 homeless veterans with benefits counseling and referrals to other VA programs. These special outreach efforts are assumed as part of ongoing duties and responsibilities. VBA has also instituted new procedures to reduce the processing times for homeless veterans' benefits claims.

VBA'S ACQUIRED PROPERTY SALES FOR HOMELESS PROVIDERS

This program makes all the properties VA obtains through foreclosures on VA-insured mortgages available for sale to homeless provider organizations at a discount of 20 to 50 percent, depending on time of the market.

VA EXCESS PROPERTY FOR HOMELESS VETERANS INITIATIVE

This initiative provides for the distribution of federal excess personal property, such as hats, parkas, footwear, socks, sleeping bags, and other items to homeless veterans and homeless veteran programs. A Compensated Work Therapy Program employing formerly homeless veterans has been established at the Medical Center in Lyons, NJ to receive, warehouse, and ship these goods to VA homeless programs across the country.

PROGRAM MONITORING AND EVALUATION

VA has built program monitoring and evaluation into all of its homeless veterans' treatment initiatives and it serves as an integral component of each program. Designed, implemented, and maintained by the Northeast Program Evaluation Center (NEPEC) at VAMC West Haven, CT, these evaluation efforts provide important information about the veterans served and the therapeutic value and cost effectiveness of the specialized programs. Information from these evaluations also helps program managers determine new directions to pursue in order to expand and improve services to homeless veterans.

CHAPTER 32

BENEFITS FOR FEMALE VETERANS

Female veterans are entitled to all of the benefits available to male veterans, including:

- Disability Compensation For Service-Related Disabilities;
- Disability Pension For Non-Service Related Disabilities;
- Education Assistance Programs;
- Work-Study Allowance;
- Vocational Rehabilitation And Counseling;
- Insurance;
- Home Loan Benefits;
- Medical Inpatient And Outpatient Care;
- Substance Abuse Treatment And Counseling;
- Sexual Trauma And Assault Counseling;
- Nursing Home Care;
- Burial Benefits;
- Burial In A VA National Cemetery;
- Employment Assistance;
- Survivors' Benefit Programs.

VA has also designed services and programs to be responsive to the gender-specific needs of female veterans. VA offers comprehensive healthcare services for female veterans, including:

- Counseling for sexual trauma;
- Breast examinations;
- Pelvic examinations;
- Pap smears;
- General reproductive health care services;

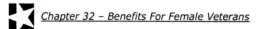

- Contraceptive services;
- Menopause management;
- Mammography;
- General reproductive healthcare.

Referrals are made for services that VA is unable to provide. Women Veterans' Program Managers are available in a private setting at all VA facilities to assist women veterans seeking treatment and benefits.

VA has also established a division within the National Center for Post-Traumatic Stress Disorder, the Women's Health Science Division. The center is based at the Boston VA Medical Center, and conducts clinical research addressing trauma-related problems of female veterans. Veterans may contact the Center at:

VA Medical Center
Women's Health Sciences Division
150 South Huntington Avenue
Boston, MA 02130
(617) 232-9500

WOMEN VETERANS COMPREHENSIVE HEATH CENTERS

Eight Women Veterans Comprehensive Heath Centers have been established to develop and enhance programs focusing on the gender-specific healthcare needs of female veterans. The locations are as follows:

Boston VA Medical Center
Boston, Massachusetts
(617) 232-9500, extension 4276

Chicago Area Network
(Hines, Lakeside, North Chicago, and West Side VA Medical Centers)
(312) 569-6168

Durham VA Medical Center
Durham, North Carolina
(919) 286-0411

Minneapolis VA Medical Center
Minneapolis, Minnesota
(612) 725-2030

Southeast Pennsylvania Network
(Coatesville, Lebanon, Philadelphia and Wilmington VA Medical Centers)
(215) 823-44496

San Francisco VA Medical Center
San Francisco, California
(415) 221-4810, extension 2174

Sepulveda / West Los Angeles VA Medical Centers
Sepulveda, California and Los Angeles, California
(415) 221-4810

Tampa VA Medical Center
Tampa, Florida
(813) 972-2000, extension 3678

STATE WOMEN VETERANS COORDINATORS

In addition to the Department of Veterans Affairs' Women Veterans Coordinators that are located at local regional offices and medical centers, there may be an *Office of State Veterans Affairs, or a State Commission for Veterans Coordinator* available within the State government veterans program. These State offices are part of the veteran-advocate community and their staff may assist female veterans in accessing State and Federal entitlements. For specific information on availability in your state, contact your local VA office.

CHAPTER 33

BENEFITS FOR GULF WAR VETERANS

With variation in exposures and veterans' concerns ranging from oil well fire smoke to possible contamination from Iraqi chemical/biological agents, VA has initiated wide-ranging research projects evaluating illnesses as well as environmental risk factors.

> *VA operates a toll-free hotline at (800) 749-8387 to inform veterans of available programs.*

The Department of Veterans Affairs (VA) offers Gulf War veterans physical examinations and special eligibility for follow-up care, and it operates a toll-free hotline at (800) 749-8387 to inform these veterans of the program and their benefits. Operators are trained to help veterans with general questions about medical care and other benefits. It also provides recorded messages that enable callers to obtain information 24 hours a day.

PERSIAN GULF REGISTRY PROGRAM

A free, complete physical examination with basic lab studies is offered to every Gulf War veteran, whether or not the veteran is ill. Veterans do not have to be enrolled in VA healthcare to participate in registry examinations. Results of the examinations, which include review of the veteran's military service and exposure history, are entered into special, computerized registries. The registries enable VA to update veterans on research findings or new compensation policies through periodic newsletters. The registries could also suggest areas to be explored in future scientific research. Registry participants are advised of the results of their examinations in personal consultations and by letters.

SPECIAL ACCESS TO FOLLOW-UP CARE

VA has designated a physician at every VA medical center to coordinate the special registry examination program and to receive updated educational materials and information as experience is gained nationally. Where an illness possibly related to military service in the Southwest Asia theater of operations during the Gulf War is detected during the examination, follow-up care is provided on a higher-eligibility basis than most non-service-connected care.

STANDARDIZED EXAM PROTOCOLS

VA has expanded its special registry examination protocol as more experience has been gained with the health of Gulf veterans. The protocol elicits information about symptoms and exposures, calls the clinician's attention to diseases common to the Gulf region, and directs baseline laboratory studies including chest X-ray (if one has not been done recently), blood count, urinalysis, and a set of blood chemistry and enzyme analyses that detect the "biochemical fingerprints" of certain diseases. In addition to this core laboratory work for every veteran undergoing the Gulf War program exam, physicians order additional tests and specialty consults as they would normally in following a diagnostic trail -- as symptoms dictate. If a diagnosis is not apparent, facilities follow the "comprehensive clinical evaluation protocol." The protocol suggests 22 additional baseline tests and additional specialty consultations, outlining dozens of further diagnostic procedures to be considered, depending on symptoms.

RISK FACTORS OF CONCERN TO VETERANS

Veterans have reported a wide range of factors observed in the Gulf environment or speculative risks about which they have voiced concerns. Some are the subject of research investigations and none have been ruled out. There appears to be no unifying exposure that would account for all unexplained illnesses. Individual veterans' exposures and experiences range from ships to desert encampments, and differences in military occupational specialty frequently dictate the kinds of elements to which service members are exposed.

Veteran concerns include exposure to the rubble and dust from exploded shells made from depleted uranium; the possibility of exposure to the nerve agent sarin or some yet-unconfirmed Iraqi chemical-biological agent; and use of a nerve agent pre-treatment drug, pyridostigmine bromide. Many other risk factors also have been raised. In 1991, VA initially began to develop tracking mechanisms that matured into the Gulf War Registry as a direct consequence of early concerns about the environmental influence of oil well fires and their smoke and particulate.

Anyone with first-hand information about "incidents" that occurred in the Southwest Asia theater of operations during the Persian Gulf War that may be related to health problems experienced by military personnel who served in the war should call the Department of Defense "Incidents" hotline at (800) 472-6719.

VA DISABILITY COMPENSATION FOR DIAGNOSED AND UNDIAGNOSED ILLNESSES

Like all other veterans, veterans of the Persian Gulf War can receive service-connected compensation for mental and physical disabilities that were incurred during, or aggravated by their service in the armed forces.

Recent legislation also authorized disability compensation for Persian Gulf veterans with chronic, ***undiagnosed*** illness resulting in a permanent disability that developed after they left the Persian Gulf. Congress created this legislation after many Persian Gulf War veterans reported they were suffering from multi-symptom disabilities that are poorly understood by the medical profession, and may be classified as "undiagnosed" by one physician, or referred to as "chronic fatigue syndrome" by another physician.

Public Law 107-103, signed by President Bush on December 27, 2001, extended the presumptive period for disabilities associated with Persian Gulf War service until December 31, 2011, or such later date as prescribed by VA.

To be entitled to disability compensation due to an undiagnosed illness, the claimant must meet the following requirements:

- The veteran must qualify as a Persian Gulf War veteran.

    - VA considers an individual to be a Persian Gulf War veteran if he or she served on active military, naval, or air service in the Southwest Asia theater of operations during the Persian Gulf War. This includes service in Iraq, Kuwait, Saudi Arabia, the neutral zone between Iraq and Saudi Arabia, Bahrain, Qatar, the United Arab Emirates, Oman, the Gulf of Aden, the Gulf of Oman, the Persian Gulf, the Arabian Sea, the Red Sea, and the airspace above these locations.

- The veteran's period of service must have included service in the designated area after August 2, 1990. Since members of the armed services are still serving in the area of operations, they qualify as Persian Gulf veterans because the end date for the Persian Gulf War has not been set.

- The veteran must suffer from a "qualifying chronic disability."

  A "qualifying chronic disability" can be any of the following (or combination of the following):

    - An undiagnosed illnesses;
    - A medically unexplained chronic multi-symptom illness (such as chronic fatigue syndrome, fibromyalgia, or irritable bowel syndrome) that is defined by a cluster of signs or symptoms;
    - Any diagnosed illness that the VA Secretary determines warrants a pres

  (VA considers disabilities to be chronic if they have existed for 6 months or more, or if they have exhibited intermittent episodes of improvement and worsening over a 6-month period. The 6-month period is measured from the earliest date that the signs or symptoms manifested.)

- The "qualifying chronic disability" must have appeared either during active duty in the Southwest Asia Theater of Operations during the Gulf War or it must have manifested to a degree of at least 10 percent during the presumptive period.

The following symptoms may be manifestations of an undiagnosed illness:

- Fatigue;
- Skin disorders;
- Headaches;
- Muscle pain;

- Joint pain;
- Neurological symptoms;
- Neuropsychological symptoms;
- Symptoms involving the respiratory system;
- Sleep disturbances;
- Gastrointestinal symptoms;
- Cardiovascular symptoms;
- Abnormal weight loss;
- Menstrual disorders;
- Any poorly defined chronic multi-symptom illness of unknown etiology characterized by 2 or more of the above symptoms.

Rates of compensation depend upon the degree of disability, and follow a payment schedule that is adjusted annually and applies to all veterans. Please refer to the charts in Chapter 4 for the current rates payable.

LOU GEHRIG'S DISEASE
AMYOTROPHIC LATERAL SCLEROSIS (ALS)

On December 10, 2001, VA reported that veterans who served in the Gulf during the period from August 2, 1990 through July 31, 1991, and who subsequently developed Lou Gehrig's Disease will be compensated.

For more information about VA's ALS registry, call (877) 342-5257.

Based on new research, VA now has evidence that veterans who deployed to the Gulf War are nearly twice as likely as their non-deployed counterparts to develop Lou Gehrig's Disease, technically known as amyotrohpic lateral sclerosis, or ALS.

The VA, together with the Department of Defense and other agencies, sponsored a study that looked for cases of ALS among the nearly 700,000 servicemembers deployed to Southwest Asia, and the 1.8 million on active duty during the period who were not deployed to the Gulf.

The study, found 40 cases of ALS among deployed veterans and 67 cases among the much larger non-deployed group. This translates to a nearly two-fold increase in the rate of this disorder in the deployed group compared to the non-deployed group.

VA has established a national ALS registry to identify veterans with the disease - regardless of when they served - and track their health status. Veterans with ALS who enroll will complete an initial telephone interview covering their health and military service, and will be interviewed twice yearly thereafter.

For more information about VA's ALS registry, call (877) 342-5257.

OBTAINING COPIES OF HOSPITAL RECORDS

A program is in place to help Gulf War veterans obtain copies of their in-patient hospital records from hospitals established during the Persian Gulf War.

Although these records were always located in the National Personnel Records Center in St. Louis, MO, they were stored only by the name of the hospital and the date of treatment.

An electronic database has been created to cross-reference patient names and social security numbers with their theater hospitals and admission dates.

Veterans may call (800) 497-6261 to find out if their inpatient record ahs been added to the database, and to obtain the paperwork necessary to request a copy.

VA-FUNDED EXAMINATION PROGRAM FOR THE SPOUSES AND CHILDREN OF GULF WAR VETERANS

In 1996, VA initiated a special program to fund health examinations for some spouses and children of Gulf War Veterans Registry participants. The results of these examinations, which are conducted under contract by non-VA physicians in non-VA medical facilities, are included in the Gulf War Registry. Funding for the program has been approved through December 31, 2003.

VA can provide examinations to any individual who:

- Is the spouse or child of a veterans, is listed in the Persian Gulf War Veterans Registry; and
- Is suffering from, or may have suffered from, an illness or disorder (including birth defect, miscarriage, or stillbirth) which cannot be disassociated from the veteran's service in the Southwest Asia theater of operations; and
- Has granted VA permission to include in the Registry relevant medical data from the evaluation.

Interested individuals should call the VA Persian Gulf Information Help line at (800) 749-8387.

Alternative Program

Eligible family members of Gulf War veterans may also have their medical information entered into the Persian Gulf War Registry by undergoing a physical examination from their private physician. The physician must complete a Registry code sheet, containing the protocol examination, and submit it to VA for entry into the database. The veteran or family member choosing this option must assume the cost of the examination and code sheet completion.

Interested individuals should contact the Persian Gulf Registry Coordinator at the nearest VA medical center for forms and information.

CONTINUING RESEARCH

A large number of studies are now in progress that will hopefully contribute to our understanding of Gulf War illnesses, including epidemiologic studies that will compare the types and frequency of illnesses in Gulf War veterans compared to veterans who did not serve in the Gulf War.

Additionally, more than 90 research studies are under way that will examine possible health consequences of exposure to a variety of factors present in the Persian Gulf, such as depleted uranium, pesticides, pyridostigmine bromide, and chemical warfare agents.

Any changes in benefits payable to Gulf War veterans as a result of this continuing research will be addressed in subsequent editions of this book, as well as in our monthly supplements.

CHAPTER 34

ENTITLEMENT AND BENEFITS FOR THOSE SERVING IN OPERATION JOINT GUARD

The following entitlements and benefits are offered to U.S. military personnel serving in Operation Joint Guard.

Reserves called to active duty in support of a contingency operation have the same entitlement to pay and allowances as active duty personnel. In addition to normal pay and allowances, U.S. troops in Bosnia-Herzegovina may be authorized the following pays:

Imminent Danger Pay -- $225 a month.

Imminent danger pay is payable for service in a designated combat zone. The current designated combat zones are: Afghanistan, Bahrain, Croatia, Kuwait, Kyrgyzstan, Macedonia, Montenegro, Oman, Pakistan, Philippines (for some), Qatar, Saudi Arabia, Serbia (Kosovo), Tajikistan, Turkey (selected units), United Arab Emirates, Uzbekistan, Yemen, and Iraq.

Update: The Department of Defense has announced that effective November 1, 2007, Angola, Georgia (The Georgian Republic), Sierra Leone, Bosnia-Herzegovina, Croatia, and Macedonia will no longer be classified imminent danger pay zones.

Hardship Duty Pay -- $50 - $150 a month.

Hardship duty pay is additional compensation paid to service members assigned to locations where living conditions are substantially below those conditions in the continental U.S. (CONUS). Following is a summary of the three different types of Hardship Duty Pay (HDP):

Military Hardship Duty Pay-Location

HDP-L is compensation paid to members assigned outside the continental United States in Quality of Life (QoL) Hardship locations -- Locations where QoL living conditions are substantially below the standard most members in the continental United States would generally experience. HDP-L is intended to recognize the extraordinary arduous living conditions, excessive physical hardship, and/or unhealthful conditions that exist in a location or assignment. Rates are payable in increments of $50, $100, or $150 a month based on the level of QoL hardship in a given area.

HDP-L Update: The Department of Defense has announced that effective November 1, 2007, the following locations will see increases to hardship duty-location (HDP-L):

- Angola, Georgia, and Sierra Leone are increased from $100 to $150 a month.
- Macedonia is increased from $0 to $100 a month.

Military Hardship Duty Pay-Mission

HDP-M is payable to members both officer and enlisted, for performing designated hardship missions. HDP-M is payable at the full monthly rate during any part of which, the member performs a specified mission. A member assigned to, on temporary duty with or otherwise under the operational control of the Defense Prisoner of War/Missing Personnel Office (DPMO), the Joint Task Force-Full Accounting (JTF-FA), or the Central Identification Lab-Hawaii (CIL-HI) may qualify for HDP-M based on performance of a hardship mission members so assigned are entitled for each month in which they perform investigative or remains recovery in a remote, isolated area (including, but not limited to, areas in Laos, Cambodia, Vietnam and North Korea) for recovery of U.S. service member remains.

Hardship Duty Pay - Involuntary Extension

Hardship Duty Pay for Involuntary extension of duty is a $200 a month HDP payable to servicemembers serving on a designated involuntary extension of duty. Only members assigned or attached to specific units deployed to the Iraqi area of operations are eligible.

To qualify for the Involuntary Extension Program for Iraq the following must happen:

- Servicemembers must be serving in a unit in Iraq.
- The unit must be specified by the Office of the Secretary of Defense (OSD) to continue to serve beyond their scheduled 12 month deployment.
- And including staging time – served 12 consecutive months or 12 months within a 15 month period.

The maximum total of HDP-L, HDP-M, and HDP- Involuntary Extension combined compensation that may be paid to an individual member in any one month is **$750**.

Family Separation Allowance -- $250 a month.

Paid anytime members are involuntarily separated from their dependents for more than 30 days.

Certain Places (foreign duty) Pay -- From $8 to $22.50 a month

Payable to enlisted members serving in the land area of the former Yugoslavia (i.e. Croatia, Bosnia-Herzegovina, Serbia, Montenegro, Macedonia or Slovenia.)

CHAPTER 35

SERVICEMEMBERS' CIVIL RELIEF ACT

Congress and state legislatures have long recognized that military service can often place an economic and legal burden on servicemembers. The Soldiers' and Sailors' Civil Relief Act of 1918 was passed in order to protect the rights of service members while serving on active duty.

> *The SCRA can provide many forms of relief to military members.*

Service members were protected from such things as repossession of property, bankruptcy, foreclosure or other such actions while serving in the military. This Act remained in effect until shortly after World War I when it expired. The Soldiers' and Sailors' Civil Relief Act of 1940 (SSCRA) was passed in order to protect the rights of the millions of service members activated for World War II. The SSCRA has remained in effect until the present day and has been amended many times since 1940 to keep pace with the changing military.

In December 2003, Congress passed legislation renaming SSCRA as the Servicemembers' Civil Relief Act (SCRA). The SCRA updates and strengthens the civil protections enacted during World War II.

The SCRA is designed to protect active duty military members, reservists who are in active federal service, and National Guardsmen who are in active federal service. Some of the benefits under the SCRA extend to dependents of active duty military members as well.

Public Law 107-330 extended protections under the SSCRA to members of the National Guard who are called to active service authorized by the President or the Secretary of Defense, or a state governor for a period of more than 30 consecutive days, for purposes of responding to a national emergency declared by the President, and supported by Federal funds.

Under previous law, the SSCRA only applied to National Guard members if they were called to FEDERAL service. The protections did not apply to Guard members performing duty under authority of the State Governor. Following September 11, 2000, President Bush asked the state governors to activate members of the National Guard to perform "homeland security" duties, such as guarding airports and other facilities that were considered terrorist targets. Because these members were called by the STATE, and not the Federal government, SSCRA protections did not apply. The new provision extends SSCRA protection to National Guard members, anytime they are performing "homeland security" duties, even if under control of State government.

The SCRA can provide many forms of relief to military members. Below are some of the most common forms of relief.

PROTECTION FROM EVICTION

If a military member is leasing a house or apartment and his or her rent is below a certain amount, the SCRA can protect the individual from being evicted for a period of time, usually three months. The dwelling place must be occupied by either the active duty member or his or her dependents and the rent on the premises cannot exceed $2465.00 a month (rate as of 2004). This rent ceiling will be adjusted annually for consumer price index (CPI) changes. Additionally, the military member must show that military service materially affects his or her ability to pay rent. If a landlord continues to try to evict the military member or does actually evict the member, he or she is subject to criminal sanctions such as fines or even imprisonment.

TERMINATION OF PRE-SERVICE RESIDENTIAL LEASES

The SCRA also allows military members who are just entering active duty service to lawfully terminate a lease without repercussions. To do this, the service member needs to show that the lease was entered into prior to the commencement of active duty service, that the lease was signed by or on behalf of the service member, and that the service member is currently in military service or was called to active-duty service for a period of 180 days or more. Proper written notice with a copy of orders must be provided to the landlord.

TERMINATION OF RESIDENTIAL LEASES DURING MILITARY SERVICE

The SCRA allows military members who receive permanent change of station (PCS) orders or are deployed for a period of 90 days or more to terminate a lease by providing written notice to the landlord along with a copy of the military orders. The termination of a lease that provides for monthly payment of rent will occur 30 days after the first date on which the next rental payment is due and payable after the landlord receives proper written notice.

MORTGAGES

The SCRA can also provide military members temporary relief from paying their mortgage. To obtain relief, a military member must show that their mortgage was entered into prior to beginning active duty, that the property was owned prior to entry into military service, that the property is still owned by the military member, and that military service materially affects the member's ability to pay the mortgage.

MAXIMUM RATE OF INTEREST

Under the SCRA, a military member can cap the interest rate at 6% for all obligations entered into before beginning active duty if the military service materially affects his or her ability to meet the obligations. This can include interest rates on credit cards, mortgages, and even some student loans (except for Federal guaranteed student loans), to name a few. To qualify for the interest rate cap the military member has to show that he or she is now on active duty, that the obligation or debt was incurred prior to entry on active duty, and that military service materially affects the members' ability to pay. To begin the process, the military member needs to send a letter along with a copy of current military orders to the lender requesting relief under the SCRA. The interest rate cap lasts for the duration of active duty service. The interest rate cap will apply from the first date of active-duty service. The military member must provide written notice to the creditor and a copy of military orders not later than 180 days after the servicemember's termination or release from military service.

TERMINATION OF AUTOMOBILE LEASES DURING MILITARY SERVICE

The SCRA allows military members to terminate pre-service automobile leases if they are called up for military service of 180 days or longer. Members who sign automobile leases while on active-duty may be able to terminate an automobile lease if they are given orders for a permanent change of station outside the continental United States or to deploy with a military unit for a period of 180 days or longer.

STAY OF PROCEEDINGS

If a military member is served with a complaint indicating that they are being sued for some reason, they can obtain a "stay" or postponement of those proceedings if the military service materially affects their ability to proceed in the case. A stay can be used to stop the action altogether, or to hold up some phase of it. According to the SCRA, military members can request a "stay" during any stage of the proceedings. However, the burden is on the military member to show that their military service has materially affected their ability to appear in court. In general, individuals can request a stay of the proceedings for a reasonable period of time (30-60 days). For example, if they are being sued for divorce, they can put off the hearing for some period of time, but it is unlikely that a court will allow the proceedings to be put off indefinitely. The stay can be granted in administrative proceedings.

DEFAULT JUDGMENTS

A default judgment is entered against a party who has failed to defend against a claim that has been brought by another party. To obtain a default judgment, a plaintiff must file an affidavit (written declaration of fact) stating that the defendant is not in the military service and has not requested a stay. If someone is sued while on active duty, and fails to respond, and as a result a default judgment is obtained against them, they can reopen the default judgment by taking several steps. First, they must show that the judgment was entered during their military service or within 30 days after they've left the service. Second, they must write to the court requesting that the default judgment be reopened while they are still on active duty or within 90 days of leaving the service. Third, they must not have made any kind of appearance in court, through filing an answer or otherwise, prior to the default judgment being entered. Finally, they must indicate that their military service prejudiced their ability to defend their case and show that they had a valid defense to the action against them.

INSURANCE

Under SCRA, the U.S. Department of Veterans Affairs (VA) will protect, from default for nonpayment of premiums, up to **$250,000** of life insurance for servicemembers called to active duty. (This amount was previously $10,000.) The protection provided by this legislation applies during the insured's period of military service and for a period of two years thereafter. The following are conditions for eligibility for protection:

- The policy must be whole life, endowment, universal life or term insurance.
- The policy must have been in force on a premium-paying basis for at least six months at the time the servicemember applies for benefits.
- Benefits from the policy cannot be limited, reduced or excluded because of military service.
- Policies for which an additional amount of premium is charged due to military service are not eligible for protection under SCRA.

The servicemember must apply for protection of their life insurance by filing *VA Form 29-380 "Application For Protection Of Commercial Life Insurance Policy"* with his/her insurance company and forwarding a copy of the application to VA.

Benefits Of SCRA Life Insurance Protection

Once the servicemember has applied for protection of their life insurance policy and VA determines that the policy is eligible for protection under SCRA:

- The servicemember is still responsible for making premium payments. However, the policy will not lapse, terminate, or be forfeited because of the servicemember's failure to make premium payments or to pay any indebtedness or interest due during their period of military service or for a period of two years thereafter.
- The rights of the servicemember to change their beneficiary designation or select an optional settlement for a beneficiary are not affected by the provisions of this Act.

Limitations Of SCRA Life Insurance Protection

Once the servicemember has applied for protection of their life insurance policy and VA determines that the policy is eligible for protection under SCRA:

- Premium payments are deferred only, not waived. *During this period, the government does not pay the premiums on the policy but simply guarantees that the premiums will be paid at the end of the servicemember's period of active duty.*

- A servicemember cannot receive dividends, take out a loan, or surrender the policy for cash without the approval of VA. (Dividends or other monetary benefits shall be added to the value of the policy and will be used as a credit when final settlement is made with the insurer.)

- If the policy matures as a result of the insured's death, or any other means, during the protected period, the insurance company will deduct any unpaid premiums and interest due from the settlement amount.

Termination Of Period Under SCRA

The servicemember has up to two years after their military service terminates to repay the unpaid premiums and interest to the insurer. If the amount owed is not paid before the end of the two years, then:

- The insurer treats the unpaid premiums as a loan against the policy.
- The government will pay the insurer the difference between the amount due and the cash surrender value (if the cash surrender value of the policy is less than the amount owed.)
- The amount the United States government pays to the insurance company under the SCRA Act becomes a debt due the government by the insured.
- If the policy matures as a result of the insured's death, or any other means, during the protected period, the insurance company will deduct any unpaid premiums and interest due from the settlement amount.

TAXATION

A service member's state of legal residence may tax military pay and personal property. A member does not lose residence solely because of a transfer to another state pursuant to military orders.

For example, if an Illinois resident who is a member of Illinois Army National Guard is activated to federal military service and sent to California for duty, that person remains an Illinois resident while in California. The service member is not subject to California's authority to tax his/her military income. However, if the service member has a part-time civilian job in California, California will tax his/her non-military income earned in the state.

The Servicemembers Civil Relief Act also contains a provision preventing servicemembers from a form of double taxation that can occur when they have a spouse who works and is taxed in a state other than the state in which they maintain their permanent legal residence. The law prevents states from using the income earned by a servicemember in determining the spouse's tax rate when they do not maintain their permanent legal residence in that state.

RIGHT TO VOTE

In addition to the protections involving debt payments and civil litigation, the act guarantees service members the right to vote in the state of their home of record and protects them from paying taxes in two different states.

CAUTION

The SSCRA does not wipe out any of an individual's obligations. Rather, it temporarily suspends the right of creditors to use a court to compel an individual to pay, only if the court finds that the inability to pay is due to military service. The obligation to honor existing debts remains, and some day the individual must "pay up."

It is important to remember that the SSCRA affords no relief to persons in the Service against the collection of debts or other obligations contracted or assumed by them **after** entering such Service.

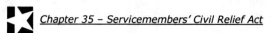

The Relief Act is highly technical. The above summary is intended only to give a general overview of the protection available. The specific nature of all the relief provided under the law is a matter about which an individual may need to contact an attorney. The Act is designed to deal fairly with military personnel and their creditors. While relief is very often available, individuals are expected and required to show good faith in repayment of all debts.

CHAPTER 36

APPEALS

Veterans and other claimants for VA benefits have the right to appeal decisions made by a VA regional office or medical center.

If a claimant wishes to appeal a VA decision, the appeal is first reviewed by the BOARD OF VETERANS APPEALS. If, after review by the Board of Veterans' Appeals, the claimant is still dissatisfied, he or she may appeal to the UNITED STATES COURT OF VETERANS APPEALS. Both entities, along with specific guidelines for the filing of appeals, are discussed in the remainder of this chapter.

BOARD OF VETERANS APPEALS

The Board of Veterans Appeals was established by law to decide appeals for benefits under laws administered by the Veterans Administration. The Board of Veterans' Appeals (BVA) is a part of the Department of Veterans Affairs, located in Washington, D.C. Decisions are made by the members of a section of the Board, appointed with the approval of the president. The Board members are attorneys experienced in veterans' law and in reviewing benefit claims. It is the mission of the Board to decide appeals with sympathetic understanding and as promptly as possible, in order to grant all benefits to which veterans and their dependents and beneficiaries are entitled. Decisions are based on a veteran's entire record.

General Information

Anyone who has filed a claim for benefits with VA and has received a determination from a local VA office is eligible to appeal to the Board of Veterans' Appeals. Some decisions, such as eligibility for medical treatment, issued by VA medical centers can also be appealed to the BVA. An appeal can be made based on a complete denial of a claim, or based on the level of benefit granted. For example, if a veteran files a claim for disability, and the local VA office awards a 10% disability, but the veteran feels he or she is more than 10% disabled, the veteran can appeal that determination to the Board of Veterans' Appeals.

An appeal must be filed within one year from the date the VA regional office or medical center mails its initial decision on a claim. If an appeal is not filed within the year, the original decision is considered final, and cannot be appealed unless the decision involves clear and unmistakable error by VA.

Decisions concerning the need for medical care or the type of medical treatment needed (such as a physician's decision to prescribe or not to prescribe a particular drug, or whether to order a specific type of treatment) are not within the BVA's jurisdiction.

UPDATE:

- On December 22, 2006 President Bush signed Public Law 109-461, the Veterans' Benefits, Healthcare, and Information Technology Act of 2006. The law allows veterans to hire an agent or attorney to represent them after a Notice of Disagreement has been filed. (A Notice of Disagreement is the written statement submitted by the veteran stating he or she disagrees with the claim decision made by the VA regional office.) Veterans will still have the option of utilizing the representation services provided without charge by many veterans' organizations, but in addition they will have the option of hiring an attorney if they so choose. Until now, the United States Code has not allowed a veteran to hire an attorney until the veteran has received a final Board of Veterans' Appeals (BVA) decision - a process that often takes years from a veterans' initial application.

How to File an Appeal and Important Time Limits

No special form is required to begin the appeal process. All that is initially needed is a written statement that the veteran disagrees with a claim decision. This initial statement is known as the "Notice of Disagreement" (NOD). The NOD must include why the veteran disagrees with a regional office decision. (For example, perhaps the veteran feels that the office making the decision overlooked or misunderstood some evidence, or misinterpreted the law.)

The Notice of Disagreement should be filed at the VA regional office where the veteran's claims file is kept. Normally, this is the same VA regional office or medical facility that issued the decision being appealed. However, if a veteran moves after a filing a claim, his or her claims file is transferred to the appropriate VA regional office, and that is where the NOD should be sent.

After the local VA office reviews a Notice of Disagreement, it is possible that the local office will agree with the NOD, and will change its original decision. However, if the local VA office does not change its decision, it will prepare and mail the veteran a *Statement of the Case*, which includes a VA Form 9 - Substantive Appeal, which the veteran must complete and return. The Statement of Case will summarize the evidence and applicable laws and regulations, and provide a discussion of the reasons for arriving at the decision.

Within 60 days of the date the local VA office issue the Statement of Case, the veteran must submit a completed VA Form 9-Substantive Appeal. (Please note that if the one-year period from the date the VA regional office or medical center mailed its original decision is later than this 60-day period, the veteran has until that later one-year date to file the VA Form 9-Substantive Appeal.)

Completion of the VA Form 9-Substantive Appeal is very important. The form should include a clear statement of the benefit being sought, as well as any mistakes the veteran feels VA made when issuing its decision. VA Form 9-Substantive Appeal should also identify anything in the Statement of Case the veteran disagrees with. In addition to VA Form 9, any additional evidence, such as records from recent medical treatments or evaluations may be included as part of the appeal.

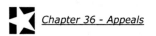

In most instances, a veteran can obtain civilian medical records and other non-government documents supporting his or her case by calling or writing directly to the office that keeps those records. VA regional office personnel and VSO representatives are experienced in locating many items that can support your case, such as service medical records, VA treatment records, and other government records. The VA does have a duty to assist veterans in the developing of their cases. However, individual veterans need to assist the VA in identifying the evidence that can prove the case.

If new information or evidence is included with VA Form 9, the regional office will prepare a Supplemental Statement of the Case (SSOC). The SSOC is similar to the Statement of the Case, but addresses the new information or evidence. If a veteran is not satisfied with the SSOC, a written statement must be mailed to the regional office within 60 days from the mailing date of the SSOC.

It is important to realize the importance of submitting the VA Form 9-Substantive Appeal on a timely basis, otherwise, the right to appeal may be lost. Remember, the VA Form 9 is due the later of:

1 year from Regional Office determination mailing date

or

60 days from Statement of Case (SOC) mailing date

(An extension of the 60-day period for filing VA Form 9-Substantive Appeal or the 60-day period following a Supplemental Statement of the Case **may** be approved if a written request is filed with the local VA office handling the appeal. An extension will only be approved if the veteran can show "good cause" (can offer a valid reason why the extra time is needed).

Docket

A veteran's VA Form 9-Substantive Appeal becomes part of his or her claims folder, and is the basis for adding the appeal to the Board's *docket.*

The Board's docket is the record of all appeals awaiting review by the Board, listed in the order that appeals (VA Form 9) are received.

When an appeal is placed on the Board's docket, it is assigned the next higher number than the one received before it. The Board reviews appeals in the order in which they were placed on the docket. Thus, the lower the docket number, the sooner the appeal will be reviewed.

Lawyers and Other Representatives

A veteran may represent himself or herself. However, over 90% of all people who appeal to the Board of Veterans' Appeals obtain representation. The majority choose to be represented by Veterans' Service Organizations (VSOs) or their state's veterans department.

A lawyer may also be hired for representation. There are strict guidelines about what a lawyer may charge for services, as well as restrictions on fees that a lawyer may charge for work performed prior to issuance of the Board's final decision.

In addition to VSOs and attorneys, some other agents are recognized by VA to represent appellants.

To authorize a VSO for representation, VA Form 21-22 must be completed. To authorize an attorney or recognized agent for representation, VA Form 22a must be completed. Both forms are available at all VA offices.

Length of Appeal Process

No one can determine exactly how long it will take form the time an appeal is filed until receipt of the Board's decision. However, veterans can expect an average of two years from the time an appeal is placed on the Board's docket until issuance of a BVA decision.

If a veteran believes his or her case should be decided sooner than others filed earlier, a *motion to advance on the docket* can be submitted. The motion should explain why the appeal should be moved ahead. Because most appeals involve some type of hardship, before a case can be advanced, there needs to be convincing proof of exceptional circumstances (i.e. terminal illness, danger of bankruptcy or foreclosure, or an error by VA that caused a significant delay in the docketing of an appeal. Veterans should be aware that, on average, fewer than 3 out of every 20 requests for advancement on the docket are granted.

Veterans can expect an average of two years from the time an appeal is placed on the Board's docket until issuance of a BVA decision.

To file a motion to advance on the docket, a written request should be sent to:

Board of Veterans' Appeals (014)
Department of Veterans Affairs
810 Vermont Avenue, NW
Washington, DC 20420

Personal Hearings

A personal hearing is a meeting between the veteran (and his/her representative) and an official from VA who will decide the case. During the hearing, the veteran presents testimony and other evidence supporting the case. There are two types of personal hearings:

- Regional office hearings (also called RO hearing or local office hearings); and
- BVA hearings.

A regional office hearing is a meeting held at a local VA office with a "hearing officer" from the local office's staff. To arrange a regional office hearing, a veteran should contact the local VA office or appeal representative as early in the appeal process as possible.

In a BVA hearing, the veteran presents his or her case in person to a member of the Board. Appellants in most areas of the country can choose whether to hold the BVA hearing at the local VA regional office, called a "Travel Board Hearing," or at the BVA office in Washington, D.C. Some regional offices are also equipped to hold BVA hearings by videoconference. (Check with the regional office for availability.)

The VA cannot pay for any lodging or travel expenses incurred in connection with a hearing.

The VA Form 9-SubstantiveAppeal has a section for requesting a BVA hearing. VA Form 9 is not used, however, to request a local office hearing. Even if a BVA hearing is not requested on the VA Form 9, a request can still be requested by writing directly to the Board. If a BVA hearing is requested, the request must clearly state where the hearing is requested - at the VA regional office, or at the Board's office in Washington, D.C. A BVA hearing cannot be held in both places. (Travel Board hearings may not be available at regional offices located near Washington, D.C.)

The requested type and location of the hearing determines when it will be held. Generally, regional office hearings are held as soon as they can be scheduled on the hearing officer's calendar.

The scheduling of BVA hearings held at regional offices (Travel Board hearings) is more complicated, since Board members must travel from Washington, D.C. to the regional office. BVA videoconferenced hearings are less complicated to arrange, and can be scheduled more frequently than Travel Board hearings.

Hearings held at the Board's offices in Washington, D.C. will be scheduled for a time close to when BVA will consider the case - approximately three months before the case is reviewed by the BVA.

Location of Claims Folder

If a BVA hearing is not requested, the claims folder remains at the local VA office until shortly before the BVA begins its review, at which time it is transferred to the BVA.

If a Travel Board hearing is requested, the claims folder remains at the local VA office until the hearing is completed, at which time it is transferred to the BVA.

If a videoconferenced BVA hearing or a hearing held at the Board's office in Washington, D.C. is requested, the claims folder remains at the local VA office until shortly before the BVA hearing is held. It is transferred to the BVA in time for the hearing and the Board's review.

When a claims folder is transferred from the local VA office to Washington, D.C., the local VA office will send the claimant a letter advising that he or she has 90 days remaining (from the date of that letter) during which more evidence can be added to a file, a hearing can be requested, or a representative can be selected (or changed).

The BVA cannot accept items submitted after the 90-day period has expired, unless a written explanation (called a "motion") is also submit, explaining why the item is late and showing why the BVA should accept it (called "showing good cause"). A motion to accept items after the 90-day period will be reviewed by a Board member who will issue a ruling either allowing or denying the motion.

Checking on the Status of an Appeal

To check on the status of an appeal, veterans or their representatives should contact the office where the claims folder is located (see previous section).

If a claims file is at the Board, veterans or their representatives may call (202) 565-5436 to check on its status (be sure to have the claim number available).

The Board Review Process

When the VBA receives an appeal from a local VA office, the veteran and/or representative will be notified in writing. The Board will then examine the claims folder for completeness, and will provide an opportunity to submit additional written arguments. The case is then assigned to a Board member for review. If a BVA hearing was requested, the Board member assigned the case will conduct the hearing prior to reaching a decision.

When the docket number for an appeal is reached, the file will be reviewed by a Board member and a staff attorney, who will check for completeness, review all evidence and arguments, as well as the regional office's Statement of the Case (and Supplement Statement of the Case, if applicable), the transcript of the hearing (if applicable), the statement of any representative, and any other information included in the claims folder. The staff attorney, if directed to do so by the Board member, may also conduct additional research and prepare recommendations for the Board member's review.

When, in the judgment of the Board member, expert medical opinion, in addition to that available within the VA, is warranted by the medical complexity or controversy involved in an appeal, the Board may secure an advisory medical opinion from one or more independent medical experts who are not employees of the VA.

The VA shall make necessary arrangements with recognized medical schools, universities, or clinics to furnish such advisory medical opinions at the request of the Chairman of the Board. Any such arrangement shall provide that the actual selection of the expert or experts to give the advisory opinion in an individual case shall be made by an appropriate official of such institution.

The Board shall furnish a claimant with notice that an advisory medical opinion has been requested, and shall furnish the claimant with a copy of such opinion when it is received by the Board.

Prior to reaching a decision, the Board member must thoroughly review all materials and recommendations. The Board member will then issue a decision.

The Board member's decision will be mailed to the home address that the Board has on file, so it is extremely important that the VA be kept informed of any address changes.

The BVA must attempt to make its decisions as understandable as possible. However, due to the nature of legal documents, laws, court cases, and medical discussions, decisions can be confusing. If an appeal is denied , the Board will send a "Notice of Appellate Rights" that describes additional actions that can be taken.

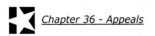

The Board annually produces a CD-ROM with the text of its decisions. Most VA regional offices have these CD-ROMS available for review, or the CD-Rom may be purchased from the Government Printing Office. For further information, contact:

Department of Veterans Affairs
Board of Veterans' Appeals (01B)
Washington, D.C. 20420

Remands

Sometimes when reviewing a claims folder, the Board member determines additional development of the case is necessary. The appeal is then returned to the local VA office. This is called a "remand." After performing the additional work, the regional office may issue a new decision. If the claim is still denied, the case is returned to the Board for a final decision. (The case keeps its original place on the Board's docket, so it is reviewed soon after it is returned to the Board.)

Depending on the reason for the remand, the regional office may provide the veteran with a Supplement Statement of the Case (SSOC). The claimant then has 60 days from the date the local VA office mails the SSOC to comment on it.

APPEALING THE BOARD OF VETERANS' AFFAIRS DECISION

Motion for Reconsideration

If it can be demonstrated that the Board made an obvious error of fact or law in its decision, a written "motion to reconsider" can be filed. Any such motions should be sent directed to the Board, not to the local VA office. A motion to reconsider should not be submitted simply because of disagreement with the BVA's decision. The claimant must be able to show that the Board made a mistake, and that the Board's decision would have been different if the mistake had not been made. A motion to reconsider should be sent directly to the Board, not to the local VA office.

Reopening

If a claimant has "new and material evidence," he or she can request that the case be re-opened. To be considered "new and material," the evidence submitted must be information related to the case that was not included in the claims folder when the case was decided.

To re-open an appeal, the claimant must submit the new evidence directly to the local VA office that handled the claim.

CUE Motion

The law was amended in 1997 to provide one more way to challenge a Board decision. A Board decision can be reversed or revised if the claimant is able to show that the decision contained "clear and unmistakable error" (CUE).

The written request for the Board to review its decision for CUE is called a "motion." CUE motions should be filed directly with the Board, and not with the local VA office.

Because CUE is a very complicated area of law, most claimants seek help from a representative to file a CUE motion.

A motion for CUE review of a prior Board decision must meet some very specific requirements, described in the Board's *Rules of Practice*. If the motion is denied a claimant can't ask for another CUE review of the way the Board decided the issues raised in the first CUE motion, so it is very important that the motion be prepared properly the first time out.

Not many CUE motions are successful, because CUE is a very rare kind of error, the kind that compels a conclusion that the Board would have decided the claimant's case differently but for the error. A difference of opinion is not enough.

A motion to review a Board decision for CUE can be filed at any time, but if it is filed after filing a timely Notice of Appeal with the Court, the Board will not be able to rule on your CUE motion.

UNITED STATES COURT OF VETERANS' APPEALS

The United States Court of Veterans' Appeals was created under Public Law 100-687, on November 18, 1988. The Court has seven judges, appointed by the President and confirmed by the Senate. Judges are appointed for a 15-year term.

If a claimant is not satisfied with the Board of Veterans' Appeals decision, an appeal can be filed with the United States Court of Veterans Appeals.

If a claimant is not satisfied with the Board of Veterans' Appeals decision, an appeal can be filed with the United States Court of Veterans Appeals (referred to as the "Court"). The Court is an independent court that is not part of the Department of Veterans Affairs. The Court does not hold trials, receive new evidence, or hear witnesses. It reviews the BVA decision, the written record, and the briefs of the parties. Claimants do not need to appear in Washington, D.C. for an appeal. (In approximately 1% of decided cases, the Court holds oral arguments in its Washington courtroom, or occasionally, by telephone conference call.)

A claimant may represent himself or herself, but may want to get advice from an attorney or from a service officer in a veterans organization or a state or county veterans' affairs office. The VA will be represented by its attorney, and a claimant's case may be better presented if he or she is represented.

The Court does not recommend or appoint attorneys to represent claimants. However, the Court does have a *Public List of Practitioners* which shows who is allowed to represent appellants in the Court, and have said that they are available. Most attorneys charge a fee.

To appeal a Board of Veterans' Appeals decision, a claimant must file a "Notice of Appeal" with the Court within 120 days from the date the Board's decision is mailed. (The first day of the 120 days a claimant has to file an appeal to the Court is the day the BVA's decision is postmarked, not the day the decision is signed.)

If a claimant filed a motion to reconsider with the Board of Veterans' Appeals within the 120 day time-frame, and that motion was denied, the claimant has an additional 120 days to file the "Notice of Appeal" with the Court. (This 120 day period begins on the date the Board mails a notification that it has denied the motion to reconsider.) If the Board denies the motion to reconsider, a "Notice of Appellate Rights" will be mailed to the claimant.

In addition to the above 120 day limit, in order for the Court to consider an appeal, a Notice of Disagreement must have been filed with the VA regional office handling the case on or after November 18, 1988.

An original "Notice of Appeal" must be filed directed with the Court at:

United States Court of Veterans Appeals
625 Indiana Avenue, NW, Suite 900
Washington, D.C. 20004
Fax: (202) 501-5848
(Appeals cannot be filed by e-mail)

The fee for an appeal is $50.00, and should be included with the "Notice of Appeal." If a claimant is unable to pay this fee, a "Motion to Waive Filing Fee" form must be completed and returned with the "Notice of Appeal."

If a claimant appeals to the Court, a copy of the "Notice of Appeal" must also be filed with the VA General Counsel at:

Office of the General Counsel (027)
Department of Veterans Affairs
810 Vermont Avenue, NW
Washington, D.C. 20420

Please note that the *original* "Notice of Appeal" that is filed with the Court is the only document that protects a claimants right to appeal a BVA decision. The copy sent to the VA General Counsel does not protect that right, or serve as an official filing.

If the Court accepts an appeal, it will send a printed copy of the rules of practice and procedure to the claimant and his/her representative, if applicable.

To obtain more specific information about the "Notice of Appeal," the methods for filing with the Court, Court filing fees, and other matters covered by the Court's rules, a claimant should contact the Court directly at:

United States Court of Veterans Appeals
625 Indiana Avenue, NW, Suite 900
Washington, D.C. 20004
(800) 869-8654

If either party disagrees with the Court's ruling, an appeal may be filed with the U.S. Court of Appeals for the Federal Circuit, and, thereafter, may seek review in the Supreme Court of the United States.

DEATH OF APPELLANT

According to the law, the death of an appellant generally ends the appellant's appeal, and the Board normally dismisses the appeal without issuing a decision. The rights of a deceased appellant's survivors are not affected by this action. Survivors may still file a claim at the regional office for any benefits to which they may be entitled.

GENERAL GUIDELINES FOR EFFICIENT PROCESSING OF CLAIMS

The following guidelines may help ensure that an appeal is not unnecessarily delayed:

- Consider having an appeal representative assist with the filing of the appeal.
- File the Notice of Disagreement and VA Form 9-Substantive Appeal as soon as possible
- Be as specific as possible when identifying the issues the Board should consider.
- Be as specific as possible when identifying sources of evidence for the VA to obtain. (For example, provide the full names and addresses of physicians, along with dates of treatment, and reasons for treatment.)
- Keep VA informed of current address, phone number, and number of dependents.
- When possible, provide clinical treatment records, rather than simply a statement from a physician.
- Be clear on the VA Form 9 about whether or not a BVA hearing is requested, and where the hearing should take place, if applicable.
- Include the claim number on any correspondence with the VA.
- Do not submit material that is not pertinent to the claim. This will only delay the process.
- Do not use the VA Form 9 to raise new claims for the first time. (VA Form 9 is only to be used to appeal decisions on previously submitted claims.)
- Do not use the VA Form 9 to request a local office hearing.

- Do not raise additional issues for the Board's review late in the appeal process. This may cause the appeal to be sent back to the regional office for additional work, and may result in a longer delay.

- Do not submit evidence directly to the Board unless a written or typed statement is included, stating that consideration by the regional office is waived. The statement must clearly indicate that the Board is to review the evidence, even though the regional office has not seen it. If a waiver is not included with any additional evidence submitted directly to the Board, the case may be remanded to the regional office for review, and may result in further delays.

- Do not submit a last minute request for a hearing or a last minute change to the type or location of a hearing unless it is unavoidable. Such a request will likely result in a delay in reaching a final decision.

- Do not miss a scheduled VA examination or hearing.

CHAPTER 37

VA REGIONAL OFFICES & BENEFITS OFFICES

Department of Veterans Affairs Headquarters
810 Vermont Avenue NW
Washington, DC 20420
(202) 273-5400

Alabama (SDN 5)
Montgomery Regional Office
345 Perry Hill Road
Montgomery, AL 36109

Alaska (SDN 8)
Anchorage Regional Office
2925 DeBarr Road
Anchorage, AK 99508-2989

Arizona (SDN 9)
Phoenix Regional Office
3225 North Central Avenue
Phoenix, AZ 85012

Arkansas (SDN 7)
North Little Rock Regional Office
2200 Fort Roots Drive
Building 65
North Little Rock, AR 72114

California (SDN 9)
Los Angeles Regional Office
Federal Building
11000 Wilshire Boulevard
Los Angeles, CA 90024

Oakland Regional Office
1301 Clay Street
Room 1300 North
Oakland, CA 94612

San Diego Regional Office
8810 Rio San Diego Drive
San Diego, CA 92108

Colorado (SDN 8)
Denver Regional Office
155 Van Gordon Street
Denver, CO 80228

Connecticut (SDN 1)
Hartford Regional Office
450 Main Street
Hartford, CT 06103

Delaware (SDN 3)
Wilmington Regional Office
1601 Kirkwood Highway
Wilmington, DE 19805

Florida (SDN 5)
St. Petersburg Regional Office
9500 Bay Pines Boulevard
Bay Pines, FL 33708

Georgia (SDN 4)
Atlanta Regional Office
1700 Clairmont Road
Decatur, GA 30033

Hawaii (SDN 9)
Honolulu Regional Office
459 Patterson Road
E-Wing
Honolulu, HI 96819-1522

Idaho (SDN 8)
Boise Regional Office
805 West Franklin Street
Boise, ID 83702

Illinois (SDN 6)
Chicago Regional Office
2122 West Taylor Street
Chicago, IL 60612

Indiana (SDN 2)
Indianapolis Regional Office
575 North Pennsylvania Street
Indianapolis, IN 46204

Iowa (SDN 6)
Des Moines Regional Office
210 Walnut Street
Des Moines, IA 50309

Kansas (SDN 6)
Wichita Regional Office
5500 East Kellogg
Wichita, KS 67211

Kentucky (SDN 3)
Louisville Regional Office
545 South 3rd Street
Louisville, KY 40202

Louisiana (SDN 7)
New Orleans Regional Office
701 Loyola Avenue
New Orleans, LA 70113

Maine (SDN 1)
Togus VA Med/Regional Office
1 VA Center
Togus, ME 04330

Maryland (SDN 3)
Baltimore Regional Office
31 Hopkins Plaza Federal Bldg
Baltimore, MD 21201

Massachusetts (SDN 1)
Boston VA Regional Office
JFK Federal Building
Government Center
Boston, MA 02114

Michigan (SDN 2)
Detroit Regional Office
Federal Building
477 Michigan Avenue
Detroit, MI 48226

Eastern Area Office
24 Frank Lloyd Wright Drive
Lobby B, 3rd Floor
Ann Arbor, MI 48106

Minnesota (SDN 6)
St. Paul Regional Office
1 Federal Drive
Fort Snelling
St. Paul, MN 55111-4050

Mississippi (SDN 5)
Jackson Regional Office
1600 East Woodrow Wilson Ave.
Jackson, MS 39216

Missouri (SDN 6)
St. Louis Regional Office
Federal Building
400 South, 18th Street
St. Louis, MO 63103

Montana (SDN 8)
Fort Harrison Regional Office
William Street
off Highway 12 West
Fort Harrison, MT 59636

Nebraska (SDN 6)
Lincoln Regional Office
5631 South 48th Street
Lincoln, NE 68516

New Hampshire (SDN 1)
Manchester Regional Office
Norris Cotton Federal Bldg
275 Chestnut Street
Manchester, NH 03101

New Jersey (SDN 2)
Newark Regional Office
20 Washington Place
Newark, NJ 07102

New Mexico (SDN 8)
Albuquerque Regional Office
Dennis Chavez Federal Building
500 Gold Avenue, S.W.
Albuquerque, NM 87102

Nevada (SDN 9)
Reno Regional Office
1201 Terminal Way
Reno, NV 89520

New York (SDN1)
Buffalo Regional Office
130 South Elmwood Avenue
Buffalo, NY 14202

New York Regional Office
245 West Houston Street
New York, NY 10014

North Carolina (SDN 4)
Winston-Salem Regional Office
Federal Building
251 North Main Street
Winston-Salem, NC 27155

North Dakota (SDN 6)
Fargo Regional Office
2101 North Elm Street
Fargo, ND 58102

Ohio (SDN 2)
Cleveland Regional Office
A.J. Celebrezze Federal Building
1240 East 9th Street
Cleveland, OH 44199

Oklahoma (SDN 7)
Muskogee Regional Office
125 South Main Street
Muskogee, OK 74401

Oregon (SDN 8)
Portland Regional Office
1220 SW 3rd Avenue
Portland, OR 97204

Pennsylvania (SDN 2)
Philadelphia Regional Office
5000 Wissahickon Avenue
Philadelphia, PA 19101

Pittsburgh Regional Office
1000 Liberty Avenue
Pittsburgh, PA 15222

Rhode Island (SDN 1)
Providence Regional Office
380 Westminster Mall
Providence, RI 02903

South Carolina (SDN 4)
Columbia Regional Office
1801 Assembly Street
Columbia, SC 29201

South Dakota (SDN 6)
Sioux Falls Regional Office
PO Box 5046
2501 West 22nd Street
Sioux Falls, SD 57117

Tennessee (SDN 4)
Nashville Regional Office
110 9th Avenue South
Nashville, TN 37203

Southern Area Office
3322 West End, Suite 408
Nashville, TN 37203

Texas (SDN 7)
Houston Regional Office
6900 Almeda Road
Houston, TX 77030

Waco Regional Office
1 Veterans Plaza
701 Clay Avenue
Waco, TX 76799

Utah (SDN 8)
Salt Lake City Regional Office
550 Foothill Drive
Salt Lake City, UT 84158

Vermont (SDN 1)
White River Junction
Regional Office
North Hartland Road
White River Junction, VT 05009

Virginia (SDN 3)
Roanoke Regional Office
210 Franklin Road SW
Roanoke, VA 24011

Washington (SDN 8)
Seattle Regional Office
Federal Building
915 2nd Avenue
Seattle, WA 98174

West Virginia (SDN 3)
Huntington Regional Office
640 Fourth Avenue
Huntington, WV 25701

Wisconsin (SDN 6)
Milwaukee Regional Office
5400 West National Avenue
Milwaukee, WI 53214

Wyoming (SDN 8)
Cheyenne Regional Office
2360 East Pershing Blvd.
Cheyenne, WY 82001

District of Columbia (SDN 3)
Washington DC Regional Office
1722 I Street N.W.
Washington, DC 20421

Puerto Rico (SDN 5)
San Juan Regional Office
150 Carlos Chardon Avenue
Hato Rey, Puerto Rico 00918

Philippines (SDN 9)
Manila Regional Office
1131 Roxas Boulevard, Ermita
0930 Manila, Philippines 96440

Note: SDN = Service Delivery Network

CHAPTER 38

STATE BENEFITS

Many states offer services and benefits to veterans in addition to those offered by the Department of Veterans' Affairs. To find out more about a particular state's programs, individuals should contact the following:

Alabama Department of Veterans' Affairs
P.O. Box 1509
770 Washington Ave, Suite 530
Montgomery, AL 36102-1509
(334) 242-5077

Alaska Department of Veterans' Affairs
P.O. Box 5800
Fort Richardson, AK 99505-5800
(907) 428-6031

Arizona Department of Veterans' Services
3839 North Third Street, Suite 200
Phoenix, AZ 85012
(602) 225-3373

Arkansas Department of Veterans' Affairs
2200 Fort Roots Drive
Room 119 – Bldg 65
North Little Rock, AR 72114
(501) 370-3820

California Department of Veterans' Affairs
1227 O Street, Suite 300
Sacramento, CA 95814
1-800-952-5626

Colorado Division of Veterans' Affairs
789 Sherman Street, Suite 260
Denver, CO 80203-1714
(303) 894-7474

Connecticut Department of Veterans' Affairs
287 West Street
Rocky Hill, CT 06067
(860) 529-2571

Delaware Commission of Veterans' Affairs
Robbins Building
802 Silverlake Blvd, Suite 100
Dover, DE 19904
(302) 739-2792
1-800-344-9900 (in state only)

Florida Department of Veterans' Affairs
Mary Grizzle Building, Room 311-K
11351 Ulmerton Road
Largo, FL 33778
(727) 518-3202

Georgia Department of Veterans' Affairs
Floyd Veterans Memorial Building
Suite E-970
Atlanta, GA 30334
(404) 656-2300

Hawaii Office of Veterans' Services
Mailing Address:
459 Patterson Road
E-Wing, Room 1-A103
Honolulu, HI 96819
Location:
Tripler Army Med Center (Ward Road)
VAMROC, E-Wing, Room 1-A103
Honolulu, HI 96819
(808) 433-0420

Idaho Division of Veterans' Affairs
320 Collins Road
Boise, ID 83702
(208) 334-3513

Illinois Department of Veterans' Affairs
P.O. Box 19432
833 South Spring Street
Springfield, IL 62794-9432
(217) 785-4114

Indiana Department of Veterans' Affairs
302 West Washington, Room E120
Indianapolis, IN 46204-2738
(317) 232-3910

Iowa Commission of Veterans' Affairs
7105 N.W. 70th Avenue
Camp Dodge - Building A6A
Johnston, IA 50131-1824
(515) 242-5331

Kansas Commission on Veterans' Affairs
Jayhawk Towers
Suite 701
700 S.W. Jackson Street
Topeka, KS 66603-3714
(785) 296-3976

Kentucky Department of Veterans' Affairs
1111 Louisville Road
NGAKY Building
Frankfort, KY 40601
(502) 564-9203

Louisiana Department of Veterans' Affairs
P.O. Box 94095
Capitol Station
1885 Wooddale Blvd.
10th Floor, Room 1013
Baton Rouge, LA 70806
(225) 922-0500

Maine Bureau of Veterans' Services
117 State House Station
Camp Keyes Building 7, Room 115
Augusta, ME 04333
(207) 626-4464

Maryland Department of Veterans' Affairs
Room 110, Federal Building
31 Hopkins Plaza
Baltimore, MD 21201
(800) 446-4926

Massachusetts Department of Veterans' Services
600 Washington Street, Suite 1100
Boston, MA 02111
(617) 210-5480

Michigan Department of Veterans' Affairs
7109 W. Saginaw
Lansing, MI 48913
(517) 335-6523

Minnesota Department of Veterans' Affairs
State Veterans Service Building
20 West 12th Street, 2nd Floor
St. Paul, MN 55155-2079
(651) 296-2562

Mississippi State Veterans' Affairs Board
3466 Highway 80 East
P.O. Box 5947
Pearl, MS 39288-5947
(601) 576-4850

Missouri Veterans' Commission
Mailing Address:
Post Drawer 147
Jefferson City, MO 65102-0147
Location:
1719 Southridge Drive
Jefferson City, MO 65109
(573) 751-3779

Montana Veterans' Affairs Division
P.O. Box 5715
1900 Williams Street
Helena, MT 59604
(406) 324-3740

Nebraska Department of Veterans' Affairs
State Office Building
301 Centennial Mall South
P.O. Box 95083
Lincoln, NE 68509-5083
(402) 471-2458

Nevada Commission for Veterans' Affairs
1201 Terminal Way, Room 215
Reno, NV 89502
(775) 688-1653

New Hampshire State Veterans' Council
275 Chestnut Street
Room 321
Manchester, NH 03101-2411
(603) 624-9230
1-800-622-9230 (in state only)

New Jersey Department of Veterans' Affairs
Eggert Crossing Road
PO Box 340
Trenton, NJ 08625-0508
(800) 624-0508

New Mexico Veterans' Service Commission
P. O. Box 2324
Santa Fe, NM 87504
(505) 827-6300

New York Division of Veterans' Affairs
5 Empire State Plaza
Suite 2836
Albany, NY 12223-1551
(518) 474-6114

North Carolina Division of Veterans' Affairs
Albemarle Building, Suite 1065
1315 Mail Service Center
325 North Salisbury Street
Raleigh, NC 27699-1315
(919) 733-3851

North Dakota Department of Veterans' Affairs
P.O. Box 9003
1411 32nd Street, South
Fargo, ND 58106-9003
(701) 239-7165

Ohio Governor's Office of Veterans' Affairs
77 South High Street
Columbus, OH 43215
(614) 644-0898

Oklahoma Department of Veterans' Affairs
2311 N. Central Avenue
Oklahoma City, OK 73105
(405) 521-3684

Oregon Department of Veterans' Affairs
700 Summer Street, NE
Salem, OR 97310-1285
(503) 373-2000

Pennsylvania Department of Veterans' Affairs
Fort Indiantown Gap
Building S-O-47
Annville, PA 17003-5002
(717) 861-2000

Rhode Island Division of Veterans' Affairs
480 Metacom Avenue
Bristol, RI 02809
(401) 462-0324

South Carolina Office of Veterans' Affairs
1205 Pendleton Street, Suite 369
Columbia, SC 29201
(803) 734-0200

South Dakota Division of Veterans' Affairs
425 East Capitol Avenue
c/o 500 East Capitol Avenue
Pierre, SD 57501
(605) 773-4981

Tennessee Department of Veterans' Affairs
215 Eighth Avenue North
Nashville, TN 37243-1010
(615) 741-6663

Texas Veterans' Commission
P.O. Box 12277
Austin, TX 78711
1-800-252-8387

Utah Division of Veterans' Affairs
550 Foothill Blvd, Room 206
Salt Lake City, UT 84108
(801) 326-2372

Vermont State Veterans' Affairs
118 State Street
Montpelier, VT 05620-4401
(802) 828-3379

Virginia Department of Veterans' Affairs
900 East Main Street
Richmond, VA 23219
(804) 786-0286

Washington Department of Veterans' Affairs
P.O. Box 41150
1011 Plum Street
Olympia, WA 98504-1150
1-800-562-0132

West Virginia Division of Veterans' Affairs
1321 Plaza East, Suite 101
Charleston, WV 25301-1400
(304) 558-3661

Wisconsin Department of Veterans' Affairs
30 West Mifflin Street
Madison, WI 53703
(608) 266-1311

Wyoming Veterans' Affairs Commission
Wyoming ANG Armory
5905 CY Avenue - Room 101
Casper, WY 82604
(307) 265-7372

American Samoa Veterans' Affairs
P. O. Box 8586
Pago Pago
American Samoa 96799
(001) 684-633-4206

Guam Veterans' Affairs Office
Mailing Address:
P.O. Box 3279
Agana, Guam 96932
(671) 475-4222
Location:
"M" Street
HSE #105
Tiyan, Guam

Puerto Rico Public Advocate for Veterans' Affairs
Mailing Address:
Apartado 11737
Fernandez Juncos Station
San Juan, PR 00910-1737
Location:
Mercantile Plaza Bldg,
Fourth Floor, Suite 4021
Hato Rey, PR 00918-1625
(787) 758-5760

Government of the Virgin Islands Division of Veterans' Affairs
1013 Estate Richmond
Christiansted, St. Croix VI
00820-4349
(340) 773-6663

CHAPTER 39

WHERE TO OBTAIN MILITARY PERSONNEL RECORDS

The U.S. Department of Veterans Affairs does not maintain veterans' military service records.

The personnel records of individuals currently in the military service, in the reserve forces, and those completely separated from military service are located in different offices. A nominal fee is charged for certain types of service. In most instances service fees cannot be determined in advance. If your request involves a service fee you will be notified as soon as that determination is made.

The personnel records of individuals currently in the military service, in the reserve forces, and those completely separated from military service are located in different offices.

A veteran and spouse should be aware of the location of the veteran's discharge and separation papers. If a veteran cannot locate discharge and separation papers, duplicate copies may be obtained (further information regarding who to contact is included later in this chapter).

Use Standard Form 180, *Request Pertaining To Military Records*, which is available from VA offices and veterans organizations. Specify that a duplicate separation document or discharge is needed. The veteran's full name should be printed or typed so that it can be read clearly, but the request must also contain the signature of the veteran or the signature of the next of kin, if the veteran is deceased. Include branch of service, service number or Social Security number and exact or approximate date and years of service.

It is not necessary to request a duplicate copy of a veteran's discharge or separation papers solely for the purpose of filing a claim for VA benefits. If complete information about the veteran's service is furnished on the application, VA will obtain verification of service from the National Personnel Records Center or the service department concerned.

WHO TO CONTACT

The various categories of military personnel records are described in the tables below. Please read the following notes carefully, to make sure an inquiry is sent to the right address. Please note especially that the record is not sent to the National Personnel Records Center as long as the person retains any sort of reserve obligation, whether drilling or non-drilling.

Special Notes For Following Tables:

- **Records at the National Personnel Records Center:** Note that it takes at least 3 months, and often 6 or 7, for the file to reach the National Personnel Records Center after the military obligation has ended (such as by discharge). If only a short time has passed, please send the inquiry to the address shown for active or current reserve members. Also, if the person has only been released from active duty, but is still in a reserve status, the personnel record will stay at the location specified for reservists. A person can retain a reserve obligation for several years, even without attending meetings or receiving annual training.

- If there were two or more periods of service within the same branch, send your request (only one is necessary) to the office having the records for the LAST PERIOD OF SERVICE.)

LOCATION OF AIR FORCE MILITARY PERSONNEL & HEALTH RECORDS

Status of Service Member or Veteran	Location of Personnel Record	Location of Health Record
Discharged, deceased, or retired before 5/1/1994	National Personnel Records Center Military Personnel Records 9700 Page Avenue St. Louis, MO 63132-5100 (314) 801-0800	National Personnel Records Center Military Personnel Records 9700 Page Avenue St. Louis, MO 63132-5100 (314) 801-0800
Discharged, deceased, or retired on or after 5/1/1994	National Personnel Records Center Military Personnel Records 9700 Page Avenue St. Louis, MO 63132-5100 (314) 801-0800	Department of Veterans Affairs Records Management Center PO Box 5020 St Louis MO 63115 (314) 538-4500
Active (including National Guard on active duty in the Air Force), TDRL, or general officers retired with pay	Air Force Personnel Center HQ AFPC/DPSRP 550 C Street West Suite 19 Randolph AFB, TX 78150 (800) 616-3775	
Reserve, retired reserve in nonpay status, current National Guard officers not on active duty in the Air Force, or National Guard released from active duty in the Air Force	Air Reserve Personnel Center /DSMR HQ ARPC/DPSSA/B 6760 E. Irvington Place, Suite 4600 Denver, CO 80280-4600 (800) 525-0102	
Current Air National Guard enlisted not on active duty in the Air Force	Adjutant General of your state	

LOCATION OF ARMY MILITARY PERSONNEL & HEALTH RECORDS

Status of Service Member or Veteran	Location of Personnel Record	Location of Health Record
Discharged, deceased, or retired (Enlisted) before 11/1/1912	The National Archive's Old Military and Civil Records Branch (NWCTB-Military) Washington, DC 20408	
Discharged, deceased, or retired (Officer) before 7/1/1917	The National Archive's Old Military and Civil Records Branch (NWCTB-Military) Washington, DC 20408	
Discharged, deceased, or retired (Enlisted) 11/1/1912 - 10/15/1992	National Personnel Records Center Military Personnel Records 9700 Page Avenue St. Louis, MO 63132 (314) 801-0800	National Personnel Records Center Military Personnel Records 9700 Page Avenue St. Louis, MO 63132 (314) 801-0800
Discharged, deceased, or retired (Officer) 7/1/1917 - 10/15/1992	National Personnel Records Center Military Personnel Records 9700 Page Avenue St. Louis, MO 63132 (314) 801-0800	National Personnel Records Center Military Personnel Records 9700 Page Avenue St. Louis, MO 63132 (314) 801-0800
Discharged, deceased, or retired on or after 10/16/1992	National Personnel Records Center Military Personnel Records 9700 Page Avenue St. Louis, MO 63132 (314) 801-0800	Department of Veterans Affairs Records Management Center PO Box 5020 St Louis MO 63115-5020 314-538-4500
Reserve; or active duty records of current National Guard members who performed service in the U.S. Army before 7/1/1972	Commander U.S. Army Personnel Command ATTN: ARPC-ZCC-B 1 Reserve Way St. Louis, MO 62132-5200	
Active enlisted (including National Guard on active duty in the U.S. Army) or TDRL enlisted	Commander USAEREC ATTN: PCRE-F 8899 E. 56th St. Indianapolis, IN 46249	
Active officers (including National Guard on active duty	U.S. Total Army Personnel Command ATTN: TAPC-MSR-S	

Status of Service Member or Veteran	Location of Personnel Record	Location of Health Record
in the U.S. Army) or TDRL officers	200 Stoval Street Alexandria, VA 22332	
Current National Guard enlisted not on active duty in Army (including records of Army active duty performed after 6/30/1972)	Adjutant General of your state	
Current National Guard officers not on active duty in Army (including records of Army active duty performed after 6/30/1972)	Army National Guard Readiness Center NGB-ARP 111 S. George Mason Dr. Arlington, VA 22204-1382	

LOCATION OF COAST GUARD MILITARY PERSONNEL & HEALTH RECORDS

Status of Service Member or Veteran	Location of Personnel Record	Location of Health Record
Discharged, deceased, or retired before 1/1/1898	The National Archive's Old Military and Civil Records Branch (NWCTB-Military) Washington, DC 20408	
Discharged, deceased, or retired: 1/1/1898 - 3/31/1998	National Personnel Records Center Military Personnel Records 9700 Page Avenue St. Louis, MO 63132-5100 (314) 801-0800	National Personnel Records Center Military Personnel Records 9700 Page Avenue St. Louis, MO 63132-5100 (314) 801-0800
Discharged, deceased, or retired on or after: 4/1/1998	National Personnel Records Center Military Personnel Records 9700 Page Avenue St. Louis, MO 63132-5100 (314) 801-0800	Department of Veterans Affairs Records Management Center PO Box 5020 St Louis MO 63115-5020 (314) 538-4500
Active, reserve, or TDRL	Commander, CGPC-adm-3 USCG Personnel Command 4200 Wilson Blvd. Suite 1100 Arlington, VA 22203-1804	

LOCATION OF MARINE CORPS MILITARY PERSONNEL & HEALTH RECORDS

Status of Service Member or Veteran	Location of Personnel Record	Location of Health Record
Discharged, deceased, or retired before 1/1/1905	The National Archive's Old Military and Civil Records Branch (NWCTB-Military) Washington, DC 20408	
Discharged, deceased, or retired (Enlisted): 1906 – 9/8/1939	Archival Program Division National Personnel Records Center 9700 Page Avenue St. Louis, MO 63132-5100	National Personnel Records Center Military Personnel Records 9700 Page Avenue St. Louis, MO 63132-5100 (314) 801-0800
Discharged, deceased, or retired (Officer): 1/1/1905 – 4/30/1994	National Personnel Records Center Military Personnel Records 9700 Page Avenue St. Louis, MO 63132-5100 (314) 801-0800	National Personnel Records Center Military Personnel Records 9700 Page Avenue St. Louis, MO 63132-5100 (314) 801-0800
Discharged, deceased, or retired (Enlisted): 9/9/1939 – 4/30/1994	National Personnel Records Center Military Personnel Records 9700 Page Avenue St. Louis, MO 63132-5100 (314) 801-0800	National Personnel Records Center Military Personnel Records 9700 Page Avenue St. Louis, MO 63132-5100 (314) 801-0800
Discharged, deceased, or retired on or after: 5/1/1994	National Personnel Records Center Military Personnel Records 9700 Page Avenue St. Louis, MO 63132-5100 (314) 801-0800	Department of Veterans Affairs Records Management Center PO Box 5020 St Louis MO 63115-5020 (314) 538-4500
Active, Selected Marine Corps Reserve, TDRL	Headquarters U.S. Marine Corps Personnel Management Support Branch (MMSB) 2008 Elliot Road Quantico, VA 22134-5030 Phone: 800-268-3710	
Individual Ready Reserve or Fleet Marine Corps Reserve	Marine Corps Reserve Support Command (Code MMI) 15303 Andrews Road Kansas City, MO 64147 Phone: 800-255-5082	

LOCATION OF NAVY MILITARY PERSONNEL & HEALTH RECORDS

Status of Service Member or Veteran	Location of Personnel Record	Location of Health Record
Discharged, deceased, or retired (Enlisted) before 1/1/1885	The National Archive's Old Military and Civil Records Branch (NWCTB-Military) Washington, DC 20408	
Discharged, deceased, or retired (Officer) before 1/1/1903	The National Archive's Old Military and Civil Records Branch (NWCTB-Military) Washington, DC 20408	
Discharged, deceased, or retired (Enlisted): 1885 – 9/8/1939	The National Archive's Old Military and Civil Records Branch (NWCTB-Military) Washington, DC 20408	The National Archive's Old Military and Civil Records Branch (NWCTB-Military) Washington, DC 20408
Discharged, deceased, or retired (Enlisted) 9/9/1939 – 1/30/1994	National Personnel Records Center Military Personnel Records 9700 Page Avenue St. Louis, MO 63132-5100 (314) 801-0800	National Personnel Records Center Military Personnel Records 9700 Page Avenue St. Louis, MO 63132-5100 (314) 801-0800
Discharged, deceased, or retired (Officer) 1/1/1903 – 1/30/1994	National Personnel Records Center Military Personnel Records 9700 Page Avenue St. Louis, MO 63132-5100 (314) 801-0800	National Personnel Records Center Military Personnel Records 9700 Page Avenue St. Louis, MO 63132-5100 (314) 801-0800
Discharged, deceased, or retired 1/31/1994 – 12/31/1994	National Personnel Records Center Military Personnel Records 9700 Page Avenue St. Louis, MO 63132-5100 (314) 801-0800	Department of Veterans Affairs Records Management Center PO Box 5020 St Louis MO 63115-5020 (314) 538-4500
Discharged, deceased, or retired on or after: 1/1/1995 (* see note on Navy Records from 1995 on)	Navy Personnel Command (PERS-313C1) 5720 Integrity Drive Millington, TN 38055 (901) 874-4885	Department of Veterans Affairs Records Management Center PO Box 5020 St Louis MO 63115-5020 (314) 538-4500
Active, reserve, or TDRL	Navy Personnel Command (PERS-313C1) 5720 Integrity Drive	

Status of Service Member or Veteran	Location of Personnel Record	Location of Health Record
	Millington, TN 38055 (901) 874-4885	
Naval Reserve members NOT currently on active duty, including those in the Ready Reserve (SELRES/IRR) and Standby Reserves (USNR-S1/USNR-S2)	Naval Reserve Personnel Command 4400 Dauphine Street New Orleans, LA 70149 (866)250-4778	

NOTE: Beginning in 1995, the United States Navy no longer retires military personnel records to the NPRC (MPR). For the conversion period between 1995 and 1997, either the NPRC or the Navy may hold the record, but it is recommended that all requests relating to Navy personnel discharged, deceased, or retired from 1995 to the present contact:

Navy Personnel Command
PERS-313C1, 5720 Integrity Drive
Millington, TN 38055-3130.

FACTS ABOUT THE 1973 ST. LOUIS FIRE AND LOST RECORDS

A fire at the NPRC in St. Louis on July 12, 1973, destroyed about 80 percent of the records for Army personnel discharged between November 1, 1912, and January 1, 1960. About 75 percent of the records for Air Force personnel with surnames from "Hubbard" through "Z" discharged between September 25, 1947, and January 1, 1964, were also destroyed.

What Was Lost

It is hard to determine exactly what was lost in the fire, because:

- There were no indices to the blocks of records involved. The records were merely filed in alphabetical order for the following groups:
- World War I: Army November 1, 1912 - September 7, 1939
- World War II: Army September 8, 1939 - December 31, 1946
- Post World War II: Army January 1, 1947 - December 31, 1959
- Air Force September 25, 1947 - December 31, 1963
- Millions of records, especially medical records, had been withdrawn from all three groups and loaned to the Department of Veterans Affairs (VA) before the fire. The fact that one's records are not in NPRC files at a particular time does not mean the records were destroyed in the fire.

Reconstruction of Lost Records

If veterans learn that their records may have been lost in the fire, they may send photocopies of any documents they possess -- especially separation documents -- to the NPRC at:

National Personnel Records Center
Military Personnel Records
9700 Page Blvd.
St. Louis, MO 63132-5100.

Alternate Sources of Military Service Data

When veterans don't have copies of their military records and their NPRC files may have been lost in the St. Louis fire, essential information about their military service may be available from a number of other sources, including:

- The Department of Veterans Affairs (VA) maintains records on veterans whose military records were affected by the fire if the veteran or a beneficiary filed a claim before July 1973.
- Service information may also be found in various kinds of "organizational" records such as unit morning reports, payrolls and military orders on file at the NPRC or other National Archives and Records Administration facilities.
- There also is a great deal of information available in records of the State Adjutants General, and other state "veterans services" offices.

By using alternate sources, NPRC often can reconstruct a veteran's beginning and ending dates of active service, the character of service, rank, time lost on active duty, and periods of hospitalization. NPRC can issue NA Form 13038, "Certification of Military Service," considered the equivalent of a Form DD-214, "Report of Separation From Active Duty," to use in establishing eligibility for veterans benefits.

Necessary Information for File Reconstruction

The key to reconstructing military data is to give the NPRC enough specific information so the staff can properly search the various sources. The following information is normally required:

- Full name used during military service;
- Place of entry into service;
- Branch of service;
- Last unit of assignment;
- Approximate dates of service;
- Place of discharge;
- Service number or Social Security number.

CHAPTER 40

CORRECTION OF RECORDS BY CORRECTION BOARDS

Retirees may feel that their records need correcting or amending for any number of reasons. Correction boards consider formal applications for corrections of military records.

Each service department has a permanent Board for Correction of Military (Naval) records, composed of civilians, to act on applications for correction of records.

In order to justify correction of a military record, the applicant must prove to a Corrections Board that the alleged entry or omission in the record was in error or unjust. This board considers all applications and makes recommendations to the appropriate branch Secretary.

An application for correction of record must be filed within three years after discovering the error or injustice. If filed after the three-year deadline, the applicant must include in the application reasons the board should find it in the interest of justice to accept the late application.

Evidence may include affidavits or signed testimony executed under oath, and a brief of arguments supporting the application. All evidence not already included in one's record must be submitted. The responsibility for securing new evidence rests with the applicant.

JURISDICTION

Correction boards are empowered to deal with all matters relating to error or injustice in official records. The boards cannot act until all other administrative avenues of relief have been exhausted. Discharges by sentence of Special Court-Martial and administrative discharges cannot be considered by correction boards unless:

- Application to the appropriate Discharge Review Board has been denied and rehearing is barred; or

- Application cannot be made to the Discharge review Board because the time limit has expired.

APPLICATION

DD Form 149, Application for Correction of Military or Naval record, must be used to apply for correction of military records. It should be submitted, along with supporting evidence, to one of the review boards listed below:

Army
Army Review Boards Agency (ARBA)
ATTN: Client Information and Quality Assurance
Arlington, VA 22202-4508
(703) 607-1600

Navy & Marine Corps
Board for Correction of Naval Records
2 Navy Annex, Room 2432
Washington, DC 20370-5100
(703) 614-1402

Coast Guard
Board for Correction of Military Records (C-60)
Room 4100
400 7th Street SW
Washington, DC 20590
(202) 366-9335

Air Force
Air Force Board for Correction of Military Records
1535 Command Drive
EE Wing 3rd Floor
Andrews AFB DC 20331-7002

DECISIONS

In the absence of new and material evidence the decision of a correction board, as approved or modified by the Secretary of the Service Department, is final. Adverse decisions are subject to judicial review in a U.S. District Court. Decisions of the Boards for Correction of Military or Naval Records must be made available for public inspection. Copies of the decisional documents will be provided on request.

CHAPTER 41

DISCHARGE REVIEW

DISCHARGE REVIEW BOARDS

Each branch of service has discharge review boards to review the discharge or dismissal of former service members. (The Navy Board considers Marine Corps cases.)

Authority

Discharge review boards can, based on the official records and such other evidence as may be presented, upgrade a discharge or change the reason and authority for discharge. Discharge review boards cannot grant disability retirement, revoke a discharge, reinstate any person in the service, recall any person to active duty, act on requests for re-enlistment code changes or review a discharge issued by sentence of a general court-martial. Discharge review boards have no authority to address medical discharges.

Application

DD Form 293, *Application for Review of Discharge or Dismissal from the Armed Forces of the United States*, is used to apply for review of discharge. (If more than 15 years have passed since discharge, DD Form 149 should be used.) The individual or, if legal proof of death is provided, the surviving spouse, next-of-kin, or legal representative can apply. If the individual is mentally incompetent, the spouse, next-of-kin, or legal representative can sign the application, but must provide legal proof of incompetence. The instruction for completing DD Form 293 must be read and complied with.

Time Limitation

Initial application to a discharge review board must be made within 15 years after the date of discharge.

Personal Appearance

A personal appearance before the Discharge Review Board is a legal right. A minimum 30-day notice of the scheduled hearing date is given unless the applicant waives the advance notice in writing. Reasonable postponements can be arranged if circumstances preclude appearance on the scheduled date. All expenses of appearing before the board must be paid by the applicant. If no postponement of a scheduled hearing date is requested and the applicant does not appear on the date scheduled, the right to a personal hearing is forfeited and the case will be considered on the evidence of record.

Hearings

Discharge review boards conduct hearings at various locations in the U.S. Information concerning hearing locations and availability of counsel can be obtained by writing to the appropriate board at the address shown on DD Form 293. Those addresses are listed at the end of this chapter.

Published Uniform Standards For Discharge Review

A review of discharge is conducted to determine if an individual was properly and equitably discharged. Each case is considered on its own merits.

- A discharge is considered to have been proper unless the discharge review determines:
- That there is an error of fact, law, procedures, or discretion which prejudiced the rights of the individual, or
- That there has been a change of policy which requires a change of discharge.
- A discharge is considered to have been equitable unless the discharge review determines:
- That the policies and procedures under which the individual was discharged are materially different from current policies and procedures and that the individual probably would have received a better discharge if the current policies and procedures had been in effect at the time of discharge; or
- That the discharge was inconsistent with the standards of discipline; or
- That the overall evidence before the review board warrants a change of discharge. In arriving at this determination, the discharge review board will consider the quality and the length of the service performed, the individual's physical and mental capability to serve satisfactorily, abuses of authority which may have contributed to the character of the discharge issued, and documented discriminatory acts against the individual.

Decisions

An authenticated decisional document is prepared and a copy provided to each applicant and council.

- A copy of each decisional document, with identifying details of the applicant and other persons deleted to protect personal privacy, must be made available for public inspection and copying. These are located in a reading room in the Pentagon, Washington, DC.
- To provide access to the documents by persons outside the Washington,. D.C. area, the documents have been indexed. The index includes case number of each case; the date, authority and reason for, and character if the discharge, and the issues addressed in the statement of findings, conclusions and reasons.

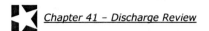

- Interested parties may contact the DVARO or the State veterans Agency for the location of an index. A copy of the index will be made available at the sites of traveling board hearings during the period the board is present.

- An individual can go through the index and identify cases in which the circumstances leading to discharge are similar to those in the individual's case. A copy of these case decisional documents can be requested by writing to:

  DA Military Review Boards Agency
  ATTN: SFBA (Reading Room)
  Room 1E520
  The Pentagon
  Washington, D.C. 20310.

Examination of decisional documents may help to identify the kind of evidence that was used in the case, and may indicate why relief was granted or denied. Decisional documents do not set precedence - each case is considered on its own merits.

Reconsideration

An application that has been denied can be reopened if:

- The applicant submits newly discovered evidence that was not available at the time of the original consideration.

- The applicant did not request a personal hearing in the original application and now desires to appear before the board. If the applicant fails to appear at the hearings, the case will be closed with no further action.

- The applicant was not represented by counsel in the original consideration and now desires counsel and the application for reconsideration is submitted within 15 years following the date of discharge.

- Changes in policy, law or regulations have occurred or federal court orders have been issued which substantially enhance the rights of the applicant.

SERVICE DEPARTMENT DISCHARGE REVIEW BOARD ADDRESSES

Army

Army Discharge Review Board
Attention: SFMR-RBB
1901 South Bell Street, 2nd Floor
Arlington, VA 22202-4508

Navy & USMC

Navy Discharge Review Board
801 North Randolph Street
Suite 905
Arlington, VA 22203

Air Force

Air Force Military Personnel Center
Attention: DP-MDOA1
Randolph AFB, TX 78150-6001

Coast Guard

Coast Guard
Attention: GPE1
Washington, DC 20593

CHAPTER 42

DECORATIONS, RIBBONS AND MEDALS

PURPOSE

The military decorations system has an important purpose – to provide tangible evidence of public recognition and national appreciation of acts of heroism performed and valuable services rendered. Military decorations are awarded in recognition of, and as a reward for heroic, extraordinary, outstanding, and meritorious acts, achievements, and services. Such visible evidence of recognition is meant to be cherished by the recipients, their comrades, and their families.

Not more than one of each military decoration will be issued to any one individual. In its place, for each succeeding award of the same decoration, an Oak-Leaf Cluster or Service Star will be issued (except in the cases of succeeding awards of the Legion of Merit and Medal of Freedom to foreigners, and posthumous awards of the Purple Heart.)

No decoration shall be awarded or presented to any individual whose entire service, subsequent to the time of the distinguished act, achievement, or service, shall not have been awarded.

MILITARY DECORATIONS AND REASONS FOR AWARD

(Year indicated in parentheses indicates year decoration was instituted)

MEDAL OF HONOR

ARMY – NAVY – AIR FORCE – MARINE CORPS – COAST GUARD

(Instituted by Army in 1862, Navy in 1861, Air Force in 1960 - prior to 1960, Airmen received the Army Medal)

For conspicuous gallantry and intrepidity at the risk of life, above and beyond the call of duty, in action involving actual conflict with an opposing armed force

UNITED STATES PERSONAL DECORATIONS

AERIAL ACHIEVEMENT MEDAL (1988)

AIR FORCE

For sustained meritorious achievement while participating in aerial flight

AIR FORCE ACHIEVEMENT MEDAL (1980)

Air Force

For outstanding achievement or meritorious service not warranting award of the Air Force Commendation Medal

AIR FORCE COMMENDATION MEDAL (1958)
AIR FORCE
For outstanding achievement or meritorious service rendered on behalf of the United States Air Force

AIR FORCE CROSS (1960)
AIR FORCE
For extraordinary heroism in action against an enemy of the U.S. while engaged in military operations involving conflict with an opposing foreign force, or while serving with friendly foreign forces

AIRMAN'S MEDAL (1960)
AIR FORCE
For heroism involving voluntary risk of life under conditions other than those of actual conflict with an armed enemy

AIR MEDAL (1942)
ARMY – NAVY – AIR FORCE – MARINE CORPS – COAST GUARD
For heroic actions or meritorious service while participating in aerial flight

ARMY ACHIEVEMENT MEDAL (1981)
ARMY
For meritorious service or achievement while serving in a non-combat area

ARMY COMMENDATION MEDAL (1945-retroactive to 1941)
ARMY
For heroism, meritorious achievement, or meritorious service

BRONZE STAR MEDAL (1944)
ARMY – NAVY – AIR FORCE – MARINE CORPS – COAST GUARD
For heroic or meritorious achievement or service not involving participation in aerial flight

COAST GUARD ACHIEVEMENT MEDAL (1968)
COAST GUARD
For professional and/or leadership achievement in a combat or noncombat situation

COAST GUARD COMMENDATION MEDAL (1947)
COAST GUARD
For heroic or meritorious achievement or service; and meritorious service resulting in unusual or outstanding achievement

COAST GUARD MEDAL (1958)
COAST GUARD
For heroism not involving actual conflict with an armed enemy of the United States

COMBAT ACTION BADGE (2005)(Badge was approved n May 2, 2005, and can be awarded retroactively to September 18, 2001.)
ARMY
For any soldier who personally engages the enemy, or is engaged by the enemy during combat operation in an area where hostile fir pay or imminent danger pay is authorized

COMBAT ACTION RIBBON (1969)
NAVY – MARINE CORPS
For active participation in ground or air combat during specifically listed military operations

COMMANDANT'S LETTER OF COMMENDATION RIBBON (1979)
COAST GUARD
For receipt of a letter of commendation for an act or service resulting in unusual and/or outstanding achievement

DEFENSE DISTINGUISHED SERVICE MEDAL (1970)
ARMY – NAVY – AIR FORCE – MARINE CORPS – COAST GUARD (ISSUED BY SECRETARY OF DEFENSE)
For exceptionally meritorious service to the United States while assigned to a Joint Activity in a position of unique and great responsibility

DEFENSE MERITORIOUS SERVICE MEDAL (1977)
ARMY – NAVY – AIR FORCE – MARINE CORPS – COAST GUARD
For noncombat meritorious achievement or service while assigned to Joint Activity

DEFENSE SUPERIOR SERVICE MEDAL (1976)
ARMY – NAVY – AIR FORCE – MARINE CORPS – COAST GUARD (ISSUED BY SECRETARY OF DEFENSE)
For superior meritorious service to the United States while assigned to a Joint Activity in a position of significant responsibility

DISTINGUISHED FLYING CROSS (1926)
ARMY – NAVY – AIR FORCE – MARINE CORPS – COAST GUARD
For heroism or extraordinary achievement while participating in aerial flight

DISTINGUISHED SERVICE CROSS (1918)
ARMY
For extraordinary heroism in action against an enemy of the U.S. while engaged in military operations involving conflict with an opposing foreign force, or while serving with friendly foreign forces

DISTINGUISHED SERVICE MEDAL
(Instituted by Army in 1918, Navy and Marine Corps in 1919, Air Force in 1960, Coast Guard in 1961)
ARMY – NAVY – AIR FORCE – MARINE CORPS – COAST GUARD
For exceptionally meritorious service to the United States Government in a duty of great responsibility

GOLD LIFESAVING MEDAL (1874)
ARMY – NAVY – AIR FORCE – MARINE CORPS – COAST GUARD – CIVILIANS
For heroic conduct at the risk of life during the rescue or attempted rescue of a victim of drowning or shipwreck

JOINT SERVICE ACHIEVEMENT MEDAL (1983)
ARMY – NAVY – AIR FORCE – MARINE CORPS – COAST GUARD (Issued by Secretary of Defense)
For meritorious service or achievement while serving with a Joint Activity

JOINT SERVICE COMMENDATION MEDAL (1963)
ARMY - NAVY - AIR FORCE - MARINE CORPS - COAST GUARD (Issued by Secretary of Defense)
For meritorious service or achievement while assigned to a Joint Activity

LEGION OF MERIT (1942)
ARMY - NAVY - AIR FORCE - MARINE CORPS - COAST GUARD
For exceptionally meritorious conduct in the performance of outstanding services to the United States

MERITORIOUS SERVICE MEDAL (1969)
ARMY - NAVY - AIR FORCE - MARINE CORPS - COAST GUARD
For outstanding noncombat meritorious achievement or service to the United States

NAVY AND MARINE CORPS ACHIEVEMENT MEDAL (1961)
Navy - Marine Corps
For meritorious service or achievement in a combat or noncombat situation based on sustained performance of a superlative nature

NAVY AND MARINE CORPS COMMENDATION MEDAL (1945 retroactive to 1941)
NAVY - MARINE CORPS
For heroic or meritorious achievement or service

NAVY AND MARINE CORPS MEDAL (1942)
NAVY - MARINE CORPS
For heroism not involving actual conflict with an armed enemy of the United States

NAVY CROSS (1919)
NAVY - MARINE CORPS - COAST GUARD
For extraordinary heroism in action against an enemy of the U.S. while engaged in military operations involving conflict with an opposing foreign force, or while serving with friendly foreign forces

PURPLE HEART (1932)
ARMY - NAVY - AIR FORCE - MARINE CORPS - COAST GUARD
Awarded to any member of the U.S. Armed Forces killed or wounded in an armed conflict

SILVER LIFESAVING MEDAL (1874)
ARMY - NAVY - AIR FORCE - MARINE CORPS - COAST GUARD - CIVILIANS
For heroic conduct during rescue or attempted rescue of a victim of drowning or shipwreck

SILVER STAR (1932)
ARMY - NAVY - AIR FORCE - MARINE CORPS - COAST GUARD
For gallantry in action against an armed enemy of the United States, or while serving with friendly foreign forces

SOLDIER'S MEDAL (1926)
ARMY
For heroism not involving actual conflict with an armed enemy of the United States

SPECIAL SERVICE, GOOD CONDUCT, & RESERVE MERITORIOUS AWARDS

AIR FORCE GOOD CONDUCT MEDAL (1963)
AIR FORCE (Air Force used Army Good Conduct Medal until 1963)
For exemplary conduct, efficiency, and fidelity during three years of active enlisted service with the U.S. Air Force

AIR FORCE RECOGNITION RIBBON (1980)
AIR FORCE
For individual recipients of Air Force-level special trophies and awards

AIR RESERVE FORCES MERITORIOUS SERVICE MEDAL (1964)
AIR FORCE
For exemplary behavior, efficiency, and fidelity during three years of active enlisted service with the Air Force Reserve

ARMY GOOD CONDUCT MEDAL (1941)
ARMY – AIR FORCE
For exemplary conduct, efficiency and fidelity during three years of active enlisted service with the U.S. Army (1 year during wartime)

ARMY RESERVE COMPONENTS ACHIEVEMENT MEDAL (1971)
ARMY
For exemplary conduct, efficiency, and fidelity during three years of service with the U.S. Army Reserve or National Guard

COAST GUARD GOOD CONDUCT MEDAL (1921)
COAST GUARD
For outstanding proficiency, leadership, and conduct during three continuous years of active enlisted Coast Guard service

COAST GUARD RESERVE GOOD CONDUCT MEDAL (1963)
COAST GUARD
For outstanding proficiency, leadership and conduct during three years of enlisted service in the Coast Guard Reserve

COMBAT READINESS MEDAL (1964)
AIR FORCE
For specific periods of qualifying service in a combat or mission-ready status

FLEET MARINE FORCE RIBBON (1984)
NAVY
For active participation by professionally skilled Navy personnel with the Fleet Marine Force

MARINE CORPS GOOD CONDUCT MEDAL (1896)
MARINE CORPS
For outstanding performance and conduct during three years of continuous active enlisted service in the U.S. Marine Corps

NAVAL RESERVE MERITORIOUS SERVICE MEDAL (1964)
NAVY
For outstanding performance and conduct during four years of enlisted service in the Naval Reserve

NAVY GOOD CONDUCT MEDAL (1888)
NAVY
For outstanding performance and conduct during four years of continuous active enlisted service in the U.S. Navy

NAVY RESERVE SPECIAL COMMENDATION RIBBON (1946) (obsolete)
NAVY - MARINE CORPS
For Reserve Officers with four years of successful command, and a total Reserve service of ten years

OUTSTANDING AIRMAN OF THE YEAR RIBBON (1968)
AIR FORCE
For airmen selected to the "12 outstanding Airmen of the Year" competition

PRISONER OF WAR MEDAL (1985)
ARMY - NAVY - AIR FORCE - MARINE CORPS - COAST GUARD
For any member of the U.S. Armed Forces taken prisoner during any armed conflict dating from World War I

SELECTED MARINE CORPS RESERVE MEDAL (1939)
MARINE CORPS
For outstanding performance and conduct during four years of enlisted service in the Marine Corps Selected Reserve

UNITED STATES SERVICE MEDALS

AMERICAN CAMPAIGN MEDAL (1942)
ARMY - NAVY - AIR FORCE - MARINE CORPS - COAST GUARD
For service outside the U.S. in the American theater for 30 days, or within the continental U.S. for one year during 1941-1946

AMERICAN DEFENSE SERVICE MEDAL (1941)
ARMY - NAVY - AIR FORCE - MARINE CORPS - COAST GUARD
For 12 months of active duty service in the Army during 1939-1941; or any active duty service in Naval Services during 1939-1941

ANTARCTICA SERVICE MEDAL (1960)
ARMY - NAVY - AIR FORCE - MARINE CORPS - COAST GUARD
For 30 calendar days of service on the Antarctic Continent from 1946 to the present

ARCTIC SERVICE MEDAL (1976)
COAST GUARD
For 21 days of service on vessels operating in polar waters north of the Arctic Circle from 1946 to the present

ARMED FORCES EXPEDITIONARY MEDAL (1961)
ARMY - NAVY - AIR FORCE - MARINE CORPS - COAST GUARD
For participation in military operations from 1958 to the present not covered by a specific war medal

ARMED FORCES RESERVE MEDAL (1950)

ARMY – NAVY – AIR FORCE – MARINE CORPS – COAST GUARD

For 10 years of honorable service in any reserve component of the United States Armed Forces Reserve or award of "M" device from 1949 to the present

ARMED FORCES SERVICE MEDAL (1996)

ARMY – NAVY – AIR FORCE – MARINE CORPS – COAST GUARD

For participation in military operations not covered by a specific war medal or the Armed Forces Expeditionary Medal from 1995 to the present

For participation in providing direct support to Hurricane Katrina or Hurricane Rita relief operations for 30 consecutive days, or 60 non-consecutive days in the continental United States from August 27, 2005 to February 27, 2006

ARMY OF OCCUPATION MEDAL (1946)

ARMY – AIR FORCE

For 30 consecutive days of service in occupied territories of former enemies during 1945-1955 (Berlin: 1945-1990)

ASIATIC-PACIFIC CAMPAIGN MEDAL (1942)

ARMY – NAVY – AIR FORCE – MARINE CORPS – COAST GUARD

For service in the Asiatic-Pacific theater for 30 days or receipt of any combat decoration during 1941-1946

CHINA SERVICE MEDAL (1940)

NAVY – MARINE CORPS – COAST GUARD

For service ashore in China or on-board naval vessels during 1937-1939 or 1945-1957

EUROPEAN-AFRICAN-MIDDLE EASTERN CAMPAIGN MEDAL (1942)

ARMY – NAVY – AIR FORCE – MARINE CORPS – COAST GUARD

For service in the European-African-Middle Eastern theater for 30 days or receipt of any combat decoration during 1941-1945

GLOBAL WAR ON TERRORISM EXPEDITIONARY MEDAL (2003)

ARMY – NAVY – AIR FORCE – MARINE CORPS – COAST GUARD (INCLUDES RESERVE AND NATIONAL GUARD)

For participation in an expedition to combat terrorism on or after September 11, 2001. This is limited to those who deploy as part of Operation Enduring Freedom.

GLOBAL WAR ON TERRORISM SERVICE MEDAL (2003)

ARMY – NAVY – AIR FORCE – MARINE CORPS – COAST GUARD (INCLUDES RESERVE AND NATIONAL GUARD)

For participation in military operations to combat terrorism on or after September 11, 2001. This is limited to Operation Noble Eagle, and to those servicemembers who provide support to Operation Enduring Freedom from outside the area of eligibility designated for the Global War On Terrorism Expeditionary Medal.

HUMANITARIAN SERVICE MEDAL (1977)
ARMY - NAVY - AIR FORCE - MARINE CORPS - COAST GUARD
For direct participation in specific operations of a humanitarian nature from 1975 to the present.
For participation in providing direct support to Hurricane Katrina or Hurricane Rita immediate relief operations for at least one day in the area of eligibility - east of and including Houston (designated as 96 degrees longitude), Alabama, Louisiana or Mississippi - from August 29, 2005 to October 13, 2005.

KOREAN SERVICE MEDAL (1950)
ARMY - NAVY - AIR FORCE - MARINE CORPS - COAST GUARD
For participation in military operations within the Korean area during 1950-1954

KOREAN DEFENSE SERVICE MEDAL (Approved as part of Public Law 107-314 – Fiscal Year 2003 Defense Authorization Act)
Requires the Secretaries of the Army, Air Force, and Navy to develop a Korean Defense Service Medal for military personnel who served in the Republic of Korea after the official end of the Korean War. The eligibility period shall be from July 28, 1954 to such time in the future that the Secretary of Defense shall designate as being appropriate for termination of the award period. The intent of this provision is to recognize that Korea is still a "hostile" area.

KOSOVO CAMPAIGN MEDAL (2000)
ARMY - NAVY - AIR FORCE - MARINE CORPS - COAST GUARD
For 30 consecutive or 60 non-consecutive days of service in the Kosovo Air Campaign between March 24, 1999 and June 10, 1999; or the Kosovo Defense Campaign from June 11, 1999 to the present

MARINE CORPS EXPEDITIONARY MEDAL (1919)
MARINE CORPS
For landings on foreign territory and operations against armed opposition for which no specific campaign medal has been authorized

MEDAL FOR HUMANE ACTION (1949)
ARMY - NAVY - AIR FORCE - MARINE CORPS - COAST GUARD
For 120 consecutive days of service participating in the Berlin Airlift or in support thereof (Medal was also awarded posthumously)

NATIONAL DEFENSE SERVICE MEDAL (1953)
ARMY - NAVY - AIR FORCE - MARINE CORPS - COAST GUARD
For any honorable active duty service during 1950-1954, 1961-1974, or 1990-1995

NAVAL RESERVE MEDAL (1938) (obsolete)
NAVY
For ten years of honorable service in the U.S. Naval Reserve during 1938-1958

NAVY EXPEDITIONARY MEDAL (1936)
NAVY
For landings on foreign territory and operations against armed opposition for which no specific campaign medal has been authorized

NAVY OCCUPATION SERVICE MEDAL (1947)
NAVY – MARINE CORPS – COAST GUARD
For 30 consecutive days of service in occupied territories of former enemies during 1945-1955 (Berlin: 1945-1990)

OUTSTANDING VOLUNTEER SERVICE MEDAL (1993)
ARMY – NAVY – AIR FORCE – MARINE CORPS – COAST GUARD
For outstanding and sustained voluntary service to the civilian community

SOUTHWEST ASIA SERVICE MEDAL (1991)
ARMY – NAVY – AIR FORCE – MARINE CORPS – COAST GUARD
For active participation in, or support of Operation Desert Shield and/or Operation Desert Storm during 1991-1995

U.S. ANTARCTIC EXPEDITION MEDAL (1945)
NAVY – COAST GUARD
For members of the U.S. Antarctic Expedition of 1939-1941 (awarded in gold, silver, and bronze)

VIETNAM SERVICE MEDAL (1965)
ARMY – NAVY – AIR FORCE – MARINE CORPS – COAST GUARD
For service in Vietnam, Laos, Cambodia, or Thailand during 1965-1973

WOMEN'S ARMY CORPS SERVICE MEDAL (1943)
ARMY
For service with both the Women's Army Auxiliary Corps and Women's Army Corps during 1941-1946

WORLD WAR II VICTORY MEDAL (1945)
ARMY – NAVY – AIR FORCE – MARINE CORPS – COAST GUARD
For service in the U.S. Armed Forces during 1941-1946

UNITED STATES MILITARY MARKSMANSHIP AWARDS

Following is a list of medals and ribbons awarded for attainment of the minimum qualifying score during prescribed shooting exercises:

- Coast Guard Expert Pistol Shot Medal
- Coast Guard Expert Rifleman Medal
- Coast Guard Pistol Marksmanship Ribbon
- Coast Guard Rifle Marksmanship Ribbon
- Naval Expert Rifleman Medal
- Navy Distinguished Marksman And Pistol Shot Ribbon (Obsolete)
- Navy Distinguished Marksman Ribbon (Obsolete)
- Navy Distinguished Pistol Shot Ribbon (Obsolete)
- Navy Expert Pistol Shot Medal

- Navy Pistol Marksmanship Ribbon
- Navy Rifle Marksmanship Ribbon
- Small Arms Expert Marksmanship Ribbon

FOREIGN DECORATIONS AND NON U.S. SERVICE AWARDS

ARMED FORCES HONOR MEDAL (REPUBLIC OF VIETNAM, 1953)
For outstanding contributions to the training and development of RVN Armed Forces

CIVIL ACTIONS MEDAL (REPUBLIC OF VIETNAM, 1964)
For outstanding achievements in the field of civic actions

CROIX DE GUERRE (FRANCE, 1941)
For individual feats of arms as recognized by mention in dispatches

GALLANTRY CROSS (REPUBLIC OF VIETNAM, 1950)
For deeds of valor and acts of courage/heroism while fighting the enemy

INTER-AMERICAN DEFENSE BOARD MEDAL (1981)
ARMY - NAVY - AIR FORCE - MARINE CORPS - COAST GUARD
For service with the Inter-American Defense Board for at least one year

KUWAITI MEDAL FOR THE LIBERATION OF KUWAIT (1995)
ARMY - NAVY - AIR FORCE - MARINE CORPS - COAST GUARD
For participation in, or support of, Operations Desert Shield and/or Desert Storm (1990-1993)

MULTINATIONAL FORCE AND OBSERVERS MEDAL (1982)
ARMY - NAVY - AIR FORCE - MARINE CORPS - COAST GUARD
For six months of service with the Multinational Force & Observers peacekeeping force in the Sinai Desert

NATO MEDAL (1992)
ARMY - NAVY - AIR FORCE - MARINE CORPS - COAST GUARD
For 30 days of service in, or 90 days outside the former Republic of Yugoslavia and the Adriatic Sea under NATO command in direct support of NATO operations

NATO MEDAL (2001)
ARMY - NAVY - AIR FORCE - MARINE CORPS - COAST GUARD
For service members and civilians who participated in operations related to Kosovo

PHILIPPINE DEFENSE MEDAL (REPUBLIC OF THE PHILIPPINES, 1945, ARMY 1948)
For service in defense of the Philippines between December 8, 1941 and June 15, 1942

PHILIPPINE INDEPENDENCE MEDAL (REPUBLIC OF THE PHILIPPINES, 1946, ARMY 1948)
For receipt of both the Philippines Defense and Philippines Liberations medals

PHILIPPINE LIBERATION MEDAL (REPUBLIC OF THE PHILIPPINES, 1945, ARMY 1948)
For service in the liberation of the Philippines between October 17, 1944 and September 3, 1945

REPUBLIC OF KOREA WAR SERVICE MEDAL (1951)
ARMY - NAVY - AIR FORCE - MARINE CORPS - COAST GUARD
For service in Korea between June 25, 1950 and July 27, 1953
(This medal was retroactively approved for Korean War veterans in May 2000.)

REPUBLIC OF VIETNAM CAMPAIGN MEDAL (1966)
ARMY - NAVY - AIR FORCE - MARINE CORPS - COAST GUARD
For six months of service in the Republic of Vietnam between 1965 and 1973; or if wounded, captured, or killed in action during the above period

SAUDI ARABIAN MEDAL FOR THE LIBERATION OF KUWAIT (1991)
ARMY - NAVY - AIR FORCE - MARINE CORPS - COAST GUARD
For participation in, or support of, Operation Desert Storm (January & February 1991)

THANK YOU AMERICA CERTIFICATE (2001)
ARMY - NAVY - AIR FORCE - MARINE CORPS - COAST GUARD
For service on French territory, in French territorial waters, or in French airspace between June 6, 1944 and May 8, 1945. (Certificate is not issued posthumously.)

UNITED NATIONS MEDAL (1964)
ARMY - NAVY - AIR FORCE - MARINE CORPS - COAST GUARD
For six months of service with any authorized UN Peacekeeping mission

UNITED NATIONS SERVICE MEDAL (1951)
ARMY - NAVY - AIR FORCE - MARINE CORPS - COAST GUARD
For service on behalf of the United Nations in Korea between June 27, 1950 and July 27, 1954

U.S. "RIBBONS-ONLY" - AWARDS HAVING NO MEDALS

AIR FORCE LONGEVITY SERVICE AWARD (1957)
AIR FORCE
For successful completion of an aggregate total of four years of honorable active service

AIR FORCE TRAINING RIBBON (1980)
AIR FORCE
For successful completion of an Air Force accession training program

ARMY OVERSEAS SERVICE RIBBON (1981)
ARMY
For successful completion of normal overseas tours not recognized by any other service award

ARMY RESERVE COMPONENTS OVERSEAS TRAINING RIBBON (1984)
ARMY
For successful completion of annual training or active duty training for 10 consecutive duty days on foreign soil

ARMY SERVICE RIBBON (1981)
ARMY
For successful completion of initial entry training

BASIC MILITARY TRAINING HONOR GRADUATE RIBBON (1976)
AIR FORCE
For demonstration of excellence in all academic and military training phases of basic Air Force entry training

COAST GUARD BASIC TRAINING HONOR GRADUATE RIBBON (1984)
COAST GUARD
For successful attainment of the top 3 percent of the class during Coast Guard recruit training

COAST GUARD RECRUITING SERVICE RIBBON (1995)
COAST GUARD
For successful completion of 3 consecutive years of recruiting duty

COAST GUARD SEA SERVICE RIBBON (1984)
COAST GUARD
For satisfactory completion of a minimum of 12 months of cumulative sea duty

MARINE CORPS DRILL INSTRUCTOR RIBBON (1997-retroactive to 1952)
MARINE CORPS
For successful completion of a tour of duty as a drill instructor (staff billets require completion of 18 months to be eligible)

MARINE CORPS RECRUITING RIBBON (1995-retroactive to 1973)
MARINE CORPS
For successful completion of 3 consecutive years of recruiting duty

MARINE CORPS RESERVE RIBBON (1945-obsolete)
MARINE CORPS
For successful completion of 10 years of honorable service in any class of the Marine Corps Reserve

MARINE SECURITY GUARD RIBBON (1997-retroactive to 1949)
MARINE CORPS
For successful completion of 24 months of cumulative security guard duty service at a foreign service establishment

NAVAL RESERVE SEA SERVICE RIBBON (1987)
NAVY
For 24 months of cumulative service embarked on Naval Reserve vessels or an embarked Reserve unit

NAVY AND MARINE CORPS OVERSEAS SERVICE RIBBON (1987)
NAVY – MARINE CORPS
For 12 months consecutive or accumulated duty at an overseas shore base duty station

NAVY ARCTIC SERVICE RIBBON (1987)
NAVY – MARINE CORPS
For 28 days of service on naval vessels operating above the Arctic Circle

NAVY RECRUITING SERVICE RIBBON (1989)
NAVY
For successful completion of 3 consecutive years of recruiting duty

NAVY SEA SERVICE DEPLOYMENT RIBBON (1981)
NAVY – MARINE CORPS
For 12 months active duty on deployed vessels operating away from their home port for extended periods

N.C.O. PROFESSIONAL DEVELOPMENT RIBBON (1981)
ARMY
For successful completion of designated NCO professional development courses

N.C.O. PROFESSIONAL MILITARY EDUCATION GRADUATE RIBBON (1962)
AIR FORCE
For successful completion of a certified NCO professional military education school

OVERSEAS SERVICE RIBBON – SHORT TOUR (1980)
AIR FORCE
For successful completion of an overseas tour designated as "short term" by appropriate authority

OVERSEAS SERVICE RIBBON – LONG TOUR (1980)
AIR FORCE
For successful completion of an overseas tour designated as "long term" by appropriate authority

RESTRICTED DUTY RIBBON (1984)
COAST GUARD
For successful completion of a tour of duty at remote shore stations (LORAN stations, light ships, etc.) without family

SPECIAL OPERATIONS SERVICE RIBBON (1987)
COAST GUARD
For participation in a Coast Guard special noncombat operation not recognized by another service award

UNITED STATES AND FOREIGN UNIT AWARDS

AIR FORCE ORGANIZATIONAL EXCELLENCE AWARD (1969)
AIR FORCE
For exceptionally meritorious achievement or meritorious service by unique unnumbered organizations performing staff functions

AIR FORCE OUTSTANDING UNIT AWARD (1954)
AIR FORCE
For exceptionally meritorious achievement or meritorious service

AIR FORCE PRESIDENTIAL UNIT CITATION (1957)
AIR FORCE
For extraordinary heroism in action against an armed enemy

ARMY MERITORIOUS UNIT COMMENDATION (1944)
ARMY
For exceptionally meritorious conduct in the performance of outstanding service

ARMY PRESIDENTIAL UNIT CITATION (1942)
ARMY
For extraordinary heroism in action against an armed enemy

ARMY SUPERIOR UNIT AWARD (1985)
ARMY
For meritorious performance in difficult and challenging peacetime missions

ARMY VALOROUS UNIT AWARD (1963)
ARMY
For outstanding heroism in armed combat against an opposing armed force

COAST GUARD BICENTENNIAL UNIT COMMENDATION (1990)
COAST GUARD
For all Coast Guard personnel serving satisfactorily at any time between June 4, 1989 and June 4, 1990

COAST GUARD "E" RIBBON (1990)
COAST GUARD
For U.S. Coast Guard ships and cutters which earn the overall operational readiness efficiency award

COAST GUARD MERITORIOUS TEAM COMMENDATION (1993)
COAST GUARD
For valorous or meritorious achievement by smaller U.S. Coast Guard

COAST GUARD MERITORIOUS UNIT COMMENDATION (1973)
COAST GUARD
For valorous or meritorious achievement (combat or noncombat)

COAST GUARD UNIT COMMENDATION (1963)
COAST GUARD
For valorous or extremely meritorious service not involving combat

DEPARTMENT OF TRANSPORTATION OUTSTANDING UNIT AWARD (1995)
COAST GUARD
For valorous or extremely meritorious service on behalf of the Transportation Department

JOINT MERITORIOUS UNIT AWARD (1981)
ARMY – NAVY – AIR FORCE – MARINE CORPS – COAST GUARD
For meritorious achievement or service in combat or extreme circumstances

KOREAN PRESIDENTIAL UNIT CITATION (1951)
ARMY – NAVY – AIR FORCE – MARINE CORPS – COAST GUARD
Awarded to certain units of the U.S. Armed Forces for services rendered during the Korean War

NAVY "E" RIBBON (1976)
NAVY – MARINE CORPS
For ships or squadrons which have won battle efficiency competitions

NAVY MERITORIOUS UNIT COMMENDATION (1967)
NAVY – MARINE CORPS
For valorous actions or meritorious achievement (combat or noncombat)

NAVY PRESIDENTIAL UNIT CITATION (1942)
NAVY – MARINE CORPS
For extraordinary heroism in action against an armed enemy

NAVY UNIT COMMENDATION (1944)
NAVY – MARINE CORPS
For outstanding heroism in action or extremely meritorious service

PHILIPPINE PRESIDENTIAL UNIT CITATION (1948)
ARMY – NAVY – AIR FORCE – MARINE CORPS – COAST GUARD
For service in the war against Japan and/or for 1970 and 1972 disaster relief

REPUBLIC OF VIETNAM CIVIL ACTIONS UNIT CITATION (1966)
ARMY – NAVY – AIR FORCE – MARINE CORPS – COAST GUARD
Awarded to certain units of the U.S. Armed Forces for meritorious service during the Vietnam War, March 1, 1961 – March 28, 1974

REPUBLIC OF VIETNAM GALLANTRY CROSS UNIT CITATION (1966)
ARMY – NAVY – AIR FORCE – MARINE CORPS – COAST GUARD
Awarded to certain units of the U.S. Armed Forces for valorous combat achievement during the Vietnam War, March 1, 1961 – March 28, 1974

VIETNAM PRESIDENTIAL UNIT CITATION (1954)
ARMY – NAVY – MARINE CORPS – COAST GUARD
Awarded to certain units of the U.S. Armed Forces for humanitarian service in the evacuation of civilians from North and Central Vietnam

UNITED NATIONS MEDALS CURRENTLY AUTHORIZED FOR U.S. PERSONNEL

Korean War (1950 - 1953)
UN Advance Mission in Cambodia (1991 – 1992)
UN Iraq – Kuwait Observation Mission (1991 – Present)
UN Military Observer Group, in India and Pakistan (1949 – Present)
UN Mission for the Referendum in Western Sahara (1991 – Present)
UN Mission in Haiti (1993 – 1996)
UN Operation in Somalia (1993 – 1995)
UN Protective Force in Former Yugoslavia (1992 – 1995)
UN Security Force on West New Guinea (1962 – 1963)
UN Transitional Authority in Cambodia (1992 – 1993)
UN Truce Supervision Organization (1948 - Present)

EARLIER SERVICE MEDALS

Earlier Service Medals include the Civil War Campaign Medal, the Indian Campaign Medal, the Spanish Campaign Medal, the Spanish War Service Medal, the Army of Cuban Occupation Medal, the Army of Puerto Rican Occupations Medal, the Philippine Campaign Medal (1899-1913), Philippine Congressional Medal (1898-1902), China Campaign Medal (1900-1901), Army of Cuban Pacification Medal, Mexican Service Medal, Mexican Border Service Medal, Haitian Campaign Medal (April 1, 1919-June 15, 1920), Second Nicaraguan Campaign Medal (August 27, 1926-January 2, 1933), and the Yangtze Service Medal (September 3, 1926-October 21, 1927).

World War I Medals

Medals related to WWI include WWI Victory Medal and the Army of Occupation of Germany Medal. Specific WWI Campaigns are recognized not by separate medals, but by clasps to be attached to WWI Victory Medal's suspension ribbon. These clasps include battle clasps and service clasps.

World War I veterans who received an honorable discharge from Armed Forces for service between April 6, 1917 and November 11, 1918, or served with the American Expeditionary Forces in European Russia between November 12, 1918 and August 5, 1919, or in Siberia between November 12, 1918 and April 1, 1920, were entitled to receive the bronze wreathed star lapel button. Wounded veterans were entitled to receive a silver one.

WEAR OF DECORATIONS, RIBBONS AND MEDALS

Decorations, ribbons and medals which have been awarded may be worn on a uniform or civilian clothing of honorably discharged and retired Armed Force members. However, it is not considered appropriate to wear skill or qualification badges on civilian attire. It is customary to wear only the highest award in miniature form on the lapel of civilian clothing. These decorations have been awarded in recognition of honorable service, and should be worn on every occasion which will reflect credit on them. Retirees are also encouraged to wear their retired pin, and World War II veterans are encouraged to wear their Honorable Discharge Pin (sometimes referred to by veterans as the "ruptured duck".

GOLD STAR LAPEL BUTTON

A Gold Star lapel button is available to identify widows, parents, and next of kin of members of the armed forces who:

- Lost their lives during World War I, World War II, or during any subsequent period of armed hostilities in which the United States was engaged before July 1, 1958;
- Lost or lose their lives after June 30, 1958 while:
- Engaged in an action against an enemy of the U.S.
- Engaged in military operations involving conflict with an opposing foreign force; or
- Serving with friendly foreign forces engaged in an armed conflict in which the U.S. is not a belligerent party against an opposing armed force.
- Lost or lose their lives after March 28, 1973, as a result of:
- An international terrorist attack against the U.S. or a foreign nation friendly to the U.S., recognized as such an attack by the Secretary of Defense; or
- Military operations whiles serving outside the U.S. (including the commonwealths, territories, and possessions of the U.S.) as part of a peacekeeping force.

Upon application, the Secretary of Defense shall furnish one gold star lapel button without cost to the widow and to each parent and next of kin of any member of the Armed Services who loses his or her life under any of the above-mentioned circumstances.

In this section, the following guidelines apply:

- The term "widow" includes widower;
- The term "parents" includes mother, father, stepmother, stepfather, mother through adoption, father through adoption, and foster parents who stood in loco parentis;
- The term "next of kin" includes only children, brothers, sister, half brothers, and half sisters;
- The term "children" includes stepchildren and children through adoption;
- The term "World War I" includes the period from April 6, 1917 to March 3, 1921;
- The term "World War II" includes the period from September 8, 1939, to July 25, 1947, at 12:00 P.M.;

- The term "military operations" includes those operations involving members of the armed forces assisting in U.S. Government sponsored training of military personnel of a foreign nation;

- The term "peacekeeping force" includes those personnel assigned to a force engaged in a peacekeeping operation authorized by the United Nations Security Council.

WHERE TO ORDER MEDALS / REPLACEMENT OF MEDALS

The Armed Forces typically issue decorations and service medals as they are awarded or earned.

Discharged veterans may request replacement of lost, stolen, or destroyed medals. Requests may also be made for awards that were earned, but never issued. The next-of-kin of deceased veterans may also make such requests. (Replacements will be issued for United States awards only, not foreign awards.)

All requests should include:

- The veteran's full name (printed or typed);
- The signature of the veteran or next-of-kin, if the veteran is deceased;
- The veteran's branch of service;
- The veteran's service number or social security number;
- The exact or approximate dates of service;
- If available, a copy of the discharge or separation document.

Requests should be sent to the following locations:

Navy, Marine Corps And Coast Guard:

U.S. Navy Liaison Office (N314)
Room 3475
9700 Page Boulevard
St. Louis, MO 63132-5100

Army

U.S. Army Reserve Personnel Center
Attn: DARP-PAS-EAW
9700 Page Boulevard
St. Louis, MO 63132-5100

Air Force

Air Force Reference Branch NCPMF
National Personnel Records Center
(Military Personnel Records)
9700 Page Boulevard
St. Louis, MO 63132-5100

PRESIDENTIAL MEMORIAL CERTIFICATES

A Presidential Memorial Certificate is an engraved paper certificate that has been signed by the current president, honoring the memory of any honorably discharged deceased veteran. Presidential Memorial Certificates may be distributed to a deceased veteran's next of kin and loved ones. More than one certificate can be provided per family, and there is no time limit for applying for the certificate. Requests for a Presidential Memorial Certificate can be made in person at any VA regional office, or by U.S. Mail. There is no form to use when requesting a certificate. A copy of the veteran's discharge documents and a return mailing address should be included with any request. Written requests should be sent to:

U.S. Department of Veterans Affairs
National Cemetery Administration (403A)
810 Vermont Avenue, NW
Washington, DC 20420

CHAPTER 43

AGENTS AND ATTORNEYS

No individual may act as an agent or attorney in the preparation, presentation, or prosecution of any claim under laws administered by the VA unless the VA has recognized such individual for such purposes.

The VA may recognize the following representatives in the preparation, presentation, and prosecution of claims under laws administered by the VA:

- National Red Cross;
- American Legion;
- Disabled American Veterans;
- United Spanish War Veterans;
- Veterans of Foreign Wars;
- Other organizations as the VA may approve.

The VA, in the discretion of the Secretary of the VA, may furnish, if available, space and office facilities for the use of paid full-time representatives of national organizations so recognized.

No individual shall be recognized unless:

- The individual has certified to the VA that no fee or compensation of any nature will be charged any individual for services rendered in connection with any claim; and
- Such individual has filed with the VA a power of attorney, executed in such manner and form as the VA may prescribe.

Unless a claimant specifically indicates in a power of attorney filed with the VA a desire to appoint only a recognized representative of an organization listed in or approved above, the VA may, for any purpose, treat the power of attorney naming such an organization, a specific office of such an organization, or a recognized representative of such an organization as the claimant's representative as an appointment of the entire organization as the claimant's representative.

Whenever the VA is required or permitted to notify a claimant's representative, and the claimant has named in a power of attorney an organization listed in or approved by the VA, a specific office of such an organization, or a recognized representative of such an organization without specifically indicating a desire to appoint only a recognized representative of the organization the VA shall notify the organization at the address designated by the organization for the purpose of receiving the notification concerned.

Recognition Of Agents And Attorneys Generally

The VA may recognize any individual as an agent or attorney for the preparation, presentation, and prosecution of claims under laws administered by the VA. The VA may require that individuals, before being recognized under this section, show that they are of good moral character and in good repute, are qualified to render claimants valuable service, and otherwise are competent to assist claimants in presenting claims.

The VA, after notice and opportunity for a hearing, may suspend or exclude from further practice before the Department of the VA, any agent or attorney recognized under this section if the VA finds that such agent or attorney:

- Has engaged in any unlawful, unprofessional, or dishonest practice;
- Has been guilty of disreputable conduct;
- Is incompetent;
- Has violated or refused to comply with any of the laws administered by the VA, or with any of the regulations or instructions governing practice before the VA; or
- Has in any manner deceived, misled, or threatened any actual or prospective claimant.

A fee may not be charged, allowed, or paid for services of agents and attorneys with respect to services provided before the date on which the Board of Veterans' Appeals first makes a final decision in the case. Such a fee may be charged, allowed, or paid in the case of services provided after such date only if an agent or attorney is retained with respect to such case before the end of the one-year period beginning on that date. The limitation in the preceding sentence does not apply to services provided with respect to proceedings before a court.

A person who, acting as agent or attorney in a case referred to in the above paragraph, represents a person before the Department or the Board of Veterans' Appeals after the Board first makes a final decision in the case shall file a copy of any fee agreement between them with the Board at such a time as may be specified by the Board. The Board, upon its own motion or the request of either party, may review such a fee agreement and may order a reduction in the fee called for in the agreement if the Board finds that the fee is excessive or unreasonable. A finding or order of the Board under the preceding sentence may be reviewed by the Court of Appeals for Veterans Claims.

A reasonable fee may be charged or paid in connection with any proceeding before the VA in a case arising out of a loan made, guaranteed, or insured under the VA's home or small business loan program. A person who charges a fee under this paragraph shall enter into a written agreement with the person represented and shall file a copy of the fee agreement with the VA at such time, and in such manner, as may be specified by the VA.

When a claimant and an attorney have entered into a fee agreement described above, the total fee payable to the attorney may not exceed 20% of the total amount of any past-due benefits awarded on the basis of the claim.

A fee agreement referred to in this chapter is one under which the total amount of the fee payable to the attorney:

- Is to be paid to the attorney by the VA directly from any past-due benefits awarded on the basis of the claim; and

- Is contingent on whether or not the matter is resolved in a manner favorable to the claimant.

(A claim shall be considered to have been resolved in a manner favorable to the claimant if all or any part of the relief sought is granted.)

To the extent that past-due benefits are awarded in any proceeding before the VA, the Board of Veterans' Appeals, or the Court of Appeals for Veterans Claims, the VA may direct that payment of any attorneys' fee under a fee arrangement be made out of such past-due benefits. In no event may the VA withhold for the purpose of such payment any portion of benefits payable for a period after the date of the final decision of the Secretary of the VA, the Board of Veterans' Appeals, or Court of Appeals for Veterans Claims making (or ordering the making of) the award.

Penalty For Certain Acts

Whoever directly or indirectly solicits, contracts for, charges, or receives; or attempts to solicit, contract for, charge, or receive any fee or compensation not specifically provided for in this chapter shall be fined as provided in Title 18, or imprisoned not more than one year, or both.

Whoever wrongfully withholds from any claimant or beneficiary any part of a benefit or claim allowed and due to the claimant or beneficiary, shall be fined as provided in Title 18, or imprisoned not more than one year, or both.

CHAPTER 44

PENAL AND FORFEITURE PROVISIONS

> *VA benefits are restricted if a veteran, surviving spouse, child, or dependent parent is convicted of a felony and imprisoned for more than 60 days.*

The first section of this chapter outlines basic information for veterans with questions concerning the effect of incarceration on VA benefits. The later sections of this chapter provide detailed information regarding misappropriation by fiduciaries, fraudulent acceptance of payments, forfeiture for fraud, forfeiture for treason, and forfeiture for subversive activities.

BASIC INFORMATION

VA benefits are restricted if a veteran, surviving spouse, child, or dependent parent is convicted of a felony and imprisoned for more than 60 days. VA may still pay certain benefits, however, the amount paid depends on the type of benefit and reason for imprisonment. Following is information about the benefits most commonly affected by imprisonment.

Please note that overpayments due to failure to notify VA of a veteran's incarceration results in the loss of all financial benefits until the overpayment is recovered.

VA DISABILITY COMPENSATION

The disability compensation paid to a veteran incarcerated because of a felony is limited to the 10% disability rate, beginning with the 61st day of imprisonment. For a surviving spouse, child, dependent parent or veteran whose disability rating is 10%, the payment is at the 5% rate. (This means that if a veteran was receiving $188 or more prior to incarceration, the new payment amount will be $98. If a veteran was receiving $98 before incarceration, the new payment amount will be $49.)

If a veteran resides in a halfway house, participates in a work release program, or is on parole, compensation payments will not be reduced.

VA DISABILITY PENSION

VA will stop a veteran's pension payments beginning on the 61st day of imprisonment for conviction of either a felony or misdemeanor.

VA MEDICAL CARE

While incarcerated veterans do not forfeit their eligibility for medical care, current regulations restrict VA from providing hospital and outpatient care to an incarcerated veteran who is an inmate in an institution of another government agency when that agency has a duty to give the care or services.

However, VA may provide care once the veteran has been unconditionally released from the penal institution. Veterans interested in applying for enrollment into the VA health care system should contact the nearest VA health care facility upon their release.

EDUCATIONAL ASSISTANCE / SUBSISTENCE ALLOWANCE

A subsistence allowance may not be paid to an incarcerated veteran convicted of a felony, buy, under certain circumstances, all or part of the veteran's tuition and fees may be paid. Individuals should contact the VA to determine individual eligibility.

CLOTHING ALLOWANCE

In the case of a veteran who is incarcerated in a Federal, State, or local penal institution for a period in excess of 60 days and who is furnished clothing without charge by the institution, the amount of any annual clothing allowance payable to the veteran shall be reduced by an amount equal to 1/365 of the amount of the allowance otherwise payable under that section for each day on which the veteran was so incarcerated during the 12-month period preceding the date on which payment of the allowance would be due.

PAYMENT TO DEPENDENTS

VA may be able to take part of the amount that the incarcerated veteran is not receiving and pay it to his or her dependents, if they can show need. Interested dependents should contact the nearest VA regional office for details on how to apply. They will be asked to provide income information as part of the application process.

RESTORATION OF BENEFITS

When a veteran is released from prison, his or her compensation or pension benefits may be restored. Depending on the type of disability, the VA may schedule a medical examination to see if the veteran's disability has improved or worsened.

MISAPPROPRIATION BY FIDUCIARIES

Whoever, being a guardian, curator, conservator, committee, or person legally vested with the responsibility or care of a claimant or a claimant's estate, or any other person having charge and custody in a fiduciary capacity of money heretofore or hereafter paid under any of the laws administered by the VA for the benefit of any minor, incompetent, or other beneficiary, shall lend, borrow, pledge, hypothecate, use, or exchange for other funds or property, except as authorized by law, or embezzle or in any manner misappropriate any such money or property derived wherefrom in whole or in part, and coming into such fiduciary's control in any matter whatever in the execution of such fiduciary's trust, or under color of such fiduciary's office or service as such fiduciary, shall be fined in accordance with Title 18, or imprisoned not more than 5 ye4ars, or both.

Any willful neglect or refusal to make and file proper accountings or reports concerning such money or property as required by law shall be taken to be sufficient evidence prima facie of such embezzlement or misappropriation.

FRAUDULENT ACCEPTANCE OF PAYMENTS

Any person entitled to monetary benefits under any of the laws administered by the VA whose right to payment ceases upon the happening of any contingency, who thereafter fraudulently accepts any such payment, shall be fined in accordance with Title 18, or imprisoned not more than one year, or both.

Whoever obtains or receives any money or check under any of the laws administered by the VA without being entitled to it, and with intent to defraud the United States or any beneficiary of the United States, shall be fined in accordance with Title 18, or imprisoned not more than one year, or both.

FORFEITURE FOR FRAUD

Whoever knowingly makes or causes to be made or conspires, combines, aids, or assists in, agrees to, arranges for, or in any way procures the making or presentation of a false or fraudulent affidavit, declaration, certificate, statement, voucher, or paper, concerning any claim for benefits under any of the laws administered by the VA (except laws pertaining to insurance benefits) shall forfeit all rights, claims, and benefits under all laws administered by the VA (except laws pertaining to insurance benefits).

Whenever a veteran entitled to disability compensation has forfeited the right to such compensation under this chapter, the compensation payable but for the forfeiture shall thereafter be paid to the veteran's spouse, children, and parents. Payments made to a spouse, children, and parents under the preceding sentence shall not exceed the amounts payable to each if the veteran had died from service-connected disability. No spouse, child, or parent who participated in the fraud for which forfeiture was imposed shall receive any payment by reason of this subsection. Any apportionment award under this subsection may not be made in any case after September 1, 1959.

Forfeiture of benefits by a veteran shall not prohibit payment of the burial allowance, death compensation, dependency and indemnity compensation, or death pension in the event of the veteran's death.

After September 1, 1959, no forfeiture of benefits may be imposed under the rules outlined in this chapter upon any individual who was a resident of, or domiciled in, a State at the time the act or acts occurred on account of which benefits would, but not for this subsection, be forfeited unless such individual ceases to be a resident of, or domiciled in, a State before the expiration of the period during which criminal prosecution could be instituted. The paragraph shall not apply with respect to:

- Any forfeiture occurring before September 1, 1959; or

- An act or acts that occurred in the Philippine Islands before July 4, 1946.

The VA is authorized and directed to review all cases in which, because of a false or fraudulent affidavit, declaration, certificate, statement, voucher, or paper, a forfeiture of gratuitous benefits under laws administered by the VA was imposed, pursuant to this section or prior provisions of the law, on or before September 1, 1959. In any such case in which the VA determines that the forfeiture would not have been imposed under the provisions of this section in effect after September 1, 1959, the VA shall remit the forfeiture, effective June 30, 1972. Benefits to which the individual concerned becomes eligible by virtue of any such remission may be awarded, upon application for, and the effective date of any award of compensation, dependency and indemnity compensation, or pension made in such a case shall be fixed in accordance with the facts found, but shall not be earlier than the effective date of the Act or administrative issue. In no event shall such award or increase be retroactive for more than one year from the date of application, or the date of administrative determination of entitlement, whichever is earlier.

FORFEITURE FOR TREASON

Any person shown by evidence satisfactory to the VA to be guilty of mutiny, treason, sabotage, or rendering assistance to an enemy of the United States or its allies shall forfeit all accrued or future gratuitous benefits under laws administered by the VA.

The VA, in its discretion, may apportion and pay any part of benefits forfeited under the preceding paragraph to the dependents of the person forfeiting such benefits. No dependent of any person shall receive benefits by reason of this subsection in excess of the amount to which the dependent would be entitled if such person were dead.

In the case of any forfeiture under this chapter, there shall be no authority after September 1, 1959 to:

- Make an apportionment award pursuant to the preceding paragraph; or
- Make an award to any person of gratuitous benefits based on any period of military, naval, or air service commencing before the date of commission of the offense.

FORFEITURE FOR SUBVERSIVE ACTIVITIES

Any individual who is convicted after September 1, 1959, of any offense listed below shall, from and after the date of commission of such offense, have no right to gratuitous benefits (including the right to burial in a national cemetery) under laws administered by the VA based on periods of military, naval, or air service commencing before the date of commission of such offense, and no other person shall be entitled to such benefits on account of such individual. After receipt of notice of the return of an indictment for such an offense, the VA shall suspend payment of such gratuitous benefits pending disposition of the criminal proceedings. If any individual whose rights to benefits has been terminated pursuant to this section, is granted a pardon of the offense by the

President of the United States, the right to such benefits shall be restored as of the date of such pardon.

The offenses referred to in the previous paragraph are:

- Sections 894, 904 and 906 of Title 10 (articles 94, 104, and 106 of the Uniform Code of Military Justice);
- Sections 792, 793, 794, 798, 2381, 2382, 2383, 2384, 2385, 2387, 2388, 2389, 2390, and chapter 105 of Title 18;
- Sections 222, 223, 224, 225 and 226 of the Atomic Energy Act of 1954 (42 U.S.C. 2272, 2273, 2274, 2275, and 2276);
- Section 4 of the Internal Security Act of 1950 (50 U.S.C. 783).

The Secretary of Defense, the Secretary of Transportation, or the Attorney General, as appropriate, shall notify the VA in each case in which an individual is convicted of an offense mentioned in this chapter.

CHAPTER 45

MILITARY PAY RATES

COMPARATIVE RANKS CHART

The charts below will assist in determining the pay of the Officer, Warrant Officer and Enlisted man.

Pay Grade	Army, Air Force And Marine Corps	Navy, Coast Guard and Coast and Geodetic Survey
O-10	General	Admiral
O-9	Lt. General	Vice Admiral
O-8	Major General	Real Admiral (Upper half)
O-7	Brigadier General	Rear Admiral (Lower half) & Commodore
O-6	Colonel	Captain
O-5	Lt. Colonel	Commander
O-4	Major	Lt. Commander
O-3	Captain	Lieutenant
O-2	First Lieutenant	Lieutenant (Jr. Grade)
O-1	Second Lieutenant	Ensign
W-4	Chief Warrant Officer	Chief Warrant Officer*
W-3	Chief Warrant Officer	Chief Warrant Officer*
W-2	Chief Warrant Officer	Chief Warrant Officer*
W-1	Warrant Officer	Warrant Officer*

(*Not applicable to Coast and Geodetic Survey)

Pay Grade	ARMY
E-9	Sergeant Major Staff Sergeant Major
E-8	First Sergeant – M. Sergeant
E-7	Sergeant 1/c – Specialist – 7
E-6	Staff Sergeant – Specialist - 6
E-5	Sergeant – Specialist - 5
E-4	Corporal – Specialist - 4
E-3	Private 1/c
E-2	Private
E-1	Private

Pay Grade	COAST GUARD
E-9	Master Chief Petty Officer
E-8	Senior Chief Petty Officer
E-7	Chief Petty Officer
E-6	Petty Officer 1/c
E-5	Petty Officer 2/c
E-4	Petty Officer 3/c
E-3	Seaman
E-2	Seaman Apprentice
E-1	Seaman Recruit

Pay Grade	NAVY
E-9	Master Chief Petty Officer
E-8	Senior Chief Petty Officer
E-7	Chief Petty Officer
E-6	Petty Officer 1/c
E-5	Petty Officer 2/c
E-4	Petty Officer 3/c
E-3	Seaman
E-2	Seaman Apprentice
E-1	Seaman Recruit

Pay Grade	MARINE CORPS
E-9	Sergeant Major Master Gunnery Sergeant
E-8	First Sergeant
E-7	Gunnery Sergeant
E-6	Staff Sergeant
E-5	Sergeant
E-4	Corporal
E-3	Lance Corporal
E-2	Private First Class
E-1	Private

Pay Grade	AIR FORCE
E-9	Chief Master Sergeant
E-8	Senior Master Sergeant
E-7	Master Sergeant
E-6	Tech. Sergeant
E-5	Staff Sergeant
E-4	Sergeant
E-3	Airman 1/c
E-2	Airman
E-1	Airman Basic

MONTHLY BASIC PAY RATES – ACTIVE DUTY - EFFECTIVE JANUARY 1, 2008

The following tables reflect the 3.5 percent military pay raise for 2008 passed by Congress. As of January 1, 2008 all servicemembers will receive a 3.0 percent increase in base pay. Once the National Defense Authorization Act of 2008 is signed into law, the 3.5% increase in base pay rates will go into effect and will be made retroactive to January 1, 2008.

The following charts show monthly base pay. A military member may be entitled to other pays, such as a housing allowance (if authorized to live off base), or a monthly food allowance (if authorized to consume meals outside of the chow halls). Unless serving in a designated combat zone, base pay is taxable (federal income tax, social security tax, medicare tax, state income tax, etc). Some states do not tax military pay.

(When a figure is not shown for a given number of completed years of service-for-pay, the amount to the left applies.)

COMMISSIONED OFFICERS

Years of Service

Grade	*Less Than 2*	*2*	*3*	*4*	*6*
O-10					
O-9					
O-8	8749.00	9035.20	9225.60	9278.70	9515.90
O-7	7269.70	7607.30	7763.70	7887.90	8112.70
O-6	5388.40	5919.40	6307.80	6307.80	6331.70
O-5	4491.70	5059.90	5410.50	5476.20	5694.60
O-4	3875.70	4486.40	4785.70	4852.50	5130.40
O-3	3407.40	3862.90	4169.40	4545.70	4763.10
O-2	2943.90	3353.10	3862.00	3992.40	4074.40
O-1	2555.70	2659.70	3215.20	3215.20	3215.20

Grade	*8*	*10*	*12*	*14*	*16*
O-10					
O-9					
O-8	9912.40	10004.60	10381.30	10489.00	10813.50
O-7	8334.80	8591.80	8848.00	9105.10	9912.40
O-6	6603.40	6639.10	6639.10	7016.40	7683.60
O-5	5825.60	6113.10	6324.00	6596.30	7013.60
O-4	5428.20	5798.90	6088.30	6288.90	6404.10
O-3	5002.20	5157.10	5411.40	5543.40	5543.40
O-2	4074.40	4074.40	4074.40	4074.40	4074.40
O-1	3215.20	3215.20	3215.20	3215.20	3215.20

Grade	*18*	*20*	*22*	*24*	*26*
O-10		14137.10	14206.30	14501.60	15016.40
O-9		12364.70	12542.60	12800.10	13249.30
O-8	11282.30	11715.30	12004.20	12004.20	12004.20
O-7	10594.30	10594.40	10594.30	10594.30	10648.00
O-6	8075.20	8466.40	8914.50	8914.50	9351.90
O-5	7212.00	7408.50	7631.20	7631.20	7631.20
O-4	6471.10	6471.10	6471.10	6471.10	6471.10
O-3	5543.40	5543.40	5543.40	5543.40	5543.40
O-2	4074.40	4074.40	4074.40	4074.40	4074.40
O-1	3215.20	3215.20	3215.20	3215.20	3215.20

Grade	*30*	*34*	*38*
O-10	15767.20	16555.50	17383.30
O-9	13912.00	14607.50	15337.80
O-8	12304.50	12612.20	12612.20
O-7	10861.00	10861.00	10861.00
O-6	9538.90	9538.90	9538.90
O-5	7631.20	7631.20	7631.20
O-4	6471.10	6471.10	6471.10
O-3	5543.40	5543.40	5543.40
O-2	4074.40	4074.40	4074.40
O-1	3215.20	3215.20	3215.20

OFFICERS WITH MORE THAN FOUR YEARS ACTIVE-DUTY AS ENLISTED OR WARRANT OFFICER

Years of Service

Grade	Less Than 2	2	3	4	6
O-3E				4545.70	4763.10
O-2E				3992.40	4074.40
O-1E				3215.20	3433.80
Grade	*8*	*10*	*12*	*14*	*16*
O-3E	5002.20	5157.10	5411.40	5625.60	5748.60
O-2E	4204.20	4423.00	4592.30	4718.40	4718.40
O-1E	3560.50	3690.30	3817.90	3992.40	3992.40
Grade	*18*	*20*	*22*	*24*	*26*
O-3E	5916.00	5916.00	5916.00	5916.00	5916.00
O-2E	4718.40	4718.40	4718.40	4718.40	4718.40
O-1E	3992.40	3992.40	3992.40	3992.40	3992.40
Grade	*30*	*34*	*38*		
O-3E	5916.00	5916.00	5916.00		
O-2E	4718.40	4718.40	4718.40		
O-1E	3992.40	3992.40	3992.40		

WARRANT OFFICERS (FOR ARMY, NAVY AND MARINE CORPS)

Grade	Less Than 2	2	3	4	6
W-5					
W-4	3521.10	3788.10	3896.80	4003.90	4188.00
W-3	3215.50	3349.70	3486.90	3532.20	3676.30
W-2	2845.40	3114.60	3197.50	3254.70	3439.10
W-1	2497.70	2765.90	2838.90	2991.70	3172.40
Grade	*8*	*10*	*12*	*14*	*16*
W-5					
W-4	4370.00	4554.70	4832.60	5076.10	5307.70
W-3	3959.80	4254.80	4393.90	4554.40	4719.90
W-2	3726.00	3867.90	4007.90	4179.00	4312.50
W-1	3438.50	3562.70	3736.60	3907.60	4041.80
Grade	*18*	*20*	*22*	*24*	*26*
W-5		6261.20	6578.90	6815.50	7077.50
W-4	5496.80	5681.80	5953.50	6176.50	6431.10
W-3	5017.40	5218.90	5339.00	5467.00	5640.90
W-2	4433.90	4578.60	4674.00	4750.00	4750.00
W-1	4165.40	4316.00	4316.00	4316.00	4316.00
Grade	*30*	*34*	*38*		
W-5	7431.50	7803.20	8193.50		
W-4	6559.60	6559.60	6559.60		
W-3	5640.90	5640.90	5640.90		
W-2	4750.00	4750.00	4750.00		
W-1	4316.00	4316.00	4316.00		

ENLISTED MEMBERS

Years of Service

Grade	*Less Than 2*	*2*	*3*	*4*	*6*
E-9					
E-8					
E-7	2421.00	2642.40	2743.60	2878.00	2982.40
E-6	2094.00	2303.90	2405.80	2504.50	2607.60
E-5	1918.90	2047.10	2145.90	2247.40	2405.10
E-4	1759.00	1849.00	1949.00	2047.70	2135.00
E-3	1587.90	1687.90	1789.70	1789.70	1789.70
E-2	1510.00	1510.00	1510.00	1510.00	1510.00
E-1>4	1346.90	1346.90	1346.90	1346.90	1346.90

Grade	*8*	*10*	*12*	*14*	*16*
E-9		4254.50	4351.00	4472.40	4615.60
E-8	3482.60	3636.90	3732.20	3486.50	3970.10
E-7	3162.10	3263.00	3443.10	3592.50	3694.60
E-6	2840.10	2930.50	3105.00	3158.70	3197.80
E-5	2570.60	2705.40	2722.20	2722.20	2722.20
E-4	2135.00	2135.00	2135.00	2135.00	2135.00
E-3	1789.70	1789.70	1789.70	1789.70	1789.70
E-2	1510.00	1510.00	1510.00	1510.00	1510.00
E-1	1346.90	1346.90	1346.90	1346.90	1346.90

Grade	*18*	*20*	*22*	*24*	*26*
E-9	4759.30	4990.40	5185.70	5391.50	5705.70
E-8	4193.60	4306.90	4499.50	4606.30	4869.60
E-7	3803.00	3845.50	3986.80	4062.60	4351.30
E-6	3243.20	3242.20	3243.20	3243.20	3243.20
E-5	2722.20	2722.20	2722.20	2722.20	2722.20
E-4	2135.00	2135.00	2135.00	2135.00	2135.00
E-3	1789.70	1789.70	1789.70	1789.70	1789.70
E-2	1510.00	1510.00	1510.00	1510.00	1510.00
E-1	1346.90	1346.90	1346.90	1346.90	1346.90

Grade	*30*	*34*	*38*
E-9	5991.10	6290.70	6605.30
E-8	4967.10	4967.10	4967.10
E-7	4351.30	4351.30	4351.30
E-6	3243.20	3243.20	3243.20
E-5	2722.20	2722.20	2722.20
E-4	2135.00	2135.00	2135.00
E-3	1789.70	1789.70	1789.70
E-2	1510.00	1510.00	1510.00
E-1	1346.90	1346.90	1346.90

Note: Basic Pay for O-7 – 0-10 is limited to Level III of the Executive Schedule
Note: Basic Pay for 0-6 and below is limited to Level V of the Executive Schedule

Monthly Basic Pay Rates – Reserve Pay
Effective January 1, 2008

The following 2008 drill pay amounts are based on a 3.5 percent pay increase, which was passed by congress, but is still pending the President's signature.

As of January 1, 2008 all servicemembers will receive a 3.0 percent increase in base pay. Once the National Defense Authorization Act of 2008 is signed into law, the 3.5% increase in pay rates will go into effect and will be made retroactive to Jan.1, 2008.

Rates shown are for four drills. (All of the figures have been rounded to the closest dollar. When a figure is not shown for a given number of completed years of service-for-pay, the amount to the left applies.)

COMMISSIONED OFFICERS

	Years of Service				
Grade	*Less Than 2*	*2*	*3*	*4*	*6*
O-10					
O-9					
O-8	1166	1205	1229	1237	1268
O-7	969	1014	1035	1051	1082
O-6	717	789	840	840	844
O-5	598	675	721	730	759
O-4	516	589	638	647	684
O-3	454	514	556	605	634
O-2	392	447	497	532	543
O-1	341	354	427	427	427

Grade	*8*	*10*	*12*	*14*	*16*
O-10					
O-9					
O-8	1321	1333	1384	1398	1441
O-7	1112	1145	1179	1214	1321
O-6	880	885	885	935	1025
O-5	776	815	842	879	935
O-4	723	773	810	838	853
O-3	667	687	721	739	739
O-2	543	543	543	543	543
O-1	427	427	427	427	427

Grade	18	20	22	24	26
O-10		1808	1808	1808	1808
O-9		1649	1649	1672	1766
O-8	1504	1562	1562	1600	1600
O-7	1412	1412	1412	1412	1419
O-6	1076	1128	1128	1188	1246
O-5	960	987	987	1017	1017
O-4	862	862	862	862	862
O-3	739	739	739	739	739
O-2	543	543	543	543	543
O-1	427	427	427	427	427

OFFICERS WITH MORE THAN FOUR YEARS ACTIVE-DUTY AS ENLISTED OR WARRANT OFFICER

		Years of Service			
Grade	Less Than 2	2	3	4	6
O-3E				605	634
O-2E				532	543
O-1E				427	457

		Years of Service			
Grade	8	10	12	14	16
O-3E	667	687	721	749	766
O-2E	560	590	612	629	629
O-1E	474	492	508	532	532

Grade	18	20	22	24	26
O-3E	789	789	789	789	789
O-2E	629	629	629	629	629
O-1E	532	532	532	532	532

WARRANT OFFICERS

	Years of Service				
Grade	*Less Than 2*	*2*	*3*	*4*	*6*
W-5					
W-4	469	504	519	534	558
W-3	427	446	465	470	490
W-2	377	398	417	431	443
W-1	332	360	378	390	421
Grade	*8*	*10*	*12*	*14*	*16*
W-5					
W-4	583	607	631	655	694
W-3	5111	541	569	600	622
W-2	474	500	518	536	548
W-1	441	457	475	489	500
Grade	*18*	*20*	*22*	*24*	*26*
W-5		806	834	861	889
W-4	718	743	768	794	820
W-3	646	655	664	687	709
W-2	558	579	597	617	617
W-1	518	532	532	532	532

ENLISTED MEMBERS

	Years of Service				
Grade	*Less Than 2*	*2*	*3*	*4*	*6*
E-9					
E-8					
E-7	322	352	365	383	397
E-6	278	306	320	333	348
E-5	256	272	285	299	320
E-4	234	246	260	272	284
E-3	211	225	238	238	238
E-2	201	201	201	201	201
E-1	179	179	179	179	179

Grade	*8*	*10*	*12*	*14*	*16*
E-9		566	580	596	615
E-8	464	484	497	512	529
E-7	421	435	448	472	484
E-6	378	390	404	415	419
E-5	338	352	356	356	356
E-4	284	284	284	284	284
E-3	238	238	238	238	238
E-2	201	201	201	201	201
E-1	179	179	179	179	179

	Years of Service				
Grade	*18*	*20*	*22*	*24*	*26*
E-9	634	664	691	718	760
E-8	559	573	599	614	649
E-7	496	502	526	541	580
E-6	422	422	422	422	422
E-5	356	356	356	356	356
E-4	284	284	284	284	284
E-3	238	238	238	238	238
E-2	201	201	201	201	201
E-1	179	179	179	179	179

Note: Guard/Reserve members are normally credited with 4 days pay for a weekend duty. The above charts show the monthly base pay, based upon the normal requirements of one weekend per month.

When performing active duty other than weekend drills, Guard/Reserve members receive 1/30th of monthly active duty pay for each day served on active duty.

BASIC ALLOWANCE FOR HOUSING.

The housing allowance for active-duty personnel combines the basic allowance for quarters and the variable housing allowance into one rate. Separate allowances are calculated for applicable regions, and vary for different regions in the country. For further information, individuals should contact their local military office.

BASIC ALLOWANCE FOR SUBSISTENCE

Officers (including commissioned officers, warrants, and aviation cadets):
$202.76 per month

***Enlisted Members*:**
$294.43 per month

MILITARY RETIREMENT PAY

The calculation of an individual's military retirement pay is an extremely complicated subject. The amount of an individual's retirement pay depends on many factors, and it is not appropriate in the scope of this book to cover this topic. Prior to retirement, it is important for individuals to attend any briefings offered by their command concerning the retirement system. The decisions an individual makes at the time of retirement affect the amounts of retirement benefits. Some decisions cannot be changed, so careful consideration of all options is crucial.

CHAPTER 46

OFFICE OF SMALL AND DISADVANTAGED BUSINESS UTILIZATION

The Office of Small and Disadvantaged Business Utilization (OSDBU) serves as the Department of Veterans Affairs (VA) advocate, to assist and support the interests of small businesses. Its purpose is to provide information, counseling, and guidance to small, women-owned, minority-owned and veteran-owned small businesses wishing to do business with VA.

OSDBU also assists VA organizations in locating and working with small businesses.
OSDBU neither awards contracts nor maintains solicitation mailing lists. OSDBU promotes the position of small businesses within the Department, maintains liaison with trade and professional organizations, and serves as the major source of information about VA for small businesses. The office monitors the performance of the Department on these programs.

Its purpose is to provide information, counseling, and guidance to small, women-owned, minority-owned and veteran-owned small businesses wishing to do business with VA.

A related mission of the office is to provide outreach and liaison support to businesses (large and small) and other members of the private sector concerning acquisition related issues. In addition, the office is responsible for monitoring VA implementation and execution of the following socioeconomic procurement programs:

CENTER FOR VETERANS ENTERPRISE

In early 2001, VA opened its first "Center For Veterans Enterprise." The center offers services to veterans who own, or want to start, their own businesses. Veterans can call the center at (866) 584-2344, or (202) 565-8336 to receive assistance from a national network of business specialists. Information will be available about loans, business management programs, online training for entrepreneurs, and procurement opportunities with federal, state, and local agencies.

To be considered a "veteran-owned business," or a "service-disabled veteran-owned business," 51% of the ownership and control of the enterprise must be maintained by veteran(s).

SMALL BUSINESS PROGRAM

The small business program implements the requirements to aid, counsel, assist, and protect the interests of small business concerns to ensure that a fair proportion of total purchases, contracts, and subcontracts for property and services for VA are placed with small businesses. For acquisition purposes, small businesses must be independently owned and operated, not dominant in the field of operation in which they are bidding on Government contracts, and otherwise qualify as small businesses under the criteria and size standards developed by the Small Business Administration (SBA).

SMALL BUSINESS SET-ASIDES

This program requires agencies to limit competition on certain contracts to qualified small businesses so that small firms do not have to compete with large ones for the same contracts. However, because the law requires the Government to buy at competitive prices, contracts are set aside only when two small businesses are expected to submit offers to ensure adequate competition. SBA establishes size standards that determine a firm's eligibility to offer on set-asides. These standards are established on an industry-by-industry basis, using dollar volume of sales or number of employees, to determine eligibility.

SMALL DISADVANTAGED BUSINESS PROGRAM

For the purpose of improving and stimulating this small business segment, VA established a realistic Department-wide goal for the award of contracts to small business concerns owned and controlled by socially and economically disadvantaged individuals. OSDBU is also responsible for the Department's program to encourage greater economic opportunity for minority entrepreneurs. To implement these requirements, goals are established for award of contracts to small disadvantaged businesses.

A business is eligible to participate under this program if it is:

- At least 51 percent owned by one or more individuals who are both socially and economically disadvantaged; and
- Managed and controlled by one or more such individuals.

Economically or socially disadvantaged individuals for government procurement purposes include:

- African Americans;
- Hispanic Americans;
- Native Americans, (American Indians, Eskimos, Aleuts, or Native Hawaiians);

- Asian Pacific Americans (persons with origins from Japan, China, the Philippines, Vietnam, Korea, Samoa, Guam, U.S. Trust Territory of the Pacific Islands, Northern Mariana Islands, Laos, Cambodia, or Taiwan);
- Asian Indian Americans (persons with origins from India, Pakistan or Bangladesh); and
- Members of other groups designated from time to time by the SBA under 13 CFR 124.105(d).

8(A) PROGRAM

OSDBU promotes increased utilization of small businesses owned and controlled by socially and economically disadvantaged individuals certified under the SBA Section 8(a) Program.

Section 8(a) of the Small Business Act, as amended, authorizes SBA to contract for goods and services with Federal agencies. SBA then subcontracts actual performance of the work to socially and economically disadvantaged small businesses that have been certified by SBA as eligible to receive these contracts. The major advantage of this program is that it provides Government contracts on a noncompetitive basis to socially and economically disadvantaged small businesses. SBA also offers managerial, technical, and financial support to participating firms.

The purpose of the 8(a) Program is to:

- Foster business ownership by individuals who are socially and economically disadvantaged;
- Promote the competitive viability of these firms by providing contract, technical, and management assistance;
- Expand acquisition opportunities for these firms.

To be eligible for the 8(a) Program a concern must qualify as a small businesses (at least 51 percent owned by a U.S. citizen who is determined by SBA to be socially and economically disadvantaged.)

Each SBA 8(a) concern is subject to a fixed program participation term.

WOMEN-OWNED BUSINESS PROGRAM

In response to the need to aid and stimulate women's business enterprises, this advocacy program directs acquisition officials to take appropriate action to facilitate, preserve, and strengthen women's business enterprises and to ensure full participation by women in the free enterprise system.

Appropriate action includes the award of prime contracts and subcontracts and counseling of women-owned businesses. "Women-owned small businesses" means small business concerns that are at least 51 percent owned, controlled, and operated by women who are United States citizens.

OSDBU is responsible for negotiating annual goals with VA acquisition officials to increase Federal prime contracts with women-owned small businesses.

VETERAN-OWNED AND OPERATED SMALL BUSINESS (VOB) PROGRAM

Consistent with its mandate and mission, VA strongly encourages the participation of VOBs in the VA acquisition program. OSDBU is the advocate that monitors the Veteran-owned small business program.

VA is not authorized to set aside contracts for veterans. However, veteran-owned small businesses are identified, targeted, and included in its existing acquisition programs.

SUBCONTRACTING PROGRAM

Recognizing that small firms often do not have the capability to perform as a prime contractor on certain large contracts, VA promotes the involvement of small businesses at the subcontract level. VA requires that any contractor receiving a contract for more than $10,000 shall agree that small business concerns have the maximum practicable opportunity to participate in contracts awarded by the Department.

Furthermore, all prime contracts not awarded to small businesses, in excess of $1,000,000 for construction and $500,000 for all others, which offer subcontracting opportunities must contain a subcontracting plan. Each subcontracting plan must contain percentage goals for the maximum practicable utilization of small business concerns, small disadvantaged business concerns, and women owned small business concerns.

To carry out this program, OSDBU:

- Recommends informational goals for solicitations;
- Reviews subcontracting plans, and offers recommendations;
- Monitors compliance with subcontracting plans;
- Participates in prebid conferences, and conducts small business workshops to provide small, small disadvantaged, women owned and veteran-owned small business firms the opportunity to present their capabilities to prime contractors;
- Publishes a directory of VA prime contractors as a marketing tool to assist small, small disadvantaged, women-owned, and veteran-owned small businesses.

Additional information on these programs may be obtained by contacting:

U.S. Department of Veterans Affairs
Director, Office of Small and Disadvantaged Business Utilization (00SB)
810 Vermont Avenue, N.W.
Washington, DC 20420
Telephone: (202) 565-8124
Toll free: (800) 949-8387
Facsimile: (202) 565-8156

CHAPTER 47

OTHER FEDERAL BENEFITS

There are a variety of benefits for veterans and their dependents that are not administered by the Department of Veterans Affairs. This chapter offers a general overview of the benefits provided by through the Department of Labor, and provides information on who to contact for additional details.

Congress created the Veterans' Employment and Training Service (VETS) as an independent agency within the Department of Labor to:

- Assist veterans making the transition from military to civilian life;
- Train for and find good jobs; and
- Protect the employment and reemployment rights of veterans, Reservists, and National Guard members.

Through cooperative efforts with each State, VETS offers employment and training service to eligible veterans through several programs.

DISABLED VETERANS' OUTREACH PROGRAMS (DVOP)

DVOP specialists develop job and training opportunities for veterans, with special emphasis on veterans with service-connected disabilities. DVOP specialists provide direct services to veterans enabling them to be competitive in the labor market. They provide outreach and offer assistance to disabled and other veterans by promoting community and employer support for employment and training opportunities, including apprenticeship and on-the-job training.

DVOP specialists work with employers, veterans' organizations, the Departments of Veterans Affairs and Defense, and community-based organizations to link veterans with appropriate jobs and training opportunities.

DVOP specialists serve as case managers for veterans enrolled in federally funded job training programs such as the Department of Veterans Affairs' Vocational Rehabilitation program, and other veterans with serious disadvantages in the job market. DVOPs are available to those veterans and their employers to help ensure that necessary follow up services are provided to promote job retention.

The U.S. Department of Labor provides grant funds to each State's employment service to maintain DVOP specialist positions in the State. DVOP specialists are employees of the State and are generally located in State employment service offices.

DVOP specialists may be stationed at regional offices and medical or veterans' outreach centers of the Department of Veterans Affairs, State or county veterans' service offices, Job Training Partnership Act program offices, community-based organizations, and military installations.

To contact a DVOP specialist, call or visit the nearest State Employment Service (sometimes known as Job Service) agency listed in the State Government section of the phone book.

LOCAL VETERANS' EMPLOYMENT REPRESENTATIVES (LVERS)

Local Veterans' Employment Representatives (LVERs) are state employees located in state employment service local offices to provide assistance to veterans by:

- Supervising the provision of all services to veterans furnished by employment service employees, including counseling, testing, and identifying training and employment opportunities;
- Monitoring job listings from Federal contractors to see that eligible veterans get priority in referrals to these jobs;
- Monitoring Federal department and agency vacancies listed at local state employment service offices and preliminary processing of complaints from veterans about the observance of veterans' preference by Federal employers;
- Promoting and monitoring the participation of veterans in Federally-funded employment and training programs;
- Cooperating with the Department of Veterans Affairs to identify and aid veterans who need work-specific prosthetic devices, sensory aids or other special equipment to improve their employability; and
- Contacting community leaders, employers, unions, training programs and veterans' service organizations to be sure eligible veterans get the services to which they are entitled.

TRANSITION ASSISTANCE PROGRAM (TAP)

The Transition Assistance Program (TAP) was established to meet the needs of separating service members during their period of transition into civilian life by offering job-search assistance and related services.

The law creating TAP established a partnership among the Departments of Defense, Veterans Affairs, Transportation and the Department of Labor's Veterans' Employment and Training Service (VETS), to give employment and training information to armed forces members within 180 days of separation or retirement.

TAP helps service members and their spouses make the initial transition from military service to the civilian workplace with less difficulty and at less overall cost to the government. An independent national evaluation of the program estimated that service members who had participated in TAP, on average, found their first post-military job three weeks sooner than those who did not participate in TAP.

TAP consists of comprehensive three-day workshops at selected military installations nationwide. Professionally-trained workshop facilitators from the State Employment Services, military family support services, Department of Labor contractors, or VETS' staff present the workshops.

Workshop attendees learn about job searches, career decision-making, current occupational and labor market conditions, and resume and cover letter preparation and interviewing techniques. Participants also are provided with an evaluation of their employability relative to the job market and receive information on the most current veterans' benefits.

Service members leaving the military with a service-connected disability are offered the Disabled Transition Assistance Program (DTAP). DTAP includes the normal three-day TAP workshop plus additional hours of individual instruction to help determine job readiness and address the special needs of disabled veterans.

Although experience shows that veterans generally enjoy a favorable employment rate in the nation's job market, many veterans initially find it difficult to compete successfully in the labor market. The TAP program addresses many barriers to success and alleviates many employment related difficulties.

THE UNIFORMED SERVICES EMPLOYMENT AND REEMPLOYMENT RIGHTS ACT OF 1994 (USERRA 38 U.S.C. 4301-4334)

The Department of Labor, through the Veterans' Employment and Training Service (VETS), provides assistance to all persons having claims under USERRA.

The Uniformed Services Employment and Reemployment Rights Act (USERRA) clarifies and strengthens the Veterans' Reemployment Rights (VRR) Statute.

USERRA protects civilian job rights and benefits for veterans and members of Reserve components. USERRA also makes major improvements in protecting service member rights and benefits by clarifying the law, improving enforcement mechanisms, and adding Federal Government employees to those employees already eligible to receive Department of Labor assistance in processing claims.

USERRA establishes the cumulative length of time that an individual may be absent from work for military duty and retain reemployment rights to five years (the previous law provided four years of active duty, plus an additional year if it was for the convenience of the Government). There are important exceptions to the five-year limit, including initial enlistments lasting more than five years, periodic National Guard and Reserve training duty, and involuntary active duty extensions and recalls, especially during a time of national emergency. USERRA clearly establishes that reemployment protection does not depend on the timing, frequency, duration, or nature of an individual's service as long as the basic eligibility criteria are met.

USERRA provides protection for disabled veterans, requiring employers to make reasonable efforts to accommodate the disability. Service members convalescing from injuries received during service or training may have up to two years from the date of completion of service to return to their jobs or apply for reemployment.

USERRA provides that returning service-members are reemployed in the job that they would have attained had they not been absent for military service (the long-standing "escalator" principle), with the same seniority, status and pay, as well as other rights and benefits determined by seniority. USERRA also requires that reasonable efforts (such as training or retraining) be made to enable returning service members to refresh or upgrade their skills to help them qualify for reemployment. The law clearly provides for alternative reemployment positions if the service member cannot qualify for the "escalator" position. USERRA also provides that while an individual is performing military service, he or she is deemed to be on a furlough or leave of absence and is entitled to the non-seniority rights accorded other individuals on non-military leaves of absence.

Health and pension plan coverage for service members is provided for by USERRA. Individuals performing military duty of more than 30 days may elect to continue employer sponsored health care for up to 24 months; however, they may be required to pay *up to* 102 percent of the full premium. For military service of less than 31 days, health care coverage is provided as if the service member had remained employed. USERRA clarifies pension plan coverage by making explicit that all pension plans are protected.

The period an individual has to make application for reemployment or report back to work after military service is based on time spent on military duty. For service of less than 31 days, the service member must return at the beginning of the next regularly scheduled work period on the first full day after release from service, taking into account safe travel home plus an eight-hour rest period. For service of more than 30 days but less than 181 days, the service member must submit an application for reemployment within 14 days of release from service. For service of more than 180 days, an application for reemployment must be submitted within 90 days of release from service.

USERRA also requires that service members provide advance written or verbal notice to their employers for all military duty unless giving notice is impossible, unreasonable, or precluded by military necessity. An employee should provide notice as far in advance as is reasonable under the circumstances. Additionally, service members are able (but are not required) to use accrued vacation or annual leave while performing military duty.

The Department of Labor, through the Veterans' Employment and Training Service (VETS) provides assistance to all persons having claims under USERRA, including Federal and Postal Service employees.

If resolution is unsuccessful following an investigation, the service member may have his or her claim referred to the Department of Justice for consideration of representation in the appropriate District Court, at no cost to the claimant. Federal and Postal Service employees may have their claims referred to the Office of Special Counsel for consideration of representation before the Merit Systems Protection Board (MSPB). If violations under USERRA are shown to be willful, the court may award liquidated damages. Individuals who pursue their own claims in court or before the MSPB may be awarded reasonable attorney and expert witness fees if they prevail.

Service member employees of intelligence agencies are provided similar assistance through the agency's Inspector General.

HOMELESS VETERANS' REINTEGRATION PROGRAM

The purpose of the Homeless Veterans' Reintegration Program (HVRP) is to provide services to assist in reintegrating homeless veterans into meaningful employment within the labor force and to stimulate the development of effective service delivery systems that will address the complex problems facing homeless veterans.

HVRP was initially authorized under Section 738 of the Stewart B. McKinney Homeless Assistance Act in July 1987. It is currently authorized under Title 38 U.S.C. Section 2021, as added by Section 5 of Public Law 107-95, the Homeless Veterans Comprehensive Assistance Act of 2001. Funds are awarded on a competitive basis to eligible applicants such as: State and local Workforce Investment Boards, public agencies, for-profit/commercial entities, and non-profit organizations, including faith based and community based organizations.

Grantees provide an array of services utilizing a case management approach that directly assists homeless veterans as well as provide critical linkages for a variety of supportive services available in their local communities. The program is "employment focused" and veterans receive the employment and training services they need in order to re-enter the labor force. Job placement, training, job development, career counseling, resume preparation, are among the services that are provided. Supportive services such as clothing, provision of or referral to temporary, transitional, and permanent housing, referral to medical and substance abuse treatment, and transportation assistance are also provided to meet the needs of this target group.

Since its inception, HVRP has featured an outreach component using veterans who themselves have experienced homelessness. In recent years, this successful technique was modified to allow the programs to utilize formerly homeless veterans in various other positions where there is direct client contact such as counseling, peer coaching, intake, and follow-up services.

The emphasis on helping homeless veterans get and retain jobs is enhanced through many linkages and coordination with various veterans' services programs and organizations such as the Disabled Veterans' Outreach Program and Local Veterans' Employment Representatives stationed in the local employment service offices of the State Workforce Agencies, Workforce Investment Boards, One-Stop Centers, Veterans' Workforce Investment Program, the American Legion, Disabled American Veterans, Veterans of Foreign Wars, and the Departments of Veterans' Affairs, Housing and Urban Development, and Health and Human Services.

VETERANS WORKFORCE INVESTMENT PROGRAM (VWIP)

The intent of the Veterans Workforce Investment Programs (VWIP), is to support employment and training programs, through grants or contracts, program to meet the needs for workforce investment activities of veterans with service-connected disabilities, veterans who have significant barriers to employment, veterans who served on active duty in the armed forces during a war or in a campaign or expedition for which a campaign badge has been authorized, and recently separated veterans.

The Office of the Assistant Secretary administers the VWIP program for Veterans' Employment and Training (OASVET). The annual funding for (VWIP) is authorized by legislation and derived as a percentage of the total annual Workforce Investment authorization. Most of the appropriated funds are used to support two-year grants awarded to eligible entities through a competitive, Solicitation-of-Grant Applications (SGA) process conducted in even-numbered years. Eligible entities include state and local governments, private, not-for-profit organizations including community based and faith based organizations.

The competitive process allows for two-year grant programs, the second year funding is based on performance and availability of funds.

These programs can provide for, but are not limited to training (formal classroom or on-the-job training), retraining, job placement assistance, and support services, including testing, counseling. Grantees may choose to supplement the core training by offering other services that also enhance the employability of participants.

FEDERAL CONTRACTOR PROGRAM

Any contractor or subcontractor who receives a contract from the federal government in the amount of $100,000 or more must take affirmative action to hire and promote qualified Vietnam-era and special disabled veterans.

Contractors and subcontractors with openings for jobs, other than executive or top management jobs, must list them with the nearest State Job Service (also known as State Employment Service) office. The requirement applies to vacancies at all locations of a business not otherwise exempt under the company's Federal contract. The job-listing requirement may be satisfied by immediate posting of the job on America's Job Bank.

Qualified Vietnam- era and special disabled veterans receive priority for referral to Federal contractor job openings listed at those offices. The priority for referral is not a guarantee that referred veterans will be hired.

Federal contractors are not required to hire those referred, but must have affirmative action plans when applicable (50 employees and a $50,000 contract). They must be able to show they have followed the plans and that they have not discriminated against veterans or other covered groups. They also must show that they have actively recruited Vietnam-era and special-disabled veterans and disseminated all information internally regarding promotion activities.

Companies must file an annual *VETS-100* report, which shows the number of Vietnam-era and special disabled veterans in their work force by job category, hiring location, and number of new hires, including Vietnam-era and special disabled veterans hired during the reporting period. Instructions, information and follow-up assistance is provided to employers who do not understand the reporting and other legal requirements.

For more information about the *VETS- 100* report contact the VETS-100 Processing Center at (334) 242 2028.

For more information about the Federal Contractor Program, contact the nearest USDOL Veterans' Employment and Training Service representative.

For information about how to list a job opening, contact the nearest State Job Service office listed in the telephone book, or the America's Job Bank.

For copies of *Affirmative Action Obligations of Contractors and Subcontractors for Disabled Veterans and Veterans of the Vietnam Era, Rules and Regulations,* contact:

ESA Office of Federal Contract Compliance Programs
U.S. Department of Labor
200 Constitution Ave., NW
Washington, D.C. 20210

NATIONAL VETERANS' TRAINING INSTITUTE

The U.S. Department of Labor, through the Office of the Assistant Secretary for Veterans' Employment and Training (OASVET), established the National Veterans' Training Institute in 1986 to provide specialized training and professional skills enhancement of State Employment Security Agency and other veterans' service providers' staff.

To perform most effectively, veterans' services specialists require specialized training; and State Employment Security Agencies' local job service office and other program management staff need more generalized training. The NVTI strives to meet both needs.

The NVTI basic training focuses on improving employment services for veterans through a professional skills-development program.

The University of Colorado at Denver operates the NVTI under a competitively awarded contract with VETS. Classes are delivered in a variety of modes, including residential weeks in Denver and selected locations around the country, and via distance learning approaches. NVTI courses are accredited by the North Central Association of Colleges and Universities; satisfactory course completion can earn participants two hours of academic credit per average five-day course. NVTI's administrative office in Denver houses the Resource and Technical Assistance Center (RTAC), a repository for a variety of materials and information resources on veterans' issues and services that offers on-going support for individuals who have completed NVTI training.

CHAPTER 48

MISCELLANEOUS BENEFITS OF INTEREST TO VETERANS

SOCIAL SECURITY AND MEDICARE

Monthly retirement, disability, and survivor benefits are payable to veterans and dependents if the veteran has earned enough work credits under the program.

In addition, a veteran may qualify at age 65 for Medicare's hospital insurance and medical insurance.

Supplemental Security Income Benefits (SSI) may also be payable to veterans who have a low income and few assets, and are 65 or older or disabled.

For information about Social Security Benefits, individuals should call (800) 772-1213.

For information about Medicare, individuals should call (800) 633-4227.

Military Service And Social Security

The earnings of people who serve in military services on active duty or on active duty for training have been covered under Social Security since 1957. Inactive duty service in the armed forces reserves (such as weekend drills) has been covered by Social Security since 1988. However, people who served in the military before 1957 did not pay into Social Security directly, but their records are credited with special earnings for Social Security purposes that count toward any benefits that might be payable. Additional earnings credits are given to military personnel depending on when they served. The following information explains how and when these special earnings are credited, and provides other general information military personnel need to know about the benefits available from Social Security.

Paying Social Security And Medicare Taxes

While in military service (from 1957 on), individuals pay Social Security taxes the same way civilian employees do. Those taxes are deducted from the individual's pay and the U.S. government as the employer pays an equal amount.

When Additional Earnings Are Added To Military Records

The amount an individual gets from Social Security depends on the earnings averaged over much of his or her working lifetime. Generally, the higher the earnings, the higher the Social Security benefits.

Under certain circumstances, special earnings can be credited to an individual's military pay record for Social Security purposes. The extra earnings credits are granted for periods of active duty or active duty for training. These extra earnings may help an individual qualify for Social Security or increase the amount of the Social Security benefit. (Social Security cannot add extra earnings credits to an individual's earnings record until the individual files for Social Security benefits.)

Following is a brief explanation of how the additional earnings are granted:

Service In 1978 Through 2001:
For every $300 in active duty basic pay, an individual is credited with an additional $100 in earnings, up to a maximum of $1,200 a year. If an individual enlisted after Sept. 7, 1980, and didn't complete at least 24 months of active duty or his or her full tour, he or she may not be able to receive the additional earnings. Check with Social Security for details.

After 2001, additional earnings are no longer credited.

Service In 1957 Through 1977:
An individual is credited with $300 in additional earnings for each calendar quarter in which he or she received active duty basic pay.

Service In 1940 Through 1956:
If an individual was in the military during this period, including attendance at a service academy, he or she did not pay Social Security taxes. However, his or her Social Security record may be credited with $160 a month in earnings for military service from September 16, 1940, through December 31, 1956, under the following circumstances:

- The individual was honorably discharged after 90 or more days of service, or was released because of a disability or injury received in the line of duty; or
- The individual is still on active duty; or
- The widow is applying for survivors' benefits and the veteran died while on active duty.

Individuals cannot receive these special earnings credits if they are already receiving a federal benefit based on the same years of service. There is one exception to this rule: if an individual was on active duty after 1956, he or she can still get the special earnings for 1951 through 1956, even if they are receiving a military retirement based on service during that period.

When applying for Social Security benefits, an individual will be asked for proof of his or her military service (DD Form 214) or information regarding his or her reserves or National Guard service.

RAILROAD RETIREMENT AND SURVIVOR BENEFITS

The Railroad Retirement Act is a Federal law that provides retirement and disability annuities for qualified railroad employees, spouse annuities for their wives or husbands, and survivor benefits for the families of deceased employees who were insured under the Act. These benefit programs are administered by the U.S. Railroad Retirement Board. It also administers the Railroad Unemployment Insurance Act, and has administrative responsibilities under the Social Security Act for certain benefit payments and railroad workers' Medicare coverage. *The information provided in this chapter is intended as a brief summary of Medicare only.*

A toll-free help line is available at (800) 808-0772, which can be used to obtain the addresses and telephone numbers of the Board's field offices. Employees can use the Help Line to obtain statements of creditable service and compensation, and beneficiaries on the rolls can use it to verify their current monthly benefit rate or secure a replacement Medicare card. Information on unemployment-sickness benefits can also be obtained by using the Help Line, which is available 24 hours a day, 7 days a week.

JOB-FINDING ASSISTANCE

State employment offices help veterans find jobs by providing free job counseling, testing, referral and placement services. Veterans are given priority when referring applicants to job openings and training opportunities.

Disabled veterans receive the highest priority in referrals.

Employment offices also assist veterans by providing information about unemployment compensation, job markets, and on-job and apprenticeship training opportunities.

Interested veterans should contact the nearest state employment office. If applying in person, veterans should present a copy of their military discharge form DD-214.

UNEMPLOYMENT COMPENSATION

Weekly unemployment compensation may be paid to discharged servicemembers for a limited period of time. Individual state laws govern the amount and duration of payments. To apply for unemployment compensation, veterans should contact their nearest state employment office immediately after leaving military service. If applying in person, veterans should present a copy of their military discharge form DD-214.

OPERATION TRANSITION

The military services provide civilian-transition counseling at least 90 days prior to each service member's discharge in a program called Operation Transition. A Defense Department document (DD Form 2586) is prepared that provides military experience, training history, civilian job equivalent experience and recommended educational credit. The document is delivered to service members 90 to 180 days before the scheduled separation.

The Defense Outplacement Referral System (DORS) refers resumes to potential employers through 350 Transition offices worldwide. Resumes are provided to employers by mail, electronic mail, or facsimile. Employers may place job ads on the electronic Transition Bulletin Board (TBB) kept by Transition offices. Those employers having the proper computer equipment are able to place their ads electronically; others may mail or fax their ads to the TBB. Servicemembers are encouraged to respond directly to employers with their resumes. The electronic bulletin board also contains business opportunities, a calendar of transition seminars and events, and other helpful information.

Two special registries have been developed at Transition offices to help separating servicemembers obtain public community service jobs. The "Registry of Public and Community Service Organizations" contains information on organizations desiring to hire servicemembers. The "Personnel Registry" lists servicemembers who desire employment in public and community service occupations. The Defense Department matches people and employers on the two registries, and counsels separating servicemembers on how to apply for positions with public and community service organizations.

SMALL BUSINESS ADMINISTRATION

Although business loans are not available through VA, the Small Business Administration (SBA) has a number of programs designed to help foster and encourage small business enterprises, including financial and management assistance.

Each SBA office has a veteran's affairs officer available to speak with.

Interested veterans should refer to the local telephone directory for the phone number of a local SBA office, or call (800) 827-5722.

FARM LOANS

VA loan guaranties are not available for farm loans, unless there is a home on the property, which will be personally occupied by the veteran. Non-realty loans for the purchase of equipment, livestock, machinery, etc. are not made.

However, loans and guaranties may be provided by the U.S. Department of Agriculture to buy, improve, or operate farms. Loans and guaranties are available for housing in towns generally up to 20,000 in population. Applications from veterans have preference.

For further information, veterans should contact local Department of Agriculture offices, usually located in county seats. Interested parties may also contact:

Farm Service Agency / Rural Economic and Community Development
U.S. Department of Agriculture
Washington, DC 20250

Other loan programs for farm financing may be available through the Farmers Home Administration, which gives preference to veteran applicants. (Interested veterans should refer to the local telephone directory for the phone number of a local office.)

HOUSING AND URBAN DEVELOPMENT - (HUD)

HUD homeless assistance grants are awarded to non-profit organizations, state and local governments, and public housing authorities to provide housing and services for the homeless, including veterans. HUD sponsors the Veteran Resource Center (HUDVET), which works with national veterans service organizations to serve as a general information center. To contact HUDVET, call (800) 998-9999. HUD also funds approved housing counseling agencies that provide free counseling services. To find a counselor, call (800) 569-4287.

DEATH GRATUITY PAID BY MILITARY COMMAND

Fallen Hero Compensation (Formerly known as the Death Gratuity)

In 2005 congress enacted The Emergency Supplemental Appropriations Act of 2005. The act increased the immediate cash payment from $12,420 to $100,000 for survivors of those *whose death was a result of hostile actions and occurred in a designated combat operation or combat zone or while training for combat or performing hazardous duty.*

2006 Update:
The Fiscal Year 2006 National Defense Authorization Act expanded eligibility for the $100,000 death gratuity, retroactively to October 7, 2001, to survivors of *any member who dies while on active duty.*

The gratuity is paid by the last military command of the deceased. If the beneficiary is not paid automatically, application should be made to the appropriate military service.

COMMISSARY AND EXCHANGE PRIVILEGES

Unlimited exchange and commissary store privileges in the United States are available to:

- Honorably discharged veterans with a service-connected disability rated at 100 %;
- Unremarried surviving spouses of members or retired members of the Armed Forces;
- Recipients of the Medal of Honor, and their dependents and orphans;
- Reservists and their dependents also may be eligible.

Update Regarding Commissary for Reservists:

Section 651 of the Fiscal Year 2004 Military Authorization Act gives almost all reservists and their dependents unlimited access to DOD Commissaries. Unlimited access is authorized for:

- Members of the Ready Reserve (which includes members of the Selected Reserve, Individual Ready Reserve and Inactive National Guard) and members of the Retired Reserve who possess a Uniformed Services Identification Card;
- Former members eligible for retired pay at age 60 but who have not yet attained the age of 60 and who possess a Department of Defense Civilian Identification Card;
- Dependents of the members described above who have a Uniformed Services Identification Card or who have a distinct identification card used as an authorization card for benefits and privileges administered by the Uniformed Services.

Previously, Guard and Reserve members were authorized only 24 shopping days per year in Defense Commissaries.

Privileges overseas are governed by international law and are available only if agreed upon by the foreign government concerned. VA certifies total disability. VA provides assistance in completing DD Form 1172, *Application for Uniformed Services Identification and Privilege Card.*

ARMED FORCES RETIREMENT HOMES

Veterans may be eligible to live in two retirement homes run by an independent federal agency, the Armed Forces Retirement Home Board.

More than 150 years ago, Congress established a home for destitute Navy officers, sailors and Marines in Philadelphia. Some 20 years later in 1851, with money demanded as booty from the Mexican War, Congress established an asylum for "old and disabled soldiers" in Washington, D.C.

Through the proceeding years, the U.S. Naval Home (USNH), now in Gulfport, Miss., and the U.S. Soldiers' and Airmen's Home (USSAH), still in Washington,

D.C., have operated under separate legislation, undergoing many changes. One of the biggest changes came as a result of the Armed Forces Retirement Home Act, Public Law 101-510, which took effect 1991.

This new law established the ***Armed Forces Retirement Home*** (AFRH), which combined the USSAH and the USNH under the unified management of the Armed Forces Retirement Home Board. Regulations such as resident eligibility, resident fees, operating funds, oversight, etc. now are standardized for both Homes.

The AFRH is an independent federal agency. Each Home has a local advisory board, administered by the AFRH Board appointed by the Secretary of Defense. Funding for the Homes comes from a Congressional trust fund that is fed by monthly, active-duty payroll deductions of 50 cents, fines and forfeitures from military disciplinary actions, interest earned on the trust, and resident fees.

In both Homes, residents can maintain an independent lifestyle in an environment designed for safety, comfort and personal enrichment.

Eligibility Criteria

Veterans are eligible to become a resident of either the U.S. Soldiers' and Airmen's Home or the U.S. Naval Home if their active duty service in the military is at least 50 percent enlisted, warrant officer or limited duty officer and who are:

- Veterans with 20 or more years of active duty service and are at least 60 years old; or
- Veterans unable to earn a livelihood due to a service-connected disability; or
- Veterans unable to earn a livelihood due to non service-connected disability, and who served in a war theater or received hostile fire pay, or;
- Female veterans who served prior to 1948.

Applicants must be free of drug, alcohol, and psychiatric problems, and never have been convicted of a felony.

Married couples are welcome, but both must be eligible in their own right.

At the time of admission applicants must be able to live independently. If increased healthcare is needed after being admitted, assisted living and long term care are available at both Homes.

For more information, contact:

Admissions Office 1094
U.S. Soldiers' and Airmen's Home
3700 North Capitol Street NW
Washington, DC 20317
(800) 422-9988

or

U.S. Naval Home
1800 Beach Drive
Gulfport, MS 39507
(800)332-3527

CHAPTER 49

LIST OF COMMON FORMS USED BY VA

While the following list is not exhaustive, following are some of the forms frequently used by VA.

General Administration Forms

Form #	*Purpose*
20-572	Request For Change Of Address / Cancellation Of Direct Deposit
20-5655	Financial Status Report

Compensation and Pension Forms

Form #	*Purpose*
21-22	Appointment Of Veterans Service Organization As Claimant's Representative
21-0304	Application For Spina Bifida Benefits
21-0510	Eligibility Verification Report Instructions
21-0514-1	Parent's DIC Eligibility Verification Report
21-526	Veteran's Application For Compensation Or Pension
21-527	Income-Net Worth And Employment Statement
21-530	Application For Burial Benefits
21-534	Application For DIC, Death Pension, And Accrued Benefits By A Surviving Spouse Or Child
21-535	Application For DIC By Parents
21-601	Application For Reimbursement From Accrued Amounts Due A Deceased Beneficiary
21-674	Request For Approval Of School Attendance
21-686c	Declaration Of Status Of Dependents
21-2008	Application For United States Flag For Burial Purposes
21-4138	Statement In Support Of Claim
21-4142	Authorization And Consent To Release Information To The Department Of Veterans Affairs
21-4502	Application For Automobile Or Other Conveyance And Adaptive Equipment
21-4703	Fiduciary Agreement
21-6753	Original Or Amended DIC Award
21-8416	Medical Expense Report
21-8678	Application For Annual Clothing Allowance
21-8940	Veteran's Application For Increased Compensation Based On Unemployability
21-8951-2	Notice Of Waiver Of VA Compensation Or Pension To Receive Military Pay And Allowances

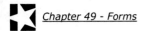

Education Forms

Form #	***Purpose***
22-1990	Application For VA Education Benefits
22-1990t	Application And Enrollment Certification For Individualized Tutorial Assistance
22-1995	Request For Change Of Program Or Place Of Training
22-5490	Application For Survivors' And Dependents' Educational Assistance
22-5495	Request For Change Of Program Or Place Of Training – Survivors' And Dependents' Educational Assistance
22-6553c	Monthly Certification Of Flight Training
22-8690	Time Record (Work-Study Program)
22-8691	Application For Work-Study Allowance
22-8873	Supplemental Information For Change Of Program Or Reenrollment After Unsatisfactory Attendance, Conduct Or Progress

Home Loan Guaranty Forms

Form #	**Purpose**
26-0826	VA Loan Summary Sheet
26-0503	Federal Collection Policy Notice
26-0592	Counseling Checklist For Military Homebuyers
26-1802a	HUD / VA Addendum To Uniform Residential Loan Application
26-1814	Batch Transmittal – Loan Code Sheet
26-1817	Request For Determination Of Loan Guaranty Eligibility – Unremarried Surviving Spouses
26-1820	Report And Certification Of Loan Disbursement
26-1839	Compliance Inspection Report
26-1847	Request For Postponement Of Offsite Or Exterior Onsite Improvements – Home Loan
26-1852	Description Of Materials
26-1880	Request For A Certificate Of Eligibility For VA Home Loan Benefits
26-6382	Statement Of Purchaser Or Owner Assuming Seller's Loan
26-6393	Loan Analysis
26-6684	Statement Of Fee Appraisers Or Compliance Inspectors
26-6705	Offer To Purchase And Contract Of Sale
26-6705b	Credit Statement Of Prospective Purchaser
26-6807	Financial Statement
26-8630	Manufactured Home Loan Claim Under Loan Guaranty
26-8712	Manufactured Home Appraisal Report
26-8736a	Non-Supervised Lender's Nomination And Recommendation Of Credit Underwriter
26-8791	VA Affirmative Marketing Certification
26-8812	VA Equal Opportunity Lender Certification
26-8937	Verification Of VA Benefit-Related Indebtedness

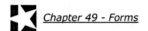

Vocational Rehabilitation and Employment Forms

Form #	Purpose
28-1900	Disabled Veterans Application For Vocational Rehabilitation
28-1902	Counseling Record – Personal Information
28-1902n	Counseling Record – Narrative Report
28-8872	Rehabilitation Plan
28-8872a	Rehabilitation Plan – Continuation Sheet
28-8890	Important Information About Rehabilitation

VA Insurance Forms

Form #	Purpose
29-336	Designation Of Beneficiary – Government Life Insurance
29-1546	Application For Cash Surrender Value / Application For Policy Loan
29-4125	Claim For One Sum Payment
29-4364	Application For Service-Disabled Insurance

Finance and Budget Forms

Form #	Purpose
24-0296	Direct Deposit Enrollment
24-5281	Application For Refund Of Education Contributions - VEAP

Miscellaneous Forms

Form #	Purpose
DD 149	Application For Correction Of Military Record
DD 214	Report of Separation From Active Duty
DD 293	Application For The Review Of Discharge OR Dismissal From The Armed Forces Of The United States
SF 15	Application For 10-Point Veteran's Preference
SF 180	Request Pertaining To Military Records
SGLV8283	Claim For Death Benefits – Form Returned To Office Of Servicemembers' Group Life Insurance
SGLV8285	Request For Insurance (Servicemembers' Group Life Insurance)
SGLV8286	Servicemembers' Group Life Insurance Election And Certificate
SGLV8714	Application For Veterans' Group Life Insurance
SGLF8721	Beneficiary Designation for Veterans Group Life Insurance
VAF 8	Certification To Appeal
VAF 9	Appeal To Board Of Veterans' Appeals
VAF 10 – 10ez	Instructions For Completing Application For Health Benefits
VAF 3288	Request For And Consent To Release Of Information From Claimant's Records
VAF 4107	Notice Of Procedural And Appellate Rights
VAF 4107b	Notice Of Procedural And Appellate Rights (Spanish Version)
40-1330	Application For Standard Government Headstone Or Marker For Installation In A Private Or State Veterans' Cemetery

CHAPTER 50

HELPFUL WEB SITES

The following list contains the addresses of some web sites we have found helpful:

American Ex-Prisoners Of War	www.axpow.org
American Gold Star Mothers, Inc.	www.goldstarmoms.com
American Legion	www.legion.org
American Veterans of World War II, Korea and Vietnam	www.amvets.org
Disabled American Veterans	www.dav.org
Gold Star Wives Of America, Inc.	www.goldstarwives.org
Gulf War Illness	www.gulflink.osd.mil
Legislative Information From The Library Of Congress	www.Thomas.loc.gov
Military Order Of The Purple Heart Of The USA, Inc.	www.purpleheart.org
National Veterans Legal Services Program, Inc.	www.nvlsp.org
The National Association For Uniformed Services	www.naus.org
The Retired Enlisted Association	www.trea.org
The Military Officers Association of America	www.moaa.org
The Society Of Military Widows	www.militarywidows.org
Tricare	www.tricare.osd.mil
U.S. House Of Representatives	www.house.gov
U.S. Senate	www.senate.gov
Veterans Administration	www.va.gov
Veterans Of Foreign Wars	www.vfw.org
White House	www.whitehouse.gov

CHAPTER 51

IMPORTANT PHONE NUMBERS

GENERAL BENEFITS

Burial, Headstones & Markers	1-800-697-6947
Disability, Compensation, Pension, Education & Training, Vocational Rehabilitation, Home Loans	1-800-827-1000
Education Programs	1-888-442-4551
Life Insurance	1-800-669-8477

HEALTHCARE BENEFITS

CHAMPVA	1-800-733-8387
National Mammography Helpline	1-888-492-7844
Emergency Medical Preparedness	1-304-263-0811
Spina Bifida	1-888-820-1756
Veterans Healthcare	1-877-222-8387
Veterans Healthcare in Canada	1-800-296-6379
Veterans Healthcare in Philippines	011-632-833-4566
Veterans Healthcare in all other Countries	1-303-331-7590

MISCELLANEOUS BENEFITS

Agent Orange Helpline	1-800-749-8387
Center For Veteran Entrepreneurs	1-866-584-2344
Debt Management Center	1-800-827-0648
Income Verification Center	1-800-949-1008

Persian Gulf Hotline	1-800-PGW-VETS
Persian Gulf TDD	1-800-829-4833
Sexual Trauma Hotline	1-800-827-1000
Telecommunication Device for the Deaf	1-800-829-4833

VAONLINE Bulletin Board Service – via data line 1-800-US1-VETS up to 28.8KBPS at 8-N-1 modem setting

INDEX

A

B

C

D

E

F

G

H

I

J

K

L

M

N

O

P

R

S

T

U

V

W

Would You or Someone You Know Benefit from Additional Copies Of
***What Every Veteran Should Know*?**

Simply tear out this form, and:

***Phone or Fax Orders:* 309-757-7760**

Mail To: VETERANS INFORMATION SERVICE
P.O. Box 111
East Moline, IL 61244-0111

ORDER ONLINE AT:
www.vetsinfoservice.com

☐ Yes! Send me _____ copies of "*What Every Veteran Should Know*", at $20.00 each (domestic shipping & handling included).

☐ Yes! I would like to subscribe to "*What Every Veteran Should Know*" monthly supplement (an 8-page newsletter which keeps your book up-to-date), and receive ______ copies of 12 monthly issues (1 year) for $30.00 per subscription (domestic shipping & handling included). ***

☐ Yes! I want to save money, and receive both the book and the monthly supplement. I would like ______ sets, at $48 per set (shipping & handling included). ***

****Again This Year* – ☐ Yes! Sign me up for an Email Newsletter edition, free with supplement subscriptions, just provide Email address, below.

____
Name

____
Address

____
City / State / Zip Code

____
Telephone Number E-mail Address

____
Amount Enclosed *(if overseas, add $10 to order)* Phone # (incl. area code)

Method of Payment:

☐ Check ☐ Visa ☐ MasterCard ☐ Money Order

____
Credit Card # Expiration Date (Month/Year)

Thank you for your order!
If you have any questions, feel free to contact us at
(309) 757-7760
www.vetsinfoservice.com or Email - help@vetsinfoservice.com

Would You or Someone You Know Benefit from Additional Copies Of *What Every Veteran Should Know*?

Simply tear out this form, and:

***Phone or Fax Orders:* 309-757-7760**

Mail To: VETERANS INFORMATION SERVICE
P.O. Box 111
East Moline, IL 61244-0111

ORDER ONLINE AT:
www.vetsinfoservice.com

☐ Yes! Send me _____ copies of "*What Every Veteran Should Know*", at $20.00 each (domestic shipping & handling included).

☐ Yes! I would like to subscribe to "*What Every Veteran Should Know*" monthly supplement (an 8-page newsletter which keeps your book up-to-date), and receive ______ copies of 12 monthly issues (1 year) for $30.00 per subscription (domestic shipping & handling included). ***

☐ Yes! I want to save money, and receive both the book and the monthly supplement. I would like ______ sets, at $48 per set (shipping & handling included). ***

****Again This Year* – ☐ Yes! Sign me up for an Email Newsletter edition, free with supplement subscriptions, just provide Email address, below.

Name

Address

City / State / Zip Code

Telephone Number | E-mail Address

Amount Enclosed *(if overseas, add $10 to order)* | Phone # (incl. area code)

Method of Payment:

☐ Check ☐ Visa ☐ MasterCard ☐ Money Order

Credit Card # | Expiration Date (Month/Year)

Thank you for your order!
If you have any questions, feel free to contact us at
(309) 757-7760
www.vetsinfoservice.com or Email - help@vetsinfoservice.com

Would You or Someone You Know Benefit from Additional Copies Of *What Every Veteran Should Know*?

Simply tear out this form, and:

Phone or Fax Orders: **309-757-7760**

Mail To: VETERANS INFORMATION SERVICE
P.O. Box 111
East Moline, IL 61244-0111

ORDER ONLINE AT:
www.vetsinfoservice.com

☐ Yes! Send me _____ copies of "*What Every Veteran Should Know*", at $20.00 each (domestic shipping & handling included).

☐ Yes! I would like to subscribe to "*What Every Veteran Should Know*" monthly supplement (an 8-page newsletter which keeps your book up-to-date), and receive ______ copies of 12 monthly issues (1 year) for $30.00 per subscription (domestic shipping & handling included). ***

☐ Yes! I want to save money, and receive both the book and the monthly supplement. I would like ______ sets, at $48 per set (shipping & handling included). ***

****Again This Year* – ☐ Yes! Sign me up for an Email Newsletter edition, free with supplement subscriptions, just provide Email address, below.

Name

Address

City / State / Zip Code

Telephone Number E-mail Address

Amount Enclosed *(if overseas, add $10 to order)* Phone # (incl. area code)

Method of Payment:

☐ Check ☐ Visa ☐ MasterCard ☐ Money Order

Credit Card # Expiration Date (Month/Year)

Thank you for your order!
If you have any questions, feel free to contact us at
(309) 757-7760
www.vetsinfoservice.com or Email - help@vetsinfoservice.com

Would You or Someone You Know Benefit from Additional Copies Of
***What Every Veteran Should Know*?**

Simply tear out this form, and:

Phone or Fax Orders: **309-757-7760**

Mail To: VETERANS INFORMATION SERVICE
P.O. Box 111
East Moline, IL 61244-0111

ORDER ONLINE AT:
www.vetsinfoservice.com

☐ Yes! Send me _____ copies of "*What Every Veteran Should Know*", at $20.00 each (domestic shipping & handling included).

☐ Yes! I would like to subscribe to "*What Every Veteran Should Know*" monthly supplement (an 8-page newsletter which keeps your book up-to-date), and receive ______ copies of 12 monthly issues (1 year) for $30.00 per subscription (domestic shipping & handling included). ***

☐ Yes! I want to save money, and receive both the book and the monthly supplement. I would like ______ sets, at $48 per set (shipping & handling included). ***

****Again This Year* – ☐ Yes! Sign me up for an Email Newsletter edition, free with supplement subscriptions, just provide Email address, below.

Name

Address

City / State / Zip Code

Telephone Number — E-mail Address

Amount Enclosed *(if overseas, add $10 to order)* — Phone # (incl. area code)

Method of Payment:

☐ Check ☐ Visa ☐ MasterCard ☐ Money Order

Credit Card # — Expiration Date (Month/Year)

Thank you for your order!
If you have any questions, feel free to contact us at
(309) 757-7760
www.vetsinfoservice.com or Email - help@vetsinfoservice.com